Ecologic-Biochemical Approaches to Treatment of Delinquents and Criminals

Ecologic-Biochemical Approaches to Treatment of Delinquents and Criminals

Edited by Leonard J. Hippchen, Ph.D.

VNR **VAN NOSTRAND REINHOLD COMPANY**
NEW YORK   CINCINNATI   ATLANTA   DALLAS   SAN FRANCISCO
LONDON   TORONTO   MELBOURNE

Van Nostrand Reinhold Company Regional Offices:
New York   Cincinnati   Atlanta   Dallas   San Francisco

Van Nostrand Reinhold Company International Offices:
London   Toronto   Melbourne

Copyright © 1978 by Litton Educational Publishing, Inc.

Library of Congress Catalog Card Number: 77-25001
ISBN: 0-442-23420-1

All rights reserved. No part of this work covered by the copyright hereon may be reproduced or used in any form or by any means—graphic, electronic, or mechanical, including photocopying, recording, taping, or information storage and retrieval systems—without permission of the publisher.

Manufactured in the United States of America

Published by Van Nostrand Reinhold Company
135 West 50th Street, New York, N.Y. 10019

Published simultaneously in Canada by Van Nostrand Reinhold Ltd.

15 14 13 12 11 10 9 8 7 6 5 4 3 2 1

Library of Congress Cataloging in Publication Data
Main entry under title:

Ecologic-biochemical approaches to treatment of
 delinquents and criminals.

   Bibliography: p. 389
   Includes index.
   1. Crime and criminals—Addresses, essays, lectures.
2. Rehabilitation of criminals—Addresses, essays,
lectures.   3. Criminal psychology—Addresses, essays,
lectures.   I. Hippchen, Leonard Joseph, 1923-
[DNLM: 1. Crime.   2. Juvenile delinquency. HV9069
E19]
HV6028.E28   364.2'4   77-25001
ISBN 0-442-23420-1

This book is dedicated to the Source of All-Knowledge, and to the men and women everywhere—the true lovers of mankind—who with open minds and pure and radiant hearts have embraced a potent portion of this knowledge, and who, thus armed, have rushed to the aid of a long-suffering humanity!

Foreword

This is a vital and significant book. The title may not attract attention; however, readers will soon discover it to be challenging and stimulating in presenting new and sound ideas, which I predict will be proved valid as programs are expanded and evaluated. This long-overdue book on the *Ecologic-Biochemical Approaches to Treatment of Delinquents and Criminals* meets a need I have felt for some time.

For many years I have been interested in the effect of diets on delinquents and criminals. In the early 1940s, while serving as superintendent of a large coeducational training school in Pennsylvania, I used routine height and weight charts to monitor the physical condition of the boys and girls. Individuals with major deviations were referred to the medical department for thorough physical examinations. Individual medical treatment was provided, and major menu changes were made where indicated.

While I was serving as Director of the Training Schools of Maryland, an intensive study of dietary deficiencies was made in cooperation with the State Department of Health. A training school for girls was selected; each girl was examined by a team of experts at the time of reception and after nine months in the institution. Although many increased in weight and appeared in better health, some continued with signs of malnutrition. As a result of this study, appropriate changes were made in the menus of all the institutions. There was occasional evidence of behavioral improvement, but there were no hard data to link these observations with the improved diets.

By coincidence, when I was reading the first two chapters of this book, we were visited by a relative who described in interesting detail a radical change he has experienced as a result of diet. He stated that for years he had been depressed, irritable, and disgusted with life in general. After his condition was diagnosed as hypoglycemia, he was placed on a rigid diet by his physician. As a result, his disposition and attitude changed drastically, so that he now has a positive outlook on life. He further stated that he is so sensitive to diet that his wife can observe a difference in his behavior the day after he eats a prohibited food. Since he has both an engineering and a legal degree, I had confidence in his objectivity.

Corrections has been seeking effective methods of providing opportunities for improvement of behavior for many years. I do not doubt that we have overlooked the importance of nutrition. The contributors to this book do not present this approach as a panacea for the treatment of all delinquents and criminals. However, we will not know who or how many can be helped until an adequate number of demonstration projects have been conducted.

I strongly urge correctional administrators and professional staffs to consider seriously the advisability of testing the concepts in this book. Correctional institutions provide excellent laboratories to test the validity of this program. The testing can be done without major interference with the regular program and does not involve expensive capital outlay. It can be conducted in harmony with the mission of the correctional service.

The major goal is to learn more about how to detect nutritional deficiencies and increase the fund of knowledge relating to the impact of diet on behavior. This information would be of great value in early recognition of these conditions in children, which should make possible the reduction of delinquent acts through diet control.

An essential element will be the pooling of the results of all projects testing this approach. I look forward to keeping in touch with developments stimulated not only by this book but also by future research in the use of the biochemical approach.

E. PRESTON SHARP, PH.D.
Former Executive Director
American Correctional Association

Cape Coral, Florida

Preface

This book is directed to the practitioner and to the student. It is designed for the person who is looking for more effective ways of dealing with the problems associated with delinquency and crime. It should be of vital interest, therefore, to the many practitioners who are involved with a wide variety of human services: basic infant and child medical care, counseling of parents, services to children with learning disabilities and behavioral disorders, programs for the mentally ill or retarded, community programs and/or institutions for the alcoholic, drug addict, delinquent, and criminal. It also would be extremely useful as a college text for students preparing for professional work in any of these fields.

The orientation and the approach of this book come from two recent areas of theoretical, research, and applied developments: the ecological and the biochemical.

The ecological area is concerned with how man in interrelationship with his environment may develop maladaptive patterns that affect his health. It is theorized that the human body through many millions of years of evolution became adapted to a *natural* environment, but that today many persons have become susceptible to some of the many *unnatural* agents of industrial society. Thus, the ecologically oriented practitioner looks at the patient's adaptability to such environmental agents as foods, chemical fumes, drugs, and food and other contaminants. Specific susceptibility is measured clinically in terms of immediacy and severity of test or nonadaptive reactions. The nonadaptive behavior often can be seen as "antisocial."

The biochemical area is concerned with how the brain may be affected by the molecular concentration of many substances that are normally present in the brain. Biochemists have discovered that the optimum concentration of these substances for a person may differ greatly from the concentration provided by his normal diet and genetic machinery. Abnormal deficits or excesses in these brain concentrations, depending upon the specific and individual needs of each person, can lead to a wide variety of pathological thought and behavior patterns, i.e., bizarre behavior, hyperactivity, and violence. Under certain conditions, in the family, school, or workplace, these behaviors may be seen as "antisocial." It is theorized that these chemical imbalances can originate from genetic factors, or they can be induced, especially during the birth process or in early childhood by improper nutrition of the mother and/or child.

The new knowledge offered by the ecologic-biochemical approaches to delinquency and crime related behavioral disorders promises to make a considerable contribution to our efforts to deal with this serious and increasing social problem. Already, practitioners using these approaches have been able to demonstrate an unusually high degree of effectiveness in treatment of these dysfunctions. Also, many of these treatments have been extended to alcoholics, drug addicts, children with learning and behavioral problems, delinquents, and criminals.

The purpose of this book is to present an initial overview of the theory, research, and applied findings that relate to this new development. The twenty chapters of the book have been organized into four sections. Section I deals with the history, need, and theory of the new approach. Section II includes an extensive survey of important empirical research findings that concern "antisocial" behavioral problems.

Section III reports on a variety of applied developments pertaining to the diagnosis and treatment of "antisocial" types of problem behavior, including that of delinquents and criminals. Section IV deals with a problem of major contemporary concern: the prevention of, and early intervention with, delinquents and criminals in the community.

It is hoped that the information contained in this book will stimulate much interest and action in using this new approach to the delinquency-crime problem. The recommendations in Section IV, which relate to the practical and effective application of the new ecologic-biochemical approaches in the community, will undoubtedly, if applied, help us to reduce the severity and scope of delinquency and crime in society.

This work would not have been possible without the dedicated assistance of many persons. In particular, I wish to thank Dr. Abram Hoffer, who provided considerable encouragement and support for this book when the idea first emerged. Also acknowledgement is made, with deep appreciation, of the help provided by the twenty-two professionals who took time from their extremely busy schedules to prepare their contributions for this book.

LEONARD J. HIPPCHEN, PH.D.

Richmond, Virginia

Contributor Sketches

GARY H. BACHARA, Ph.D., the Institute for Child Study, University of Maryland, is a clinical associate with the Eastern Virginia Medical-Psychiatric Associates, Ltd., in Chesapeake, Va. A former court psychologist, Bachara serves as a member of the Special Education Advisory Board to the Norfolk Public Schools and as a consultant to the Tidewater Juvenile Court. He has published and presented numerous papers in the area of learning disabilities and their effect on social and emotional development. Co-author WILLIAM R. LAMB, M.D., a clinical psychiatrist specializing in adolescent and family psychiatry, is in private practice with the Eastern Virginia Medical-Psychiatric Associates, Ltd. He is an assistant professor of psychiatry at the Eastern Virginia Medical School, consultant to numerous local facilities, the founding president of the Virginia Society of Adolescent Psychiatry, and a member of the Academy of Orthomolecular Psychiatry.

JEFFREY B. BLANCHARD, O.D., has been actively engaged in visual perception training in youngsters for the past six years. He has a B.S. in Physiological Optics, an O.D. from the Ohio State University College of Optometry, and a residency certificate in visual training from the Optometric Center of New York. He has worked extensively in New York school systems in Rochester, Victor, and East Bloomfield, as well as in Broward County, Fla. Co-author FRANK MANNARINO, a licensed Medical Hypnotist in Florida, has worked extensively in the use of hypno-therapy as an adjunct to perceptual training, and established a private practice in Lauderhill in 1974. Currently he is director of the Fort Lauderdale School of Hypnosis. His experience with juvenile delinquents stems from a career in law enforcement in New York City and service as a volunteer counselor in the Pompano Juvenile Detention Center.

PHILIP L. BONNET, M.D., is a staff psychiatrist at the Brain Bio Center in Princeton, N.J. CARL C. PFEIFFER, Ph.D., M.D., is director of the Center. Dr. Bonnet completed his psychiatric residency at Hahnemann Hospital, Philadelphia, and joined Dr. Pfeiffer as a research fellow at the New Jersey Neuro-Psychiatric Institute in 1972. Dr. Pfeiffer is well known for his many years of research directorships at the University of Illinois, Emory University, and the New Jersey Neuro-Psychiatric Institute, and for his more than 180 publications in pharmacology and physiology.

ALLAN COTT, M.D., F.A.P.A., has been an innovator in psychiatric practice since his earliest medical training in Ohio in 1936. Following psychiatric practice in World War II, Dr. Cott has investigated and practiced character analysis (Reich), and studied hypoglycemia and depression, LSD, megavitamins in treatment of childhood schizophrenia and autism, and orthomolecular approaches to treatment of children with learning disabilities. He is President of the Academy of Orthomolecular Psychiatry, practices in New York City, and has published more than 20 papers and books on orthomolecular subjects. His latest work, *The Orthomolecular Approach to Learning Disabilities*, excerpts of which are included in this volume, is available from Academic Therapy Publications.

R. GLEN GREEN, M.D., C.M., has had a lengthy and varied practice in Prince Albert, Saskatchewan, Canada, since 1948, specializing in general medicine, pediatrics, obstetrics, surgery, anesthesia, and, more recently, orthomolecular medicine. He discovered and named "subclinical pellegra" in 1969 while he was serving as attending doctor to the maximum security prison in Prince Albert. His recent work on hypoglycemia and food allergies has led him to conclude that today food allergies are the main causes of man's physical and mental problems.

LEONARD J. HIPPCHEN, Ph.D., was trained in social and counseling psychology, and has worked with criminal/delinquency programs for the past 20 years. He has served as Research Director of the U.S.A.F. Prisoner Retraining Program in Texas; as a research associate with the Juvenile Delinquency Research Division, Children's Bureau, DHEW, Washington, D.C.; and as a consultant and/or director of 12 criminal justice demonstration/research projects in Texas, California, Georgia, New Jersey, and Virginia. He is the author of numerous correctional publications and serves as chairman of the Committee on Classification & Treatment of the American Correctional Association. Dr. Hippchen is on the faculty of Virginia Commonwealth University.

ABRAM HOFFER, M.D., Ph.D., who received training in biochemistry and psychiatric medicine, developed the first biochemical hypothesis of schizophrenia and initiated megavitamin therapy. He also has done extensive study of criminal behavior and the addictions. Dr. Hoffer has written more than 200 scientific journal publications and is the author of several books on orthomolecular psychiatry. He is a Fellow of the International College of Applied Nutrition and a Founder of the Academy of Orthomolecular Psychiatry.

JOHN NASH OTT, Sc.D., Honorary, best known for his extensive research, lecturing, and publications on the effects of light on human behavior, has served as Chairman and Executive Director of the Environmental Health and Light Research Institute since 1966. He has been a Visiting Lecturer and Research Associate in the College of Natural Sciences and Department of Biology at the University of South Florida.

WILLIAM H. PHILPOTT, M.D., conducts clinic and research practice, specializing in psychiatry and allergy reactions, in Oklahoma City. He was Assistant Medical Director and Psychiatrist at the Fuller Memorial Hospital in Massachusetts from 1969-1974. Dr. Philpott has published widely in the research literature, is Second Vice-President of the International Academy of Metabology, and is Editor of the *Journal of the International Academy of Metabology*.

ELIZABETH LODGE REES, M.D., F.A.A.P., is a pediatrics specialist practicing in Castro Valley, Calif. A founding member of the California Orthomolecular Medical Society and a charter member of the Academy of Orthomolecular Psychiatry, she has lectured extensively before lay groups, has published widely, and has served as an extension faculty member at the University of California.

HAROLD ROSENBERG, M.D., is in private practice in New York City, and has for many years emphasized nutritional guidance with his patients. He has served as president of the International

xvi   Contributor Sketches

Academy of Preventive Medicine, and is author of the Book-of-the-Month Club selection, *The Doctor's Book of Vitamin Therapy.*

SIDNEY H. SLAVIN, O.D., a 1963 graduate of the Southern College of Optometry, conducts private practice in Richmond, Va., and specializes in optometric research in visual therapy. He serves as a consultant to the Committee on Children and Visual Development of the American Optometric Association, is a frequent contributor to journals of the field, and is the author of a new text on the developmental examination of children.

RUSSELL F. SMITH, M.D., well known nationally for his clinical and research work on alcoholism, is a former medical director of Brighton Alcoholic Hospital in Michigan, where he conducted extensive studies on alcoholic patients. He also has served as clinical and research coordinator of Guest House Sanitariums in Lake Orion and Rochester, Mich. He is the author of a number of journal papers on alcoholism, as well as two books.

HENRY TURKEL was awarded the M.D. in 1936 from the University of Michigan. While working on his medical degree, he developed a new type of instrument for bone-marrow biopsies and intraosseous infusions. These were accepted as the standard instruments for emergency infusions by the armed forces during World War II. At the same time he perfected his treatment of genetic diseases by the method of removing depositions in patients with adult-onset diabetes, arteriosclerosis, allergies, or other diseases associated with metabolic accumulations. In 1952 he did a crossover study with Patient Evelyn, whose progress with treatment and regression when treatment was prematurely discontinued helped to establish the efficacy of the "U" series. The "U" Series has been used to treat retarded persons throughout the world. Co-author ILSE NUSBAUM received the B.A. in English and Philosophy from Radcliffe College in 1955, and the M.A. in English Language and Literature from the University of Michigan in 1956. Following ten years of teaching at Ohio University and in Detroit public and parochial schools, she joined Dr. Turkel as a psychometrist in 1968.

M. ELLIS WARE, M.S., was awarded the master of science degree in clinical psychology at Virginia Commonwealth University in 1971. The study reported on in this volume was conducted as part of her degree requirements. At the time, she was serving as a staff psychologist with the Mobile Psychiatric Clinic, Virginia Division of Youth Services, in Bon Air, Va. Following this study she served as clinical psychologist at the Beaumont Learning Center in Beaumont, Va., a training school for boys.

ROY C. WUNDERLICH, JR., M.D., St. Petersburg, Fla., is a pediatrician by training, but now is practicing preventive medicine and health maintenance, emphasizing allergies, learning disorders, mental illness and degenerative disease of adulthood. Dr. Wunderlich has written numerous articles for professional journals, lectures extensively, and is the author of five books on allergies and learning disorders.

JOSE A. YARYURA-TOBIAS, M.D., widely known for his extensive psychiatric research studies, both in the United States and Argentina, has served on the faculty of the University of Argentina in Buenos Aires, and presently is Research Director of the North Nassau Mental Health Center in Manhasset, N.Y. He has practiced as a psychiatrist and consulting psychiatrist in a number of mental health settings, and is a founding member of the World Federation of Biological Psychiatry.

Contents

Foreword / *E. Preston Sharp, Ph.D.*
Preface / *Leonard J. Hippchen, Ph.D.*

SECTION I
THE NEED AND BACKGROUND OF THE NEW APPROACH

Introduction	1
1 The Need for a New Approach to the Delinquent-Criminal Problem / *Leonard J. Hippchen, Ph.D.*	3
2 Alcoholism and Criminal Behavior / *Russell F. Smith, M.D.*	20
3 Some Theoretical Principles Basic to Orthomolecular Psychiatric Treatment / *Abram Hoffer, M.D., Ph.D.*	31

SECTION II
ECOLOGIC-BIOCHEMICAL RESEARCH IN DELINQUENCY-CRIME RELATED PROBLEMS

Introduction	57
4 The Etiology of Learning Disabilities, Drug Abuse and Juvenile Delinquency / *Allan Cott, M.D., F.A.P.A.*	61
5 Information Processing Defects in Delinquents / *Sidney H. Slavin, O.D.*	75
6 The Effects of Light and Radiation on Human Health and Behavior / *John N. Ott, Sc.D., Hon.*	105
7 Ecological Aspects of Antisocial Behavior / *William H. Philpott, M.D.*	184
8 Biological Research on Violent Behavior / *Jose A. Yaryura-Tobias, M.D.*	138
9 Some Effects of Nicotinic and Ascorbic Acids on the Behavior of Institutionalized Juvenile Delinquents / *M. Ellis Ware, M.S.*	153

SECTION III
ECOLOGIC-BIOCHEMICAL APPROACHES TO DIAGNOSIS AND TREATMENT

Introduction	179
10 Biochemical Diagnosis of Delinquent Behavior / Philip L. Bonnet, M.D., Carl C. Pfeiffer, M.D.	183
11 Symptoms and Treatment of Children with Learning Disorders / Allan Cott, M.D., F.A.P.A.	206
12 Neuroallergy as a Contributing Factor to Social Misfits: Diagnosis and Treatment / Roy C. Wunderlich, M.D.	229
13 Treatment of the "Slow Learner" / Henry Turkel, M.D., Ilse Nusbaum, M.A.	254
14 Treatment of Penitentiary Inmates / R. Glen Green, M.D., C.M.	269
15 Diagnosis and Treatment of Alcoholism / Russell F. Smith, M.D.	284

SECTION IV
PREVENTION-INTERVENTION APPROACHES TO DELINQUENCY AND CRIME

Introduction	297
16 Family Planning, Nutrition, and Crime / Harold Rosenberg, M.D.	301
17 Early Diagnosis and Treatment of Childhood Disorders / Elizabeth Lodge Rees, M.D.	327
18 Academic, Perceptual, and Visual Levels of Detained Delinquents / Jeffrey B. Blanchard, O.D., Frank Mannarino, L.M.H.	341
19 Intervention with Juvenile Delinquents / Gary H. Bachara, Ph.D., William R. Lamb, M.D.	352
20 A Model for Community Programs Dealing with Antisocial Persons / Leonard J. Hippchen, Ph.D.	371
Bibliography	389
Index	393

Section I | # THE NEED AND BACKGROUND OF THE NEW APPROACH

INTRODUCTION

Everyone today is aware of the fact that delinquency and crime are on the increase and that crime is among the most serious problems facing our nation. Since crime has been dealt with as a national problem at least for the past ten years, one might be puzzled at the fact that so little progress has yet been made in understanding, controlling, or preventing it.

The authors of this section attempt to shed some light on the problem of understanding, which is the first step toward more effective control and possible prevention. In the first paper, Dr. Hippchen suggests that our approach to the study of causative factors has been too limited, and outlines ways in which new biochemical knowledge can make important contributions to better understanding of criminal behavior. He also suggests that new biochemical approaches to the diagnosis and treatment of persons with antisocial behavior can greatly aid our correctional and preventive efforts. Dr. Hippchen emphasizes that if we are to make a significant impact on crime, we will need to find more effective ways of dealing with, especially, alcoholism, drug abuse, and the restiveness of our children and youth, since this is such a large part of the underlying problem.

The paper by Dr. Smith focuses on the devastating problem of alcoholism and its relation to the criminal problem. More arrests are made for alcohol-related problems than any other category of crime, and our youth today appear to be moving somewhat away from drug use to alcohol use. Further, a majority of violent crimes are reported to have been committed under the influence of alcohol. Dr. Smith describes the long history of alcohol use by man and shows how alcohol use can change from simple social usage to alcoholism and possible criminal behavior. He also indicates why he feels that we have avoided facing the problem of social drinking and alcoholism.

In the final paper, Dr. Hoffer explains some of the important historical events and discoveries related to the new biochemical approach to human problems. As one of the pioneers of the field, he outlines some of the significant persons and ideas which led him from a purely psychosocial psychiatric practice into the more holistic orthomolecular approach. Dr. Hoffer gives a detailed explanation of how orthomolecular medicine theoretically views the development of a wide variety of human symptoms related to abnormal and antisocial forms of behavior. He also defines the means that orthomolecular medicine has developed to treat these disorders with improved effectiveness. He emphasizes that orthomolecular psychiatry uses not just biochemical, but both psychosocial and biophysical knowledge.

Chapter 1

The Need for a New Approach to the Delinquent-Criminal Problem

Leonard J. Hippchen, Ph.D.
Administration of Justice and Public Safety
Virginia Commonwealth University
Richmond, Virginia

INTRODUCTION

The need for a new way to deal with problems associated with juvenile delinquency and crime can be seen by examining three areas of contemporary development: (1) the continuing trend for reported delinquency and crime to increase throughout the country; (2) our seeming inability to resolve successfully a large proportion of these kinds of socially disruptive behavioral problems; and (3) the inadequacies of criminological efforts to identify the key causative factors underlying these forms of behavior.

The purpose here is first to review these three areas, which indicate the need for a new approach to the delinquent-criminal problem. A discussion of how biochemical knowledge and approaches can make important contributions to a solution of these problems will follow.

DELINQUENCY-CRIME TRENDS

Determining the actual amount of delinquency and crime in the United States each year is a difficult, if not impossible, task. The Federal Bureau of Investigation attempts to make an annual assessment of the number of crimes committed in the country, but their data are limited to include only those crimes for which an arrest has been made. It has been estimated that only one-fifth of all serious crimes result in an arrest; thus, it is probable that the F.B.I.'s data report represents a considerable underestimate of the actual volume of crime. However, in spite of this serious limitation, this annual report, called the *Uniform Crime Report*,[1] still is the most valid and most nearly complete source of data on crime available.

One of the most striking facts reported by the F.B.I. in the *Uniform Crime Report* is that the total number of offenses in the nation has increased each year since 1960. There has not been a single year since that time in which the data have shown a decrease in the total amount of crime committed in the United States. The percentage increase in the Total Crime Index for the period 1960-1974, even accounting for population increases, was 157%. This crime index, which is used to study trends, is based upon the more serious crimes, such as murder, manslaughter, rape, robbery, assault, burglary, larceny-theft, and motor vehicle theft.

For the 1969-1974 period, total crime increased 38%. The violent crimes, such as murder, rape, robbery and assault, were up a startling 47%, while property crimes increased 37%. The F.B.I. quarterly report for Jan.-Mar., 1976, showed this same tendency for crime to continue to increase. It showed a 4% increase over the same period for 1975.

These data give ample testimony to the claim that crime continues to increase throughout the country despite our best efforts to curb it. A 1973 Gallup Poll reported that more than one of every five people across the nation had been victimized by crime during the past year. In center cities one of three citizens had been crime victims. Respondents listed crime as the worst problem in their community.[2]

In the area of juvenile delinquency, the *Uniform Crime Report* suggests that teen-age crimes have been increasing at a rate much greater than that for adult crimes. In one comparative study of the years 1960-1974, the increase in arrests of persons under 18 was 138%, while for those 18 years of age and over the increase was only 16%. The most notable category of arrest during this period for teenagers was for violation of narcotic drug laws—an increase of 3,778%!

Of the 1,709,137 arrests of juvenile offenders in 1974, the police themselves handled 44% of the cases, using the typical warning to the youngster. Another 47% were referred to the juvenile court for processing. Many of these youngsters in the court also are merely put off with a warning, or they may be placed on a short period of probation. The effect of the warning type of approach to the juvenile delinquent, both by police and the juvenile court judge, is questionable in view of the large number of repeaters in crime among the teen-age group. A reprimand or warning to a youngster by a loving father or mother may have deterrent value; this action with a chronic offender by a policeman or judge is likely to have only a limited effect in changing behavior.

THE NATURE OF THE CRIMINAL ACT

It is natural to think of crime primarily in terms of the violent crimes, especially murder, rape, assault, and robbery, because these are most publicized and of greatest perceived threat to the average citizen. However, the crime picture is much broader than the one we get from crimes of violence.

The latest F.B.I. *Uniform Crime Report* shows that of the total 9,055,800 arrests in 1974, only 429,350 were for violent crimes. Even property crimes—burglary, larceny, and auto theft—only accounted for 1,731,000 of this total. What, then, does account for the bulk of these arrests?

The largest single group of offenses in the Report relate to alcohol use. A total of 2,486,200 arrests were made in 1974 for alcohol-related offenses, i.e., drunkenness, driving under the influence of alcohol, and liquor law violations. This does not include the many violent and vice types of crimes with which alcohol use frequently is involved.

It should be noted, however, that the 1,372,600 reported arrests for drunkenness do not represent that number of individuals. The criminal justice system has done very little more with chronic drunks than to arrest and sentence them to jail or the county farm for 30 days. Thus, it is conceivable that a chronic drunk could be arrested 12 times during a single year. Cases have been reported where one person had been arrested as many as 250 times during his career of alcoholism!

The 1974 F.B.I. report also shows that 843,600 arrests were made for driving under the influence of alcohol. But the National Safety

Council has estimated that the chances of being arrested for driving while intoxicated are one in 2,000. Thus, the arrest figures vastly underestimate the extent of this problem.

Further, the U.S. Dept. of Transportation has reported that only 5% of the drivers initially charged with drunken driving are ever convicted of the offense. It appears that it is very difficult for an officer to prove to the court's satisfaction that social drinkers can't hold their liquor while driving. And yet, the drunk driver is a considerable danger on the road, as has been attested to by the National Safety Council, which says that alcohol is a factor in at least half of the motor vehicle fatalities each year. This would represent, for example, about half of the 56,300 persons who were so killed in 1972.

To further indicate the problem of alcoholism and its relation to crime, we will quote from a 1974 study of prison populations throughout the country, which was conducted by the U.S. Bureau of the Census. It reported that of the 191,400 inmates in state prisons at the time, 43% said that they had been drinking at the time they committed the offense for which they were arrested and later imprisoned.[3]

Another large category of crime arrests is for violation of the narcotic drug laws. Drug use, especially use of marijuana, has increased greatly among teen-agers in recent years. Arrests in this category totaled 642,100 in 1974.

The U.S. Department of Justice has estimated that the number of heroin addicts in the United States has increased 12-fold in the last ten years—from 50,000 to 600,000. Further, the U.S. Bureau of the Census reported that 26% of the inmates in state prisons in 1974 said that they were under the influence of drugs when arrested for the crime for which they were incarcerated. Drug usage is known for its relation to robbery, burglary, and larceny, since the drug user often must steal to support his expensive habit once it is acquired.

Offenses typical of children and youth also have a high arrest incidence, according to the *Uniform Crime Report*. Reported in this category are: runaways, 239,600; vandalism, 221,000; and curfew and loitering law violations, 151,000. Restive and mobile youth are truly a sign of the times. They represent an increasing problem of control for law enforcement personnel in every community, especially the large cities.

The fight against crime today tends to focus on crimes of violence, for politically they appear to be most important. However, our investigation of the number of arrests for specific types of crime indicates that few, if any, inroads can be expected in curbing crime unless more attention is paid to the problems of alcohol, drugs, and our restive children and youth. It is true that the increasing number of crimes of violence represent a serious threat to society, but our analysis of crime data should lead us to conclude that the major part of our crime problem lies elsewhere.

OUR LIMITED EFFECTIVENESS IN DEALING WITH DELINQUENCY AND CRIME

Our nation's juvenile delinquent correctional institutions are filled with chronic delinquents. Most have lengthy careers of repeated forms of antisocial behavior. Most have had problems of this type from their earliest years—in the family, in the school, and in their peer and other social groups.

Most of these delinquents have had numerous contacts with the police and with the juvenile court, but to no avail. Their behavior has been neither understood nor corrected, either by themselves or by the social institutions with which they have had contact. And now, in the correctional institution, they may well be preparing for an adult life of crime. Unfortunately, these institutions have not been too effective in helping many of these youth. The 1974 U.S. Bureau of the Census study, mentioned earlier, found some evidence for this conclusion: 33% of the nation's 191,400 adult prisoners in the survey said that they had been charged in their younger years one or more times as juvenile delinquents. Most of the remaining group of adult criminals probably had been delinquent but had not been caught or charged. This last statement can be substantiated by reading the case histories of most of the adult criminals in any of our typical state or Federal prisons: most acknowledge the delinquency of their earlier years.

The problem in the area of the adult criminal is even more striking. The majority of persons filling our nation's prisons have been described as "career criminals" by the F.B.I. The 1974 *Uniform Crime Report* provides information on a special study by the F.B.I. on these persons. They followed up 207,748 offenders during the period 1970–1974 and found that 135,470 or 65% had been arrested two or more times. In fact, these persons had an average "criminal career" of five years and five months, during which time they were arrested an average of four times each. They had a total of 835,000 documented charges against them, with 227,014 reported convictions and 109,657 imprisonments of six months or more.

In the 1974 U.S. Bureau of the Census study, more data on repeat behavior of adult criminals were uncovered. This study found that 23% of the 191,400 prison inmates had had two prior sentences, 19% had had three prior sentences, 12% had had four prior sentences, and 18% had had five or more prior sentences.

These data clearly indicate what the average citizen today already knows: that many of our criminals are out on the streets perpetrating new crimes every day! The criminal justice system neither is effective in deterring nor correcting large numbers of our juvenile delinquents and adult criminals. Yet, most remain free: undetected or uncharged, on suspended sentences, on probation, on parole, or on release from prison after only a short stay in that prison.

This failure to deter, hold, and/or correct has led to the point where the large number of repeat offenders in the community not only represent serious crime threats in themselves but contaminate, and set a poor example for, large segments of other parts of society, especially our children and youth.

Many attempts have been made over the past several decades to develop more effective approaches to the correction of offender groups. Social casework, psychotherapy, group therapy, psychiatric approaches, academic and vocational training, and other methods have been used. Probation and parole have been extensively expanded throughout the country. And yet, several studies of the correctional methods in common use today show that they are relatively ineffective in reducing repeat delinquent-criminal behavior.

For example, Bailey, in 1966, examined 100 reports dealing with correctional programs conducted between 1940 and 1960, and reported the evidence of treatment efficacy to be only slight.[4] Also, in 1971, Martinson published a report on his study of 231 correctional treatment programs throughout the country since 1945 and concluded that there was little evidence that these programs had a decisive effect in reducing recidivism of convicted offenders.[5]

It should be mentioned that the Bailey and Martinson selection and evaluation criteria were quite rigid in their screening of correctional treatment programs. They only selected studies which had been evaluated with acceptable scientific methods, and improvement had to be clearly shown to be significant. Undoubtedly, effective correctional treatment is being carried on in some areas of the field, but the research evidence to support this effectiveness to this time has not been presented in sufficient quantity. In general, correctional evaluators have tended to be critical of the great bulk of the correctional treatment efforts now in progress throughout the country.

SOME LIMITATIONS OF CONTEMPORARY CRIMINOLOGICAL THEORIES OF CAUSATION

For more than a hundred years, criminologists have conducted numerous investigations into the causes of criminal behavior. Establishing cause can be important to the finding of a remedy for the crime problem.

Traditionally, the nineteenth-century work of Cesare Lombroso, an Austrian, is regarded to have initiated the scientific study of crime. In his studies of criminals, Lombroso, a physician, found numerous physical defects in the typical criminal. He also found evidence of mental retardation, epilepsy, and pellegra. He concluded that the criminal had been born as a biological error, and that he was a reversion to a primitive or subhuman type of man.

Since these earlier studies, criminologists have conducted extensive investigations of crime phenomena, and many theories have been propounded. The biological theories, which were the earliest, have tended to stress the general inferiority of the criminal, identification of body types and physical features, abnormal sex chromosomes, and psychosomatic conditions that stimulate criminal activity.

Psychological theories emphasize the destructive instinctive forces of the subconscious mind as causative to crime. They also have suggested that mental degeneration or psychosis and mental defects may be causative elements.

Sociological theories, which have been most predominant since the end of World War II, tend to see the criminal as one who has been estranged from society by rejecting social forces and who is undersocialized. They stress the importance of social structures, such as family, religious, school, and economic structures, in the normal socialization process, and consider that the normal social interaction process of human development has failed in the case of the criminal. They also include such factors as class conflict, subcultural influences, and anomie.

In spite of the fact that a very large number of theories of crime causation have been developed, no single criminological theory is recognized as a fully valid explanation. Each has some factual support, but each fails to explain large amounts of the behavior included in the labels "delinquent" or "criminal." As Shafer has concluded from his review of criminological theory: "No criminological theory has established the 'truth' or shown us the causes of crime."[6]

One of the limitations of current criminological theory appears to be its partial approach to the criminal; that is, criminologists with psychological orientations tend only to look at the psychological aspect of behavior, sociologists concentrate on social factors, and so on. Also, while the earlier biological theories today are in poor repute, the sociological theories tend to be emphasized; but this emphasis limits the approach to the subject too much. What may be needed is a more holistic, total view of criminal behavior.

Second, criminologists may be missing the causative links by concentrating too much merely on studying the "average" criminal or the "average" society. It has been suggested that we need to study more a "self-actualized" or more fully functioning and healthy group of humans, so that we develop a better understanding of the potentialities of man. Then, with this new base of understanding, the "criminal" may better be understood. From this viewpoint it may be discovered that the criminal primarily is a person who was born with unusually high potentialities for growth, but has been blocked in growth expression and turned to crime out of frustration!

Finally, criminological theory has not yet benefited from the extensive research that has been conducted in biochemistry in recent years. This research has produced something of a revolution in that it has generated a number of new ideas about man and his problems. The findings from this relatively new field of knowledge have clearly been shown to relate to delinquent and criminal types of behavior, primarily identifying many of these kinds of behavior as originating in specific biochemical deficiencies and/or abnormalities. Certainly, criminological theory would be advanced considerably by incorporating the findings of biochemical research into their theoretical models of causation.

PROBLEMS OF DEFINITION: WHAT IS DELINQUENT AND CRIMINAL BEHAVIOR?

Before we consider the contributions of biochemistry to the crime problem, it is important to clarify the definition of delinquency and crime. One of the handicaps involved in studying or dealing with the criminal is in the tendency to think in terms of labels rather than people. The terms "delinquent" and "criminal" are labels that we put on certain people when they pass through to a certain point in the criminal justice system. These terms do not necessarily relate to human behavior, but are helpful labels which society uses to identify those who break the criminal laws.

Precisely because labels are not people it is difficult to develop knowledge about persons who are called "criminals" by just studying those criminals. For one thing, a person can be arrested for a crime but not convicted. Or, a person can commit a crime but not be arrested. Thus, there are many more persons who are involved with delinquent and criminal behavior than there are those convicted of crimes. Then, even a number of those convicted may be released, have their sentences suspended, or be put on probation. They, too, would not be included among the criminals placed in prison.

It is not too difficult to see that just studying criminals in jail or prison may not help us understand criminal behavior. The small proportion of the persons who commit criminal acts who end up in prison certainly are not likely to be representative of the ones who avoid institutionalization. We know that a high proportion of the criminal population comes from minority groups, from those in low-income areas of the community, and from those who are mentally retarded and/or poorly educated academically and vocationally. We also know that this institutionalized population is not representative of all those in our society who commit delinquent and criminal acts. Those who commit crimes among the middle and upper classes are called "white-collar" criminals, but their crimes are hard to detect and convict!

Further, what is the relationship between criminal behavior and other forms of behavior, such as speaking back to one's parents or teachers, being disruptive in a classroom, or failing to brush one's teeth or pick up one's room at home? Or, when does criminal behavior begin? Before birth, at birth, after birth? When? Certainly not when the crime is committed for which the arrest is made.

Again, as we have seen earlier, when we study crime, should we limit our study to the basic crimes of violence and property? Do we not, as the statistics indicate, have to study alcoholism and drug addiction, and why these behaviors are so intricately tied-in with the crime problem? Do we not also have to ask questions related to our restive youth, i.e., why the vagrancy, why the vandalism, why the loitering, why the breaking of curfew laws, why the truancy, why the school dropout? And of the parents, too: why the neglect, why the child abuse, why the lack of care and guidance of the children?

It seems that our search to the answers to the crime problem cannot be found merely by looking at the prison inmate, an approach that has been typical of much of our criminological thinking to this time; but we must think deeper and look further. We must identify the role of heredity, the importance of biophysical as well as biosocial factors in the environment. And we must include a deeper understanding of the biopsychology of the developing infant, child, and adolescent before we can understand the delinquent and criminal.

We must not understand merely what is *normal* biopsychosocial development at each of these important stages of human development, but we should strive to understand what is *optimum*—optimum chemistry, optimum physiology, optimum psychology, and the optimum socioculturally. Then, it seems, we will have a means of understanding why humans engage in behavior which, if there is detection, arrest, and conviction, we will call "delinquent" or "criminal."

BIOCHEMICAL CONTRIBUTIONS TO THE DELINQUENT-CRIMINAL PROBLEM

Biochemistry can make important contributions to the delinquent-criminal problem in at least four major areas: (1) development of a more nearly complete criminological theory; (2) treatment of institutionalized delinquents and criminals; (3) programs designed for early detection and diversion of delinquents and criminals from the criminal justice system; and (4) prevention of delinquency and crime.

Criminological Theory

Criminological theory today tends to emphasize the social nature of crime, probably because in the United States the bulk of the scientific study of delinquents and criminal behavior has been conducted by

The Need for a New Approach to the Delinquent Criminal Problem 13

sociologists. Psychological theories of crime causation would rank second in volume, but little, if any, consideration has been given in recent years to biochemical or biophysiological factors.

However, the great volume of recent research in the biochemistry of the body and mind suggests that our current emphasis on sociopsychological factors is too one-sided. This biochemical research has led to development over the past two decades of a new field of practice known as "orthomolecular medicine." This term was coined by Dr. Linus Pauling of Stanford University, a Nobel Peace Prize winner for his discoveries in biochemistry.[7]

Orthomolecular theory suggests that behavior associated with delinquency and crime can be caused by chemical deficiencies or imbalances in the body, or by brain toxicity. These problems can originate from genetic factors, or they can be induced, especially during the birth process or in early childhood by improper nutrition of the mother and/or child.

Biochemical research has revealed that the functioning of the brain is affected by the molecular concentrations of many substances that are normally present in the brain. The optimum concentrations of these substances for a person may differ greatly from the concentrations provided by his normal diet and genetic machinery. Abnormal deficits or excesses in these molecular brain concentrations, depending upon the specific and varying individual needs of each person, will lead to a variety of pathological thought and behavior patterns, some of which, under some conditions, may be seen as "antisocial."

Four major groups of symptoms may accompany biochemical deficiencies or abnormalities in the body, and may be seen as "antisocial": (1) perceptual changes due to nutritional disorders; (2) perceptual changes due to brain allergy; (3) hyperactivity due to nutritional deficiencies; and (4) hyperactivity due to hypoglycemia. These groups recently were defined by Dr. Abram Hoffer, a leader in the orthomolecular medicine movement.[8]

A broad group of perceptual changes can be caused by either vitamin deficiencies or by vitamin dependencies. If a person with a normal need for vitamins does not consume food that provides these needs he will suffer from a *vitamin deficiency*. If a person has requirements for certain vitamins far in excess of the normal amounts, he may suffer from a vitamin deficiency even with a normal diet. This condition is called a *vitamin dependency*.

For example, research has shown that alcoholics develop an excessive need for thiamine, which is caused typically by their poor diets. If they are not given large doses of thiamine, they may develop a very serious, deadly disease called Wernicke-Korsakoff. Or, a person may have an extremely high requirement for the B-3 vitamin and on a normal diet may develop pellagra; he has a vitamin dependency, probably due to a genetic or birth defect. Whereas the *deficiency* was produced by a poor diet for a person with normal needs, the dependency was produced by a normal diet for a person with abnormal needs for a specific vitamin.

A person with a vitamin deficiency-dependency disease can suffer severe distortions in seeing, hearing, and the other special senses. The person also can become very violent at times. The changes in perception can lead to behaviors that can be identified as "antisocial" or "criminal." Usually, neither the person involved nor those around him understand the source of the behavior, and they may impute erroneous motivations to this behavior.

A large number of studies to this time have found that these vitamin deficiencies-dependencies are common among "criminal" groups. In studies of alcoholics and drug addicts, for example, a majority were discovered to be suffering from vitamin dependency disease. Studies of several institutionalized criminal groups also showed that a majority were vitamin B-3-B-6 dependents. It also has been estimated that a major proportion of all acute and subacute schizophrenics and children with learning and behavior disorders are vitamin B-3-B-6 dependents.[9]

A second major cause of perceptual changes is food allergies. Researchers have found a large number of substances that in some persons can trigger violent behavior. Perceptual distortions were highest on a selected group of subjects for such foods as wheat, corn, and milk.[10] A study of prison inmates concluded that at least one-third of the prisoners were suffering from serious perceptual distortions that were being caused by allergies to certain foods. Their behavior had been classified as "psychopathic," a largely untreatable diagnostic entity.

Hyperactivity frequently is seen as an "antisocial" form of behavior. But it may be caused either by nutritional deficiencies or by a condition of low blood sugar (hypoglycemia).

An overactive child is too distractable, too restless, to learn or to respond appropriately to cues for social learning. Thus, the overactive child easily can be labeled a "problem child" by parents and teacher, and early made to feel rejected or a misfit in society. Many of these children, it appears, because they are unable to learn, grow into adulthood with a wide variety of deficiencies in knowledge and skills. A large number become our truants and school dropouts, and possibly later our delinquents and criminals.

Medical research has identified as one aspect of hyperactivity a vitamin B-3 dependency. A person with untreated hyperactivity at an early age has a high possibility of developing schizophrenic symptoms before age 25. This condition has been identified as the *primary cause* of restlessness among youth today, leading them into such activity as smoking, alcohol and drug use, running away, truancy, vandalism, violence, delinquency, and crime.

A second major cause of hyperactivity has been identified through research to be hypoglycemia (low blood sugar). Nutritionists relate this symptom to high consumption of products containing large quantities of refined sugars and starches, and to poisonous food additives. This eating pattern—very common today especially among children and youth—can produce a reaction in the body in which now and then there are major fluctuations in blood sugar levels.

Medical experts in the field report that hypoglycemia can have an amazing effect on behavior, in some cases producing symptoms of lethargy and depression, and in other cases, irritability, suspiciousness, bizarre thoughts, hallucinations, extreme mania, anxiety, and violent behavior. These persons certainly are capable of such acts, for example, as stealing, rape, arson, assault, and homicide.

It has been estimated from several studies that about 90% of the criminal homicides found in prisons, diagnosed as paranoid schizophrenics, are in reality suffering from hypoglycemia or some vitamin deficiency. Also, a high proportion of alcoholics and drug addicts have been found to be similarly affected.

Biochemistry thus has developed a wide range of evidence and theory suggesting a possible biochemical basis for much behavior seen as "antisocial" or "delinquent-criminal." This knowledge can be combined with knowledge relating to socio-psychological factors to develop a much more nearly complete theory of crime-related types of behavior. Once the behavior is understood causatively, then it can be subjected to greater prediction and control, one of the major aims of scientific endeavor.

Treatment of Institutionalized Delinquents and Criminals

Orthomolecular medicine has developed a wide range of diagnostic and treatment techniques, which could be used to treat inmates of our delinquent-criminal institutions. As was earlier noted, the effectiveness of modern-day correctional programs has been seriously questioned. Orthomolecular approaches could greatly increase the effectiveness of treatment, based upon what now is known of this new means of treatment for criminal types of behavior.

Hard-core alcoholics have shown a 71% recovery rate with biochemical treatment. Penitentiary inmates, as well as drug addicts, have shown significant improvements in their violence tendencies. More research is yet needed, but the evidence suggests that recidivism rates among prison populations could be reduced 25–50% with the addition of orthomolecular treatment.

Programs for Early Detection-Diversion

The early diagnosis and treatment of delinquent-crime behavior would undoubtedly be one of the most effective areas of application of orthomolecular treatment. The approach would involve establishment of community-based treatment programs, utilizing early detection of the problem, especially in the schools. Children showing evidence of hyperactivity or perceptual distortions could be identified by a teacher or counselor and referred to the community center for appropriate diagnosis and treatment.

The same process of early detection and referral could be used by truant officers, police, juvenile court personnel, and caseworkers from other community agencies. Pre-delinquents and first offenders thus could be identified and their behavior corrected before the label of delinquent had been used and reinforced. Adult criminals coming into the criminal justice system also could be similarly identified and treated in the community. The combined efforts of these activities together with the demonstrated efficacy of biochemical treatment certainly could divert a major proportion of all of these kinds of problems from the criminal justice system.

The evidence for biochemical treatment success in the community is far more extensive and impressive than that available on institutionalized offenders. Alcoholics and drug addicts in large numbers have been successfully treated, with 80–85% effectiveness. More than 90% success has been achieved with large numbers of children with learning disabilities and behavioral disturbances. And 90% success has been accomplished with treatment of first-offender delinquents-criminals in the community.[12]

Prevention of Delinquency and Crime

Undoubtedly, biochemical knowledge offers the greatest potential value in the area of prevention. The goal of prevention is to develop *superhealth* wht *supernutrition*. It involves the practice of super-nutrition in the home—in the striving for optimum nutrition for the infant, and for the mother, even before the time of conception. It involves maintaining optimum nutrition for all family members from birth to old age.

Prevention involves identification and correction of any *genetic defects* that might be found in the infant and child. It involves the early identification and correction of any *birth defects* that can be observed in the child.

In essence, prevention involves the early detection and correction of all biochemical and physiological abnormalities, as well as maintenance of a super-nutritional diet for all family members. But it also includes general knowledge of, and abstention from, those substances, such as tobacco, alcohol, drugs, and other toxins, known to be injurious to the full and healthy functioning of the body and mind. The prevention approach, although still some time away, holds out the greatest possibility, it is felt, for the reduction of anti-social forms of behavior. Attainment of an optimum biochemical environment, of course, would need to be matched by attainment of an optimum socio-psychological environment, but this would be more of a long- than a short-term goal of prevention. Man lives in both an internal biochemical-psychological and an external socio-cultural world. The two are inextricably interrelated; thus, ideally all areas need to be functioning at optimum levels if full health and development of man's potentialities are to be realized for all persons.

SUMMARY AND CONCLUSIONS

There is great need for a new approach to the delinquency-criminal problem. As has been shown here, crime is on the increase, with the major volume of arrests in the areas of alcoholism, drug abuse, and the restiveness of our children and youth.

There is widespread discontent with the apparent ineffectiveness of most of our contemporary correctional treatment programs, programs which have not appreciably reduced recidivism rates to this time. The limitations of current criminological scientific efforts were discussed here, as well as the fact that treatment of delinquency and crime would be greatly aided if scientists could identify the causative factors behind this behavior more clearly. The terms "delinquent" and "criminal" are not adequate to a full understanding of this behavior, because they really do not describe behavior but are merely labels that society uses to identify persons convicted of breaking the criminal laws.

Biochemical knowledge can make important contributions to criminological theory, and to the diagnosis and treatment and prevention of delinquent and criminal behavior. A discussion of these contributions was presented, merely indicative of the many means and ways in which biochemistry and orthomolecular medicine can aid in resolving this problem. In this introductory paper to more specialized writing on the subject, I have attempted to give a broad outline of ideas that are greatly expanded upon by writers of the subsequent papers in this collection.

It is hoped that through this book the reader will be made more aware of the real nature of the problem of delinquency and crime, and encouraged to investigate more fully the possible contributions of the biochemical approach to resolution of this problem. Only through an open mind can new knowledge seep! The challenge ahead, then, for those who are open to new discoveries, is to conduct more extensive research and applied programs until we clearly know just what this new field of biochemistry has to offer to the solution of this serious and increasing social problem.

References

1. *Uniform Crime Reports: Crime In the United States*, Federal Bureau of Investigation, U.S. Department of Justice, Washington, D.C., 1974. (Note: All statistics used in this paper are taken from the 1974 report.)
2. *A National Strategy to Reduce Crime*, National Advisory Commission on Criminal Justice Standards and Goals, U.S. Government Printing Office, Washington, D.C. 1973, p. 1.
3. *Survey of Inmates of State Correctional Facilities*, Advance Report, U.S. Bureau of the Census, Washington, D.C., 1974.

4. Bailey, Walter, C., Correctional outcome: An evaluation of 100 reports," *J. Criminal Law, Criminology and Police Science* 57: 153–160, 1966.
5. Martinson, Robert M., "Treatment evaluation survey," Division of Criminal Services, New York, 1971 (reported in Adams, Stuart, *Evaluation Research in Corrections: A Practical Guide*, U.S. Department of Justice, LEAA, Washington, D.C., 1975).
6. Shafer, Stephen, *Theories in Criminology*, Random House, New York, 1969.
7. Pauling, Linus, Orthomolecular psychiatry, *Science* 160: 265–271, 1968.
8. Hoffer, Abram, *Humanist in Canada* No. 34: 4–9, 1975.
9. Pawlak, Vic, "Megavitamin Therapy and the Drug Wipeout Syndrome," Phoenix, Ariz.: Do It Now Foundation, 1972.
10. Newbold, H. L., et al., "Psychiatric Syndromes Produced by Allergies: Ecological Mental Illness," annual meeting Academy of Orthomolecular Psychiatry, Dallas, Tx., 1972.
11. Brereton, Lloyd, "Subclinical Pellegra among Penitentiary Inmates," *Humanist in Canada*, No. 34, pp. 10–11, 1975.
12. Cott, Alan, "Orthomolecular Approach to the treatment of Learning Disabilities," New York: Huxley Institute for Social Research reprint, 1972.

Chapter 2 | Alcoholism and Criminal Behavior

Russell F. Smith, M.D.
W. J. Maxey School for Boys
Whitmore Lake, Michigan

INTRODUCTION

Few civilizations reach maturity without the need for a recreational drug; however, the costs of using a chemical compensating mechanism in our societies, though variable, have usually been quite high. The role of alcohol, our civilization's nontaboo recreational drug, has long been a matter of controversy, especially in the area of its relationship to criminal behavior. Alcohol currently exacts an awesome price in money, productivity, injury, death, and criminal acting out. Estimates of these costs are variable but of an order that cannot be ignored. The National Council on Alcoholism estimates the annual costs of its use in industrial waste, tax, law enforcement, and welfare dollars at over 22 billion dollars. The Federal Office of Transportation estimates that nearly half of all fatal automobile and pedestrian deaths are related to alcoholism.

Often we ignore, excuse, or attempt to justify the problem caused by our recreational drugs. Perhaps this response arises from the fact that we cannot conceive of our society without alcohol. Other reasons for such an illogical approach might include collective guilt, unwillingness to accept the fact that our venerated ancestors perhaps made a mistake, or lack of individual or collective alternatives. Recreational drugs tend to become mysterious and gather a folk lore through the centuries. On the subject of recreational drugs, particularly our own, it is difficult even for trained scientists to be completely objective. Disciplinary myopia is common and tends to confuse the literature even more.

We will attempt to cover the subject of alcohol's relationship to crime with a broad brush. In the process we hope to highlight some basic principles and concepts that can be applied as this area is explored. In this way you, the reader, can evaluate the possible role of alcohol and its physiological effects in contributing to social and criminal behavior in most societies.

Alcohol impacts on crime and criminal behavior in several ways: (1) there are the direct criminal activities that result from its being a regulated and taxed substance; (2) there are the indirect behavioral effects of alcohol acting as an anesthetic with a mixed potential to help achieve or frustrate social goals; (3) the acts that result from true addiction and physical dependence on alcohol and other sedative drugs complete the spectrum.

Let us discuss first the illegal production and distribution of alcoholic beverages, which did not disappear with the re-legalization of such beverages following prohibition. One would be naive to believe that illegal distillings, smuggling, and hijacking are not common today. The alcohol, firearms, and tobacco division of the Treasury Department actively expends manpower and dollar resources in the millions each year in a slowly losing battle to stem illegal production and distribution of alcoholic beverages. Illegal alcohol production has become so highly organized and sophisticated that it is nearly respectable. Truck highjacking has become so sophisticated, as has smuggling, that the majority goes undetected or simply ignored, for seldom does anyone or anything get harmed. These activities have attained so much pseudo-respectabilty they are largely ignored or even condoned; many experts place them in the category of victimless crime or, at worst, white-collar crime. Moreover, the crime resulting directly from alcohol's production and distribution is dwarfed by the vast quantities of enforcement dollars and resources expended in the efforts to contain alcohol's behavioral effects.

With respect to behavioral effects, alcohol is one of mankind's great recreational drugs, as such serving as a social lubricant. Its ability to relax inhibitions and thus produce a modified, somewhat unreal world into which we can escape is a necessity in a highly competitive complex society. As instant recreation and relaxation, it serves as a compensating mechanism in many social and emotional situations that we might not otherwise be able to handle unassisted.

Alcohol in this context has been important to many of us individually and as an important facilitator in our society and way of life.

Alcohol has come to enjoy its special, privileged position in Western civilization through a series of progressively changing relationships. Originally our ancestors used psychoactive substances as part of organized religious observance. In this context even relatively dangerous substances are used safely because they are used under the supervision of religious leaders believed to have awesome power to punish here and in the hereafter. Next, the same substances were used as instruments of death. Many present-day pharmaceuticals were once used as poisons. With simple dosage reduction the poisons of the past became the medicines of today, used to restore and maintain health. Finally, as our civilization became more complex and impersonal, an easily transported, highly efficient, economical form of recreation was needed. Logically, psychoactive substances were discovered and adopted by the major civilizations of our world to fit their goals and lifestyle.

Western man has always been achievement-oriented. He has always aspired to master all knowledge and conquer all new horizons. The attitude persists today in our preoccupation with the pursuit of excellence and perfection. We still cherish the all-A report card and seek positions of power, fame, or fortune. One's success as a human being is measured in terms of achievement. Almost all of us secretly aspire to leave our footprints on the moon. For one to achieve at this level, the basic personality trait that must be preserved is native aggression. Alcohol, while permitting relaxation of inhibitions and physical sedation, preserves native aggressional behavior, and the desire to achieve. Persons who are atoxic and incoherent still attempt to become involved in barroom brawls. Persons incapable of walking still attempt to drive home.

Alcohol has many forms. The Canaanites taught the Israelites to make beer and mead. The Turks taught the Macedonians, who in turn taught the Greeks to make wine. With these discoveries Western man found his recreational drug. During another exposure to Middle Eastern culture, during the Crusades, he learned the process of distillation. The more concentrated form of our recreational drug has had us distilling barely mash, oats, wheat, rye, potatoes, corn, and the like ever since. In recent years, solid sedative substances whose psychoactive effects differ very little from those of alcohol have been developed, even further complicating the picture.

The overprescription and illegal diversion of these alcohol-equivalent sedatives and tranquilizers has contributed to the expanding picture of crime produced by the illegal production and distribution of our recreational drugs. As long as demand is high and money can be made, these so-called victimless crimes will flourish, often partially facilitated and approved through the mechanisms of social apathy and indifference. Considered from this vantage point, sedatives other than alcohol represent a large part of our current illegal drug problem.

The behavioral problems that arise from alcohol's use as a recreational drug stem from the fact that it is one of the general anesthetics. Alcohol depresses the central nervous system in progressive stages by causing localized loss of oxygen being carried to the base of the brain. Key to this function is the reduction of oxygen being carried to the reticular area, which is the central communications switchboard between the body and the brain. This process begins with toxic changes in the highest centers and progresses through atoxia to death by respiratory and cardiac arrest. With prolonged anesthesia alcohol's effect on liver causes a toxic low blood sugar, magnesium deficiency, and important shifts in potassium and zinc metabolism. These toxic effects tend to potentiate the effect of oxygen loss with time.

The use of alcohol and its chemical cousins in the recreational sense is certainly not as a general anesthetic. No one would consider it fun to spend his time at a party unconscious on a sofa or the floor. Intoxication to this point is not socially sanctioned and is considered a highly undesirable subjective effect. As a rule, alcohol, its sedative chemical cousins, and, for that matter, all recreational drugs are used in subclinical or, in this case, subanesthetic doses.

These subanesthetic effects are produced by alcohol's interference with the highest and most complicated centers of the brain. Alcohol has subtle progressive effects on recent memory. The subclinical toxic brain syndrome resembles the classical organic brain syndrome by progressively interfering with judgment as well. Judgment is a complex integration of perceived status as reflected by the various senses, relating them to past experience, and then deciding what to do in response. Behavior then reflects accumulated judgment and experience. Alcohol and other sedatives in doses too small to produce any of the familiar symptoms of intoxication or anesthesia do have the capability of causing progressive loss of recent memory and of progressively dissolving accumulated judgment and behavior restraints, uncovering more primitive and unsuccessful behaviors.

Man's earliest behavior is obviously the most primitive, unrestrained, egocentric, and aggressive. A newborn infant simply lies in a crib and kicks, screams, and cries until someone provides a warm bottle or dry diaper. Such simple, demanding aggressive behavior would be unsuccessful in a large group. By age three it is no longer condoned and is labeled a temper tantrum. Multiple appeals to the bare bottom side persuade us all to change our approach. At age three most children adopt the primitive direct approach. If they want another child's sand pail, they walk up, give the other a shove, grab the pail and run. In more complex social settings, such as school, this type of behavior is unacceptable, so less aggressive techniques must be developed and used. The passive aggressive nagging and whining of an elementary school child develops. These techniques are inappropriate in a peer society and must be modified into pseudo-adult mechanisms by early adolescence. In adolescence one must further modify behavior to adjust to the fact that Detroit puts a 380-horsepower engine in an automobile not to be used. In young adult life behavior must be further modified and restrained to permit marriage, employment, and successful incorporation into social units, such as neighborhoods, work forces, political subdivisions, and the like. With advancing years additional experience lays down more sophisticated and successful layers of controls.

Often man's acquired restraints interfere with relaxation, and they can become oppressive. Alcohol and its chemical cousins dissolve off these restraints in a controlled and measured manner, from the most recently acquired back. It is this pharmacological character of alcohol that is prized while posing the greatest personal and social hazards. Greater knowledge of who can drink and what constitute safe individual limits is required before truly responsible drinking can and will occur. Insight alone may not cure all of our social difficulties with alcohol, simply because not everyone can be motivated to behave in a socially responsible way through insight. Biochemistry may actually make this an impossible goal for some.

ALCOHOL AND CRIME

Let's examine this restraint-dissolving mechanism's potential for producing crime and criminal behavior. For purposes of discussion, let us focus on a hypothetical young man and woman in their twenties, married, well adjusted, who go to a cocktail party.

At very low blood alcohol levels, considered insignificant at this age, the marriage vows dissolve off very quickly. Both become resident swingers. Each resents the philandering and flirtations of the other. Harsh words follow. Each becomes angry and resentful of the actions of the other. Verbal abuse may follow. The feelings are difficult to control, and the discomfort that follows prompts the intake of more alcohol. The adjustments of adolescence and young adulthood dissolve off. She becomes competitive and nags incessantly. He throws her coat and scarf in her face and drives the car up to the front entrance and impatiently leans on the horn. Now both are angry, seething with hostility and acting aggressively toward each other.

The pattern produced by alcohol's dissolving off the most recently acquired behavior restraints, uncovering and facilitating underlying anger and hostility while rendering behavior more primitive and aggressive, can have serious personal and political consequences. The native American has had perhaps an undeserved reputation for not being able to handle alcohol well. This characteristic is mostly artifact caused by this mechanism. After years of bitter hostilities, treaties were signed, but resentment and hostility were only recently and superficially controlled. Very little alcohol was required to dissolve off these restraints, producing an angry, aggressive, hostile, acting-out, potentially homocidal person, so often described as being under the influence of "fire water."

Recently a similar drama has been played out in Jamaica. Our State Department succeeded in convincing the Jamaican government that the practice of chewing native marijuana, common since the sixteen hundreds, was unacceptable. The people immediately switched to 150-proof Jamaican rum, converting a Caribbean island and tourist paradise into Dodge City overnight. Not even the infamous Gun Court has been able to stem the tide. The neo-affluent of the emerging African nations have also taken to alcohol, and this single social change has unleashed centuries of tribal rivalries, bitterness, and violence.

To preserve a prized characteristic, achievement, even in our recreational drug, Western man has shown his willingness to accept its companions, aggression and violence. Had our young couple been black and reared in an inner city where self-preservation is instinctive, latent anger and rage would have surfaced as the thin layers of control dissolved off. If a gun, knife, or other weapon is available in such situations, an involuntary homocide can and often does result. Where weapons are not available, serious physical assaults often result. Alcohol and the toxic brain syndrome it produces are implicated in the majority of incidents of mayhem, physical assaults, rapes, and voluntary and involuntary homicides on or off the highways.

These same principles of chemically dissolving behavior restraints apply less frequently to nonviolent crime against property. Uncapping hidden anger, hostility, and aggression can lead to acts of vandalism, arson, or theft. Revenge for real or imagined wrongs may be taken against the property, real estate, or even the savings of others. Alcohol may so commonly be a companion to crime simply because it is the catalyst that makes the crime possible. Years of personal experience support this view, particularly in juvenile offender cases. Often sexual adjustment problems are well controlled except under subclinical alcohol and sedative anesthesia, which permits overt acting out and conflict with society and its laws. A few more drinks, and the blood alcohol approaches about one-half the legal limit most states set for clinical intoxication. Now a young subject becomes an adolescent. In a car the foot goes to the floor, tires squeal in the drive, and ten minutes later a ticket, not for impaired driving but for reckless driving, is issued. The need to prove oneself even at risk of life, a need common in the teens, returns. Again conflict with the law is inevitable.

Such offenses as public intoxication, reckless driving, and disorderly person commonly originate from this level of intoxication on into deeper planes. Driving while under the influence has been determined by the Federal Department of Transportation to be responsible for nearly half the highway and pedestrian fatal accidents. Besides highway homicide, property damage and injuries, negligent homicide, hit-and-run accidents, and hunting and recreational fatal accidents can be traced to adolescent behavior and risk-taking while under the influence of alcohol. Although public intoxication, disorderly person, and drunk and disorderly person are now considered "victimless" crimes, many states are moving to decriminalize these offenses and seek other social solutions. The savings realized in law enforcement resources, although considerable, may not be real or lasting, since these offenses are cut from the same fabric as drunk driving and driving under the influence.

At deeper levels of intoxication the subject becomes a whining, nagging child in adult form. This stage is followed by the primitive acting out of an unrestrained two-year-old. At this level all the potential to restrain violent acting out against persons or property is lost.

Just before intoxication becomes apparent we find a demanding, angry, crying child insisting on immediate gratification. Now, finally, staggering gait, slurred speech, and other symptoms of impaired motor function are so disabling that criminal activity is prevented by the degree of impairment.

Loss of recent memory can cause embarrassing encounters with the law enforcement establishment—the person found in the parking lot trying to pry open the side vent of the car that resembles the one he used to drive; the person who is apprehended trying to pry open the kitchen window to the apartment he lived in two years earlier. These memory problems could well be excellent reasons for the frequent and often illogical circumstances under which many persons are arrested. It may not be accidental that most incarcerated criminals can implicate alcohol in some way in their apprehension.

Alcoholism, with actual increasing tolerance to all sedative drugs, adds several new dimensions to the toxic brain syndrome. Motor impairment is more difficult to induce. A potential homicide, suicide, rape, assault, or bank robbery is more difficult to predict. In addition, in order to permit the central nervous system to adapt to higher and higher levels of sedation, higher levels of adrenaline-like substances are released. Basically, adrenaline functions, as Dr. Selye points out, to ready us for combat or to flee the scene of an emergency. High levels of adrenaline produce a hostile, hyperactive, paranoid state. It takes little imagination to see what some paranoid thinking can do to precipitate murder, violence, rape, assault, and similar criminal acting out.

Alcoholism exacts its human cost at every level. During acute stages, paranoia along with impaired judgment and heightened aggression sets the stage for a number of problems. During withdrawal the person is even more belligerent, agitated, and hostile. Here, premeditated murder, arson, and similar criminal activity are likely. Finally, after the acute agitated phase of withdrawal passes, in a few days a reciprocal profound depression sets in, which can and does precipitate individual, family, and mass suicide.

As physical symptoms become severe during withdrawal in the physically dependent alcoholic, securing and protecting the supply of alcohol and sedatives become central concerns to his life and survival. Like any other addict who uses a substance to stay well, the alcoholic will trade wealth, family, and friendship in order to stay well. Since alcoholism develops often in successful persons in the mainstream of society, their connections provide more frequent opportunities to direct money to their ends. White-collar crime, such as prescription fraud, bunko, extortion, blackmail, embezzlement, and similar criminal activities, is common. Many alcoholics are so adept at rationalization that they often believe they are not committing any crime at all.

The final criminal-behavior–precipitating mechanism seen in alcoholics is the occurrence of permanent irreversible brain changes. Initially a loss of personal pride results. Dress becomes slovenly, appearance unkempt. This is followed by loss of the person's sense of responsibility. These two factors increase the problems of the alcoholic by decreasing his employability while also decreasing any inhibitions he might have in securing and protecting his sedative supply by illegal means. These changes slowly progress into paranoia. This paranoia can progress to the point where subjects will act on misinformation, possibly killing persons whom they believe to be their enemies. Daily papers describe persons who kill their entire families with gas, fire, or firearms, then commit suicide, because they believe their families guilty of unforgiveable sins or caught in a terrible conspiracy. Again the organic brain syndrome caused by alcohol in the alcoholic facilitates criminal acts by distorting the alcoholic's perception of reality, eliminating all barriers to acting out. The desperate pursuit of the means of maintaining an alcohol supply results in more clumsy criminal behavior. Apprehension is the eventual result, with prolonged detention or custodial care the final disposition.

To complete the picture of alcohol's role in producing crime and criminal behavior, its indirect effects on persons other than the user must be explored. Recent studies carried out by the Washingtonian Hospital implicate alcoholic parents in a high number of cases of child abuse and neglect. Many demographic studies of juvenile delinquency implicate alcoholism in one or both parents. Parental alcoholism appears consistently to be statistically more important in childhood problems than broken homes, ghetto background, or serious personal drug involvement. It is reasonable to assume that the alcoholic feels a great deal of guilt. This guilt is generated because the alcoholic needs to drink, yet if he continues he must accept a socially determined definition that is highly distasteful and punitive. In order to reduce his guilt, the alcoholic projects it onto those around them. The spouse is made to feel responsible; constant fighting ensues, which destroys most of the children's role models and personal resources. Most children of alcoholics are constantly told that the parents drink because they, the children, are bad. Eventually, after years of being told they are bad, they decide to deliver as expected.

CONCLUSION

In reviewing the literature implicating alcohol and crime, I find a frightening pattern. Alcohol may actually be implicated in a majority of violent crimes of passion, impulsive murder, assault, and rape. The spectrum continues to implicate alcohol consumption in crimes against property, vandalism, arson, and robbery. Alcohol continues to be a significant factor in such white-collar crimes as embezzlement, confidence schemes, and fraud. A large number of professional-license revocations and legal disbarments can be traced to alcoholism. Control of the public inebriate and drinking driver consumes huge law enforcement resources. This investment of law enforcement manpower results only in congested courts and constantly growing numbers of highway and pedestrian fatalities and injuries. When one adds the law enforcement problems caused by efforts to enforce alcohol tax laws and regulations, and to deal with the child abuse and delinquency accompanying alcoholism, we may well be talking about our nation's number one law enforcement as well as public health problem.

Why can we ignore a problem that costs us thousands of lives each year? A problem that cripples millions more each year, and costs us billions annually in welfare and law enforcement dollars. Alcohol remains our largest public nuisance; our largest highway enforcement problem; our largest drug enforcement problem; our major industrial source of waste; a significant cause of white-collar crime, child abuse, and juvenile delinquency; a major catalyst in murder, assault, and rape. If a single substance were found implicated so completely in the total spectrum of crime, a national attack would be launched to root it out—and, indeed, this has been attempted, but our society has proved to be too immature to survive without its traditional recreational drug. A long hard look at benefits compared to costs will have to be taken sometime in the future. Depending on how we deal with, and assign priorities to, our recreational drug, we may actually find that significant proportions of America's crime problem have a biochemical key.

References

Alcohol and Health, DHEW Publication No. (HSM) 739031, 1972. Calanzero, Ronald J., *Alcoholism*, Charles C Thomas, Springfield, Ill., 1968.
Chafetiz, Morris E., and Blanc, Howard T., *Frontiers of Alcoholism*, Hill Majorie Science House, New York, 1970.
Criteria Committee, *Criteria for the Diagnosis of Alcoholism*, National Council on Alcoholism, New York, 1972.
Davis, V. E., et al., *Advances in Mental Science*, Vol. 1, *Alcohol Dependence*, University of Texas Press, Austin.
Lennard, Henry L., *Mythification and Drug Misuse*, Harper & Row, New York, 1972.
Sexias, Frank A., and Egglshan, Suzie, Work in progress on alcoholism, *Ann. N.Y. Acad. Sci.*, 273: 1976.
Sexias, Frank A. and English, Suzie, Alcohol and the central nervous system, *Ann. N.Y. Acad. Sci.*, 215: 1973.
Smith, Russell, F., A five-year field trial of massive nicotinic acid therapy in alcoholics in Michigan, *Orthomolecular Psychiatry* 3 (4): 209–221, 1974.
Sumers, Marcia J., et al., *Our Chemical Culture*, Stash, Madison, Wis., 1975.
Tarter, Ralph E., and Sugerman, Arthur A., *Alcoholism*, Addison-Wesley, Reading, Mass., 1976.

Chapter 3

Some Theoretical Principles Basic to Orthomolecular Psychiatric Treatment

A. Hoffer, M.D., Ph.D.
Orthomolecular Psychiatrist
Victoria, British Columbia, Canada

INTRODUCTION

Dr. H. Osmond and I were the first physicians to test the therapeutic effect of megadoses (over 3 grams per day) of Vitamin B-3 on schizophrenic patients. We found that the first eight acute or subacute patients admitted either to a mental hospital[6] or to a psychiatric ward[2] were much improved or had recovered when given vitamin B-3. They had all failed to respond to the current best treatment, ECT (electroconvulsive therapy), or insulin coma. This pilot clinical experiment preceded our second double blind controlled experiment (the first in the field of psychiatry), where we compared nicotinic acid, nicotinamide, and placebo in combination with ECT for very depressed and/or aggressive patients and with psychotherapy. This original double blind controlled randomized experiment has since become established as the prototype for the only acceptable way for measuring drug efficacy. For this I am sorry, for with the hindsight of 25 years it is clear it is a very poor method, full of error and bias, more apt to prevent development of useful new treatments than it is to promote them.

These experiments introduced megadoses of vitamins into psychiatry. Unluckily, most psychiatrists were too preoccupied with other matters to pay any attention. Looking backward, I find it strange that this work did not reawaken my earlier interest in human nutrition. Before I entered medicine, I had been a cereal biochemist and had been involved in a peripheral way in the controversy over enrichment of flour with thiamine, riboflavin, and nicotinamide in the U.S., and later in Canada. I must give credit to my four years in medical school, which effectively wiped out my earlier interest in nutrition.

The megavitamin concept did not draw me back into nutrition, I think, because I did not realize that malnutrition was so common, nor was the concept of human individuality yet established. We looked upon the vitamins as drugs, such as insulin or cortisone or even penicillin. It required so much work to establish that vitamin B-3 was effective that we neglected other vitamins, except for some preliminary work with ascorbic acid. We had planned to study thiamine and riboflavin as well, but the inadequacy of the double blind type of experiment forced us to restrict our studies to one vitamin.

In 1966, I was reintroduced to the concept of relative hypoglycemia. I had been aware of it since 1951, when the early studies were reported. But at that time I was too much under the influence of psychoanalytic thought and later swung into schizophrenia research, which left no room for anything else. In 1966, I met Dr. R. Meiers, then on staff at Twin Pines Hospital, Belmont, California. He was enthusiastic about this new concept. He found that a large number of patients suffering from severe depression, tension and other symptoms became well when sugar was eliminated from their diet. A 5- or 6-hour sugar tolerance test had shown them to have very peculiar curves. They most often showed massive increases in blood sugar in the first few hours, followed by severe decreases later on. The clinical data and Bob's enthusiasm were convincing. Within a year I was able to accumulate over a hundred similar cases. It was no longer possible to ignore the pathological role of sugar in the genesis of many of the psychiatric diseases. But still, I had no overall concept of nutrition and its relationship to psychiatry. Fortunately, simply eliminating sugar markedly improves the nutritional quality of any diet.

About five years ago my interest in nutrition in general was finally reawakened by two major contributions, one by Professor Roger Williams, one of the most productive and creative biochemist nutritionists, and one by a team of English physicians, Cleave, Campbell, and Painter.[1] Williams emphasized the unique requirements of nutrients of individuals and the need to meet these unique requirements, while the latter three researchers demonstrated the vital role of fiber, the food components considered indigestible and therefore of little value. But there was still a glaring gap in my own nutritional awakening. Where were the minerals? Did they play a role too? The dedicated research of Dr. C. Pfeiffer and his associates soon demonstrated what we should have suspected all along.

Too little or too much of the essential minerals is just as apt to interfere with cerebral metabolism as is the wrong quantity of vitamins. The brain must function at its optimum level biochemically if it is to carry out its main human function of perception, thinking, feeling, and ordering behavior.

The final addition to orthomolecular psychiatry was made by a few psychiatrists, e.g., W. Philpott and H. L. Newbold, who followed the lead of a few allergists (clinical ecologists) and showed that any psychiatric syndrome can be caused by an idiosyncratic (or allergic) reaction to a variety of chemicals in the environment. With this addition, the relation of the individual to both the psychosocial and biophysical environment seems about complete. Not enough interest has yet been shown in the effect of radiation to which we are exposed, such as light, X-ray, etc., but it will surely be found one day to play a major role for some individuals.

This account of my development in and with orthomolecular psychiatry is given to illustrate how the concept has rapidly expanded from the simple use of one vitamin to its present wide breadth of interest in all aspects of nutrition and other elements of the biophysical environment. There has been no degradation of interest in the psychosocial environment; but there is an increasing awareness of the role of the biophysical. It has been neglected by psychiatrists for far too long.

THEORETICAL PRINCIPLES

The theoretical principles stem from the interrelationship between the individual and two environments. The psychosocial environment includes all those psychological and social factors that shape and mold an individual during his/her lifetime. It also includes conflicts within an individual in the presence of normal biochemistry and physiology of the body. Modern psychiatry has been almost totally interested in this relationship only. It has paid only lip service to the biophysical environment. The latter environment includes all the physical and chemical factors with which we react, such as contact chemicals (food, dust, chemicals in the air, pollutants). These are substances that come into contact with any part of the body. The most enduring and intimate chemical contacts are with ingested substances which touch and are absorbed by the large area that is the inner wall of the gastrointestinal system. But other influences exist as well. These are the various forms of energy in which we are immersed—radiation from cosmic rays to X-rays to ultraviolet radiation, temperature, gravity, atmospheric changes in pressure, and so on. The organization, the Huxley Institute for Bio-social Research, in its name spans both environments, one to honor Sir Julian Huxley for his work in biology, and the other to honor Aldous Huxley for his work in the psychosocial field.

Psychosocial interaction determines how a person with disturbed brain function will behave, whereas biophysical interaction will determine whether the brain functions normally. There is an interaction between psychosocial and biophysical environments that is very complex and to which the individual must react, but I will not deal with this complex system; the other two interrelationships are more directly concerned with psychiatric problems. The psychosocial reaction, by determining the quality of the individual's reaction, also determines how that individual will be diagnosed. There are thus several main theoretical areas fundamental to an understanding of orthomolecular psychiatry, which may be studied in the following two relationshps:

1. *The relationship between the individual and the psychosocial environment.* This leads to a consideration of how changes in brain function lead to abnormality in perception, thought, mood, and behavior. It will be shown that brain abnormality can lead to a variety of psychiatric syndromes, that the presence of a syndrome does not reliably indicate the nature of the disturbance.

2. *The relationship between the individual and the biophysical environment.* A number of factors are known to disturb brain function. These include all biochemical factors which interfere with brain function, from infections to malnutrition to allergies. In this area we have to consider *individuality*, in nutritional requirements as well as psychological individuality. The remarkable variation in individual nutritional needs leads to a consideration of deficiencies. It also leads to a consideration of foods generated by nature as

against those created by man, and finally to a consideration of unusual or allergic responses to foods, chiefly common or staple foods.

Psychosocial Environment

Life reacts with the environment from the simplest one-celled animal swimming about in a drop of fluid to the most sophisticated animal of all—man. But there can be no reaction unless the life form has an awareness of its environment. For this reason, animals have well developed sensory apparatus, which is used to obtain information about the world. These include the senses of vision, hearing, feeling, taste, smell, gravity, and perhaps a number of others still undefined. If two people in the same environment experience the world in the same way, they can both understand each other, especially in matters dealing with the environment. They will agree it is light or dark, raining or snowing; how far they are from each other; and so on. Their sensory information is more or less similar. If, however, as an extreme example, one person is blind, then there may be great difficulty in achieving a consensus. The blind person will not know whether it is light or dark unless he uses other senses, such as noise level, to help. But he will agree with the sighted individual on whether or not it is raining.

Minor perceptual changes may produce major differences in reaction. They need not come from gross anatomical defects such as deafness or blindness, but may arise from disharmony between the sensory end organ, the eye, for example, and the brain, which interprets the information submitted to it. These are the types of sensory changes that commonly lead to psychiatric problems.

Psychiatry has developed a method for examining whether the brain is working correctly. Each examination will cover about four main functional aspects. Different psychiatrists will emphasize them in different ways. In my opinion, no mental state examination is complete unless *perception, thought, feeling* (or mood), and *behavior* have been examined. This examination is as vital to the psychiatrist as is the physical examination to the surgeon.

Mental Functions

Perception. There are two main classes of changes, illusions and hallucinations. Illusions are changes in objects that are really present. The best examples are those changes induced by some of the hallucinogens, e.g., lysergic acid diethylamide (LSD). There are some changes in form, shape, color, and movement. Sounds may be too loud, too soft, or distorted. Taste may become flat or different. Any of the senses may be involved. These changes are considered minor changes but can be as disturbing as the major changes—the hallucinations. Hallucinations are experiences that are independent of things actually present. They include visions or voices or unusual sounds.

The impact of these changes depends upon the kind of change, the sense affected, the role this sensation normally plays for that individual, and the determination of whether the changed world is due to changes within the person or to environmental changes. In the first instance, the impact is less as the individual is aware of the sensory distortions. A normal subject who knows he/she has taken LSD will usually ascribe the illusions to the LSD and will react in a nonpsychotic way. If someone were to place LSD in his drink, the same kind of reaction will produce an entirely different response. In some it has led to suicide—in a moment of psychosis.

About 150 years ago, J. Conolly defined insanity as a disease of perception combined with an inability to tell whether the changes are real or not. This is an amazingly accurate definition, as good today as it ever was, and much superior to current definitions. It combines perceptual changes and thought disorder. According to Conolly, if a person experiences visual hallucinations but recognizes that they are unusual, i.e., the product of a disordered brain, he will be ill but not insane. If, however, he ascribes reality to the hallucinations and reacts accordingly, he will have passed the border from sanity to insanity. A person who believes there is poison in his food because it tastes bitter is insane. If he realizes the bitter taste is due to a taste misperception, he is not. Dr. Osmond and I have developed this theme in detail in our book, *How To Live with Schizophrenia*.[2]

Illusions may be just as frightening and disabling. Many years ago a patient consulted me because she could not keep her eyes on a line from which she was transcribing. Even a ruler placed underneath did not help. This minor visual illusion made her job as secretary very difficult.

Thought. Thought disorder may be divided into two categories—content and process. Content disorder is present when ideas obviously wrong are present and adhered to with great tenacity. I exclude wrong ideas shared by a large number of people, but include those that most people would consider wrong. Delusions, ideas of reference, are examples. Thought content is determined culturally, as well as by the nature of the perceptual changes. Thinking that occurs while observing a visual hallucination is different from the state of mind while listening to hostile voices. The specific details of the content disorder are not as important for diagnosing the syndrome as is the fact that it is present. An obsessive interest by therapists in the details of the delusions, referential ideas, and so on has been of *no* value in the diagnosis and treatment. On the contrary, Freud's single-minded preoccupation with latent homosexuality as a basis for paranoid ideas has been very harmful, because it is wrong, to large numbers of schizophrenic patients. Contrary to the ideas promulgated by psychoanalysts and by the psychobiology of Adolf Meyer, not every idea is important, even though a variety of meanings may be applied to them; a content disorder indicates the presence of a defect in the biochemistry of the brain.

A more advanced and therefore more serious form of thought disorder is thought process disorder. Here, thinking, the act of thinking, is interfered with. The process of thinking has an inherent natural rhythm. Ideas flow at a certain pace, which varies with people, but if it varies beyond certain limits, becomes socially unacceptable. Recall when you last spoke to a person who took a minute to reply instead of a few seconds. There may be changes in speed, such as becoming too slow as in a depression, or too fast as in a manic state. It may cease, as in some forms of catatonia. It may be interrupted frequently by pauses (blocking) or by extraneous ideas.

Memory and concentration problems are forms of thought disorder. Memory disturbances of old age are not so much problems of recall as they are problems in learning. Old people becoming senile may remember their past with little difficulty but have great difficulty in remembering what they ate for breakfast. They have lost the ability to learn quickly and to impress on their memory what they have learned. Their problem differs from the memory problem following a concussion or after a series of ECT, where the past is lost as well as the present. Fortunately, this sort of disorder is shortlived.

Thought disorder also includes judgment—the ability to differentiate between reality and unreality. This, in itself, may determine whether a person becomes crazy or not. As I have pointed out, this was the basis for J. Conolly's excellent description of insanity.

How does one judge that a visual hallucination is a hallucination and not a real person, angel, or devil? The process of deciding brings into play all those elements that have formed a person's ability to reason, to judge. A person living in a culture that accepts every hallucination as real would be much more apt to judge his hallucinations as real. Fortunately, every culture which has been studied does not accept these phenomena as real. The definition of insanity seems to be the same across all cultures. This is not surprising, since any culture which did not so define it could not long survive. The more familiar a person is with hallucinations as an expression of some internal change, the less threatening they are. A psychiatrist ought to have less difficulty deciding his own hallucinations are unreal. Many people who have experienced the perceptual changes produced by LSD are much less fearful of similar perceptual changes that they experience later on as they become schizophrenic. They are not pleased with them, but their knowledge that they once were produced by a drug takes away the terror of the hallucinations.

There are ways of testing the reality of one's perception. Most people are aware that on occasion one of their senses may be faulty even if only for a moment. They may experience a flash of light or see a person who on first inspection looks like a friend. A more careful look reveals the difference. Most people have dreamt and are aware that there are ephemeral sleep hallucinations, whose content is not to be taken very seriously. If, therefore, an individual sees a vision, its reality can be tested by calling upon the other senses, as well as by calling upon logic. If the apparition clearly visible does not speak, then the visual sense is the only one which informs that there is something there. This sense can be ignored. Many years ago Dr. H. Osmond described a normal sailor who heard a voice saying to him each morning as he shaved, "Cut your bloody throat!" He stoically informed Dr. Osmond he knew it was a lot of nonsense and ignored it. He had a perceptual change but he was not insane. One sense may be ignored. Suppose however, that the visual apparition begins to speak. Two senses now proclaim the presence of something. It would be much more difficult to judge it as unreal and few people would do so. A double perceptual disturbance would likely be accepted as real by most people. They would have stepped across the border into insanity. Very rarely, three of the senses are involved. The visual apparition speaking to one might cross over and touch him. According to Conolly, no human would resist the evidence of three senses. Many years ago I had a patient who was convinced an atomic bomb had been dropped on his community. He had seen the flash, heard the explosion, and felt the wave of heat. Three senses were concordant. Only after treatment, when he recovered, did he relinquish his delusional belief. I doubt that anyone else would have disbelieved three senses reporting an event so consistently.

Another way to test reality is to reason about the event. A patient who heard prophetic utterances eventually realized that what was prophesied did not later occur. Slowly he lost his faith in his auditory hallucinations, probably because loss of faith coincided with his recovery. A patient may see an apparition come through a closed door and therefore conclude that the apparition is not real. Yet another way is to test the reaction of other people. If the patient discovers that no one else can experience the same event, he may relinquish his belief in it. For this reason relatives and friends must act as a link between the patient and reality.

Mood. Changes in mood are secondary for schizophrenia—they arise from a combination of perceptual and thought disorder in a person who is suffering from a physical illness. However, schizophrenia and manic-depressive mood swings may coexist, in which case, the depression is primary in its own right and will require specific antidepressant treatment.

Behavior. It should be clear why schizophrenia, a disease of perception and thinking, could be a causative factor in antisocial behavior. This does not mean that patients with schizophrenia are more apt to engage in criminal behavior, but it does mean that when the disease is present, the criminal behavior may be more bizarre, more difficult to understand. (For example, it was hard to understand why a minister should suddenly attack a young girl. To his astonishment he found himself locked in a psychiatric ward. But he had only obeyed God's command. While he was walking downtown, the heavens suddenly opened with a vast illumination, and he heard God command "You have syphilis and only intercourse with a young virgin will cure you!") It also means that every person who commits a major crime, and many who engage in minor crime, ought to be examined for perceptual changes. A surprising proportion will have them. Their antisocial behavior is a product of an illness.

Syndrome

A syndrome is a combination of signs and symptoms that have become known to be associated with an organ or a system of the body. Thus, when a patient complains of a pain in the chest on breathing, with fever and cough, the physician recognizes a pneumonia syndrome. But its cause remains unknown. It may be tuberculosis, pneumococcus, a virus, and so on. If a patient complains of excessive hunger and thirst, weight loss, and excessive output of urine, he has the diabetic syndrome. Again, the cause is unknown until other investigation is completed.

The same principle applies to psychiatric syndromes. They arise from certain abnormalities in brain metabolism. Since there are four main areas of brain function, i.e., *perception, thinking, feeling,* and *behavior*, it follows that combinations involving these areas will produce syndromes. A combination of perceptual and thought changes causes the schizophrenic syndrome. These are primary changes and lead to mood and behavioral changes. If there are no changes in perception and in thinking but only depression or mania, one has a manic-depressive or depressive syndrome. If there are only behavioral changes, one may be dealing with antisocial behavior due to psychosocial factors alone, or due to changes in brain biochemistry.

The main syndromes are composed of:

1. Perceptual and thought changes producing schizophrenia in adults, learning and behavioral disorders in children and adolescents.
2. Mood disorders with anxiety, depression, tension, fatigue, or mania.
3. Behavioral disorders.
4. Mixed syndromes.

A fair number of patients have both the schizophrenic syndrome and the manic-depressive syndrome. In some patients the two may occur independently of each other, and each may respond to its own specific treatment. One patient has been free of all perceptual and thought changes for five years on megavitamin therapy, but still suffers from his manic-depressive mood swings. Both syndromes, when they coexist, must be treated with the most specific treatment known.

Schizophrenic Syndromes

The presence of the schizophrenic syndrome merely points to the brain, certain as yet unidentified portions of the brain, as the seat of the disorder. But it does not tell us what has caused it. The cause can be any one of a number of disorders, each causing a schizophrenic syndrome. This means that there will be no rational treatment until the particular cause of the syndrome is determined. It also means that genetic studies are necessarily crude since there was no attempt to segregate patients into three homogenous syndromes.

Over the past one hundred years or so the definition of these syndromes has become more accurate. At the turn of the century a psychiatrist working in a mental hospital in the U.S., especially in the South, would consider four diagnoses in the differential of insanity (dementia praecox). These were scurvy, pellagra, general paresis of the insane, and, of course, dementia praecox. That is, these four conditions (diseases) were enough alike that it required some investigation to determine which disease was present. Three of the diseases are today under control, having been ripped away from psychiatry to become the property of internists, neurologists, and family physicians. The fourth disappeared by changing its name to schizophrenia. Since then a number of other syndromes have been characterized, including phenyl pyruvic oligophrenia, chronic rheumatic fever, other chronic infections, and some intoxications such as by atropine (belladonna).

Over the past 20 years, the hallucinogens have come into use and have produced a large number of schizophrenic syndromes. Within the past 15 years, orthomolecular psychiatrists have added several new ones, which probably account for the majority of schizophrenic patients seen today. They include the vitamin B dependencies, primarily B-3, B-6 and B-12, in descending order of frequency, the cerebral allergies, and the syndromes due to excess of certain toxic elements such as lead, copper, and mercury and deficiencies of trace elements such as zinc and manganese. The vitamin B dependencies make up the majority of cases of acute and subacute schizophrenia, while the cerebral allergies make up a substantial proportion of chronic schizophrenics. The proportion of all schizophrenics in each group is not known, as no surveys have been made. Since the cerebral allergies will not respond as well as the others to all standard medication, they tend to accumulate in the chronic group.

Undoubtedly other types of dependencies will be discovered when physicians begin to look for them. It is already known that thiamine dependency produced by excessive consumption of alcohol will cause Wernicke Korsakoff disease. I expect that other B vitamins will be found to be related to diseases today considered baffling.

Theoretically, multiple dependencies should exist. I have treated at least one patient who relapsed without either vitamin B-3 or vitamin B-6. Both were required. It is possible that Huntington's Chorea is a multiple dependency—on vitamin E and vitamin B-3. Perhaps multiple sclerosis is a double dependency as well—on thiamine and vitamin B-3.

Antisocial Behavior

Antisocial behavior may be tolerated without being labeled criminal, as it is for many people drunk on alcohol. A crime is any act declared to be against the law. The definition changes continually. Antisocial behavior is a wider term and perhaps more accurate.

For decades every possible psychosocial factor has been invoked as a cause for criminal behavior. At the same time scant attention has been given to biophysical factors. Perhaps it is for this reason that the results of all psychosocial corrective measures have been so ineffective. The explosive development of theory and practice in psychology and sociology has not been accompanied by any improvement in either our understanding of or the prevention and treatment of antisocial behavior. This volume may well be the first concerted attempt to correct the imbalance.

Conolly's definition of insanity, as a disease of perception combined with an inability to judge these changes unreal, provides a direct link between nutrition of the brain and behavior. The most effective way to demonstrate the link is to outline a few cases.

Several years ago,[3,4] a young schizophrenic patient named Skafte killed his employer's son and severely wounded his employer. After a long history of serious difficulty, after a previous shooting episode when he had shot his sister, after a period in jail and four admissions to a psychiatric ward, he had been discharged. He suffered from a variety of perceptual and thought changes. On the morning of the shooting he decided to kill himself. He had already made several serious suicidal attempts before, each one leading to his admission.

That morning he heard voices. He later told the police, "So I went behind the barn and got the gun back in. But something was saying not to kill, wait, and kill the rest when they got home." When Skafte was examined in a mental hospital, he told his psychiatrist that he had shot the boy and his father because a man's voice had told him to. Unfortunately, none of the psychiatrists or psychologists really believed that Skafte heard voices. They were so impressed with the diagnosis "immature personality" that the voices could not be real. The preconception prevented any additional accurate observations.

The defense centered on the Conolly definition of insanity, perhaps the first time it was ever thus used in North America. As an expert witness for the defense, I outlined the perceptual theory of schizophrenia. I showed the jury the results of tests with HOD and EWI.* Every psychiatrist for the Crown attempted to prove that the defendant was not insane (legal definition). The judge in his summation stated that the jury did not have to consider the evidence of the psychiatrists at all, because in his view there was ample evidence of this young man's insanity quite apart from the evidence of the psychiatrists. He was found "not guilty because of insanity" and is still in an institution.

Mickey Hleboff,[4] represents another such case. Hleboff was sentenced to a provincial correctional institute, having been found guilty of a number of offenses involved with or arising out of excessive alcoholism. While he was in prison, his behavior became very odd. The change was not recognized by the guards, who considered him bad or evil. Hleboff concluded that he would die in prison because there was a plot among the guards to kill him. His conclusion was based upon the following perceptual evidence:

1. He could smell gas coming into his cell from the air ventilator. He tried to deal with this by plugging the vent with paper. This act annoyed his guards, who had to remove it.
2. When he ate, he tasted poison in his food. After he ate, he often suffered from nausea and vomiting.
3. He could hear the guards talking against him.

He explained that this was all evidence that he was being poisoned by gas and by poison in his food.

*These are the Hoffer-Osmond Diagnostic and Experimental World Inventory screening instruments.

At the first opportunity he escaped—in order to save his life. Surely this was a rational decision from his point of view. He was insane by the Conolly definition. The courts agreed, and he was found "not guilty on account of insanity."

A third patient, Hofman,[5] killed nearly all the members of one family. This young man had been schizophrenic for many years. After one month in a mental hospital he had been discharged. About a month later he committed the mass murder. On examination I discovered that he suffered from a large variety of perceptual changes, which he accepted as real. He was torn between his fear of, and wish to obey, the devil, whom he had seen frequently, and the instructions from his guardian angel, also clearly visible to him. On one occasion he had also heard and touched her. The devil demanded he kill; the angel persuaded him not to. On the night in question he obeyed the devil. He was also found "not guilty because of insanity," and languishes in a psychiatric prison, probably never to be discharged.

There is no need to keep on giving examples. They will be found in any book written by recovered schizophrenic patients. They will be found by any clinical psychiatrist who is curious enough to examine a patient for perceptual changes. They will not be surprising to any person who has experienced the impact of the minor perceptual changes produced by the hallucinogens. In my opinion, every person charged with a crime, especially if there is an element of the bizarre about it, should be given a thorough perceptual examination, using the HOD and the EWI tests. Anything less constitutes a failure in the examination, and may cause the person grave harm.

There are patients who no longer suffer perceptual changes, but whose illness has become chronic. It is characterized by thought disorder and antisocial behavior. Several years ago it was shown that childhood schizophrenics who were observed into adolescence followed two main pathways. One group were chronic schizophrenics in state hospitals; the other group were typical psychopaths who could not remember ever having had perceptual changes. Every one had clearly documented hallucinations before puberty. Whether or not he wound up as a chronic schizophrenic in an institution or as a psychopath roaming the streets of New York City depended upon whether his hallucinations remained or vanished. I have seen many adolescent patients who could not ever remember having had hallu-

Some Theoretical Principles Basic to Orthomolecular Psychiatric Treatment   45

cinations, although they had been present during childhood. In fact, it is the rule, rather than the exception, that once these perceptual symptoms are gone, they tend to fade from memory. Like nightmares or dreams, in general, the further they are backward in time, the less apt they are to be remembered. It may be very difficult to diagnose the psychopath as a chronic schizophrenic, simply because he will deny perceptual changes. It might be better to include all bizarre forms of behavior as evidence for thought disorder and, therefore, for schizophrenia. Unless detailed childhood descriptions are available, I suspect many chronic schizophrenics will continue to be diagnosed as psychopathic.

Recently D.M., age 27, came for his final examination before my move to Victoria, B.C. D.M.'s father is a chronic paranoid schizophrenic divorced from his mother. D.M.'s younger brother is a chronic not yet hospitalized schizophrenic. D.M. became sick when he was five years old. He became a nervous, high-strung, destructive child, who displayed many temper tantrums. Play therapy for three years yielded no improvement. When he was 12 he was very depressed, sometimes incoherent and inaccessible. Two years of psychotherapy and tranquilizer therapy were of no value. I first saw him in December, 1963, when he was 14. There was no doubt about his schizophrenic psychosis. He heard voices all the time, was very paranoid, believed he had left his body, and was very apathetic. He was started on vitamin B-3 therapy, but in June, 1964, required a series of seven ETC. By November, 1964, he was much better. By 1965, voices were less troublesome. Until January, 1966, he was given various experimental preparations with no additional improvement. On January 28, 1966, he was started on nicotinamide adenine dinucleotide (NAD), 1 gram per day. All other medication was discontinued. One week later he was nearly well. His grandmother, who had been looking after him, reported she had never before seen him so well. He still heard voices, but rarely, and he was not concerned about them. On March 2, 1966, no more NAD was available. His previous megavitamin tranquilizer program was resumed. Two days later he reverted to his pre-NAD condition. He continued to improve slowly.

By September, 1967, all voices were gone. He still remained socially inept. Eventually he was placed in a rehabilitation workshop to learn a trade. But he still tended to remain passive and disinterested, and developed a tendency to become obese. Therapeutic visits once every three months were designed to check his medication and his psychosocial progress. In June, 1968, he was given lithium carbonate, an antihistamine in the evening, and a tricyclic antidepressant. When seen last, he had lost his craving for food, was eating normally. He would be considered normal today except that at age 27 he has been deprived of the normal life experiences he should have had. He is still at the workshop, looking hopefully toward a job. He is honest, reliable, gentle, and thoughtful, and will one day be a good worker, but at a relatively simple task. He has no recollection of ever having heard voices. If he were antisocial, there would be no present basis for even suspecting childhood schizophrenia. His present medication includes: nicotinic acid, one-half gram after each meal; nicotinamide, the same; ascorbic acid, 1 gram after each meal; and thiamine and pyridoxine, 250 mg per day. He is also on zinc sulfate and trifluoperazine, 2 mg per day.

But there are other causes of antisocial behavior. A disorder of judgment is a very important one. It may occur in the absence of perceptual changes. Hypoglycemia, cerebral allergy, and even tranquilizers may so distort judgment as to lead to antisocial behavior. It may be associated with hyperirritability or depression. These factors will be discussed elsewhere in this volume.

The Biochemical Environment

The biophysical environment includes all those forces or energies that impinge on a person and in which he is immersed, as well as the chemicals with which he is in contact all the time, or on occasion. I will not deal with the physical factors, such as temperature, gravity, humidity, and radiation (light, ultra-violet, X-ray, and so on); or with the biological factors, such as molds, viruses, parasites, and so on. There is no doubt that they are all relevant. I propose to deal with one particular biochemical environment, our food, our nutrition. For the biochemical environment that is our food very quickly becomes or influences the chemical environment of each cell in our body. It is becoming increasingly clear, even among scientists who have not embraced orthomolecular medicine, that foods have a major impact on behavior.

Nutrition

Most plant cells require inorganic nutrients, air, light, and a habitat, a place in which to grow. They synthesize every organic compound required, including proteins, fats, carbohydrates, and all the accessory factors, such as enzymes, vitamins, and hormones. They are marvelous, complete, minute chemical factories. But all the energy available to them is consumed in synthesis and in growth. There is none left over for locomotion. A major evolutionary step occurred when one cell learned to engulf another. These cells were our first animal ancestors. For when one cell ate another, all the essential nutrients already present in the one eaten became available to the other. This process freed an immense amount of energy, which was diverted into movement. I am convinced that without the principle of eating, rather than of making everything, there would be no life on earth as we see it today. This process was very slow, but once started, irreversible. The presence of all the essential nutrients made superfluous much of the synthetic machinery present in the cell. It became possible to discontinue or drop this aspect of the cell's biochemistry. However, new functions such as movement and thinking would require a new synthetic apparatus within the cell. The animal cell would retain some of the old apparatus, drop some, and attain new apparatus. The old machinery (enzymes, etc.) would be what is common to plant and animal metabolism. The new machinery would serve locomotion and thought functions unknown to plants. The discarded machinery would include enzymes no longer necessary.

An example is the enzyme required to complete the conversion of glucose into ascorbic acid. It is lacking in every human, causing what Stone[6] calls the genetic disease "hypoascorbemia." The explanation of how dropping some synthetic machinery from cells could enhance survival was clearly outlined by Pauling in 1968.[7] Over the years, a large number of molecules have become essential nutrients, i.e., the animal cells are no longer able to make them. They include vitamins and essential amino acids. Those substances were always available by eating plants or other animals, and there was no point in retaining the ability to make them. There is no reason to believe that the evolutionary process has stopped. It is likely that animals will continue to drop unessential machinery. Elsewhere, I have suggested that schizophrenia due to B-3 dependency is the price we are paying for discontinuing the synthesis of NAD (vitamin B-3) from tryptophan. Perhaps, one day, every human will be unable to convert tryptophan into NAD. We had better make sure there is enough vitamin B-3 in our diet. We can then enjoy all the advantages of not needing to make NAD from tryptophan while suffering none of the disadvantages of a vitamin B-3 deficiency.

Nutrition is thus the process of providing the essential nutrients that we require.

Supernutrition

Over the years nutritionists have slowly recognized more and more essential nutrients. By now some seem to believe that every essential nutrient is known and that man can create an optimum complex of nutrients, which will be as healthy as the foods from which the nutrients have been extracted. But this preoccupation with technology has blinded most nutritionists to the fact that we evolved and adapted to food and not to food artifacts. Modern technology produces a large variety of food artifacts, all of which are inferior in quality compared to the original foodstuff, which was the basic material. Man adapted to food, which is a complex mixture of protein, fat, and carbohydrate, all present in a pattern generated by a living plant or animal. One component may be the most abundant in a food, but it will contain smaller quantities of the others. The vitamins and minerals which were required by the plant or animal to create its own structure and to function are also present. The protein, fat, and carbohydrates are not present in a pure form in nature. They are pure only when they have been extracted from food. Thus, in order to make wheat starch, the wheat must be ground, the flour extracted, and the protein, fat, vitamins, and minerals removed. When protein is extracted from soybean, all the other constituents are removed. But all the other constituents are essential foods. It is not possible to isolate all the constituents of any food, reconstitute them, and expect to get back a product as nutritious as was the original product. Not only is there a net loss of nutrients, but there is the addition of trace amounts of chemicals used to extract the components. Proteins, and so on, are in reality food artifacts. They are products created by chemists from food and never exist in a pure state in nature. But because nutritionists have equated protein, whether in the original food or extracted, as having the same nutritive value, they have allowed a massive deterioration of our national food.

We have adapted to whole foods, which must be digested slowly in our digestive tract. The food components are released slowly and simultaneously. The vitamins and minerals are released along with amino acids, fatty acids, and sugars. There is a slow absorption into the bloodstream, not a sudden massive influx of material, such as occurs when one consumes any sugar-enriched food. The whole digestive apparatus and the control mechanisms are adapted to perform slow digestion efficiently, and not adapted to massive influxes of sugars, starches, fats, and so on. Even vitamins and minerals are best given along with food and in a form that will release them gradually and continuously. No preparation concocted by man can approach the nutritive value of whole foods unless the following measures are carried out:

1. Provision of all the original food components.
2. Provision of some mechanism for releasing them slowly, as occurs in the digestion of real food.
3. Provision of equivalent activity for the digestive tract, its enzymes, and its motor activity.

In short, the only food which can match nature's food is natural food. Agriculturists and nutritionists should be concerned with the breeding and production of food that is superior to present varieties. There is no especial virtue in breeding for square tomatoes if at the same time they contain less ascorbic acid. No new variety should be licensed until it can be shown that it is nutritionally equal, or superior, to the present standard varieties. Recently it was announced that a new variety of apricot had been perfected, which matured earlier, yielded larger fruit, and ripened more uniformly. Significantly, nothing was said about its nutritive value. It was assumed that all apricots are equal. Ross Hume Hall titled a recent report "Beware of Those Fabricated Foods." His book,[8] published in 1974, *Food For Nought, The Decline in Nutrition*, is an essential textbook for every person, especially for nutritionists and physicians. He writes: "The all-American diet has largely become the all-fabricated diet—consisting of foods that have been taken apart and put together in a new form." His advice to ensure good health from optimum nutrition includes:

1. Avoid canned, bottled, or packaged food as much as possible. Use fresh fruit and vegetables prepared at home. Eat fruit and vegetables raw as much as possible.
2. If you must eat fabricated foods, eat those with the shortest list of chemical additives.

3. Avoid foods adulterated by sugar and salt. Sugar is labeled inverted sugar, dextrose, corn syrup. All are sugar.
4. Use only whole, grain cereal products.
5. Avoid all precooked and frozen prepared foods.
6. Avoid all fabricated snack foods.
7. Vitamin supplements may be required.
8. Exercise.

My rule is that you should avoid (1) all junk food, i.e., any preparation containing added sugar (a rule that will exclude most foods with additives since the two groups tend to run together), as well as food prepared from refined flour; (2) all foods you know make you sick, i.e., foods to which you are allergic.

Individuality and Variability

Scientists have known for a long time that the superficial aspects of an organism are quite variable. Every student has heard of the normal curve of distribution, of means, and of standard deviations. These terms have been applied to height, weight, color, fingerprints, and so on. Variability is such a common property of life that it is unobserved. In the same way that we remain unaware of our atmosphere when the air is quiet, so do we remain unaware of the ubiquity of variability. It is only when it is absent that we are astonished. Identical quintuplets command worldwide attention.

We live in an atmosphere of variability. Without variability there could have been no evolution. Elsewhere I have developed the theme that variability (or in other words, individuality) was essential for mammalian psychosocial development. One of the essential problems nature had to face was to establish a bond between mother and infant. In the absence of such a bond, the infant and the race would perish. This means that the infant must be able to distinguish its parent from a host of similar (but not identical) adults. Visualize an infant surrounded by a large number of adults, all identical in every aspect—smell, color, shape, form, and behavior. Humans have a remarkable gift of being able to distinguish their fellow humans, one from the other, in spite of slight variations in color, shape, and so forth. When this ability is lost, a person's life may disintegrate. A few years ago a young schizophrenic man was brought to me by his minister, to save him from suicide. With great anxiety and depression he told me that there was a plot against his life. His evidence was that wherever he was, the same person was near him. When he was sitting in my waiting room, the man sat next to him. When he was driving in his truck, the man was in the car behind him. He naturally concluded that he was being followed, as part of a plot against him. On further examination he reported that all faces were blurry at the edges, and they all looked alike. Is one of the difficulties of the autistic child an inability to distinguish Mother?

Most anatomists know that our internal organs also vary enormously. The unwary surgeon, not aware of this, may cause his patient serious harm. Police departments depend upon the individuality of fingerprints. Recently, voice prints have been coming into vogue. But in spite of all this evidence that no two individuals are alike, even identical twins, nutritionists and physicians alike have seldom given much thought to the enormous variability of human nutritional requirements. Something known intuitively by man (one man's meat is another man's poison) has been almost totally ignored. This matter has been brought to our attention forcefully by Roger Williams[9] and his colleagues. We now know that individual requirements for protein, fat, carbohydrate, vitamins, and minerals vary enormously. The requirements for bulk components such as protein, fat, and carbohydrate can not vary nearly as much because of their sheer bulk, but vitamin requirements can vary up to 1,000-fold. Most people remain well on 1 microgram (1/1,000 of a milligram) of vitamin B-12 per day. However, a very few require 1,000 micrograms per day. The individual's requirement for vitamins may be far outside the normal range of variation. Once this is recognized, it becomes clear that average requirements designed to guide governments with respect to population needs are of no value to the individual and must not be so used. The recent attempt of the FDA to apply these kinds of standards to individuals in the U.S. was defeated by an act of Congress. The citizens were wiser than the bureaucrats of the FDA and their advisors, and from the pressure they generated persuaded Congress to strip the FDA of its power to interfere with the right of each individual to solve his/her own unique nutritional needs.

The majority of people have requirements within a broad average range. For them a program of good nutrition may be adequate. A smaller proportion have much greater requirements, which are impossible to meet even with a perfect nutritional program; those individuals are then said to be dependent. If a person lives on a diet containing too little vitamin B-3, he will, in turn, develop pellagra. Here the problem arises from his special increased requirement. In the first case, the deficiency disease, pellagra, results. In the second case, he is said to have a dependency. I have provided ample evidence in many reports to suggest that a vitamin B-3 dependency can cause a schizophrenic syndrome.

Individuals with a dependency will require vitamin or mineral supplementation.

Antisocial Malnutrition

Any form of malnutrition can cause deviant behavior. In each case this cause should be examined for. The common forms of criminal malnutrition are (1) the saccharine disease, especially its psychiatric component; (2) the vitamin B dependencies, especially B-3, B-6, and B-12; and (3) the cerebral allergies.

The Saccharine Disease. This is the term originally applied by Cleave et al., to a large number of physical diseases at first glance not related to each other. They include conditions like obesity, diabetes, peptic ulcer, diverticulitis, constipation, even cancer of the large bowel. The diet responsible for these conditions is typically very high in refined carbohydrates, such as sugar, starch, and syrup, and low in fiber. The average American and English diet is designed to cause these diseases. Cleave and his colleagues did not apply the term to the psychiatric aspects of these conditions. In my opinion, the emotional components of obesity, ulcer, and so forth, are a direct expression of the same diet. It is not that peptic ulcer causes depression, anxiety, or tension. Rather both are caused by the saccharine diet—high sugar, low fiber. A large number of patients have none of the physical diseases, but suffer from severe fatigue, anxiety, depression. They swell the offices of psychiatrists. Generally they are ungrateful patients for good reason—they do not respond well to current psychiatric therapy. They are no different psychiatrically from patients with the physical aspects, but there is a selective sorting out. The family physicians screen out those who have physical symptoms, such as ulcers, because they are familiar with those conditions and can prescribe universally used remedies. The rest are referred to psychiatrists.

My use of the term saccharine disease is meant to highlight the cause of these conditions. These patients are the same as those found to have relative hypoglycemia or functional insulinism. Not only are they our typical neurotics, but they may show enough confusion and thought disorder to engage in antisocial behavior. In 1966, a man, aged 60, came to see me. He was charged with petty theft; but it was quite bizarre. He was a very wealthy man. One afternoon, about 4:00 P.M., he was caught shoplifting a 20¢ bauble. A 5-hour glucose tolerance test, started at 12:00 noon, showed a very low blood sugar level at about 4:00 P.M. He had gone into a hypoglycemic spell, became confused, forgot his wife had been dead for two years, and saw the 20¢ item, which he felt she would like. On the basis of this evidence the charge against him was dismissed.

How many major crimes are committed during hypoglycemia episodes? We will not know until all persons charged with criminal behavior are examined. Generally, hypoglycemia leads more to antisocial behavior characterized by confusion, or simple lack of social judgment.

The Vitamin B Dependencies. The classical prototype is pellagra. A study in Egypt many years ago showed that pellagrins often committed violent bizarre crimes. Since pellagrins suffer from the same perceptual and thinking disorders as do schizophrenics, this is not surprising. Subclinical pellagra was described over 40 years ago as pellagra without typical skin changes. Children in 1935 with subclinical pellagra were typical of the child with learning and behavioral disorders today. They responded promptly to vitamin B-3. Many of these children are involved in antisocial behavior during adolescence, even though they do not become schizophrenic.

I have used megadoses of vitamin B-3 to treat antisocial schizophrenics. One young boy while ill shot at his mother and father, who were in bed. The bullet hit the pillow between them. The court on the basis of my testimony suspended sentence on condition that he come under my care. He received a series of ECT plus vitamin B-3 therapy, and has remained well since 1968. Today he is married and getting on well, and has shown no more antisocial tendencies. Another man, a graduate student, was arrested for firing at passing cars. On the basis of my testimony he was not charged. He started on megadoses of vitamin B-3, completed his Ph.D., and is today a professor in a U.S. university. He has not had any more antisocial tendencies. I have no doubt that most orthomolecular psychiatrists have made similar observations. How many such patients on tranquilizers have recovered? There is a tendency with patients on tranquilizers alone for their judgment to be disrupted and for antisocial behavior to be accentuated.

Cerebral Allergies. This type of antisocial behavior is similar to that caused by the saccharine disease, or by the vitamin B dependencies. Both mechanisms may operate. I believe that the vast majority of the addictions—to heroin, morphine, amphetamines, alcohol, and so on—fall into this group. The addicted persons suffer from a variety of vitamin dependencies and the saccharine disease. I believe a good case could be made for the hypothesis that these causes are behind the explosive development of all the addictions. In my view, there will be no control of the addictions until the basic role of malnutrition as a main cause is acceptable and acted upon. I have found that alcoholics who adopt the principles of supernutrition have much less difficulty abstaining from alcohol; this also applies to obesity. If sugar disappeared from nutrition, we would soon not require TOPS, Weight Watchers, and the other organizations that attempt to deal with the problem.

SUMMARY

Orthomolecular psychiatry recognizes the two major environments—(a) the psychosocial and (b) the biophysical. When the nutritional environment is inadequate, there are changes in perception or in thinking. These in turn change the normal relationship between the individual and the psychosocial environment. Often this problem is responsible for antisocial behavior.

Orthomolecular nutrition recognizes (1) the need to provide the type of food to which we have adapted, whole unprocessed food; (2) the individuality (or variability) of people; (3) the need to provide an optimum nutrition environment for each individual.

Orthomolecular physicians dealing with criminal behavior recognize that a substantial proportion of their patients have committed antisocial acts while under the influence of changes in perception and in thought. The three most common forms of criminal malnutrition are (1) the vitamin B dependencies; (2) the saccharine diseases (the relative hypoglycemias); (3) the cerebral allergies.

References

1. Cleave, T. L., Campbell, G. D., and Painter, N. S., *Diabetes, Coronary Thrombosis and the Saccharine Disease*, John Wright and Sons, Ltd., Bristol, England, 1969.
2. Hoffer, A., and Osmond H., *How to Live with Schizophrenia*, University Books, New Hyde Park, N.Y., 1966, 1975.
3. Kahan, F. H., Skafte: A 'symptom-free' murderer, *J. Orthomolecular Psychiatry* 2: 169–181, 1973, and 3: 37–64, 1974.
4. Kahan, F. H., A strange case, *J. Orthomolecular Psychiatry*, 3: 111–132, 1974.
5. Kahan, F. H., Schizophrenia, mass murder and the law, *J. Orthomolecular Psychiatry*, 2: 127–146, 1975.
6. Stone, I., *The Healing Factor. Vitamin C Against Disease*, Grosset and Dunlap, New York, 1972.
7. Pauling, L., Orthomolecular psychiatry, *Science* 160: 265–271, 1968.
8. Hall, R. H., *Food for Nought. The Decline in Nutrition*, Harper and Row, New York, 1974.
9. Williams, R. J., *Biochemical Individuality*, John Wiley and Sons, New York, 1956. See also Williams R. J., *You Are Extraordinary*, Random House, New York, 1967.

Section II: ECOLOGIC-BIOCHEMICAL RESEARCH IN DELINQUENCY-CRIME RELATED PROBLEMS

INTRODUCTION

An increasing number of research studies in recent years have been directed toward the ecological and biochemical aspects of human behavior. Much of this research appears to have been originated by medical practitioners who were stirred to investigative action by their patients. An increasing number of the patients in these studies were children who were chronically hyperactive or who had episodes of violent or bizarre behavior. Other patients were children and youth referred by the juvenile court who were having similar but more extreme types of "antisocial" behavior. Some were inmates of juvenile training schools or youth and adult prisons.

Since these problem types largely were unresponsive to classical psycho-medical approaches many of these physicians began to investigate some of the findings that were being uncovered by nutrition-conscious research biochemists. Some of these practitioners even began to explore some of these research leads with groups of their own patients. Even though the research is far from complete at this time, this ecologic-biochemical research has begun to suggest some interesting causative patterns. These patterns also tend to show a common link with delinquency-crime related problems.

One important pattern that has emerged from this research deals with the behavioral problems of hyperactivity and violence. Hyperactive behavior tends to show itself as a chronic symptom, whereas violence appears to be more sporadic. Either form of behavior can be severely maladaptive, whether it occurs in the family, the school, or society at large. The result can be failure to develop appropriate social behavior in most areas of life. Also, since the behavior is misunderstood as to its origin, most parents and school and court authorities tend to react to it with punitive attitudes and methods. This punishment approach to hyperactivity and violence can further frustrate the individual, and may drive him into more antisocial forms of behavior.

A second pattern that has emerged from study of various forms of "antisocial" behavior relates to sensory abnormalities, especially those relating to sight, hearing, and feeling. Persons with these disabilities tend to receive sensory signals that are distortions of reality. Their behavior can easily be misinterpreted as bizarre or as resistant to normal learning processes. Thus, a child may appear to be a slow learner or to be poorly motivated for learning; but, in fact, a mere sensory malfunction may exist. These children cannot function competitively in a normal classroom. Typically they will fail and be stigmatized by peers, and sometimes even by parents and teacher, because of this failure. The resulting frustration then can lead to further emotional turmoil, and to such behavior as dropping out of school, running away, truancy, vandalism, and, possibly, delinquency or crime.

Certainly, not all delinquent and criminal behavior can be traced to ecologic-biochemical factors, either exclusively or primarily. The research evidence presented here, however, suggests that these factors are important, and that they may be primary in many cases. School and court decisions regarding disposition certainly should not be made until these factors have been properly assessed and treated.

The authors of this section present an extensive review of the research findings and etiological explanations related to these several forms of behavior. Dr. Cott first discusses the causative factors involved with learning disabilities in children, and relates this problem to drug abuse and delinquency.

Next, Dr. Slavin presents an extensive review of the research literature, which strongly supports the hypothesis that there is a very high relationship between learning disabilities and delinquency. He also presents evidence to show that the delinquency recidivism rate can be significantly reduced through appropriate treatment of these learning disabilties, especially those related to perception and vision.

Dr. Ott then presents evidence on the ecologic effects of light and radiation on human behavior. His research indicates how exposure to X-rays and certain types of classroom lighting can result in hyperactivity in children and disrupt their normal learning and social adjustment.

Dr. Philpott focuses on the ecological impact of foods and chemicals on human behavior. He discusses the etiological factors that can lead to a variety of allergies, addictions, and endocrine imbalances, and which may be seen as maladaptive and antisocial by parents and school and court personnel.

Next, Dr. Yaryura-Tobias presents an extensive review of research on the biological aspects of violent behavior. He stresses that our courts need to differentiate between delinquents and criminals whose violent behavior may be caused by ecologic-biochemical or genetic factors and those whose violence results from socio-politico-economic reasons.

In the final paper of this section, psychologist Ware reports on a controlled experimental study that she conducted utilizing biochemical treatment with institutionalized delinquents. Her findings, which are supportive of her hypotheses, suggest the need for additional and more extensive research in this area.

Chapter 4

The Etiology of Learning Disabilities, Drug Abuse and Juvenile Delinquency

Allan Cott, M.D., F.A.P.A.
New York, New York

LEARNING DISABILITY CAUSATION

There is no single etiological factor for learning disabilities, nor is it likely that one will be found. Dr. William Wendle,[1] director of research of the New York University Institute of Rehabilitation Medicine, states that the cause seems to be malfunctioning of one area or another of the brain. In many cases, the malfunction is caused by physical damage to the brain, although the presence of such damage is difficult or impossible to prove. Because damage is subtle, states Dr. Wendle, no electroencephalogram (EEG) abnormalities are found in about 50% of the cases. In experiments with rhesus monkeys, development of a group of 130 subjects in which asphyxia was deliberately induced during or after birth was compared with that of uninjured controls. In the early years, the differences were obvious. The asphyxiated monkeys had extreme difficulty carrying out simple motor tasks and had noticeable sensory problems. By the fourth year of life, the monkeys seemed to have made a normal adjustment, although a lack of manual dexterity and a low level of spontaneous activity were visible signs of neurological deficit. In most cases, the EEGs were normal, but autopsies showed that brain injury induced by the asphyxia had not been repaired. There was widespread nerve cell damage in several parts of the brain.

In humans, brain damage due to trauma before, during, or after birth is not believed to be responsible for many cases. The mother's health and general nutrition before conception and during pregnancy are of the utmost importance, for subtle or gross disasters occurring during these periods or during labor and delivery can compromise the child in learning and behavior.[2]

Learning disabilities associated with minimal brain dysfunction in children of normal or superior intelligence can readily be distinguished from cases of mental retardation or severe emotional disturbance. For this group of children, the diagnosis of *specific learning disabilities* (SLD) has been suggested. The term *general learning disabilities* should be reserved for the mentally retarded child, or the child suffering from severe disorders of behavior and communication (childhood schizophrenia, autism).

Evidence is accumulating that learning disabilities are frequently of genetic origin. Because of the worldwide scope of the problem, the World Federation of Neurology Meeting in Dallas, Texas, considered terminology related to *reading problems of genetic origin*.[3] Case studies further reveal that frequently more than one learning-disabled child is found in a single family. Additional statistics show that serious disorders of behavior, communication, and learning occur far more frequently in adopted children than in natural children. The incidence of minimal brain dysfunction with learning disabilities, furthermore, is estimated to be four to five times more frequent in boys than in girls.

A diagnosis of minimal brain dysfunction based on a cluster of deviant behaviors, including impaired concentration, short attention span, hyperactivity, impulsivity, and aggression, frequently masks a borderline psychotic condition and exposes the child to an improper approach to treatment, which may not only have adverse effects but may delay early intervention and proper treatment. In the genetically predisposed child, the minimal brain dysfunction syndrome can often be the early signs of schizophrenia. In eliciting a carefully detailed family history during the examination of a child with minimal brain dysfunction, I have frequently found siblings described as "slow learners" or other relatives diagnosed schizophrenic, diabetic, or alcoholic. In obtaining detailed case histories of adolescent or adult schizophrenic patients, moreover, I have found a high incidence of hyperactivity and learning disabilities reported early in life. In my experience, approximately 50% of delinquent children and juvenile drug abusers (including alcohol abusers) suffered from a significant degree of learning disabilties in the elementary grades.

PRENATAL INFLUENCES

In his book *Life Before Birth*, Ashley Montagu[4] states that life begins at conception and that the happenings in the interval between conception and birth are far more important for our subsequent growth and development than we have realized. The thinking about this period of the child's life had for so many years for the majority of people been rather simplistic. It was stated with confidence that the child was safe, warm, and snug in the mother's uterus, shielded and protected from all external influences while he floated in his fluid-filled sac, which, by its hydraulic effect, made him safe even from physical pressures. It was believed the placenta acted as a "barrier" against the transmission of toxic substances from the mother's bloodstream.

Not until the past decade of research has it been learned that during the prenatal period—the nine months between conception and birth—a human being is more susceptible to his environment than he ever will be again in his life. What happens to him in the prenatal period can help sustain normal development or hinder him from ever achieving his full genetic potential. The events that take place before his birth can exert a lifelong influence, for part of the child's environment consists of his mother's immediate state of health, her general physical condition, her age at the time of conception, and how fatigued she becomes each day. A pregnant woman's nutrition must be more than merely adequate, it must be the best her circumstances allow.

Montagu emphasized, "A mother's nutrition is the most important single environment influence in the life of her unborn child and by means of the food she eats a mother can have the most profound and lasting effect on her child's development—by the simple act of improving her diet where improvement is necessary she can greatly influence the development of her child toward normal healthy growth." He cites a study of malnutrition and pregnancy from which a surprising finding emerged—none of the mothers in either group, the well-fed or the poorly fed, showed any signs themselves of malnutrition or deficiency disease, yet the diet of the pregnant woman can be so seriously inadequate that her child is endangered without producing any recognizable symptoms that might give warning to her or her doctors.

This finding corroborates the report of Williams et al.[5] that greater concern must be shown for the quality of the internal environments in which our cells and tissues function, because these environments can vary through the full spectrum, from those which barely keep cells alive up through hundreds of gradations to levels supporting something like optimal performance. It is an obvious undeniable conclusion that an unborn child should be given the advantage of growing to term in an optimum molecular environment. Proper diet based on wholesome foods, vitamin and mineral supplements, and the elimination of "junk foods" helps create such an environment for prenatal development and growth; cigarette smoking, stimulant drugs, diuretic drugs, tranquilizers, and dieting with or without the use of amphetamine-containing appetite suppressors do not provide an optimum environment.

In my clinical practice, detailed prenatal histories and the histories of labor and delivery reveal that some complications of pregnancy and delivery occurred in a majority of the children who show evidence of brain injury, behavior disorder, or learning disabilities.

Dr. Benjamin Pasamanick and his co-workers, in a series of papers describing their research in these areas, postulated "a continuum of reproductive casualties extending from fetal deaths through a descending gradient of brain damage manifested in cerebral palsy, epilepsy, mental deficiency and behavior disorders in childhood." Pasamanick and Kawi extended the continuum of reproductive casualties to include reading disorders in childhood.[6] They compared the prenatal and birth records of 372 white male children with reading disorders born in Baltimore between 1935 and 1945 with the records of a similar number of matched controls. The results of the study "appear to indicate there exists a relationship between certain abnormal conditions associated with birth and the subsequent development of reading disorders in the child."

Those children with reading disorders had a significantly larger proportion of premature births and abnormalities of the prenatal and delivery periods than their control subjects. They found that toxemias of pregnancy and bleeding during pregnancy constituted those complications largely responsible for the differences between the two groups. The investigation suggested that some of the learning disabilties in children constitute a component in the continuum of reproductive casualties, previously hypothesized by Pasamanick, with a lethal component consisting of stillbirths and neonatal deaths and a sublethal component consisting of cerebral palsy, epilepsy, mental deficiency, and behavior disorders in children.

I have formed impressions leading to similar conclusions from my clinical experiences, based on detailed histories of learning-disabled children. The interview with the parents generally begins with the request that they describe the pregnancy. With very few exceptions in the hundreds of pairs of parents interviewed, the opening response is, "The pregnancy was perfectly normal." It is appalling to contemplate the disasters that can await the child in what women have been led to believe are quite the usual and, therefore, normal experiences of pregnancy. Many mothers report with a feeling of pride their accomplishment of having carried a pregnancy to full term and delivered a baby of normal weight without having gained a single pound in nine months of the pregnancy! Nausea and vomiting occurs in the great majority of mothers and is accepted as a normal occurrence. Many mothers attempt to minimize the importance of "morning sickness" by adding, "but I was sick every day with all my pregnancies."

Many mothers reported dieting severely throughout the pregnancy at the demand of their doctor, because he preferred that his patients have small babies. Amphetamines were frequently prescribed to suppress the appetite or to combat fatigue. Tranquilizer and sedative medications were used freely throughout the pregnancies, but the most frequently prescribed medication seemed to be the diuretic drugs, which mothers took throughout the pregnancies and which were in very few cases taken along with an increase in potassium-rich foods. Anemia during pregnancy was frequently reported.

The frequency of occurrence of complications during the perinatal period is higher in children with learning disabilities. A prolonged period of labor and a difficult delivery is the most commonly encountered history in the birth record of a learning-disabled child. In a study reported by Dr. Mary Hoffman,[7] 25% of a group of children who were failing students were products of difficult deliveries, while difficult delivery occurred in only 1.5% of the histories of the able students. Cyanosis occurred in 11% of the learning-disabled and in only 0.5% of the able students. Prolonged labor, blood incompatability, premature births, postmature births, breech deliveries, and induced labor were also found to be highly significant factors in the historical background of children with learning disabilities, since these casualties occurred far more frequently than in able children.

Even though research cannot at this time provide an unequivocal or full answer to the question of what effect malnutrition or malnourishment has on intellectual development, this is not a valid reason to delay programs for improving the nutritional status and eating practices of mothers and fathers. Information demonstrating the benefits of good nutrition in improved health, physical growth, and improved learning already justifies such efforts.

VISUAL FUNCTIONS

The examination of a child who suffers from a disorder of speech, communication, or learning cannot be considered complete without a visual examination, for the investigation of sight and vision is as important as any other part of the total examination and more important and revealing than many other routines. The majority of the children treated by the author have all had examinations that included electroencephalograms, but very few have been examined for vision by a vision specialist. If an examination had been done, it was performed for sight; and if the child demonstrated 20/20 vision on the Snellen Chart, the parents were informed there was nothing wrong with the child's eyes. This may be true for distance eyesight, but overlooks all the near-point visual activity so important to the dynamic visual process of reading.[8] The child who has a school or learning problem must have an examination performed by a specialist who investigates the function of the eyes as well as their structure. Such a specialist could be an ophthalmologist (an M.D. specializing in diseases of the eye) or an optometrist specializing in developmental vision. At the present time, few ophthalmologists perform these examinations, so one is more apt to find a developmental vision specialist among optometrists. Sight is the ability of the eye to see clearly. It refers only to the ability to resolve detail. Vision is the ability to gain meaning from what is seen.

Too often parents are lulled into a false sense of security when they are told that their child's eyes are "fine," for here, also, early detection and treatment will produce a more rewarding response, and the results of the remedial efforts will be more successful. As just mentioned, there can be significant deviations from normal vision even if a child has 20/20 on the Snellen Chart. Farsightedness can be overlooked in a distance vision screening examination, for example, and can cause difficulties when a child does near work. There can be problems if one eye is different from the other in refractive power. Convergence of the eyes noseward for looking at things close up is also of vital importance in centering with two eyes on a near-point task. Convergence bears an important relationship to focusing: the two processes are combined. If this link is not proper, a child can be out of focus and be completely unaware that he is, just as a child who sees a separate image with each eye has no way of telling us about this, since he believes everyone sees in this way. The out-of-focus child cannot tell us about his blurred vision until he can be helped to see in sharp focus with the aid of lenses.

The author has seen many children who had not seen near things in sharp focus or looked at the world through binocular vision until their eyes were treated successfully by a developmental optometrist or by an ophthalmologist interested in developmental vision. Yet these children are daily trying to learn to read when the printed page presents nothing but a blur. Lack of smooth eye muscle control makes a difficult task of trying to follow successive words in a line of print as the eyes sweep across a page. Often the eyes will not make the repeated necessary convergences if the focusing is not proper; and the child will skip words in the line, lose his place, or be unable to find the first word on the next line, and as a result not comprehend what he reads. Significantly, hyperactivity is frequently reduced when the visual systems work efficiently.

Developmental visual training is another vital link in the creation of an optimum molecular environment for the mind. Neither improved nutrition, vitamin and mineral supplements, enriched educational opportunities, nor visual and perceptual motor training alone can be successful in fully helping the child with learning disabilities—all must be used in a coordinated program to develop each child's potential.

RESEARCH

The following sections deal with significant findings in areas relevant to learning disabilities.

Hypoglycemia

Experimentally induced hypoglycemia, hypoxia (lack of oxygen), and hyperbilirubinemia (jaundice) can produce lesions in newborn experimental animals not unlike those found in mentally retarded children or in those with a history of comparable biochemical disturbances in the perinatal period. The situation is exceedingly complex and controversial in infants with hypoglycemia, many of whom are of low birth weight and have suffered from intrauterine malnutrition. There is good evidence of antenatal brain damage in a significant proportion of these children. Severe symptomatic hypoglycemia rarely occurs on its own, and it is, therefore, not surprising that the lesions found in children or experimental animals dying after hypoglycemic episodes are not specific and are difficult to distinguish from those produced by other causes. Dr. Gerald F. Lucey has reported that hypoglycemia in the newborn is much more prevalent than many physicians believe. He stated that anyone not finding two or three cases per 1,000 live births is probably missing it. He reports the incidence among premature infants is 43 per 1,000. A blood sugar level of less than 20 mg per 100 ml in a premature infant or 30 mg per 100 ml in a full-term infant is too low. He concludes there is strong evidence that hypoglycemia causes brain damage. He cites tremors and cyanosis as early signs of hypoglycemia in the newborn: apnea, apathy, and a high-pitched cry are other early signs. Convulsions are a late sign of hypoglycemia. Dr. Lucey recommends that all small-for-birthdate infants also be checked, as well as the large infants of diabetic mothers. He concludes that the symptoms of hypoglycemia are caused by a deprivation of glucose in the brain. It reflects inadequate intrauterine nutrition of inadequate glucose homeostasis.

Neurotransmitters: Dopamine

Administration of 6-hydroxydopamine to neonatal rats produced a rapid and profound depletion of brain dopamine. Total activity of treated animals was significantly greater than that of controls between 12 and 22 days of age, but then declined, an activity pattern similar to that seen in affected children. This suggests a functional deficiency of brain dopamine in the pathogenesis of minimal brain dysfunction.[9]

Niacinamide

Niacinamide has been shown to increase rapid eye movement (REM) sleep in mice by 17%. In adult human volunteers the administration of 1 gram of niacinamide three times daily increased REM sleep by

40%. Several volunteers in this study reported to the author they slept fewer hours and awakened more refreshed during the period when they were taking the niacinamide.[10]

The results of this study show that high doses of niacinamide may have behavioral effects unconnected with its role as a vitamin. The best-known drug that increases REM is reserpine, which suggests that further pharmacological study of niacinamide in this light might be of interest. One study (Beaton, in press) reports that administration of 250 to 500 mg per kg of niacinamide reduced the wheel-running activity of gerbils by 30%. The lower dosages of niacinamide, although inducing an initial decrease in activity, were inactive. This report also concludes that niacinamide must have central effects unrelated to its role as a vitamin, and the degree to which the therapeutic effects of niacinamide are related to the observed sedative effects is worthy of further investigation.

5-Hydroxytryptophan

Burkhard Scherer and Wolf Kramer[11] reported that the ability of some niacin compounds to inhibit the tryptophan-pyrrolase or to repress the *de novo* synthesis of this enzyme is possibly responsible for the increase of brain 5-hydroxytryptophan by 17% after niacinamide administration. The sedation observed at the same time may be due to this 5-HT increase. They concluded: "How far the sedative effects and the repeatedly published therapeutic effects on psychoses can be based on an increased 5-HT formation should be studied by further analysis of the 5-HT turnover. The doses applied by us to rats in any case are far above the doses given to man for therapeutic reasons." D. J. Boullin and colleagues (1970) were able to report highly significant abnormalities in platelet 5-HTP efflux in autistic children, as compared to normal controls. In a second study[12] the abnormality was found in nearly all cases diagnosed as autistic, but in *no* case diagnosed "psychotic but not autistic." The laboratory work was done without knowledge of the clinical diagnoses.

At the symposium on orthomolecular psychiatry in the First World Congress on Biological Psychiatry, which convened in Buenos Aires in September, 1974, the research team of Drs. G. Buyze, W. J. H. Driss, A. J. Schakellar, and W. R. P. Schreurs of the Netherlands reported that, according to Linus Pauling's[13] concept of orthomolecular psychiatry, the treatment of mental illness should benefit by optimalization of the molecular environment of the mind. In this connection, the effect of multiple vitamin administration was studied in 80 hospitalized psychiatric patients divided into two equal groups matched in age, sex, diagnosis, and psychiatric treatment. During the experimental period of three months, treatment and medications were kept constant. One group received a daily vitamin mixture of thiamine, pyridoxine, B-12, nicotinamide, and folic acid of three times the recommended daily allowance (RDA). The second group received placebo. The vitamin blood levels were determined before and after the experimental period. Assessment of the psychiatric effect was made by measurement of the scores with an ego-strength scale and with a social adjustment scale. In a number of patients, subnormal or borderline values for one or more of the vitamin concentrations were found. Statistical analysis of the scores in the two rating scales used showed an improvement in the vitamin-supplemented group. Dr. Buyze and colleagues will publish their findings this year in the Congress Proceedings.

Pyridoxine

In a study reported in the *Journal of Nutrition and Metabolism*,[14] the authors reported that vitamin B-6 (pyridoxine) is involved in some way in regulating glucose levels in the blood of stressed mice, possibly by affecting the levels of the enzyme phosphorylase or by affecting the metabolism of tryptophan in the kynurenine pathway. It also seems that B-6 plays a role in regulating a methylation process that could be related to the production of psychogenic substances, specifically di/methyl/oxy/phenyl/ethylamine. This regulation could come about as a result of augmentation of the production of nicotinic acid in the kynurenine pathway. Thus, pyridoxine would seem to have a regulatory effect on tryptophan metabolism, but does not appear to affect the production or metabolism of scrotonin from tryptophan.

The role played by pyridoxine in the production of norepinephrine is not clear, since the effects of elevated levels of glucose (associated with administration of B-6) on the levels of norepinephrine in the brain are uncertain. Finally, a decrease in ulcer formation was noted in the mice receiving B-6, which tends to implicate the vitamin in an antistress role. A study reported to the Canadian Mental Health Association in 1972 described the use of the vitamin pyridoxine

(B-6) in the treatment of certain types of schizophrenia, and its role in the potentiation of therapeutic effects of nicotinic acid by pyridoxine in chronic schizophrenics.[15] Other investigators reported that nicotinic acid, one of the products of pyridoxine-dependent pathways, was useful in the treatment of some psychiatric patients.

DRUG ABUSE AND JUVENILE DELINQUENCY

When the widespread use of marijuana, the major hallucinogens, and other illicit drugs began in the late 1950s, a correlation was noted in drug use, failing academic performance, and loss of interest in school in able students. The onset of schizophrenia in early adolescence is most often manifested by depression, loss of concentration, impaired attention span, and loss of interest, which leads to a marked decline in academic performance. These signs are manifest early in the illness, and may precede by a year or more the develoment of the more dramatic perceptual distortions and delusions characteristic of schizophrenia. Similar symptoms may be considered premonitory signs of the first stages of drug abuse in a child.

Because the learning-disabled child is not readily accepted by his peer group, who have over the years labeled him "a retard," "just stupid," and ridiculed his clumsy ineffectiveness in sports or other group games or activities, he ultimately is brought to the point in his life when he may pay any price to anyone granting acceptance. He happily and willingly becomes a follower of any member of his peer group who accepts him without ridicule or reservation. In the classroom he becomes the clown who makes the other children laugh at his bizarre antics, his foolish talk. His classmates certainly do take notice of him, and the other nonconformists in the school accept him. In my clinical experience, I have found this to be the route by which a large percentage of learning-disabled children drop into the drug culture and juvenile delinquency. I have examined and treated many hundreds of learning-disabled adolescents who began the use of marijuana while in the elementary grades and lost what little interest in learning remained as they were pushed through the grades, finally to drop out of school. Many expressed the feeling they had "better things to do than go to school." Too often, the "better" thing they did was to graduate to the use of major hallucinogens like LSD and mescaline. If engaging in regular use of illicit drugs or in actual delinquent behavior such as theft or burglary is the fee to be paid for acceptance, he readily agrees.

When a child decides he is better off out of school, he has made a decision about a lifestyle that will ease the unbearable tension and anxiety which daily attendance coupled with daily failure creates for him. The decision is soon implemented by acts of truancy that in most cases is the precursor to delinquency. Dr. MacDonald Critchley, the British authority in reading and language disorders, found 75% of a group of delinquents illiterate. Wherever groups of delinquent children have been surveyed, 60 to 80% read below grade level and many aged 18 to 22 could not perform on a fourth grade reading level. In 1967, the U.S. Public Health Service reported that 75% of delinquent children in New York were illiterate. Howard James has quoted in the book *Something's Wrong with My Child*, a book dealing with the juvenile justice system, that in at least 80% of all cases which come to the juvenile courts it can be found that a school problem was an important factor. A Bureau of Prisons report reveals that 90% of the inmates of Federal prisons have reading problems. Society adds hundreds of thousands of new school dropouts each year to the millions who preceded them to roam our city streets unable to find work because they can't read.

In a report presented to the First World Congress of Biological Psychiatry in Buenos Aires in September, 1974, Dr. Eugene Ziskind, Professor of Psychiatry at the UCLA School of Medicine, reported a study whose major thesis was based on the tendency of sociopaths to undergo spontaneous remission at midlife. Ziskind and his coworkers made the assumption that those sociopaths who do not undergo remission have failed because their pathological behavior has ruined the possibilities of such an outcome. The report continued that their data are consistent with the hypothesis that most sociopaths are the subjects of a lag in behavioral development, and stressed that the earliest treatment efforts should be focused on preventing incarceration. Therefore, energetic treatments of disabilities should be made available early in life for those who have symptoms of the minimal brain dysfunction syndrome with specific learning disabilities. Rejection by parents, teachers, and peers must be reduced to the lowest possible level by securing adequate understanding for the subject's disability. Suspension from school should be discouraged, and school dropouts not permitted. Assessment should be made of the unique patterns of learning of which each subject is capable. Dr. Ziskind described a treatment approach involving a variety of experts, whose particular expertise would be to create a constructive climate to prevent or replace "bad company" and criminal contacts. Group therapy, feedback, behavioral therapy, and chemotherapy with psychoactive drugs are also being explored in their multidimensional approach to treatment.

In a 30-year follow-up study of 524 child psychiatric patients by Dr. A. P. Derdeyn of the University of Virginia Medical Center, it was found that not a single child developed an antisocial personality as an adult in the absence of antisocial symptoms as a child. Fifty percent of the antisocial children continued their antisocial behavior as adults; of the other half of the adults who had been antisocial as children, 90% were exhibiting maladaptive behavior consisting of alcohol addiction, major mental illness, or severe marital or employment problems.[16]

References

1. Wendle, W. F., Faro, M. D., Barker, J. N., Barsky, D., and Guteirrez, S., Developmental behaviors: Delayed appearance in monkeys asphyxiated at birth, *Science* 171(3976):1173–1175, 1971.
2. Pasamanick, B., Rogers, M. E., and Lilienfeld, A. M., Pregnancy experience and development of behavior disorders in children, *Amer. J. Psychiat.* 112: 613–618, 1956.
2. Tarnopol, Lester, ed., Learning Disorders in Children (Procedings of the World Federation of Neurology meeting in Dallas, Texas, 1968), Little, Brown, New York, 1969.
4. Montague, Ashley, *Life Before Birth*, New York: New American Library, 1964.
5. Williams, R. J., Heffley, J. D., and Bode, C. W., The nutritive value of single foods, Paper presented to the National Academy of Sciences, April 28, 1971.
6. Pasamanick, B., and Kawi, A. A., Association of factors of pregnancy with reading disorders in childhood, *J.A.M.A.* 22:1420–1423, 1968.
7. Hoffman, M. S., Early indications of learning problems, *Academic Therapy* 7(1):23–35, 1971.
8. Wunderlich, R. C., *Kids, Brains and Learning*, Johnny Reads, Inc., St. Petersburg, Fla., 1970.
9. Shaywitz, B. A., Selective brain dopamine depletion in developing rats: An experimental model of minimal brain dysfunction, *Science* 191:305–308, 1976.
10. Beaton, J. M., Pegram, G. V., Smythies, J. R., and Bradley, R. J., Niacinamide, *Separatum Experientia* 30:926, 1974.
11. Scherer, B., and Kramer, W., Influence of niacinamide administration on brain 5-HT and a possible mode of action, *Life Sci.* 1:189–195, 1972.

12. Boullin, D. J., Coleman, M., and O'Brien, R. A., Abnormalities in platelet 5-hydroxytryptamine efflux in patients with infantile autism, *Nature* 226:371, 1970.
13. Pauling, Linus, Orthomolecular psychiatry, *Science* 160:265–271, 1968.
14. Lindenbaum, E. S., and Mueller, J. J., Effects of pyridoxine on mice after immobilization stress, *J. Nutr. Metab.* 17:368–374, 1974.
15. Ananth, J. V., Ban, T. A., Lehmann, H. E., and Bennett, J., Nicotinic acid in the prevention and treatment of methionine induced exacerbation of psychopathology in schizophrenics, J. Canad. Psychiat. Assoc. 15:15, 1970.
16. Derdeyn, A. P., Personality development and personality disorders, with emphasis on anti-social personality, *Psychiatry Digest* 10:28, 1974.

Chapter 5 | Information Processing Defects in Delinquents

Sidney H. Slavin, O.D.
Richmond, Virginia

Obviously, delinquents are in trouble, but not just with the law. The typical potential juvenile delinquent was developmentally handicapped even long before starting school. But, unfortunately, he never outgrew the effects of his handicaps. Even today as a teen-ager or young adult, he still continues to demonstrate subtle but disguised childhood impairments in many of his essential sensory-motor modalities and perceptual-cognitive information processing abilities. His central nervous system contains readiness or developmental gaps for which adequate compensation has not been made. These readiness problems result in formation of "inefficient, ineffective adaptive behavior abilities." Under such conditions, how could the delinquent expect maximum payoff from his social, cultural, or educational environments?

The delinquents also contain a statistically higher proportion of learning-disabled and reading-retarded youngsters than does the general school population. Is it any wonder that the majority of this population are dropouts? It is my contention that their learning disabilities are symptomatic of these subtle untreated information processing defects.[1] Impairment in verbal and nonverbal perceptual and conceptual spheres influences their adaptive behavior perhaps more than social and economic class variables affect it.

I feel that professionals in corrections will have more effective rehabilitation success after they recognize that processing defects affect "learning to learn and learning to adjust to life" skills. Effective reading skills cannot be acquired if the foundation of learning and the various central nervous system information acquisition mechanisms are underdeveloped or undermined. Acceptance of the concept of diagnosis and treatment of processing defects in juvenile delinquents is an ideal. But to reach that goal will require major philosophical changes in our corrections department.

We preach rehabilitation of these youngsters, yet we still practice "incarceration." When society really intends to rehabilitate its charges, then it will be forced to provide adequate therapeutic staff and financial resources to individually test, counsel, and treat specific learning disabilities. Continuing to teach reading skills in our juvenile institutions, using techniques and strategies identical with those of public school education, is an exercise in futility, for the average juvenile delinquent is a child with special problems and special needs. The public schools previously failed these children. They taught them without understanding that symptoms are not causes of learning disabilities. They did not understand that these children never were ready for conventional learning and thinking activities using conventional teaching methodology. Why does the correction department's educational system insist on continuing the same errors?

Conventional wisdom should be replaced with functional wisdom. Why not treat the specific problem areas that impair functioning in the juvenile delinquent's basic learning adaptive skills? Perhaps then we might be able to dramatically and positively alter behavior! Recidivism rates should plunge if this suggested approach is successful.

In Section 1, I will review selected literature from the professions of education, social work, optometry, clinical psychology, occupational therapy, audiology and speech therapy, and biostatistics. Results from these studies stress that there are a pervasive lack of developmental readiness and diffuse central nervous system dysfunction in this population. I will specifically review the classical study by Berman and Siegal of Rhode Island[2] and the multidisciplinary study of the Thirteenth District Juvenile Court Project in Richmond, Virginia.[3] Both studies emphasize the importance of a good diagnostic work-up to identify particular skill defects that affect behavior. Specific follow-up therapy, the necessary second stage, and the rationale for that needed detailed diagnosis will be emphasized. Such therapy is not based on a psychiatric-medical model. It is behavioral, holistic, functional, and academically specific to filling in developmental gaps and learning abilities.

Section 2 will examine three functional treatment programs of juveniles, comparing their recidivism rates with conventional correctional figures. A typical visual therapy case will be briefly described.

SECTION 1

Why emphasize the importance of learning disabilities so soon in this discussion? Cruickshank,[4] a giant in the field of exceptional children, points out that several major problems in learning disabilities remediation must be clarified:

> One does not remediate a vacuum and this is essentially the case in the child with perceptual processing difficulties . . . involving one or another of all of the sensory modalities . . . in this child, appropriate learning has not taken place because of neuroperceptual processing problems. A technique of education has to be developed which will provide the child with the necessary initial skills, regardless of chronological age, and which will give him a sound base for the acquisition of more complex learnings later. This is not remediation, it is a new learning. It is immediately obvious that one is dealing with a complex developmental problem, not a problem of remediation . . . learning disability is a matter relating to children of any intellectual level . . . perceptual processing defects are to be found in children of every intellectual level and are respectors of no given intelligence range.
>
> If the child's disability involves perception or perceptual processing, it logically follows that one is dealing with a neurological dysfunction of some sort . . . definitions of learning disabilities which ignore the concepts of either perceptual processing or the neurological base are misleading. Such is not to state that the specific neurological dysfunction can always be identified . . . I reiterate, once again, however, the long term issue is not of medicine . . . but is of education.

Hobbs[5] gives a very specific and cogent definition of learning disabilities, emphasizing the role of the central nervous system and information processing skills. Hobbs wrote that the concept includes

> those children of any age who demonstrate a substantial deficiency in a particular aspect of academic achievement because of perceptual or perceptual-motor-handicaps, regardless of

etiology or other contributing factors. The term *perceptual* as is used here relates to those mental (neurological) processes through which the child acquired his basic alphabets of sound and form. The term *perceptual handicap* refers to inadequate ability in such areas as the following: recognizing fine differences between auditory and visual discriminating features all underlying the sounds used in speech and the orthographic forms used in reading; retaining and recalling those discriminated sounds and forms sequentially, both in short and long term memory; ... ordering the sound and form sequentially both in sensory and motor acts ... distinguishing figure ground relationships ... recognizing spatial and temporal orientations; obtaining closure ... integrating intersensory information ... relating what is perceived to specific motor functions.

Cruickshank adds several other specifications to the above operational definition of LD and perceptual handicap:

Inadequate ability to conceptualize parts into meaningful wholes; the sometime presence of perseveration; the inability to refrain from reacting to unessential environmental stimuli; and the resulting immature or faulty self concept or body image.

Finally, Cruickshank writes that:

Unless general elementary education understands the nature and needs of the problems of processing deficits ... and knows how to adapt the learning situation and teaching materials to the child's needs, the potential for continued failure on the part of the child is present. ... In my considered opinion, the status of learning disabilities in the public schools of this nation is one of educational catastrophe.

If an expert feels it is this way in the regular public school systems, how much better should we expect our correction institutions to be?

Let us now review some of the research on reading disabilities specifically in a typical state correctional system.

On March 4, 1977, the Comptroller General of the United States,[6] in a report on learning disabilities and its link to juvenile delinquency, stated that 26% of the delinquents tested in Virginia had *primary* learning problems and 51% in Virginia had *secondary* learning problems. Thus 77% of the Virginia delinquents had learning disabilities. Virginia was one of several participating states in a national study.

According to a 1976 study, *all* committed students in Virginia correctional institutions read below acceptable performance levels. One-half of all students read two to three years below acceptable reading levels. One-third read three or more grades below acceptable reading levels.[7] The long-term implication of reading deficiencies also dramatically affects vocational education. The study showed that one-third to one-half of Virginia's vocational students had difficulty in reading the instructional materials related to their occupational preparation programs.

Even in typical elementary schools there is evidence that perceptual processing deficiencies are present in the earliest academic years. The Glen Haven Achievement Center in Virginia recently assessed psychomotor skills in selected schools of the state. The instrument chosen to assess eight areas of psychomotor performance was the Purdue Perceptual Motor Survey. A wide range of deficiencies was revealed in kindergarten through fourth grade. In kindergarten 53% of the children failed in one or more psychomotor skill areas. In the fourth grade, the percentage of failures was 44%. Seventeen percent had deficits in ocular control and 15% were deficient in visual motor control. It was also disturbing to note that by grade four, rather than a drop, there was an upward trend in these deficiency skills. Such a pattern may indicate that for a large number of children, continued improvement in psychomotor skills will not occur without intervention.[7]

The Thirteenth District Project

The Thirteenth District Juvenile and Domestic Relations Court Project in Richmond, Virginia, was a unique study utilizing data from five specialty professions, whose investigators simultaneously published their independent findings.[8-12]

This project was originated and directed by Charlene Baum, the Court's social worker supervisor. Mrs. Baum wanted to verify a previous courtroom pilot study, which suggested that many of her clients had not only a high incidence of reading retardation, but also a high incidence of parallel specific learning disabilities which required specialized referral services. The purpose of this study was to determine whether this population had sensory-motor, discriminative problems in determining similarities and differences, perceptual-cognitive processing defects, or developmental gaps which may have been handicapping juvenile offenders' learning and adaptive skills. It was obvious that if these problems did exist, they were not being attended to by the courts or the state school system.

Approximately 56 youngsters were independently examined by a multidisciplinary team. Each child received a physical examination by the public health department, a psychological examination, a language-speech-hearing evaluation, an optometric examination by a six-man optometric team, and a perceptual-motor assessment by an occupational therapy team.

The education evaluations were conducted by five graduate students at Virginia Commonwealth University, Department of Special Education. No single profession investigator knew what the other professionals found in their separate evaluations. The average chronological age of the 56 subjects was 13.2 years. The youngest was 10.4 and the oldest was 16.0 years. Only two subjects read two grades above the expected level. One subject read on grade level. The average reading level for 40 subjects was four grades behind. Twenty-eight of the 56 subjects had verbal IQs below 50. Of 44 tested, 42 were below expected math level. Performance IQ exceeded verbal IQs in the majority of cases. All tests except the audition and vision batteries were given at the court. All juveniles participating in this project had to volunteer. Each youngster involved in the study was under the jurisdiction of the juvenile court between February 1, 1975, and June 30, 1975, with birthdays not lower than 1960. Twenty-six parents or children declined. Those who declined were mainly from middle and upper-middle class families.

Occupational Therapy Battery and Factor Analysis

Using Ayres' Southern California Sensory Integration test, Reynolds found only two out of the 56 youngsters functioning adequately for their chronological age. (See Malkin and Castex for data on non-juvenile delinquent youngsters having behavior and academic difficulties.[13])

The 17 subjects in this battery describe a child's integrative functioning in the areas of balance, postural and bilateral integration, visual form and space perception, fine and gross motor planning, and kinesthetic-tactile skills.

The original Ayres data were standardized on 1,000 youngsters, ages 4-9, with functional perceptual motor age scores broken down into six-month intervals. Even though the youngest child in the court study was 10 years old, 54 out of the 56 delinquents had adjusted perceptual motor age scores less than 8 years, 11 months.

The psychological diagnostic battery was conducted by Etkin, under less than ideal circumstances. In many cases, because of personnel changes, the data were incomplete. Generally, a wide range of diagnostic instruments was used. Some, but not all, of the following tests were used: WISC; Bender-Gestalt; TAT; WRAT; and a half-hour interview. Of 30 subjects tested, only one showed no problem. The six most common problems were:

1. Cultural, education, and emotional deprivation — 29 subjects
2. Perceptual motor problems — 26 subjects
3. Immaturity — 24 subjects
4. Anxiety — 21 subjects
5. Sexual identity crisis — 20 subjects
6. Poor self-concept — 19 subjects

For purposes of statistical analysis, Etkin used a count of presenting problems, i.e., the higher the count the more problems the subject had. At the completion of the study, a factor analysis was performed, using the Statistical Analysis System Procedure Factor. Of 21 variables, a total of seven factors were obtained that explained 100% of the variability. The variable that loaded highest on a given factor was used to name this factor. They were: IQ (30.45%); (2) age (18.25%); (3) Wepman Test (12.32%); (4) offense level–family coherence–sex (10.72%); (5) screening test for auditory perception (STAP) (11.23%); (6) psychological problems–hearing–perception problems (hearing-discriminating factor) (8.07%) and (7) race (8.97%). If one combines factors 3, 5, and 6, there is slightly over 32% clustering in auditory-speech-language modalities. There can be no doubt of the pervasive influence of this important developmental skill complex in influencing reading readiness. Etkin writes:

> No vision factor emerged from the data. A careful perusal of the data, however, exposes an even more dominant role for vision. Every factor had a moderate loading from vision, (from ± .22 to .41). This means virtually everyone had some problems in one or more of the areas in addition to vision. No particular pattern of

combination emerges, just a complete permeation of vision problems throughout the structure of the study.

What we have here is a handicapped population. They are handicapped in the sensory-perceptual areas necessary for interpreting and understanding the world. At best their perceptions of their environment are quite distorted. Their behavioral problems are for the most part their attempts at adapting to their inability to cope with the complex world around them. When these attempts cannot work, then they are seen at Juvenile Court.

The Vision Study of Juvenile Subjects

The optometric vision examination is a dynamic analytical procedure that probes "understanding of what we see." It investigates three separate aspects of visual behavior:

1. The *visual physiological aspects*, i.e., the accommodative-convergence system, binocularity.
2. The *integrative aspects* of vision with other sensory-motor modalities, i.e., eye-hand-body coordination; visual tactile; auditory-verbal-visual; bilaterality; antigravity with vision.
3. The *perceptual-cognitive aspects* involving concrete and abstract concepts of space, i.e., symbolic representation, language, words, numbers and thinking.

The average examination was from 45 minutes to 1½ hours.

From the following core procedures, the optometric examining team picked the tests that they felt were appropriate for diagnosing the patient: (1) detailed general health and developmental case history; (2) detailed visual case history; (3) academic and reading skill history; (4) habitual visual acuity for near and far using both prescription and no prescription; (5) ocular pathology examination including external, ophthalmoscopy—direct and/or indirect as needed, tonometry and slit lamp as required; (6) color perception; (7) chair side visual abilities assessment including monocular and binocular pursuits, saccadics, and versions; (8) push-up convergence; (9) complete cover testing; (10) diplopia tendency; (11) pupillary reflex assessment; (12) posture observation, including bilateral and midline skills both ocular and physical; (13) any of the 21 point OEP analytical battery procedures; (14) gross and fine motor coordination assessment, including performance on a walking rail, hopping and skipping as it relates to ocular-motor control; (15) preferred eye, hand, and foot and their coordination interrelationship; (16) copy forms or other writing tasks; (17) assessment of stereopsis using the Titmus Fly & Wirt Stereo test circles; (18) use of Keystone Stereoscopic Basic Binocular Visual Skill Battery for near and far; (19) reading assessment—listening to the oral fluency of reading and the types of reading errors; (20) clues of discriminative problems in other sensory-motor areas as determined from all of the above visual procedures.[14]

Table 5-1 shows our doctor's composite checklist observations, which were filled out following each examination, on 59 delinquents. The three parts on the check list are artificial and arbitrary. The doctor felt free to terminate the examination when he could accurately answer the visual analysis summary sheet. Table 5-1 indicates potential near point stress items with X's. Table 5-2 summarizes the visual characteristics of that juvenile delinquent population.

Of interest, note that 73% of the youngsters' refractive measurements were within acceptable average emmetropic limits. Even though they had what is commonly considered "Perfect Vision: or 20/20," 59% had testable near point discomfort. Because reading is a near center activity (within 16 inches of the eye), it was felt that any problem in this near zone would mitigate against maximum development and use of one's reading skill potential. Differences in any one of the following three areas were considered hard evidence of major developmental or visual discriminative problems: (1) cross cylinder findings which resulted in minus projection indicated excessively reduced near-point focusing reserve power;[15] (2) inadequate performance on the Titmus-Wirt stereotest indicated poor near depth perception and difficulty in binocular circuitry integration; (3) poor ocular-motor controls presented evidence of minimum skill level for visual tracking and localization.

TABLE 5-1   Summary of all Optometric Patient Profiles

n	59 Pats.	\multicolumn{2}{l}{(Three additional patients were seen only by the optometric team.)}
Pat. No.'s	%	Item	Section I
4	6.8	(1)	Poor general coordination.
17	29	(2)	Faulty bilaterality and/or midline difficulties.
13	22	(3)	Eye/hand coordination or other fine motor control.
5	8.5	(4)	Fingers required for near reading fixation.
32	54	(5)X	Faulty eye movement, related to general reading difficulty.

TABLE 5-1 (*Continued*)

Pat. No.'s	%	Item	Section I
24	41	(6)X	Inadequate fixation ability.
29	49	(7)X	Inadequate focusing F to N and N to F difficulty.
25	42	(8)X	Inadequate ability to maintain near focus under stress.
29	49	(9)X	Inadequate visual teaming at near, affecting attention span.
33	56	(10)X	Near stress from excess effort focusing and aligning eyes.
35	59	(11)X	Near point discomfort.
13	22	(12)	Inadequate form perception for near visual discrimination.
4	6.8	(13)	Difficulty in visual size relationships.
7	12	(14)	Inadequate visualization abilty.
19	32	(15)	Visual inabilty to adapt to learning stress.

Pat. No.'s	%		Section II
45	76	(1)	Eyes normal and healthy.
10	17	(2)	Referral for additional health care.
15	25	(3)	No ocular defects at present. Acuity satisfactory without stress.
21	36	(4)	Possibly developing a refractive problem, amblyopia for strabismus.
26	44	(5)	Counter-stress near point lenses might reduce near stress.
8	14	(6)	Overdependent upon senses other than vision.
6	10	(7)	Suppression reading.
23	39	(8)	Visual development problem affecting learning.

Pat. No.'s	%		Section III
21	36	(1)	Vision adequate now. Re-examination in one year.
29	49	(2)	Compensatory lenses for clear vision restoration, far or near or both.
17	29	(3)	Developmental and/or remediation lenses now during and after training.
24	41	(4)	Optometric vision training to develop adequate visual motor abilities and skills.
11	19	(5)	Reading help required following visual training.
12	20	(6)	Visual training with near corrective lenses.

X = near stress items.

TABLE 5-2 Selected Visual Characteristics of the Juvenile Delinquent Population

(1) 31 of 52 or 60% had unacceptable ocular-motor control. (Minimum Developmental Visual Skill)
(2) 22/52 or 42% had unacceptable near binocular stereo test skills. (Titmus Stereo Test)
(3) 23/52 or 44% had unacceptable cross cylinder near nets where the plus at near was less than the distance subjective. (minus projection)
(4) Refractively, 73%, 38 of all 52 patients tend to range in the emmetropic zone— between −50 and +1.00 diopters.
(5) 45 or 76% had no problems requiring additional medical or optometric referral.
(6) From the following data, roughly 40–50% of our patients would be expected to have to adapt or compensate for the following inadequate visual skills if they desired to read.
   A. 56% of the patients demonstrating excess effort focusing and aligning eyes at near. (Item 10)
   B. 59% of the patients demonstrating testable near point discomfort. (Item 11)
   C. 49% of the patients demonstrating inadequate focusing far and near and near and far. (Item 7)
   D. 54% of the patients demonstrating faulty eye movement related to general reading difficulty. (Item 5)
   E. 49% of the patients demonstrating inadequate visual teaming at near, affecting attention span. (Item 9)
   F. 42% of the patients demonstrating inadequate ability to maintain near focus under stress. (Item 8)
   G. 41% of the patients demonstrating inadequate fixation ability and reading. (Item 6)
(7) 73% could benefit from either compensating glasses or visual training glasses.
(8) Any of the following items: poor eye control, poor near stereopsis, and minus projection, individually or in combination, would pick up 85% of the juvenile delinquents with potential vision problems, none of which necessarily respond exclusively to eyeglass treatment.
(9) 92% of all patients have at least one potential near vision stress problem.
(10) 80% had at least two potential near vision stress problems.
(11) 67% of our vision population had at least four presenting problems.
(12) 8% of all patients had not even one, or zero (0), potential vision stress problem.
(13) 33% of the entire population would have been picked up by any one of the other examining clinical disciplines, regardless of which one first did the testing. Putting it another way, 33% had such extensive sensory-motor, discriminative, developmental, or perceptual motor problems in all major areas concurrently, that no one would have misdiagnosed them.
(14) 59% diagnostic agreement with the optometrist would have resulted by at least two other diagnosing professions.

These near-area deficits (poor eye control, 60%; poor near binocular stereoscopic depth, 42%; and minus projection, 44%), individually or in any combination, would identify up to 85% of juvenile offenders with minimally one potential major vision problem. In none of the above skill deficiencies are maximum benefits obtained exclusively from a lens therapy program. Some additional type of supplementary regimen of visual therapy is required. Forty-two percent of our population demonstrated two out of three of the above near-area deficiencies. One important conclusion from this study is that near-zone vision skills assessment presents a more reliable picture of impaired visual functioning than standardized distance acuity and refractive assessment at 20 feet.

Ninety-two percent of all cases had at least one near stress item and 67% of the cases had at least four potential near stress items. Stress is considered by Hans Selye as "the rate of all wear and tear caused by life.[16] Near visual stress could be considered the rate of all wear and tear on the body (covert or overt) caused by society's educational and cultural near-centered activities and demands through the use of light.

There was a logical reason why the optometric team felt the highest frequency of potential stress items would occur with near vision testing. Research has shown that an infant first learns and develops his spatial coordinate system at near. Then it slowly develops and expands outward into far space. Further, this near developmental adaptation process should be efficient, purposeful when necessary, facile, automatic, and when sustained require minimal effort and concentration. Presumably, our clinicians judged these patients as having stress when their visual behavior on near tasks failed to meet the above acceptable criteria.

In the past, these youngsters have avoided close-up symbolic manipulation. Their behavior more characteristically has been oriented for concrete object manipulation, not more abstract tasks such as reading. These youngsters would rather play in the streets (distance activities) than to assemble a complex puzzle (near activities). I feel that avoidance of near-point abstract activities has been reinforced throughout the school years because of the associated near-zone unpleasantness of "school learning." For example, suppose I am overweight. It is just as natural for me to avoid diets which are unpleasant for me, as it is for a poor reader to avoid reading a best seller.

Probably only the most essential required reading was ever attempted, for that reason. Obviously, by limiting his visual system to minimum time periods, the learning disabled-juvenile delinquent could minimize near-vision discomfort. Because we found roughly 80% of the population operating in an emmetropic range, it is tempting to speculate that if you avoid reading, you also will avoid development of so-called refractive measurements.

The results from this study and others provide evidence that impaired vision negatively affects learning and reading behavior of juvenile delinquents.[17-21] These findings are in agreement with the literature that juvenile delinquents have the same number and characteristic type of presenting visual skill deficits as an underachieving learning-disabled population and twice the visual problems of a general school population.[22] One should not be surprised to see how similar are the LD and JD populations.[23] Our data also are in basic agreement with the Tarnopol Study,[24] which found 66% failure on the Bender-Gestalt. The functional neurological examination by Peters, Romine and Dykman on both learning-impaired and average achieving youngsters most impressively demonstrates the pervasiveness and subtlety of vision as a major behavior factor of learning. In this latter study, 65% of all statistically significant items which could differentiate the reading-disabled youngster from the control group had developmental vision content.[25]

Juvenile delinquents are multihandicapped. It was rare that they demonstrated only a single-modality impairment (see Table 5-3). Each of the four professions (optometry, psychology, auditory-speech pathology, and occupational therapy) specifically viewed the same patient from its discipline's specific perspective. We attempted to see which participating professions would "red flag" that same youngster as "at risk." Since much of the psychological, occupational, and speech-language-hearing procedures required vision as an essential component of their assessing instruments, it seemed reasonable to assume that a response weakness in any of the other information processing batteries indirectly implicated vision.

In general, there was 33% agreement that when optometry identified a vision problem, all other diagnosing professions similarly "red flagged" that child as "at risk." Our common criterion was the presence of a developmental discriminative or information processing weakness in a specific modality, regardless of which profession

TABLE 5-3 Percentage of Multidisciplinary Team Diagnostic Overlap

Cases	%		
19/56	33	(1)	Overlapping in diagnosis with optometry by all participating professions.
33/56	57	(2)	Overlapping in diagnosis with optometry by at least two other professions.
33/56	57	(3)	Overlapping in diagnosis with optometry by OT.
31/56	55	(4)	Overlapping in diagnosis with optometry by speech/hearing.
0	0	(5)	Overlapping in diagnosis with optometry by psychology. (uncompleted psychology data)
1/56	1.7	(6)	No confirmation of diagnosis with optometry by other professions.
1/56	1.7	(7)	No confirmation of diagnosis with OT by other professions.
50/56	89	(8)	Total cases involving vision diagnosis.
51/56	92	(9)	Overlapping diagnosis between any two professions.

diagnosed first. There was 59% agreement with optometry by at least two other professions that other problems independently existed. In 51 of 56 cases (91%), there was an independent but overlapping diagnosis between any combination of two professions. This was in agreement with a 1973 Colorado Study of 444 subjects in which 90.4% had multiple learning disabilities with combinations of problems in vision, audition-speech, and language processing, as well as in sociological and psychological areas.[26]

The Auditory Battery

A unique battery of central-auditory perceptual testing was conducted on 48 of these 56 juvenile delinquents by Martin Lenhardt, Ph.D., a professor of audiology at MCV, Virginia Commonwealth University. Three experiments previously validated on a "so-called normal achieving population" and on 60 reading-impaired second and third graders were also conducted on these same youngsters, as follows:

1. *Auditory discrimination* (*pitch, loudness, beat*). Experiment one, on auditory discrimination, had the children seated in a sound-attenuated chamber or acoustic environment. Exposed were tones of 1000 HZ at a comfortable 70 decibels sound pressure level. They were to indicate when they detected a change in either loudness or pitch. The amount of intensity or frequency change was systematically

reduced until the children failed to detect a change. The data were recorded as the Just Noticeable Difference Threshold for Loudness (L-JND) or Pitch (P-JND). Next tones (500 HZ) were presented binaurally using different sound oscillators. The frequency was gradually increased (13 HZ min) in one earphone until the subject reported hearing the sound change. The point of just hearing the sound change in this manner is called the *threshold of binaural beat perception*.

2. *Listening skills for speech.* In experiment two phonetically balanced (PB) words were delivered to each ear, and a speech discrimination score was obtained. Next PB words were presented *dichotically*, that is, a test word was presented softly to one ear and simultaneously to the other ear but with a frequency distortion (passing through a low pass filter). The child was required to listen to both the soft, clear word and the louder, distorted word, and then sum this information to correctly identify the word (*binaural summation*).

3. *Ability to perform on phonological* (*speech sound*), *semantic meaning, and memory tasks.* In experiment three:

(A) (Blending) Children were given sound-out words as C-A-T, B-O-A-T, and asked to identify the word in a phonetic fusion task. One-second pauses helped to distort the temporal sequence of phonemes.
(B) (Closure) They were next given phoneme-deleted words as tele–one or super–arket in this phonetic closure task.
(C) (Memory) Estimates were made of their short term memory by asking them to repeat digits, letters, and serial commands. (These tests are standardized ITPA subtests.)

Neither group (reading-impaired or juvenile delinquents) significantly differed in hearing acuity level or speech discrimination. No child had a hearing loss, although there were children with low-normal hearing both groups.

The achieving delinquent children matched the expected normal mean just noticeable difference (JND) threshold of 1 db for loudness discrimination. The JND for the abnormal juvenile delinquent group on the average was more than twice that amount. Since decibels are logarithmic and nonlinear, a decibel difference is a considerable amount in sound pressure. In the binaural summation test for listening skills, the normal scored an average 84.6% (normal range 80–100%) versus the abnormal group of 59.4%. Lenhardt states:

> This means that understanding by these children dropped from about 100% for words in quiet to about 60% during difficult listening conditions. . . . This situation is even more dramatic when

TABLE 5-4 Comparison of Typical Unimpaired and Juvenile Delinquent Auditory Performances

	Hearing acuity	Speech discrimination	Auditory discrimination	Listening skills	Figure ground	Memory bytes
Control expected normal	ND	ND	1 db	85.2%	84.6%	6.5
Delinquent performance	ND	ND	2.2 db	59.4%	37%	4.8

noise competes with speech in the auditory figure/ground test. Here the normal average was 84.6%, whereas, the abnormal group averages only 37%. Remember, this means that when a competing sound was present, these children misunderstood almost twice as much as they understood.

Lastly, the normal group had an average short-term auditory memory of 6.5 bytes, which is close to the adult level, 7 bytes. Of interest, an average unimpaired four-year-old can process 4 bytes, a seven-year-old can handle 5 bytes, and a ten-year-old can process 6 bytes. The abnormal group had an average short-term auditory memory of less than 5 bytes, which was a performance of 50% less than their chronological expected. Overall, 90% of the juvenile delinquents had at least one or more auditory processing deficits. This compares to a 40% deficit for a control group of 60 reading-impaired youngsters from a previous study. (See Tables 5-4 and 5-5.)

The 37.5% of this juvenile delinquent population that showed normal auditory perceptual skills was an "extremely small percentage

TABLE 5-5 A Comparison of Auditory Skill Deficits of Reading-Impaired vs. Delinquent Youngsters

Control Population from a Previous Study

Reading-Impaired Youngsters		Juvenile delinquents
1. All normal	40%—Auditory skills and auditory linguistic skills.	1. All normal 10%
2. Mixture	60% { 20%—Normal auditory skills and abnormal auditory linguistic skills. 40%—Abnormal auditory skills and abnormal linguistic skills.	2. All abnormal 90%
3. All abnormal		

of normal finding for a population referred not specifically because of a suspected auditory processing disturbances." Lenhardt comments:

> The most common deficits for this population were: auditory figure-ground; listening skills; and short term memory. In addition, multiple defects were found, with lower incidences almost universally involving one or more of the above mentioned areas. ... There then can be inferred that poor processing of speech can lead to poor development of verbal skills, and possibly contribute socially deviant behavior.

These data cast sufficient doubt on the concept that eventually with enough time for CNS motor maturation, one can outgrow processing disturbances.

Additional evidence of word and language discrimination problems were gathered by Charlie Graham, speech correctionist in two Richmond public schools.[27] He examined 29 normal-hearing-acuity juvenile delinquents with the Wepman test, a single-sound discrimination instrument, and the STAP (screening test for auditory perception) a multiple-sound discrimination instrument. The Wepman consists of 40 pairs of monosyllable words, 30 different and 10 similar. The subject merely had to mark an X by the pairs that sounded alike. The examiner pronounced the words without the subject being able to watch his mouth or lip movements. Examples are: pen–pin; pork–cork; bum–bomb. Sixteen out of 29 failed the Wepman test.

The STAP test consisted of five subtests. One was similar to the above Wepman. The other four measured: (2) perception of long vs. short vowels within 12 monosyllabic words, repeated twice; (3) ability to hear the differences between initial single consonants and blends, again in 12 words; (4) application of auditory memory span to recognize rhyming vs. nonrhyming words; (5) immediate memory span for and the ability to recognize rhythmic tapping sound patterns. Graham writes:

> Twenty rate very poor, below the 20th percentile. Five rated poor—20th to 40th percentile; two rated average—40th to 60th percentile: and two rated very good—80th to 100th percentile. Twenty-five of the 29 juvenile court cases tested had problems with word and sound perceptions. The subtests that the cases did the best on was the subtest which was similar to the Wepman.

The Rhode Island Study

Berman and Siegal's investigation represents the largest-scale, matched study of adaptive skills and neuropsychological defects of delinquent and nondelinquent boys in the LD-JD literature. These investigators feel that there is ample evidence that children who are labeled delinquent show an "ability constellation which differs from that of normal non-delinquent children and many of the subtle psychophysiological performance defects of this population resemble those of neurologically impaired youngsters."[28]

Berman and Siegal cited several preliminary studies. Because of relevancy to their monograph they are mentioned here. Graham and Kamano demonstrated that performance IQ was greater than verbal IQ in juvenile delinquents having reading disorders.[29] Hurvitz, Bibace, Wolff, and Rowbothan observed sensory-motor skills impairment as well as difficulty in symbolic sequencing involving rhythm in learning-disability and juvenile delinquent youngsters.[30] Further, they could differentiate these children from a normal control population.

Using the Halstead-Reitan Battery enabled Fitzhugh to study neurophysiological differences between matched emotionally disturbed (nondelinquent) controls and delinquent youths.[31,32] Despite the fact that only a small sample of 19 juvenile delinquents and 10 emotionally disturbed youngsters was used, and that all subjects had negative findings on a clinical neurological examination, the performance of the delinquents was significantly worse. The experimental groups in this study consisted of 45 males, 15–18 years of age (average 16), 32% black and 68% white. All were first-time-incarcerated youngsters and were examined within the first week of confinement. The control group consisted of 45 nondelinquents from a Providence, Rhode Island, inner city public high school, the same one from which 80% of the delinquents came. This latter group thus served also as a rough control for socioeconomic variables.

All were evaluated using the Halstead-Reitan neuropsychological battery, for adults, which took a full day to administer. The battery included: the Category Test; the 10-block Tactual Performance Test with time, memory, and location scoring for dominant and nondominant hands; the Seashore Rhythm test; the Finger Oscillation Test; and the Halstead Speech Sounds Perception Test. Administered but not included in the summary impairment index were the Trailmaking Test (A and B); the Reitan Examination for Sensory Imperception; the Halstead-Wepman Aphasia examination; and the Wechsler Adult Intelligence Scale (WAIS), which is used as part of the Halstead-Reitan Battery.[33]

The six subtests comprising Reitan's Examination for Sensory Imperception were collapsed, and the total number of errors of these sections constituted the raw scores that were used to compare the means between the delinquent and the nondelinquent populations. The composite scores expressed auditory, tactile, and visual sensory imperception. Additionally included were measures of the intactness of tactile perception (fingertip, number writing, tactile form recognition, and finger agnosia).

Ratios and probabilities were calculated. The results were striking. The delinquents performed worse on nearly all tasks in the Wechsler Scale and on all of the Halstead tasks with the exception of rhythm and the Finger Oscillation test. The Examination for Sensory Imperception failed to yield any significant difference between the two populations. Although the performance IQ was greater in both populations, the magnitude was significantly greater for the delinquent groups. The WAIS tests can cluster performance into three distinct constellations of adaptive abilities: verbal comprehension, perceptual organization, and memory. When able, Berman grouped the statistically significant differences between the two populations under these categories. Verbal comprehension skills had differences between the groups with a probability of less than .001 chance on the subsections of information, comprehension, similarities, and vocabulary. Perceptual organization manifested differences with a P less than .01 on block design and object assembly. The Trailmaking Test A and B differences also were significant in this area. Digit span differences were not significant. Hence, one could find no differences under the simple short term memory task.

The Trailmaking Test, Part A, required the subject to locate the numbered sequence 1 to 25 on a printed page and to connect the numbers with a continuous line. Part B added a verbal-symbolic manipulation to the spatial and perceptual demands of Part A. Here, they had to locate an interdigitated series of alternating letters and numbers. One had to proceed from 1 to A, A to 2, 2 to B, B to 3, and so on. Even though both groups' scores were within acceptable norms, the delinquents performed so poorly on Part B with its strong verbal component, that their performances fell within the range of major neurological impaired subjects.

The delinquents performed significantly worse than the nondelinquents on five out of seven of the variables that compose the Impairment Index. The overall Impairment Index was significant at P .001. The most profound deficiency in performance on the Halstead Neurophychological Battery occurred with the Category Test, a nonverbal concept formation test ($P < .001$). The subject was asked to effectively integrate past experiences that had positive and negative reinforcements into an actual problem, and then utilize this information to modify his behavior. The procedure required a projection apparatus for presenting stimulus materials, from which various abstract principles, such as size, shape, brightness, numbers, position, color, and so forth, could be used to organize one's responses. Grouping of stimulus materials by criteria allowed problem solving. Also the responses required one either to recognize similarities in different contexts or the pattern of recurrent similarities, and to organize the relevant aspects of a Gestalt.

Berman wrote: "An inability to project from experience and the repeated use of poor judgment seem to characterize the delinquent's performance on both the Category Test and his overall life style." (See modified chart from Berman and Siegal, Table 5-6.)

The delinquent population's performance was distinctly different (P .01) from that of the controls when asked to remember a tactile form, draw it from memory, and then locate it on a "cognitive map": here again was evidence that basic tactile-visual-motor information processing was impaired more in the delinquent and could limit perceptual organizing skills.

As Berman stated: "This research suggests that skill impairments are more clearly involved in the background of delinquents than are social class variables . . . delinquents also seem to show more extreme impairment in the verbal, perceptual and non-verbal conceptual spheres."

The authors conclude that any attempt at changing delinquent behavior by purely psychological or sociological techniques when the "central problem is neuropsychological or perceptual distortion or deficiency is a needlessly absurd and a useless waste of time, money and effort." They felt that no meaningful rehabiltation can be pos-

TABLE 5-6 Comparison of 48 Male Juvenile Delinquents with Matched Controls on the Halstead and Wechsler Batteries from Berman and Siegal

WAIS	Delinquent Score	Control Score	P
Verbal IQ	87.49	101.78	<.001
Performance IQ	95.78	103.91	=.001
Full Scale IQ	90.56	103.09	<.001
Information	6.33	8.73	<.001
Comprehension	6.98	11.00	<.001
Arithmetic	7.00	9.04	<.001
Similarities	8.04	11.44	<.001
Digit Span	8.84	9.33	NS
Vocabulary	6.58	8.51	<.001
Digit Symbol	6.49	9.07	<.001
Picture Comp.	9.69	10.93	=.05
Block Design	9.47	10.78	<.01
Picture Arrang.	8.73	9.87	<.05
Object Assem.	9.53	11.35	<.01
PIQ−VIG	8.29	2.13	<.005
Halstead neuropsychological battery:			
Category Test	59.96	44.56	<.001
TPT (Time)	13.93	12.14	=.05
TPT (Memory)	6.87	7.78	=.01
TPT (Location)	4.16	5.82	<.01
Speech Test	9.71	7.27	<.05
Rhythm Test	26.33	26.67	NS
Finger Oscil.	46.27	45.18	NS
Impairment Index	0.46	0.30	=.001
Trailmaking Test A— Time in Seconds	34.89	25.01	<.001
Trailmaking Test B— Time in seconds	109.68	78.40	<.01
Sensory Imperception	2.78	2.13	NS
TPT dominant hand	6.65	5.97	NS
TPT non-dominant hand	4.74	3.82	<.05
TPT both hands	2.58	2.37	NS

sible until we first learn to determine which delinquents require which specific or alternate treatment programs. Rehabilitation must be on an individual basis, tailored to an individual youth's unique neuropsychological, physiological, and emotional problems.

SECTION 2

Effective Treatment

Thus far we have shown that careful diagnostic examinations by appropriate specialists consistently reveal that juvenile delinquents have multiple perceptual processing defects involving inaccurate discrimination and developmental disabilities, with resulting maladaptive behavior. It is particularly sad that often nothing more is done for the child, even after an appropriate diagnosis. This happens for several reasons. He may leave the court's jurisdiction too soon, the original charges may be dismissed, or, perhaps, institutional budget limitations may minimize professional services available to such youth.

If rehabilitation is to be meaningful, however, several events must transpire: (1) skill deficits that can affect maladaptive behavior must be eliminated or materially lessened: (2) vocational opportunities should be enhanced with improved literacy; (3) a positive self-image should be restored to youngsters who have never demonstrated developmental processing success before in academic or social situations.

Three meaningful rehabilitative studies have recently been published, which involved visual training, reading skill enhancement, and improvement in other perceptual deficit areas. These studies show that a significant reduction of recidivism rates occurred in the experimental therapy population which did not occur in the untreated control populations.

The Plainfield Study

In 1972, a vision testing and training program for 391 juvenile delinquents was initiated at the State Boys School at Plainfield, Indiana.[34,35] Fewer than 10% passed the visual-perceptual-motor test battery. Prescription glasses were prescribed for 172. One hundred fifty-eight received therapy in the special visual-perceptual-motor training clinic at the school. Those youngsters who participated in the ten-week training program gained nearly two grade levels in reading ability. Only 11 of the 158 youngsters had to return to the school. Compare this 6.5% recidivism rate with the overall return rate of 31% at the school.

The Tidewater Study

Bachara and Zaba conducted a 3½-year study of 79 status offenders in the Tidewater (Virginia) Juvenile Court.[36] The purpose of the study was to evaluate the "effectiveness of utilizing appropriate academic therapies with the juvenile offender." This experimental population group was compared to a control group of juvenile delinquents with primary learning disabilities who did not receive academic treatment and who were committed to state institutional care or on probation without any outside intervention. The experimental group consisted of status offenders charged with such offenses as incorrigibility, truancy, and disruption in school.

Each youngster in this study had an extensive evaluation—psychiatric, psychological, social case work histories, visual-perceptual, audiological, neurological, and so on. No serious emotional, family dysfunction or diagnosis other than learning disability was permitted. Also excluded were those youngsters who received individual psychotherapy or family counseling. But the experimental population in many cases received supportive counseling and family educational counseling that accompanied their academic and other appropriate remedial therapies. The majority of delinquents referred for academic therapy were involved in a visual-therapy, perceptual-motor program in connection with remedial reading classes or tutoring. The remaining subjects were placed in a self-contained learning disability class or some variation of this within a public or private special education course. They were referred to appropriate professionals, such as developmental optometrists, occupational therapists, educational remediators, or tutors.

The recidivism rate for the experimental group was 4.3%. The control population (Group B) had a 44% recidivism rate. Group A (mixed control) showed a recidivism rate of 55%. This rate was computed from a composite of previous studies conducted in the Chesapeake Juvenile Court, none of which involved learning disability diagnostic cause or treatment.

The Denver Study

Roger Dowis, an optometrist, diagnosed and provided optometric visual therapy to 78 children aged 12–18, with a mean age of 14.9

years.[37] These youngsters were seen at the Denver, Colorado, Optometric Center through a contract with the Colorado Division of Youth Services to provide complete visual care, especially vision training to those most in need. The initial testing battery included entrance skills, pathology, OEP 21 point analysis, Kirshner ocular-motor tests, Keystone skills, accommodative facility, and Visual III. When necessary, form boards, gross motor skills, and pencil-paper tests were conducted. Both glasses and visual training were prescribed when needed. When visual therapy was recommended, subjects were then placed in Lookout Mountain School, an educational treatment facility for committed delinquents.

The subjects were seen for one hour of weekly therapy at the optometric center. Their programs were individualized for their needs. Additionally, the physical education and reading teachers not only accompanied the students to the center, but participated there as well. They were instructed in take-home therapy, which was to be conducted daily. Large motor and general movement skills were programmed for the PE teacher. Fine motor and perceptual activities were assigned the reading teacher. Four hours of therapy a week, two hours per instructor, were conducted by this Lookout staff.

The results from initial testing were in conformity with other vision studies: 56% of the teen-agers had less than the expected near-focusing power for sustained periods of reading. Basic eye control skills deficiencies ranged from 46% on pursuits to 58% on saccadics.

The entire accommodative complex of skills was below what was expected. Deficiencies ranged from 56% for reduced positive relative accommodative findings below -3.00 diopters to an 80% reduction in speed of amplitude stimulation and inhibition (to clear a blur instantly within 2 seconds).

This study incorporated two new visual procedures that could be quantified. Using the Kirshner Rotations for Dynamic Acuity, only 7 of 73 youngsters achieved a score higher than 45 revolutions per minute. The expected score was 47.1; the mean score was 32.9 rpms. The subject viewed a 20/40 Snellen letter spinning in a projected 4 feet wide (diameter) circle on a wall 10 feet away. This was accomplished by sending a reverse picture onto a mirror, which spun simultaneously on the common shaft of a variable-speed 10-100 rpm motor. Head movements were not permitted while following the moving letter. The examiner reduced the rotational speed of the spinning letter until four consecutive individual letters could be correctly read. When head control was measured, the subjects had to aim a Burgess headlight ahead on a moving red-green target. Scored was the highest speed at which the patient could maintain the light coincident on the target for three consecutive rotations. Only 9 scored the expected 35 rpms. The mean score was 18.9 rpms, much slower than expected. The slow speed of identification and inaccurate visual localization and tracking underline the suspicion of neurological timing lags and problems in the integrative mechanism of the CNS information processing channels.

This was also the first optometric battery measuring visualization and short term memory using the Monroe III Test as described at the Gessel Institute. Here the subject had to reproduce a series of complex figures or designs from memory. The expected score for age 10 was 11.2 with expectation that attempted figures would be made correctly 74% of the time. Seventy-three of 78 delinquents were tested. They had a mean score of 9.0, with a mean percentile of 58%, the expected score for persons 7 and 8 years old. Only 12 subjects achieved a score greater than 11.0. Twenty-one percent of the subjects approached a 70% correct-attempted-figure score. This test shows juvenile delinquents have an inadequate ability to visually organize symbolic information in their "mind's eye," for adequate periods of time.

During 1970–1973, there were 48 students who remained in the training program for a period of 4½ months. They had a recidivism rate of 4.1%. From this group only two students were returned after release. This compared to a recidivism rate of 18% for the total population during that same time interval. The definition of recidivism was based on the premise that JD did not return to the Division of Youth Services for violation or suspension before the two-year parole commitment was completed. This difference, analyzed by the binomial distribution method, was found to be significant at the .005 level.

A Case Study

Dowis and Dickerson describe one typical vision therapy case. Paul, a 12-year-old, was suffering from a long standing learning difficulty when he first appeared at the state receiving and diagnostic center.

He had been sniffing glue since age 7. He first appeared before the court at age 10 for theft and curfew violations. He was then declared beyond parental control. At 12, he was committed to state care for burglary, conspiracy, and malicious mischief.

His score on the Gilmore Oral reading test, word-call accuracy, was grade 3.0, and comprehension was 1.9 years. He read silently second grade material and could spell only two words. On the Bender-Visual Motor Integration Test, he scored 5 years, 3 months, with severe visual perceptual problems. His reading of letters and words both were riddled with reversals, transpositions, and upside-down words. He even turned around characters and events within paragraphs. Psychiatric examination showed an abnormal EEG with other soft neurological signs. Anticonvulsive drugs were prescribed for four months. The psychiatrist after labeling him "probable organic brain impairment" recommended enrollment in a program for perceptually handicapped youngsters.

His initial uncorrected acuity was 20/20 for each eye. Both focusing or accommodative flexibility and eye control vertically and diagonally were poor, with lots of head movement. Basic visual skills indicated fusional or binocular instability, overconvergence with normal depth perception. On one nonverbal reading test, his left eye performed 20% slower than the right or both eyes together. On the Monroe Visual III Test his visual memory was less than age 5.

His visual therapy program was designed to develop the following abilities: adequate skills in eye movement, convergence, accommodative flexibility, visual attention, eye-hand-body coordination, directionality, form perception, figure-ground relationships, spatial organization, sensory integration, and visualization.

He was given the following help: reading remediation at his reformatory, weekly therapy sessions at Colorado Optometric Center, and four sessions per week in perceptual motor classes at Lookout Mountain School. Five students were in each class. The reading teacher used a token reward system. Paul spent two years at Lookout Mountain. Though released at 11 months, he had to be returned because of inadequate outside supervision.

At final dismissal, these new findings had resulted: His initial WRAT was 2.6. Now, after 15 months of special effort of his part, he was reading at the 5.4 grade level. His Gilmore Test Reading went from 3.0 accuracy and 1.9 comprehension to 5.3 and 8.0, respectively.

Accommodative flexibility went from 2 to 22 cycles per minute. On the Kirschner Oculo-Motor Skills, he went from 35 to 55 rpms. Head control went from 15 to 45 rpms. On his nonverbal tests, he went to no difference between right and left eyes. The Monroe Visual III test showed a gain from 3.0 (age 5) to 12.5 (greater than 10 years).

Observation showed a more self-confident and happier boy who could return to school with a chance of making it. Paul has remained out of court custody for three years now, a fact which speaks for itself.

SUMMARY

1. The attempt has been made to show that juvenile delinquents have deficiencies in their basic neuropsychological information processing abilities. These developmental and perceptual inadequacies continue to affect learning in general and symbolic manipulation in particular. Failure in school can be considered the end product of impoverished adaptive skills.

2. Delinquent and learning-disabled children share several characteristics. One of the more prominent is retarded reading performance. Untreated perceptual-cognitive skill deficits continues to affect development negatively and undermine academic progress long after the critical years of their initial impact. The classical mode of delinquency treatment has been incarceration, with minimal attempts to remediate the causes of multiple developmental processing difficulties. Such an approach is not supported by the research presented in this paper. The outmoded psychiatric medical model should embrace functional behavioral principles.

3. A more realistic approach to rehabilitation is to treat the multiple underlying developmental processing problems, which appear to be major contributors in creating learning disabilities and faulty adaptation of delinquents.

4. To maximize the juvenile delinquent's educational and vocational experiences, specialized therapists are required for rehabilitative programming. An obvious and common sense approach to rehabilitation requires not only expert diagnosis but, even more important, expert treatment in particular. Each skill deficit must be treated by various specialists in a multidisciplinary team. We must develop a rational, holistic approach first to understand the unique

problems of each individual delinquent so that our therapy programs can be correctly designed for their specific needs.

5. A 4 to 6% recidivism rate for a therapy population is dramatically lower than the present-day conventional incarceration-probation rates.

References

1. Bachara, Gary H., Zaba, Joel, and Raskin, Larry, Human figure drawings and learning disabled children, *J. Academic Therapy* XI (2):75-76, Winter 1975-76.
2. Berman, Allan, and Siegal, Andrew, Delinquents are disabled: An innovative approach to the prevention and treatment of juvenile delinquency, University of Rhode Island, Kingston, 1974.
3. Slavin, Sidney H., The 13th District Juvenile and Domestic Relations Court project. An optometric study, *Transactions of Eastern Seaboard Invitational Skeffington Symposium on Visual Training*, Transcript by Caryl Croisant, O.D., Phoenix, Oregon, 1976.
4. Cruickshank, William, Myths and realities in learning disabilities, *J. Learning Disabilities* 10 (1): 1977.
5. Hobbs, N., Ed., *Issues in the Classifications of Children*, Vol. 1, Jossey-Bass, San Francisco, 1975.
6. U.S. Government, *A Report on Learning Disabilities of Juvenile Delinquency*, Report GGD-76-97, U.S. Central Accounting Office, Distribution Section, Washington, D.C., 1977.
7. Virginia, State of, *The State of the Art of Reading in Virginia*, State Department of Education, Richmond, Va., 1976.
8. Baum, Charlene, Richmond's 13th District Juvenile and Domestic Relations Court project—Overview from a social worker, *Transactions of Eastern Seaboard Invitational Skeffington Symposium on Visual Training*, January 1975, Transcript by Caryl Croisant, O.D., Phoenix, Oregon, 1976.
9. Etkin, Michael, Biostatistical analysis of the 13th District Juvenile and Domestic Relations Court project, *Transactions of Eastern Seaboard Invitational Skeffington Symposium on Visual Training*, Transcript by Caryl Croisant, O.D., Phoenix, Oregon, 1976.
10. Reynolds, Carol B. Perceptual-motor functioning of delinquent adolescents—The occupational therapist's role in juvenile and domestic relations court, *Transactions of Eastern Seaboard Invitational Skeffington Symposium on Visual Training*, Transcript by Caryl Croisant, O.D., Phoenix, Oregon, 1976.
11. Lenhardt, Martin L., Richmond's 13th District Juvenile and Domestic Relations Court project. Part A—Auditory and speech discrimination in reading impaired children. Part B—Central auditory processing abilities in children with confirmed delinquent behavior, *Transactions of Eastern Seaboard Invitational Skeffington Symposium on Visual Training*, Transcript by Caryl Croisant, O.D., Phoenix, Oregon, 1976.

12. Slavin, Sidney H., Historical perspective on selected literature on vision and juvenile offenders, *Transactions on Eastern Seaboard Invitational Skeffington Symposium on Visual Training*, Transcript by Caryl Croisant, O.D., Phoenix, Oregon, 1976.
13. Malkin, Joyce, and Castex, G. M., The effects of perceptual-motor dysfunctions on behavior, Research in partial fulfillment for degree of M.S.W., School of Social Work, Virginia Commonwealth University, Richmond, Va., 1976.
14. Borish, Irvin, *Clinical Refraction*, The Professional Press, Chicago, 1970.
15. Robinson, B. N., A study of visual function in institutionalized juveniles who are demonstrated unachieving readers, *Am. J. Optometry* and Archives American Academy of Optometry. 50 (2):, 1973.
16. Selye, Hans, *The Stress of Life*, McGraw-Hill, New York, 1956.
17. Koch, C. C. Note: Juvenile delinquency & refractive errors, *Am. J. Optometry* 10 (7):, 1933.
18. Christie, Amos, *J. Juvenile Research* 8:13, 1934.
19. Brooks, Charles, Juvenile delinquency as an optometric problem. *J. A.O.A.* 18 (6):307–311, 1947.
20. Dzik, David, Vision and the juvenile delinquent, *J. A.O.A.* 37 (5):, 1966; A Symposium on Juvenile Delinquency, B'Nai B'rith, Stanley Lachman, Lodge #446, 2nd Annual Symposium on Juvenile Delinquency, Chattanooga, Tenn., April 6, 1967 (available from A.O.A. Library).
21. Shearer, Robert V., Eye findings in children with reading difficulties, *J. Pediat. Ophthal.* 3 (4):, 1966.
22. Peters, Henry B., Blum, H. L., Bettman, J. W., Johnson, F., and Fellows, V., The Orinda study, *Am. J. Optometry* and Archives of American Academy of Optometry 36, September 1959 (available from A.O.A. Library).
23. Coleman, Howard, Visual perception and reading dysfunction, *J. Learning Disabilities* 1 (2):, 1968; The West Warwick visual perception story, Part 1, *J. A.O.A.* 43 (4):, 1972.
24. Tarnpol, Lester, Delinquency and minimal brain dysfunction, *J. Learning Disabilities* 3 (4):, 1970.
25. Peters, J. E., Romine, J. S., and Dykman, R. A., A special neurological examination of children with learning disabilities, *Develop. Med. Child. Neur.* 17:63–78, 1975.
26. Dowis, Roger, The effect of a visual training program on juvenile delinquency, *J. A.O.A.*, 48:9, 1977.
27. Graham, Charlie, Word and language discrimination tests given to juvenile court cases, unpublished, 1976.
28. Berman, Allan, and Siegal, Andrew, Adaptive and learning skills in juvenile delinquent. A neuro-psychological analysis. *J. Learning Disabilities* 9, (9): 1976.
29. Graham, E. E., and Kamano, D., Reading failure as a factor in the WAIS subtest patterns of youthful offenders, *J. Clin. Psychol.*, 14:302–305, 1958.
30. Hurvitz, I., Bibace, R. M., Wolff, P. H., and Rowbotham, B. M., Neurological function of normal boys, delinquent boys, and boys with learning problems, *Perceptual Motor Skills* 35:387–394, 1972.

31. Reitan, R. H., Investigation of the validity of Halstead measures of biological intelligence, *Arch. Neurol. Psychiat.* 73:28–35, 1955; The comparative effects of brain damage on the Halstead impairment index & the Wechsler-Bellevue Scale, *J. Clin. Psychol.* 15:281–285, 1959.
32. Fitzhugh, B., Some neuropsychological features of delinquent subjects, *Perceptual Motor Skills* 36:494, 1973.
33. Berman, Allan, Neurological dysfunction in juvenile delinquents: Implications for early intervention, *Child Care Quart.*, 264–271, 1972.
34. The Plainfield project—Optometry Indiana, July, 1970, 9–15 (copy from A.O.A. Library, St. Louis, Mo.).
35. Keystone communique—Correlation between juvenile delinquency and vision problems shown in studies, *Keystone Communique Quarterly*, No. 7, Keystone-Mast Co., Davenport, Iowa.
36. Bachara, Gary H., Empathy in learning disabled children, *Perceptual Motor Skills* 43:, 1976. Bachara, Gary H., and Zaba, Joel N. Learning disabilities and juvenile delinquency beyond the correlation, in press, 1977.
37. Dowis, Roger, and Dickerson, Della, Case study—The effect of a visual therapy program on juvenile delinquency, *J. A.O.A.*, 48:9, 1977.

Chapter 6

The Effects of Light and Radiation on Human Health and Behavior

John Ott, Sc.D., Hon.
Center for Light Research
Roswell Park, New York

INTRODUCTION

The effects of sunlight, both beneficial and harmful, on the human skin have long been recognized. However, more recently neurochemical channels leading from the retina to the pituitary and pineal glands have been reported. These master glands control the endocrine system, which produces and releases the hormones that control body chemistry. Thus, the basic principles of photosynthesis in plants, sometimes referred to as the conversion of light energy into chemical energy, appear to carry over into animal life, a fact that has not heretofore been recognized.

Life on this earth since the beginning has evolved under the full spectrum of natural sunlight. Recent experimental studies have indicated specific endocrine responses through sensitive photoreceptor mechanisms in both the skin and the retina to narrow bands of wavelengths within the entire electromagnetic spectrum, and not just to the difference between light and dark. Some of these wavelengths of general background radiation penetrate ordinary building material as readily as visible light penetrates window glass.

Various skin and suntan lotions block certain light rays from penetrating the skin, and ordinary window glass, windshields, and eyeglasses filter most of the ultraviolet light from entering the eyes.

Tinted contact lenses, deeper-colored sunglasses, and different artificial light sources also grossly distort the natural spectrum of light entering the eyes. These distortions are creating a condition now referred to as malillumination, which is similar to malnutrition, resulting primarily from what is lacking in a proper diet.

Man-made radiation from TV sets, fluorescent tubes, radar and radar ovens, telephone microwave relay towers, computers and office machines using cathode ray tubes, and other similar electronic devices are creating levels of artificial radiation many times greater than the natural general background radiation.

SOME EXPERIMENTAL STUDIES

A serious question now exists as to what effect this relatively recent drastic change in our light and radiation environment may have on human health and behavior. The seriousness of the problem has become more apparent as the result of the hobby of taking time-lapse pictures of flowers growing, which I started 50 years ago while still in high school. My professional career was for 20 years with a Chicago bank, until I retired from banking in 1948 to devote full time to time-lapse photography. It became my good fortune and priviledge to prepare many of the sequences of flowers growing for some of Walt Disney's films, such as "Nature's Half-Acre," "Secrets of Life," and others. Pumpkins would produce only staminate blossoms when I was using ordinary cool-white fluorescent tubes in my studio. When these tubes became old and started to flicker, I replaced them with new ones that just happened to be daylight-white, with more energy in the blue or shorter wavelengths. All the pumpkin plants then produced only pistillate blossoms. In the Department of Biology at Loyola University in Chicago, a controlled study showed similar results, with different kinds of lights influencing the sex of tropical fish. Today the chinchilla industry on a worldwide commercial basis is obtaining approximately 95% males or females in the litters depending on the lights used in the breeding rooms.

More recently I was asked by Paramount Pictures to make the time-lapse sequences of geraniums and other flowers for the film "On a Clear Day," featuring Barbra Streisand. The pictures clearly showed that the geraniums would grow better near the center of the fluorescent tubes than directly under the ends where the cathodes are located.

These unusual and abnormal growth responses in plants under different types of artificial lights, which were lacking certain wavelengths or contained peaks of energy in others when compared to the full spectrum of natural outdoor sunlight, led to controlled experiments with laboratory animals kept under different types of fluorescent lights.

The most significant abnormal conditions were found in the animals under pink fluorescent, which represents a concentration of the wavelength energy in a narrow part of the spectrum towards the red end of the visible spectrum. The animals used in this particular experiment were mice and rats, which are both nocturnal in nature and do not see into the far red end of the spectrum. This is why red lights are used in the so-called night rooms of many zoos, so that these nocturnal animals are more active and not asleep in a corner of their cage while the zoo is open to the public during the daytime.

The abnormal responses in the animals under the pink fluorescent consisted of excessive calcium deposits in the heart tissue, smaller numbers of young in the litters and lower survival rate, significantly greater tumor development or cancer, plus a strong tendency toward their becoming irritable, aggressive, constantly fighting with one another, and cannibalistic.

Our first thought: The particular wavelengths that we see as pink might be responsible for these abnormal results. However, these wavelengths are a part of the total spectrum and present in natural outdoor daylight. It therefore is suggested that the abnormal responses result from the wavelengths that are missing in the pink fluorescent light and thus causing the condition of malillumination, mentioned above. The balance of this paper will be devoted to further discussion of the effects of light and radiation on behavioral problems.

Former Warden Regan of Stateville Penitentiary in Illinois was a great believer in horticultural therapy. He was a guest on my TV gardening program on several occasions to tell of the work done by the inmates at the penitentiary. I also visited him several times and was amazed by the beautiful gardens within the prison walls and also the very extensive prison farms. Warden Regan stated on many occasions that it was only through horticultural therapy that he was able to rehabilitate some of the most extreme psychological cases, making them actually eligible for parole. He said that the other forms of manual therapy, including painting and sculpture done indoors, did not have the same beneficial effects. Maybe the results of the horticultural therapy were purely psychological, as the men got closer to nature and worked with flowers. And maybe getting them outdoors into the natural sunlight was a very important factor, especially when consideration is given to how poorly the average jail cell is lighted.

Sometime later, visiting the Miami Seaquarium, I noticed one area where black light ultraviolet fluorescent tubes had been placed over some of the aquariums. I asked the Director about this, and he explained that in view of the increasing interest in psychedelic lighting, it was done just to create an eerie effect. He went on to state that he had noticed within ten days after installing the black light ultraviolet fluorescent tubes that a severe condition of popeye or excothalmus in some of the fish completely disappeared. He and his co-workers also noted that this added small amount of ultraviolet eliminated another very common problem, that of fin-nipping. He also mentioned that he was now able to keep many rare species of fish thriving that never could be kept in captivity before.

We have experimented in breeding rats under standard cool-white fluorescent and the new full spectrum type of fluorescent tube. Under ordinary types of fluorescent light, it has been common practice to remove the male from the cage before the litter arrives because of the tendency toward cannibalism. However, under the new type of fluorescent tubes it is no longer necessary to remove the male, as he invariably will show a more normal parental instinct in helping to take care of the young.

At the State of Florida Marine Research Laboratory, where I have been fortunate in having the opportunity to serve as a consultant, a new laboratory building has been constructed, using ultraviolet transmitting plastic in all the skylights and windows, as well as a new type of full spectrum fluorescent tubes with radiation shields that more closely duplicate natural outdoor sunlight. Dr. Frank Hoff and his assistant were both working on a project to find a way to raise shrimp on a commercial farming basis, as has been done in the past with catfish. In the old laboratory under standard cool-white fluorescent lights, the chief problem encountered was that of cannibalism. In the new laboratory under the ultraviolet transmitting plastic and the full spectrum fluorescent tubes, this problem of cannibalism has completely disappeared.

In another experiment conducted at a small college, a professor of psychology submitted a questionnaire to all the students asking, among other things, whether or not they wore tinted contact lenses or sunglasses, and if so, what color. The answers, though not satistically significant because only three cases were involved, did indicate that three students constantly wore "Hot-Pink" sunglasses, and a check with the faculty ratings indicated that these same students were also considered to be the most psychologically disturbed students in the college.

EFFECTS OF TELEVISION ON CHILDREN

The November 6, 1964, issue of *Time* carried a very interesting and provocative article entitled "Those Tired Children." It told of a report presented by two Air Force physicians at a meeting of the American Academy of Pediatrics in New York City. No explanation for the symptoms of 30 children being studied could be found after they made all the usual tests for infectious and childhood illnesses. Both the food and water supplies were checked. The symptoms included nervousness, continuous fatigue, headaches, loss of sleep, and vomiting. Only after further checking was it discovered that children in this group were all watching television three to six hours a day during the week and six to ten hours on Saturdays and Sundays.

The doctors prescribed total abstinence from TV. In 12 cases the parents enforced the rule, and the children's symptoms vanished in two to three weeks. In 18 cases the parents cut the TV time to about two hours a day, and the children's symptoms did not go away for five or six weeks. But in 11 cases the parents later relaxed the rules and the children were back again spending their usual time in front of the picture tube. Their symptoms returned as before.

The report concluded that watching TV, in itself, is not necessarily bad, but that some children become addicted to it and fall into a vicious cycle of viewing for long hours. Thus they become too tired to do anything more strenuous than to continue watching the TV set. Other reports have suggested psychological overstimulation in children as a result of the program content of too many western thrillers and murder mysteries. Little or no consideration seems to have been given to the question of possible radiation problems. However, epileptic seizures in some children have been reported as being caused by flicker from TV sets in the visible light range.

It will be remembered that the X-ray–type shoe-fitting machines, commonly used in many shoe stores, were found to be giving off excessive X-rays and were banned from use.

In order to determine if there might be any basic physiological responses in plants or laboratory animals to some sort of radiation being emitted from TV sets, an experiment was set up in our laboratory at Environmental Health and Light Research Institute using a large-screen color TV. One-half of the picture tube was covered with one-sixteenth-inch solid lead, which is customarily used to shield X-rays, and the other half was covered with ordinary heavy black photographic paper that would stop all visible light but allow other areas of radiation to penetrate. Six pots, each containing three bean seeds, were placed directly in front of the portion of the TV tube covered with the black photographic paper, and six pots were placed in front of the lead shielding; also six pots were placed outdoors at a distance of 50 feet from the greenhouse where the TV set was located. At the end of three weeks all the young bean plants in the six pots outdoors and the six pots with lead shielding showed approximately six inches of normal-appearing growth. All the bean plants in the six pots shielded only with the black photographic paper showed an excessive vine-type growth ranging up to $31\frac{1}{2}$ inches. Furthermore, the leaves in the paper-shielded group were all approximately two and one-half to three times the size of those of the outdoor plants or those protected with the lead shielding.

These results prompted an additional similar experiment using white laboratory rats. Two rats, approximately three months old, were placed in each of two cages directly in front of the color television tube, and the set was turned on for six hours each weekday and ten hours on Saturday and Sunday. One cage was placed in front of the half of the tube covered with black photographic paper, and the other cage in front of the lead shielding, which was increased to one-eighth-inch thickness. The sound was turned off.

The rats, protected only with the black paper, showed stimulated abnormal activities for three to ten days after the experiment started and then became progressively lethargic. At 30 days they were extremely lethargic, and it was necessary to push them to make them move about the cage. This experiment was repeated three times, and the same results were obtained.

When the color television set was placed in the greenhouse area of our laboratory, the location was 15 feet from our animal breeding room, with two ordinary building partitions in between. We observed that immediately following the placing of the color television set in the greenhouse, our animal breeding program, which had been going on very successfully for over two years, was completely disrupted. Whereas litters of the rats had previously averaged eight or twelve or more young, the number immediately dropped off to one or two, many of which did not survive. After removal of the TV set, approximately six months' time was required before the breeding program was back to normal.

This information was given in testimony to the House Sub-Committee on Public Health and Environment and credited by its Chairman, Rep. Paul G. Rogers, for getting things started toward control of radiation from electronic products and passage of the 1968 Radiation Control Act.

The TV sets in the homes of 12 hyperactive children being sent to a special adjustive education center in Sarasota, Florida were tested and all found to be giving off low levels of X-rays. When these sets were discarded or repaired, all the children within a few months could be returned to their regular school classes.

More recent medical reports indicate that air traffic controllers are experiencing abnormal health problems identical to those of the tired-child syndrome and possibly radiation-oriented rather than due to the psychological stress from their responsibilities alone.

LIGHTING AND ITS EFFECTS ON SCHOOL CHILDREN

During the 1972–1973 school year the Environmental Health and Light Research Institute of Sarasota, Florida, undertook a study of the effects of lighting on behavioral problems of first grade students.

In a pilot project conducted in four windowless elementary classrooms, children showed dramatic reactions to an improved lighting environment.

Under their normal classroom lighting, some first graders in the study demonstrated nervous fatigue, irritability, lapses of attention, and hyperactive behavior. After full spectrum lighting was installed, with lead foil shields over the cathode ends of the fluorescent tubes to stop suspected soft X-ray, and an aluminum screen grid over the entire fixture to stop known RF radiation, which is characteristic of all fluorescent tubes, a marked improvement appeared in the youngsters.

Without any use of drugs, the first graders settled down and paid more attention to their teachers. Nervousness diminished and teachers reported that overall classroom performance improved. The children were unaware of the special cameras mounted near the ceiling that snapped sequences of time-lapse pictures during the class day. With the standard type of unshielded lights still in operation, students could be observed fidgeting to an extreme degree, leaping from their seats, flailing their arms, and paying little attention to their teachers. After the full spectrum shielded lighting was installed, the same children were filmed two and three months later. Behavior was entirely different. Youngsters appeared calmer and far more interested in their work. One little boy, who stood out in the first films because of his constant motion and who was inattentive to everything, had changed to a quieter child, able to sit still and concentrate on routine. According to his teacher, he was capable of doing independent study and had even overcome a severe learning disability and learned to read during the short period of time.

This may indicate that hyperactivity is a radiation stress condition. The improvement occurred when that part of the visible spectrum which is lacking in standard artificial light sources was supplied and excessive radiation was eliminated. The fact that no drugs were used is of particular significance, since warnings are now being heard about the widespread use of amphetamines and other psychoactive drugs on children thought to be hyperactive.

Estimates of the number of children in this country now taking drugs range as high as one million, a situation which prompted the Committee on Drugs of the American Academy of Pediatrics to propose regulations to the U.S. Food and Drug Administration to prevent abuses. Psychoactive drugs have been shown helpful in treating hyperkinesis, a restlessness that some experts believe derives from minimal brain damage or chemical imbalances. What will become of the hyperactive boy in our study and the many other children like him?. If he gets relief through drugs from stress caused by malillumination and radiation, will that lead to later addiction to drugs or alcohol?

Dr. Irving Geller, Chairman of the Department of Experimental Pharmacology at Southwest Foundation for Research and Education in San Antonio, has found that abnormal conditions of light and darkness can affect the pineal gland, one of the master glands of the endocrine system. Experimenting with rats, Dr. Geller discovered that rats under stress preferred water to alcohol until left in continuous darkness over weekends. Then they went on alcoholic binges. Nobel prize winner Dr. Julius Axelrod had earlier found that the pineal gland produces more of the enzyme melatonin during dark periods. Injections of melatonin to rats on a regular light-dark cycle turned these rats into alcoholics.

Many biological responses are to narrow bands of wavelengths within the total light spectrum, and we have found that if these wavelengths are missing in an artificial light source, the biological receptor responds as in total darkness.

RADIATION AND HYPERACTIVITY

The hyperactive reaction to radiation from unshielded fluorescent tubes may have a correlation to the hyperactivity symptoms and severe learning disorders triggered by artificial food flavors and colorings. Dr. Ben F. Feingold, of the Kaiser-Permanente Medical Center, found that a diet eliminating all foods containing artificial flavors and colors brought about a dramatic improvement in 15 of 25 hyperactive school children studied. Any infraction of the diet led within a matter of hours to a return of the hyperkinetic behavior.

This suggests the possibility of an interaction between wavelength absorption bands of these synthetic color pigments and the energy peaks caused by mercury vapor lines in fluorescent tubes. This could explain the reaction or "allergy" to fluorescent lighting. (Increased sunburn reaction has been found to occur in individuals taking particular drugs, who are not so "sun-reactive" when not on medication.)

This reaction could be eliminated in two ways: by eliminating the absorbing material consumed when the child eats artifical coloring, or by eliminating the energy peaks in fluorescent tubes.

At the American Association for the Advancement of Science meeting in Chicago, December 26–31, 1970, Lewis W. Mayron, Ph.D., presented a paper entitled "Environmental Pollution: Its Biological Effects and Impact on the Bioanalytical Laboratory," in which he explored the biological effects of radiation from television sets and fluorescent lighting tubes.

In discussing the published results of our experiments with the bean plants and white rats placed in front of a television set, Dr. Mayron comments as follows:

> Thus it appears that the radiation emitted from the TV set has a physiological effect both on plants and animals and it is likely that

this effect, or these effects, are chemically mediated. If "Those Tired Children" are any indication of a trend, the bioanalytical laboratory may be called upon to chemically determine low-grade radiation toxicity.

Although there is as yet no indication of the body chemicals involved in the physiological effects of TV radiation, there is some indication of a chemical effect of the radiation of Ultra High Frequency (UHF) radio fields. Gordon (*Science*, 133: 444, 1961) has found that UHF fields result in the accumulation of acetylcholine along nerve fibers. Korbel and Thomspon (*Psychological Reports* 17: 595–602, 1956) reported on the behavioral effects of stimulation by UHF radio fields, which just happens to correlate with the behavior of the rats in front of the color TV screen and which also correlates with behavioral effects due to the accumulation of acetylcholine. Acetylcholine in small concentrations leads to a decrease in activity (Crossman and Mitchell, *Nature* 175: 121–122, 1955, Koshtoiants and Kokina, *Psychological Abstracts* 32: 3584, 1957; Russell, *Bulletin British Psych. Society* 23: 6, 1954 (abstract)). Nikogosyan found significant reductions in blood cholinesterase activity in rabbits after a program of UHF exposure (In Letavet and Gordon, Eds., *Biological Action of Ultra-high Frequencies*, OTS 62-19175, Moscow: Academy of Medical Sciences USSR, 1960). Thus, perhaps cholinesterase activities ought to be determined on man and laboratory animals exposed to TV radiation.

Dr. Mayron then further comments: "The implications of this are enormous when one considers the magnitude of the use of fluorescent lighting in stores, offices, factories, schools, and homes."

The fluorescent cathode, as a source of soft X-ray, has been recognized by such scientists as Dr. K. G. Emeleus, professor of physics at Queen's University, Belfast, in his book *The Conduction of Electricity Through Gases*.

In our experiments we found that the trace amount of suspected radiation from the ends of fluorescent tubes was not consistent and that as a rule it varied significantly between one end and the other of the same tube. Some tubes seem to give off more radiation than others, and, generally speaking, the older the tube, the more noticeable were the abnormal growth responses in the bean plants. This is a similar situation to the problem of X-ray emission from TV tubes, which also varied considerably from one tube to another with respect to the amount of X-ray emissions.

CONCLUSIONS

There is increasing evidence of the harmful biological effects of artifical light sources and low levels of man-made radiation, with a strong indication that what first appears as hyperactivity and learning disabilities in young children is positively correlated with incidence of such radiation. The problem of to what extent these effects constitute a major contributing factor in the more serious problems of alcoholism, drug addiction, crime, and violence facing today's modern society and civilization, should be further investigated.

Chapter 7 | Ecological Aspects of Antisocial Behavior

William H. Philpott, M.D.
Psychiatrist
Oklahoma City, Oklahoma

INTRODUCTION

Hippocrates reportedly observed that when frequently eaten foods are avoided for four days, a re-exposure to these foods may cause symptoms.

In 1621, in England, a book was published entitled *The Anatomy of Melancholy*, in which milk is incriminated as a frequent cause of depression and headache, and beans as a cause of nightmares.[1]

In Charles Dickens's *A Christmas Carol*, Jacob Marley, Scrooge's former partner, appeared to Scrooge in a ghostly apparition. "You don't believe in me," observed the ghost. "I don't," said Scrooge. "What evidence would you have of my reality beyond that of your senses?" "I don't know," said Scrooge. "Why do you doubt your senses?" "Because," said Scrooge, "a little thing affects them. A slight disorder of the stomach makes them cheats. You might be an undigested bit of beef, a blot of mustard, a crump of cheese, a fragment of undone potato. There is more of gravy than the grave about you whatever you are!"[2]

There is the story from an Oklahoma restaurant truck stop of a waitress coming to work on her first day and not being familiar with the truckers' language. A trucker ordered two hubcaps, two headlights, and a cup of coffee. She took the order back to the cook and asked for an explanation. He said, "That is two pancakes and two eggs sunny side up." She decided to get back at the trucker and placed in front of him a bowl of beans. He said, "What is this for?" And she replied, "While you are waiting for your parts, don't you want to gas up?"

Hippocrates knew that some people react to foods with symptom formation. In 1621 England, central nervous system reactions to foods were known. Charles Dickens knew of visual and auditory hallucinations in response to foods. Even a waitress at a truck stop in Oklahoma knows that foods can evoke symptoms. Why is it that only the modern psychiatrist is having difficulty recognizing that reactions to foods can be responsible for physical and mental symptoms? In view of this common knowledge about emotional symptoms being evoked by foods, should not these psychiatrists examine for these reactions as one of the possible numerous causes for emotional reactions? But it is *not* only the psychiatrists who are having trouble recognizing the significance of foods and emotional reactions. There is a state board examination for nurses with a multiple-choice questionnaire which runs like this: "Your patient is having visual hallucinations. What should you do? 1. Tell him to talk it over with his doctor. 2. Tell him to forget it, that it is of no significance. 3. Tell him it is due to something he ate." If you wish to fail the exam, it is likely that all you have to do is check the statement "Tell him it is due to something he ate."

Some medical professionals are in the dilemma of waiting for five-year double blind studies of 100 cases which then have to be confirmed by two other independent five-year double blind studies before they will venture even a feeble spark of recognition about that which the public considers already to be common knowledge.

Psychologist K. E. Moyer reported in the July, 1975, issue of the magazine *Psychology Today* on the subject of allergy and aggression. "For an allergic person, eating may lead to beating, biting and battle. While a person who is allergic to pollen suffers a stuffy nose, a person allergic to chocolate or bananas may pass out bloody noses. The intensity of the symptoms varies from a mild irritable reaction, in which a person is a little more easily annoyed than usual, to a psychotic aggressive reaction."[3]

Moyer attributes these cerebral allergic reactions evoking aggression to focal swelling of the brain with activation of neural networks occurring when the allergen is contacted.

Howard G. Rapaport, M.D., states, "It is factually established that one of five school children has a major allergic disease."[4] He views allergy considerations as belonging in the differential diagnosis of causes of learning disabilities.

Starting in 1970, I began to take a serious look at the claims made by some allergists that an assortment of emotional reactions are sometimes observed to occur during deliberate exposure to single foods and chemicals. Under the guidance of the allergists Marshall Mandell, Theron G. Randolph, and Sol D. Klotz, I learned how to test patients so as to induce symptoms during exposure to single items. For food testing the patient avoids his commonly used foods by either a four- to six-day fast using water only, or by eating only foods he seldom uses.

The symptoms evoked during testing range in scope from mild to severe and involve numerous physical as well as mental symptoms, including psychosis and seizure.

The following case histories involving aggression were observed during induction testing of my patients.

A 20-year-old paranoid schizophrenic became quite symptom-free by the fourth day of a fast on water only. When test-smoking a cigarette he became disoriented and delusional, and defied anyone to come near him. It took four men to subdue him and place him in a seclusion room. He had been well until two years before, when he went off to college, at which time he also introduced cigarette smoking.

An 18-year-old paranoid schizophrenic had to be restrained, since he would strike out to kill anyone who came near him because he believed the person wanted to kill him; so he was attempting to kill first in self-defense. By the fourth day of his fast he was not delusional and could be trusted about the hospital. At this time he phoned his father stating, "I love you. Please come and see me." When given a test meal of wheat he became hostile and agitated, phoned his father, and yelled into the phone, "I hate you. You made me sick. I don't ever want to see you again." When tested for a reaction to tobacco by smoking a cigarette, he became paranoid, hostile, and struck the examiner because he hallucinated horns on the examiner's head and thought the examiner was the devil. (Others tell me I am not the devil and do not have horns!) It was necessary to physically restrain him. Later he had no memory of the incident.

A 52-year-old woman with a neurotic depression, tested for wheat, developed a stiff neck and tightness in the chest and throat; but, worst of all, she felt like hitting or punching someone. She was so frightened that she might act on these compulsive urges that she went to a room by herself until the reaction subsided.

A 12-year-old boy diagnosed as hyperkinetic had the following symptoms on testing spinach: was overtalkative, physically aggressive, and hot; had excessive saliva, flatus, a stomach-ache, and cried.

Symptoms evoked by cantaloupe: aggressive teasing of other patients, itching head. Watermelon: irritability, teasing, depression, flatus. Perch: fought with his sister, had stuffy and itching nose.

In a 36-year-old psychoneurotic woman, pineapple evoked: irritability, blocking of thought, dizziness, headache. Oranges: was violently angry, fought with her son, and loudly told another patient to shut up, following which she became sleepy and her mind functioned so poorly she could hardly carry on a conversation. Rice: she loudly scolded her son for speaking while she was speaking. When the examiner observed that this behavior was a reaction to the test meal of rice, she denied it and said she was just teaching her son to be respectful. A few minutes later she began uncontrollable giggling, followed by crying. At this time she admitted she was reacting to rice.

A four-year-old boy with a diagnosis of hyperkinesis had these reactions. String beans: very hyperactive, wanted to fight, coughing. Garbanzo beans: first overly happy, followed by hunger and grouchiness. Navy bean: very hyperactive, teasing, and eyes watering. Cod fish: coughing, cried and said he thought there would be a storm, afraid of having nightmares and seeing scary monsters, and afraid his cat would turn into a lion. Carrots: fighting and grouchy. Celery: stomachache, crying and grouchy. Strawberries: angry, hyperactive and coughing. Unrefined cane sugar: irritable, stuffy nose and coughing.

A 12-year-old hyperkinetic boy. Banana: listless, depressed, crying. Then he became aggressive and picked up a stick and tried to hit another patient. Oranges: first singing, then tired, impatient, wild and wanted to strike someone. Tomato: irritable, defensive, upset stomach. Rice: hot, silly, teasing, followed by rebelliousness and hyperactivity. Apple: at first he felt stimulated, then started to fight.

A 12-year-old autistic girl grabbed and broke her mother's glasses during a food reaction. In response to another food she picked up a rock as a door stop and attempted to hit someone.

A 20-year-old paranoid schizophrenic in response to a food test for duck felt like choking his mother and others and secluded himself until the urge subsided.

A 40-year-old schizophrenic woman's response to a sublingual test for petrochemical hydrocarbons, using glycerinated exhaust fumes, was trying to find a way to kill herself and had to be restrained to prevent suicide. Repeatedly she had attempted suicide by opening the door of the car in an attempt to jump out while the car was going down the road. She would be normal when starting on a ride but within a few minutes she would try to jump from the running car and had to be restrained by her husband. He found a faulty exhaust system on the car, which leaked exhaust fumes into the car.

One patient, in response to a test for oranges, lost his voice and was so irritable he slapped his son. One 69-year-old grandmother argued and fought with her grandchildren in response to a food test.

I could go on and on and on with case histories which show that objectively observed induction testing of foods and chemicals reveals the cause and effect relation between maladaptive reactions to foods and chemicals and aggressive behavior, as well as numerous other physical and central nervous system reactions.

WHAT IS THE CAUSE OF MALADAPTIVE REACTIONS TO FOODS AND CHEMICALS?

Doctors have been taught to be comfortable in making their diagnoses on the basis of chronic symptoms, the tissues involved in symptom production, invading organisms, or the autoimmune reaction. Traditionally, the allergist is comfortable with consistent evidence given by a skin test and, by and large, has disowned another group of allergic-like fluctuating symptoms not diagnosable by skin testing. No specialty such as allergy, internal medicine, neurology, or psychiatry has assumed responsibility for teaching how to examine for or understand these nonantibody (and therefore assumed to be nonallergic) fluctuating allergic-like symptoms. However, there are those allergists who venture beyond the narrow boundaries usually defined by their specialty and who examine and treat these nonantibody reactions. This group consists of about 10% of allergists, who are now being joined by other specialists. Arthur F. Coca, M.D., is a good example of those allergists contributing to this enlarged view of allergy, which is perhaps better termed clinical ecology. Arthur Coca was an allergist and immunologist, as well as founder and first editor of the *Journal of Immunology*.[5] He recognized that a large number of reactions to foods and chemicals do not give evidence of antibodies, do not evoke skin reactions, and are not justly classified as a group of immunological reactions. Another way to look at it is simply to say that a definition disagreement exists over what the medical profession wishes to call allergy.

In any event, these maladaptive reactions to foods and chemicals require methods other than skin testing to reveal their presence.

Observing the emergence of symptoms during a planned single exposure after a period of avoidance in an environmental control setting, has become a standard of establishing a cause and effect relationship between substances and symptoms.[6] Theron G. Randolph, M.D., Allergist, was the first to demonstrate by a blind technique the existence of mental reactions to foods. He coined the term "ecologic mental illness."[7]

Jules M. Weiss, M.D., Psychiatrist, and Herbert S. Kaufman, M.D., Allergist,[8] made a significant contribution in giving case histories of either allergic or allergic-like reactions affecting the central nervous system function. They concluded that psychiatrists have not been trained to recognize subtle organic reactions to environmental substances, and that the pathophysiology has not as yet been clearly defined but presumably involves several components, such as allergy and metabolic errors. They observed that the family histories of these patients were heavily laden with allergic reactions and also with carbohydrate-related metabolic disease.

For some years there have been those who observed a frequent relation between the carbohydrate disorder hypoglycemia and emotional reactions. It has also been common knowledge that hypoglycemia often precedes adult onset diabetes mellitus. It is also known that acute metabolic acid states exist when either hypoglycemia or diabetes mellitus is observed. Diabetic acidosis is, of course, well known.

Theron G. Randolph, M.D., observed some years ago that a state of acidosis exists at the time maladaptive reactions to foods and chemicals occur. Based on this evidence, he developed a frequently effective method of giving sodium and potassium biocarbonate to relieve these symptoms. Of course, soda baths for skin reactions and baking soda applied to insect bites have long been household remedies.

A significant article has recently been published in the journal *Diseases of the Nervous System* entitled "Glucose-Insulin Metabolism in Chronic Schizophrenia."[9] Glucose as well as insulin metabolism was examined in 18 schizophrenic subjects. The authors write:

> It is evident that the insulin-glucose levels in basal conditions are normal in our patients. However, the glucose load brings to light a severe metabolic impairment, which, for its characteristics, could be defined as chemical diabetes. In fact it includes:
>
> 1. Increased and delayed insulin peak levels, with prolonged hyperinsulinemia. The presence of a chemical diabetes, and its eventual

correlation with the schizophrenic process, is difficult to be explained. We can exclude the possibility that the phenomenon is casual, as it is present in 100% of our patients.

To establish a connection between specific psychic symptomatologies and biochemical damages seems rather difficult in our patients. In fact, we have observed that the most severe glucose-insulin alterations go in parallel constantly with the presence of deep mental deterioration, mood flattening, withdrawal from reality and autism. This datum suggests that only the long-deteriorating processuality of the disease correlates with the metabolic impairment. In conclusion, we suggest that the impaired glucose-insulin metabolism is related in our patients only to the deep deteriorating processuality of the mental disease. We can suggest also that the same metabolic derangement is probably responsible for both the mental disease and the endocrine alteration.[9]

What is this metabolic derangement that is responsible for both chemical diabetes and schizophrenia? Before we attempt to answer this question let us take a look at an internal medicine textbook on diabetes. *The Principles and Practice of Medicine* gives this picture of diabetes mellitus:

> Diabetes mellitus is a complex disorder characterized in most cases by a relative or absolute insulin deficiency. The idiopathic form of diabetes mellitus is familiar although its mode of inheritance is complex and controversial. Several phases have been suggested: 1. A prediabetic period—that is, no metabolic abnormalities are recognized, but the subject is genetically a diabetic. 2. *A chemical diabetes phase*, during which the patient is asymptomatic but abnormalities in glucose tolerance are recognized on standard tests or upon provocation. And 3. A phase during which the subject is frankly diabetic.[10]

The syndrome may be symptomless; or accompanied by symptoms fairly directly attributed to insulin lack or responding to the administration of the hormone, or by a constellation of manifestations (complications) occurring singly or together and involving the kidney, the retina, the vascular, and the neurologic systems, or by both. These abnormalities may not be correlated by, and may well not be causally related to, a deficiency of insulin. Indeed, *there is accumulating evidence that the complications of diabetes mellitus can be found with-*

out any detectable disturbances in carbohydrate metabolism. This suggests that the syndromes of insulin insufficiency and the late complications are both related to a more fundamental, but at present obscure, metabolic disturbance.

What is this as yet obscure common denominator between diabetes mellitus and the numerous symptoms of the body and central nervous system often called complications of diabetes but also present in many other chronic diseases, which also include schizophrenia? What is this obscure metabolic derangement responsible for both mental disease and endocrine alterations?

I have monitored the saliva pH before and serially after induction food and chemical tests hundreds of times. Consistently, and with only a rare exception, when a symptom reaction occurs, the saliva becomes acid. I also have monitored blood sugar before and serially after induction food and chemical tests several hundred times. Characteristically, about half of the time when symptom reactions occur there also occurs a blood sugar level beyond 160 mg% at one hour post-test; also sometimes hyperglycemia occurs without observable symptoms occurring. There are many hyperglycemic reactions of 300 to 400 mg% and beyond. The acid reaction is present even when glucose remains normal, thus revealing that the pH shift is an even better or earlier sign of a reaction than the blood sugar shift.

To understand the acid reaction we can draw from knowledge about diabetes mellitus and why acid reactions occur in diabetes. The end products of carbohydrate and lipid metabolism are CO_2 and water. However, there are several acid steps in the metabolic process, and if the carbohydrate or lipid metabolism is interfered with and thus cut short, the consequences will be a metabolic acid state. The evidence from my work is that all these maladaptive reactions, to carbohydrate, fat, protein, various chemicals, tobacco, cat, dog, pollen, and so forth, have this common denominator of an acid reaction occurring due to interference with carbohydrate and lipid metabolism. It matters not whether it is termed a true allergy with antibodies or a metabolic disorder due to metabolic errors, nutritional deficiencies, toxins, and so forth. The fact of an acid state on exposure to the reacting substance is the same.

We can conclude there are diabetics without schizophrenia, just as there are diabetics without other so-called complications involving the eyes, kidneys, or vascular or central nervous system. However, we are forced to question whether there are any schizophrenics without diabetes mellitus. In a schizophrenic this disorder only rarely proceeds to a full-blown diabetic picture, but usually remains in the chemical diabetes phase, which is not diagnosable by a fasting blood sugar but is diagnosable by (1) a combined glucose-insulin metabolism examination, as Brambilla et al. have performed, or (2) monitoring blood sugar, as I have done, before and one hour after induction testing, which has been preceded by a four- to six-day period of avoidance before the test is given. This period of avoidance is necessary, as it reverts the addictive phase characteristically causing hypoglycemia at three to four hours after exposure to an acute reactive phase that evokes hyperglycemia, which is usually at its highest after one hour.

Thus, we characteristically see miniature diabetes reactions occurring in our schizophrenic patients. This hyperglycemic reaction occurs about 50% of the time when symptoms develop on exposure to a substance. And, as Brambilla et al. observed, there is a higher consistent correlation between symptoms and hyperglycemia in the more mentally deteriorated. Hyperglycemia occurs as a reaction to all types of substances, whether they are carbohydrates, lipids, proteins, or chemicals. Thus I have observed evidence of carbohydrate interference rather than the customary view of carbohydrate intolerance. It is clear there are many noncarbohydrate substances that give indications of interference with carbohydrate metabolism. We see that inherent in these reactions is such an interference. Repeatedly I have observed patients who are just as diabetic from a reaction to tobacco or petrochemical hydrocarbons as they are to corn or grape sugar.

The disease process producing such chronic diseases as schizophrenia, manic-depressive illness, those neurotic or so-called psychosomatic reactions that are caused by maladaptive reactions to food or chemicals, learning problems such as dyslexia or minimal brain dysfunction, autism, or diabetes mellitus, appears to be the same, but the difference lies in the area of the body that is primarily affected. This process consists of maladaptive (allergic and allergic-like) reactions to foods, chemicals, and inhalants, plus the superimposed infections that inevitably follow, all this made possible by the chemically defective state, best termed a nutritionally defective state, even though metabolic errors and frequency of use have a major role in the nutritionally defective state developing.

Virginia Livingston, M.D., and I have observed a common denominator between cancer and schizophrenia.[11] My observation is that 10 to 12 infectious agents can be isolated from the schizophrenic, but that one, *Progenitor cryptocides*, can routinely be cultured from the urine and/or feces and observed in the blood by dark field microscopic examination. The blood of a small series of schizophrenics studied by dark field microscopic examination by Virginia Livingston revealed the presence of *Progenitor cryptocides* in all cases studied. There is a suggested correlation between the degree of pleomorphic proliferation and red cell invasion of the infection and the degree of mental deterioration. The degree of infection in the blood of a deteriorated schizophrenic and that of a debilitated cancer patient are similar. These findings agree with those of James Papez, M.D., who observed parasitized red blood and consistent culturing of a pleomorphic microbe from the brains of schizophrenics.[12] It has long been known that diabetics have a low resistance to infection. We can now understand why the schizophrenic is predisposed to chronic infections. It seems evident that each time a maladaptive reaction to a food or chemical occurs, it produces local edema, lowered oxygen supply, and pH shift; and these conditions encourage an infectious flare-up with its toxins and local damage.

NUTRITIONAL DEFICIENCY

What chemical state can be behind these nonantibody-allergic maladaptive reactions? By trials of intravenous nutrients I have succeeded in demonstrating that intravenous vitamin B-6 alone in doses of around 1,000 mg is capable of relieving most of these maladaptive reactions evoked during induction testing.[13] The best results are obtained when vitamin C and magnesium are associated with B-6. The most effective means of administration is to give B-6 1,000 mg, sodium ascorbate 12.5 grams, magnesium sulfate 2 grams, Calphosan 10 cc or calcium gluconate 10 cc, added to 150 cc of normal saline for IV drip.

It is known that edema is characteristic of B-6 deficiency.[14] Thus, in B-6 deficiency we see edema evoked the same as in a true antibody-allergic type reaction. In a clinical setting where immunological reactions are not measured, one cannot tell which is an antibody reaction and which is a B-6 deficiency reaction. In either event, symptoms will be produced in the specific tissues involved with the edema. Edema of the central nervous system during symptoms has been objectively observed by Bassoe[15] and Galtman.[16]

Antibodies cannot be formed in the presence of B-6 deficiency, according to Axelrod.[17] Thus, we see our patient is in an immunologically defective state and unable to adequately defend against infections.

How does the B-6 deficiency develop? It can occur in many ways, such as (1) lower B-6 in the diet; (2) chronic infections demanding nutrients; (3) toxins (endogenous from infections and exogenous from such sources as food preservatives, insecticides, and so forth); (4) metabolic errors, which make demands for B-6. Each amino acid and sugar can have its metabolic error that, if present, would make such demands. In my observation, controlled provocation test conditions revealed that 30% of my patients have porphyria and 20% have galactocemia. Henry Peters likewise observed a porphyric-schizophrenic syndrome.[18] Perry has also observed that there are occasional adult patients with phenylketonuria.[19] It is suspected there are numerous as yet undiagnosed metabolic errors in schizophrenics. (5) The deficiency may develop from frequent use of foods making demands for specific enzymes. *The most obviously demonstratable of these sources of deficiency of B-6 is that of frequency of contact with foods and chemicals.* The habit of using foods daily or several times a day uses up the chemistry necessary to metabolize those particular foods. It has been demonstrated that the minimum of four-day spacing of food contacts markedly increases tolerance for that food and nearly always prevents addiction from occurring (see results of Rinkle et al.,[20] Randolph,[7] Carwin,[21] and Philpott et al.[22]). Even nutritious foods such as milk, whole grain cereals, and so forth, when used frequently, create a malnourished state by the demand for other nutrients necessary in their metabolism. Of course, the more depleted the foods are of nutrients, the quicker the maladaptive reactions will occur.

It is likely true that the greatest single health principle we could institute as a protection against chronic physical and chronic mental disease is that of a diversified four-day or more rotation of 50 or more foods replacing the customary dozen or so frequently eaten foods. Nutrition would be markedly increased, and food addiction virtually nonexistent. Thus a major process leading to chronic physical and mental illnesses would be reversed.

PANENDOCRINE DISORDER

There is good evidence that maladaptive reactions to foods and chemicals produce a state of panendocrine disorder. The disorder can be either over- or underproduction of hormones. From symptoms one would judge that there usually are low adrenocortical hormones except in acute excitement states when they are high—high ACTH production with its clinging to symptoms effect (Levine);[23] low estrogen, disturbing menstruation; high progesterone, producing premenstrual tension and even a state of autoimmune reaction to progesterone; a delayed rise to high insulin finally producing an autoimmune reaction to insulin with a reversal to low insulin, which if and when it occurs produces a frank diabetes mellitus state. In involuntional women, hot flashes and other symptoms disappear when symptom-incriminated foods and chemicals are removed from the diet. Menstrual cramps, premenstrual tension, and menstrual irregularity usually disappear with the removal of incriminated foods and chemicals.

Thyroid function deserves special comment. Frequently it is low but occasionally high in schizophrenics and manic-depressives. I routinely do a thyroid survey, and if it is abnormal, repeat it after the food and chemical reactions have been managed.

Here is the case history of a 59-year-old woman, with a history of 18 years of manic-depressive illness and treated with thyroid the last five years by an endocrinologist. On entry to the hospital her thyroid profile placed her as having a low functioning thyroid in spite of her continued use of thyroid. The findings were T3 22% (normal 25-35%), T4 6 mcg (normal 5.3-14.5 mcg), T7 1.3 (normal 1.5-5), PBI 3.9 mcg (normal 4-8 mcg).

Twenty-three days later when food reactions had been sorted out and incriminated foods involved removed, her thyroid profile was normal as indicated below: T3 32% (normal 25-35%), T4 8.2 mcg (normal 5.3-14.5 mcg), T7 2.61 (normal 1.5-5), PBI 5.3 mcg (normal 4 to 8 mcg).

Someone might object because this is only a single case. However, I can say low thyroid function is common in schizophrenia, and I have found only rarely a low or high thyroid function uncorrected by avoiding the symptom-incriminated foods and chemicals.

Jim was an adult onset diabetic of five-year duration. In spite of strictly following his assigned diet and insulin three times a day, he had never been in good control. Because he was a brittle diabetic, he was under the care of a diabetes specialist. Perceptual distortions, obsessions, paranoia, and depression developed, justifying the diagnosis of schizophrenia. I first saw him when he tried to hang himself.

His fasting blood sugar on entry to the hospital was 250 mg%. By the fourth day of the fast his blood sugar was 100 mg%, and it remained at 100 on the fifth day when food testing began. I tested his blood sugar before and one hour after each test meal and introduced no test meals until his blood sugar was normal before the test. There was an assortment of foods, proteins as well as carbohydrates, to which he reacted with hyperglycemia. The effect of whole wheat was especially striking. His blood sugar was 250 mg% in one hour, and at the same time he wished to die. Also there were carbohydrate foods that did not evoke hyperglycemia. Avoidance of the symptom-producing, hyperglycemia-evoking foods managed both his diabetes and his schizophrenia. The fundamental error that had been made in his diet for diabetes was inclusion of a small amount of whole wheat bread on a daily basis. This wheat was evoking both his diabetes and the schizophrenia.

My experience tells me that maladaptive reactions to foods and chemicals are a common cause of disorder in any and all endocrine glands. The evidence is strong that no true judgment can be drawn about primary endocrine disorders until maladaptive reactions to foods and chemicals are first corrected. I believe there is a great deal of low level of efficiency use of thyroid, insulin, estrogen, testosterone, ACTH, and adrenal cortical hormones, in which the symptoms being treated will be reduced with a high level of efficiency by avoidance and later spacing of symptom-incriminated foods and chemicals.

ALLERGY, ADDICTION, HYPOGLYCEMIA, HYPERGLYCEMIA

By serially studying the blood sugar before and after exposure to addictants in known narcotic, alcohol, and food addicts I have arrived at convincing evidence that hypoglycemia can consistently be observed as relating to the stress of the addictive withdrawal state. A glucose tolerance test that evokes hypoglycemia reveals a single fact to us, namely, that is the person is addicted to corn if corn sugar was used as a source of the glucose. Addiction is observed to be specific substances and does not cross-react, except that the taxonomic relationship (common antigenicity) such as exists between cereal grains (grass family) is significant, so that a person has a greater chance of reacting, for example, to wheat if reactive (allergic, allergic-like, addictive) to corn. There is convincing evidence by several other workers (Randolph,[7] Campbell[24]), as well as my own observations, that addiction is an adaptive adjustment to the chronic stress of a substance to which a person is maladaptively reactive. This appears true whether these are antigen-antibody type allergic reactions or deficiency type allergic-like reactions. When adaptive addiction fails, because of some degree of metabolic failure, to be able to maintain the adaptive addictive adjustment, chronic illnesses then emerge, with the most biologically central inherent disease being diabetes mellitus.

REVERSAL EFFECT

Why is it that a person may hate, attack, or even kill a person he loves when maladaptively reacting to foods or chemicals? Experiments with rats, I believe, give us the answers to this question.[25,26] When acetylcholine is injected into rats, a reversal of the usual behavior occurs. Highly learned and recently learned responses are blocked, and responses that had been trained out emerge again. This behavior can be comprehended when it is understood that the adaptive highly learned and recently learned responses occur in response to stimuli by evoking a specific amount of acetylcholine at synaptic junctions. But when this amount is exceeded by an additional source of acetylcholine, then the response is blocked instead of activated. This blocking effect is known to occur in any response that is overdone. The response that was trained out would no longer produce acetylcholine when meeting the stimulus, but when an exogenous source of acetylcholine was present, the stimulus then evoked the unlearned response.

These animal experiments become significant when we realize that a rise in acetylcholine is evident in cerebral allergic and allergic-like reactions.[27] Thus a person maladaptively reacting to a food or chemical can behave in a way opposite to the way in which he was reared, and thus hate and attack a person he loves. Other synaptic transmitting agents undoubtedly follow the same rules that acetylcholine does. It is likely true that in aggression there is also a nonspecific rise in norepinephrin. While a nonspecific rise in acetylcholine would produce tension and facilitate aggression, a nonspecific rise in norepinephrin would specifically evoke hostility and aggression, since it would tend to activate areas of the brain involved in evoking aggression.

TREATMENT

It follows that treatment should logically include the following: (1) A four-day rotation of all foods, avoiding for an initial three months those demonstrated to cause symptoms and returning to the rotation diet only those foods that do not evoke symptoms after three months of initial avoidance. The four-day rotation of foods prevents the development of new maladaptive reactions to foods. (2) Therapeutic supernutrition, emphasizing B-6, zinc, manganese, vitamin C, vitamin A, and pantothenic acid, along with a balance of other supporting nutrients. Monitoring of body fluids for vitamins and minerals and hair for minerals can aid as a guide. Carl Pfeiffer confirms the significance of B-6, zinc, and appropriate supportive nutrients in the emotionally ill.[28] (3) Immunologic treatment, which should include autogenous vaccine for *Progenitor cryptocides*. This infection should initially be diagnosed by dark field and/or flourescent microscopy, and monitored for improvement as treatment proceeds. Autogenous vaccines from all isolatable bacteria are in order; if they are not used, then use stock respiratory vaccine.

Other useful stock vaccines are such ones as flu vaccine, poison ivy-oak vaccine, sheep cell erythrocyte and spleen vaccine, and most of all BCG vaccine, which is known to suppress *Progenitor cryptocides*. It is helpful to develop a broad immunological defense, since the patient has been living in an immunologic deficit state. (4) We should never assume that the only stimuli to which emotionally ill persons will respond are foods and chemicals, but should understand that even when they are not maladaptively reacting to these items, there still remains for them a vulnerability to maladaptive responses to sensory imputs of sight, sound, feeling, and interpersonal relationships based on a chronic state of central nervous system irritation resulting from nutritional deficiencies, metabolic errors, infections, and the toxicity resulting from all of these factors. In removal of the symptom-incriminated substances we simply have taken away the cause of the patient's more serious symptoms and greatest vulnerability; but a residual maladaptive response capacity is still available, which is due to his central nervous system irritation as well as his past learning experiences. Therefore, it can be understood that corrective psychotherapeutic training is needed as well as biochemical correction.

CONCLUSIONS

Induction testing of foods and chemicals after a period of four or more days of avoidance reveals an abundance of physical and mental symptoms to specific individualized foods and chemicals. Antisocial aggression is a common symptom evoked and can even involve murder or suicide. These reactions are usually reactions of nutritional deficiency, the most likely common cause being metabolic errors and frequent use of foods, either of which makes demands for specific nutrients. There is evidence from the ability to relieve by IV injection these acute reactions that B6 deficiency is the central deficiency.[13] Vitamin B-6 deficiency produces edema of tissues and thus mimicks the edema of antibody reactions. Clinically, B-6 deficiency and immunological reactions behave similarly. Not only are the majority of these maladaptive reactions not immunological in nature, but an immunologic deficit state exists due to the B-6 deficiency, in which antibodies cannot be formed against infectious agents and thus infections are encouraged and are found when examined for.

The stress of these maladaptive reactions (addictive and allergic-like) causes a panendocrine disorder usually suppressing and sometimes overexciting endocrine glands. This panendocrine disorder is characteristically corrected when the incriminated foods are initially avoided and later spaced in a diversified four-day rotation diet.

Addiction is observed to be an adaptive mechanism that occurs because of the necessity of metabolically adjusting to immunological allergic and allergic-like deficiency reactions. Hypoglycemia, when present, is observed to be due to the stress of an addictive withdrawal state, and can only be observed when the withdrawal phase is on a three- to four-hour cycle. This would be a severe degree of addiction, since the most adaptive addiction is on a three-day cycle, with reduction in time as the adaptive addiction is metabolically failing. After a four-day period of avoidance of the addictant, the addictive withdrawal phase disappears and hyperglycemia emerges on test exposure instead of the hypoglycemia. This conversion of hypoglycemia to hyperglycemia confirms the observation that hypoglycemia is a precursor to adult onset diabetes. Characteristically, many mentally and behaviorally disordered subjects are observed to be in the state of chemical diabetes, which involves all the features of hypoglycemia, hyperglycemia, addiction, episodic hypoinsulinism and hyperinsulinism.

In the early stage, the hyperglycemia, as well as the addictive withdrawal hypoglycemia, is sufficiently separate from the symptoms to give the appearance of two separate or only loosely related metabolic problems. However, as the disease process proceeds, there finally develops a state where hyperglycemia and symptoms are consistently associated. Thus, in the more mentally deteriorated, symptoms and the carbohydrate disorder are observed as associated on a timed basis. Serial monitoring of pH shifts and blood glucose, as well as objective and subjective observations of emerging symptoms during induction testing of single items in an environmentally controlled situation, reveals maladaptive reactions to foods and chemicals to be the cause of pH shifts and glucose malfunction, as well as the symptoms. These maladaptive reactions are indeed the common metabolic cause between diabetes mellitus and its so-called complications, and also between diabetes and many mental disorders. If, and when, and only when, the disease process has reached a very serious degree of metabolic failure, do all the varied features coalesce on a time basis, thus revealing beyond a shadow of a doubt their common cause.

Hans Selye understood that foods and toxins were among the stressors leading to chronic illnesses. What he did not understand was that these stressors are among the major stressors leading to disease. In view of this evidence it is profitable to reassess his monumental work on stress and chronic disease.[29]

During food and chemical induction testing the patient serves as his own control in these respects: (1) Avoidance for four to six days leads to metabolic recovery or at least partial recovery. (2) Exposure to single items under environmental control conditions selectively precipitates symptoms. (3) There is evidence that no direct relationship exists between amounts of food ingested or food categories of incriminated substances and the symptoms evoked. These conclusions are reinforced by this evidence: (a) minute sublingual drops of the incriminated substances evoke symptoms; (b) intradermal injections of the incriminated substances evoke symptoms plus local edema of the skin; and (c) stress test meals, such as "all you wish to eat," reveal carbohydrates, fats, and proteins which do not evoke symptoms or hyperglycemia, and other carbohydrates, fats, and proteins which for that particular person selectively do evoke symptoms, hyperglycemia, and rarely hypoglycemia. *These evidences reveal that the symptoms and blood sugar shifts are independent of the class of foods or the amount used and that they truly represent chemically mediated maladaptive reactions rather than an overload factor.*

Treatments consist of supernutrition emphasizing B-6, vitamin C at bacterial supression levels, and vitamin A at levels which suppress *Progenitor cryptocides*. Autogenous and stock vaccines are in order, especially an autogenous vaccine of *Progenitor cryptocides* and stock BCG vaccine.

A four- (or seven-) day rotation of foods followed in families is most biologically sound and therefore the most efficient diet, since it avoids the development of new maladaptive food reactions. Test-incriminated foods are withheld for a three-month period, which provides for the development of a refractory phase. Ninety-five percent of the time these incriminated foods can be returned to the diversified rotation diet after three months of avoidance without symptoms developing. The addition of therapeutic supernutrition emphasizing B-6 and zinc supported by balanced nutrition further reduces the potential for maladaptive reactions to foods and chemicals.

Behavioral corrective training for overlearned responses trained in by the frequently evoked maladaptive responses and life experiences is usually needed if the illness has existed for more than two years.

James Papez observed from crushed brain cultures that a pleomorphic microbe grew from intercellular inclusion bodies in the neurons. When neurons were killed by an infectious flare-up, the adjacent perivascular and supportive tissues reacted to the infection with gliosis formation. Judging by the age of the casts of neurons killed by infectious episodes, he was able to accurately predict when in the patient's history there had been acute psychotic episodes.[12]

The work of James Papez correlates well with that of M. Fisman,[30] in which glial nodules and perivascular infiltration suggestive of an encephalitic process occurred in hallucinating and delusional schizophrenics. Microscopic brain stem examinations revealed that seven of ten hallucinating or delusional patients had sclerosis, ischemic changes of neurons, and occasional petechiae, while only one of the fourteen controls from the mental hospital not subject to hallucinations or delusions had such lesions, and none of the ten non–mentally ill from a general hospital had brain stem lesions.

Virginia Livingston gives evidence that *Progenitor cryptocides* enters by way of the colon and resides in the colon, as demonstrated by culturing the feces.[11] Carl Pfeiffer[28] raises the question about bacterial production of toxic amines produced in the gut. *Progenitor cryptocides* culture has a fetid odor, the same as with schizophrenic and cancer patients.

The final irreversible deteriorated state of psychosis is viewed as most likely due to an infection of *Progenitor cryptocides*, which in its viral size stage lives in neurons. When B-6 deficiency reactions or true allergic reactions occur in the brain, an infection of *Progenitor cryptocides* flares up, killing neurons. After repeated infections a stage is reached in which there are not enough neurons of the right kind left for normal function, at which stage the psychosis is irreversible.

These preliminary observations give evidence that these minor to major central nervous system reactions ranging from learning problems and behavioral disorders to psychosis, which give evidence of soft neurological signs, have the characteristic of multiple causative factors that are interrelated. These observations beg for large-scale, long-term definitive statistical studies in correlating the varied, multiple organic causative factors of central nervous system malfunction, including: (1) maladaptive reactions to foods, chemicals and inhalants; (2) metabolic errors; (3) nutritional deficiencies; and (4) infections associated with the foregoing.

That obesity is a precursor to diabetes mellitus is well documented. That obesity is a frequent manifestation of food addiction has been objectively demonstrated. It has been understood for a long time that addiction predisposes to diabetes. This relationship has been known especially about alcohol addiction. Only more recently has it been understood that alcohol addiction is a manifestation of food addiction, and that all food addictions produce the same metabolic disorder as alcohol addiction. Also, only recently has it been appreciated that food addiction is common. Even more recent is our understanding relative to addiction to nonfood chemicals, and inhalants. Now objectively controlled test exposures have repeatedly and in numerous subjects demonstrated the disordered carbohydrate metabolism that occurs in addictions to foods, chemicals, and inhalants. As long as metabolic processes remain sufficiently intact to maintain the adaptive addiction adjustment, this carbohydrate disorder (acidosis, hypoglycemia, hyperglycemia) is of brief duration, and usually goes unsuspected and, therefore, undetected. But when adaptive addiction cannot be maintained, then a chronic carbohydrate disorder emerges, producing a chronic state of acidosis and hyperglycemia. At this stage, the diagnosis of clinical primary overt diabetes mellitus is made. The identification of addiction as a manifestation of allergic (usually nonreagenic type) reactions to foods, chemicals, and inhalants has done much to tie together cause and effect relationships.

Monitoring blood sugar during food testing of single foods preceded by a period of avoidance identified chemical (latent) diabetes mellitus as a central metabolic disorder in many chronic degenerative physical and mental diseases. Secondarily, this diabetic process produces biological conditions favorable for opportunist microbes to flourish, invade tissues, and produce toxins poisoning vital metabolic systems. Moreover, symptom induction testing using autogenous vaccines composed of microbes and toxins frequently evokes acute physical and mental symptoms, which are the same symptoms in miniature as those of the chronic degenerative diseases. Thus a chain reaction in many chronic degenerative physical and mental diseases can be objectively observed, which starts with selective nutritional deficiency for numerous reasons, such as metabolic errors, dietary causes, and infections, proceeding to reactions to foods, chemicals, and inhalants due to enzymatic deficiencies, proceeding to carbohydrate interference as part of the chemistry of these reactions, proceeding to infectious invasion and diminished immunological defense against infectious microbes.

References

1. Burton, R., in Dell, F., and Jordan-Smith, P., eds., *The Anatomy of Melancholy*, 1621, Tudor, New York, 1955.
2. Dickens, Charles, *A Christmas Carol*, 1843.
3. Moyer, K. E., The physiology of violence; Allergy and aggression, *Psychology Today*, July 1975.
4. Rapaport, Howard G., and Flint, Shirley H., Is there a relationship between allergy and learning disabilities? *J. School Health*, XLVI (3):, 1976.
5. Coca, Arthur F., *Familial Nonreagenic Food Allergy*, 1st ed., Charles C Thomas, Springfield, Ill., 1942. See also ibid., 2nd ed., 1943, and ibid. 3rd ed., 1953; *The Pulse Test*, Arco, New York, 1956.
6. Dickey, Lawrence, D., *Clinical Ecology*, Charles C Thomas, Springfield, Ill., 1976, p. 7.
7. Randolph, Theron G., Beet sensitivity: Allergic reactions from ingestion of beet sugar (sucrose) and monosodium glutamate of beet origin, *J. Lab. Clin. Med.* 36:407-415, 1950. See also Ecologic mental illness—Levels of central nervous system reactions, *Proc. Third World Congress of Psychiatry*, Vol. 1, University of Toronto Press, Montreal, 1961, pp. 379-384; Adaptation to specific

environmental exposures enhanced by individual susceptibility, *Clinical Ecology*, Dickey, Lawrence D., ed., Charles C Thomas, Springfield, Ill., 1976, pp. 45–66; Hospital comprehensive environmental control program, ibid., pp. 70–85; Biological dietetics, ibid., pp. 107–121; The enzymatic, acid, hypoxia, endocrine concept of allergic inflammation, ibid., pp. 577–596.
8. Weiss, Jules M., and Kaufman, Herbert S., A subtle organic component in some cases of mental illness, *Arch. Gen. Psychiat.* 25:, 1971.
9. Brambilla, F., Guerrini, A., Riggi, F., Rovere, C., Zanoboni, A., and Zanoboni-Muciaccia, W., Glucose-insulin metabolism in chronic schizophrenia, *Dis. Nerv. Syst.* 37 (2):, 1976.
10. Harvey, A. McGehee, Johns, Richard J., Owens, Albert H., and Ross, Richard S., eds., *The Principles and Practice of Medicine*, Appleton-Century-Crofts, New York, 1972, p. 879.
11. Livingston, Virginia Wuerthele-Caspe, and Alexander-Jackson, Eleanor, A specific type of organism cultured from malignancy; Bacteriology and proposed classification, *Ann. N.Y. Acad. Sci.* 174 (2):636–654, 1970. See also Livingston, A., Livington, V., Alexander-Jackson, E., and Wolter, Gerhard H., Toxic fractions obtained from tumor isolates and related clinical implications, ibid., 675–689; Livingston, V., and Livingston, A., Demonstration of *Progenitor cryptocides* in the blood of patients with collagen and neoplastic diseases, *Trans. N.Y. Acad. Sci.* 34 (5):433–453, 1972; Livingston, V., and Livingston, A., Some cultural, immunological and biochemical properties of *Progenitor cryptocides*, *Trans. N.Y. Acad. Sci.* 36 (6):569–582, 1974; Livingston, V., *Cancer: A New Breakthrough*, Los Angeles, Nash Publishers, 1972.
12. Papez, James W., Inclusion bodies associated with destruction of nerve cells in scrub typhus, psychoses and multiple sclerosis, *J. Nerv. Ment. Dis.* 108:5, 1948. See also Papez, J., and Batement, J. F., Cytological changes in cells of thalmic nuclei in senile, paranoid and manic psychoses, *J. Nerv. Ment. Dis.* 112:5, 1950; Papez, J., Form of living organisms in psychotic patients, *J. Nerv. Ment. Dis.* 116:5, 1952; Papez, J., Living organisms in nerve cells as seen under dark contrast, phase microscope, *Trans. Am. Neur. Assoc.* 1952; Papez, J., A study of polyzoan organisms in brains of young and old mentally ill patients, *J. Geront.* 7:3, 1952; Papez, J., and Papez, B. Pearl, The hypophysis cerebri in psychosis, *J. Nerv. Ment. Dis.* 119:4, 1954; Papez, J., and Papez, B., Drops of protein in brains of hospital patients in stupor, uremia, edema, clouded, and catatonic states, *J. Nerv. Ment. Dis.* 124:4, 1956; Papez, J., and Papez, B., Arteriolar mycosis associated with chronic degenerative brain disease (A new look at sclerotic patches), *Dis. Nerv. Syst.* 16:4, 1957.
13. Philpott, William H., Methods of relief of acute and chronic symptoms of deficiency-allergy-addiction maladaptive reactions to foods and chemicals, *Clinical Ecology*, Dickey, Lawrence D., ed., Charles C Thomas, Springfield, Ill., 1976, pp. 496–509.
14. Ellis, John M., *Vitamin B6, The Doctor's Report*, Harper & Row, New York, 1973.
15. Bassoe, P., The auriculotemporal syndrome and other vasomotor disturbances about the head: "Auriculotemporal syndrome" complicating diseases of paratid gland: Angioneuronic edema of brain, *Med. Clin. N. Am.* 16:405, 1932.

16. Galtman, A. M., Mechanisms of migrain, *J. Allergy*, 7:351, 1936.
17. Axelrod, A. E., Nutrition in relation to acquired immunity, *Modern Nutrition in Health and Disease*, Goodhart, Robert S., and Shild, Maurice E., eds., Lea & Febiger, Philadelphia, 1973, pp. 493–505. See also Axelrod, A. E., and Trakatellis, Anthony C., Relationship of pyridoxime to immunological phenomena, *Vitamins Hormones* 22:591, 1964.
18. Peters, Henry A., Eichman, Peter L., and Reese, Hans H., Therapy of acute, chronic and mixed hepatic porphyria patients with chelating agents. *Neurology* 8:8, 1958. See also Peters, H., Trace minerals, chelating agents and the porphyrias, *Fed. Proc.* 20:3, 1971.
19. Perry, Thomas L., Hansen, Shirley, Tischlet, Bluma, Richards, Frances M., and Sokol, Marlene, Unrecognized adult phenylketonuria: Implications for obstetrics and psychiatry. *N. Engl. J. Med.* 289:8, 1973.
20. Rinkle, H. G., Randolph, Theron, G., and Zeller, M., *Food Allergy*, Charles C Thomas, Springfield, Ill., 1951, p. 8.
21. Carwin, A. H., The rotating diet and taxonomy, *Clinical Ecology*, Dickey, Lawrence, D., ed., Charles C Thomas, Springfield, Ill., 1976, pp. 472–486.
22. Philpott, William H., Neilsen, Ruth, and Pearson, Virginia, Four-day rotation of foods according to families, *Clinical Ecology*, Dickey, Lawrence D., ed., Charles C Thomas, Springfield, Ill., 1976, pp. 472–486.
23. Levine, Seymore, *Hormones and Conditioning*, University of Nebraska Press, Lincoln, 1968.
24. Campbell, M. D., Allergy and behavior, neurologic and psychic syndromes, *Allergy of the Nervous System*, Spears, Frederick, ed., Charles C Thomas, Springfield, Ill., 1970, pp. 28–46.
25. Carlton, Peter L., *Brain-Acetylcholine and Inhibition: Reinforcement and Behavior*, Academy Press, New York, 1969.
26. Hearst, E., Effects of scopolamine on discriminated responding in the rat, *J. Pharmacol. Exp. Ther.*, 1959.
27. Speer, Frederick, *Allergy of the Nervous System*, Charles C Thomas, Springfield, Ill., 1970.
28. Pfeiffer, Carl C., *Mental and Elemental Nutrients*, Keats Publishing Inc., New Canaan, Conn., 1975 p. 419.
29. Selye, Hans, *The Stress of Life*, McGraw-Hill, New York, 1956. See also *Stress Without Distress*, Lippincott, Philadelphia, 1974.
30. Fisman, M., Brain stem lesions in schizophrenia, *Roche Report: Frontiers of Psychiatry*, No. 3, 1976.

Chapter 8 | Biological Research on Violent Behavior

Jose A. Yaryura-Tobias, M.D.
Director of Research
The North Nassau Mental Health Center
Manhasset, New York

INTRODUCTION

Aggression can be defined as an attack or an act of hostility that can be inwardly or outwardly directed, and violence as "an unfair exercise of power or force." This definition has led me to conclude that if the application of power or force is fair, the act is not any longer violent (e.g., a fair war). Aggression as an instinct was postulated by Freud in conjunction with death and sex (Thanatos and Eros) and by Dollard et al.[1] as a consequence of frustration.

It has been reported[2] that there is no satisfactory definition of aggression and/or violence, whereas what people label as aggression is of utter importance (i.e., aggressive people react more aggressively towards family members than towards strangers where the reverse is true for nonaggressive individuals[3]). One country may have a Ministry of War, while another country will call the same department "Secretary of Defense." While in one culture, raising the voice implies aggressive behavior, in another it does not; the same applies even for human killing.[4] Moreover, from the medical viewpoint, surgery is an act of aggression, where the aggressor is not the surgeon but the instrument that injures the cell; accordingly, the response to this action is a stress mechanism or act of self-defense.[5,6] For research purposes, to define aggression and violence is important, but definitions are still controversial; thus in this chapter the terms aggression and violence may be used interchangeably. Aggression can be classified as verbal or physical; the latter includes destructiveness and assaultiveness.

To evaluate aggression, precipitant factors, objects of aggression, intensity, and frequency are important variables that should be measured in any experimental design dealing with aggression.

ANIMAL STUDIES

Spontaneous aggression is not alien to the zoological scale from ants,[7] spiders, fish such as the piranha, to primates. Aggressive behavior may be the result of efforts to survive (e.g., food competition, killing in order to eat), to defend one's self, to protect one's territoriality;[8] or it may constitute acts of depredation or cannibalism, unless the latter is done for the purpose of nutritional survival, becoming an act of instinctual conduct. This type of aggressive behavior is applied to animals living only in their natural habitats; a laboratory or domesticated animal will usually lose its natural aggressiveness.

The centers that regulate violent behavior are anatomically located in the rhinencephalic structures, also called hippocampus. Surgical extirpation of both temporal lobes in monkeys, including the cingulate gyrus, the olfactory bulb, olfactory tubercle, septal area, amygdala, hippocampus, and hypothalamus, produces a taming effect.[9]

Aggressive behavior can also be induced by anatomical lesions in the circuit given by olfactory routes, and the hypothalamus, which integrates vegetative, emotional, and motor impulses, including aggressiveness, sexuality, appetite, thirst, and sleep, and participates in the regulation of some important biochemical reactions, such as glucose metabolism.[10] Therefore, aggressive behavior may be accompanied by symptoms that reflect a disturbance of other functions that are regulated in the same anatomical regions.

Stimulation of the lateral hypothalamus in the cat is also known to be related to aggressive behavior.[11] The amygdala seems to be crucial in the regulation of aggression, and its centromedial lesions reduce aggression in the muricide behavior of the rat.[12] Furthermore, the stimulation of septal nuclei in connection with the amygdala depresses both emotion and reaction motor activity.[13] Therefore, electrical stimulation or surgical extirpation of an anatomical area may produce excitatory or inhibitory responses of centers usually considered in intimate relationship with behavioral modifications.

The fundamental works of Cannon[14] have shown that the adrenals actively participate in the mechanism of aggressive behavior, thus suggesting biochemical changes. Recently, it has been shown that biogenic amines including catecholamines and indolamines (serotonin, noradrenaline, dopamine, dopa) are present in regions of the brain which determine emotional behavior.

Pharmacological aggression can be elicited by the administration of drugs that increase catecholamine levels in the brain, such as monoamine oxidase inhibitors (MAOI), LSD and mescaline,[15] amphetamines,[16] and serotonin (5HT).[17] Moreover, amphetamines are more toxic in aggressive than in normal mice,[18] and show an inhibitory effect on induced aggressiveness.[19] On the other hand, serotonin-induced aggression is still controversial, since its synthesis is slower in aggressive males,[20] and its metabolite, 5-hydroxyindolacetic acid (5HIAA), is higher in normal than in aggressive animals. Moreover, predatory behavior that is very low in laboratory rats can be stimulated by administration of p-chlorophenylalanine (pCPA),[21] a drug that inhibits the synthesis of serotonin. Further, pCPA tames the aggressive behavior of rats with lesions in the septal area of the brain[22] that contains serotonin. This indicates that aggression is related inversely to serotonin. In the rat, 6-hydroxydopamine facilitates aggression[23] by destruction of dopaminergic fibers. Amantadine, a substance which appears to have similar activity to levodopa, inhibits the aggressogenic effect of apormorphine in the rat.[24]

Cholinergic and anticholinergic drugs also trigger aggressive behavior.[25-27] Therefore, the chemistry of aggressive behavior may be the result of an adreno-cholinergic imbalance, and this mechanism is probably controlled by the biogenic amines.[28]

Hormonal participation in the causation of aggressive behavior has also been reported in various experimental studies. It seems that male animals are more aggressive than female, as in the case of female mice, and that testosterone is a causative factor of aggressiveness, as observed in monkeys,[29] or in the ranacide aggression in the female rat.[30]

Genetic work in the area of violent behavior has begun to draw the interest of researchers; for instance, aggressive behavior appears to be correlated to genetic factors and cyclic AMP content in brains of mice.[31]

Further, aggression in the albino rat can be induced by pain stimulation, utilizing a food electric shock; it is well known that an animal in pain is more irritable.

There is empirical evidence that a relationship between nutrition and aggressive behavior exists. In this regard, some experimental work has been performed by Resnick,[32] who stated that a reduced protein diet fed to rats was linked to brain lesions that led to aggressive behavior. Furthermore, undernutrition in early life of some mice strains may increase the fighting responses.[33,34]

It is known that drug responses are very much influenced by environmental changes, such as temperature, noise, painful stimulus, isolation,[35] or aggregation (crowding), and these factors should be taken into account in studying aggressive behavior.

In fighting animals, aggression can be reduced by the administration of psycholeptic drugs, such as phenothiazines, butirophenones, or meprobamates, which exert a calming and also an analgesic effect, thereby enhancing their sedative properties.

So far, no selective drug for aggressive behavior seems to exist.

Summarizing this review of animal studies, present knowledge of the biological aspects of aggressive and violent behavior indicates a definite participation of environmental, social, and organic factors in inducing aggression, where as the utilization of psychosurgery, chemotherapy, and diet modification might be of value in controlling it.

HUMAN STUDIES

Lorenz's observations on aggression in animals could be extended to humans, who also seem to manifest violence of instinctual origin, but without the proper internal mechanism to control it; for the only inhibitory mechanism that humans utilize is learned and social controls. In humans, as previously seen in animals, territorial defense plays an important role in various forms of behavior,[36] including the behavior of violent prisoners.[37] In humans, aggression may not be a simple instinctual response, but an intrinsic reaction precipitated by neuroendocrine mechanisms.

The reviewed animal data support evidence that some forms of human violence may be the result of cerebral dysfunction. The fight and flight reactions described by Cannon and related to an adrenergic-cholinergic mechanism must undoubtedly be integrated at higher cerebral levels, where electrophysiological and biochemical interactions may take place in order to process not only external but internal input, which may trigger the mechanism of violence in man, as well as in animals.

Violent behavior may be the result of structural brain damage caused by oxygen deprivation, drug intoxication, physical injury, or nutritional and environmental factors, and may not be permanent. Violent behavior can be observed in many neuropsychiatric disorders, such as mental retardation, hyperkinesis, drug addiction, Gilles de la Tourette Syndrome, Lesch Nyhan Syndrome, self-mutilation, tumors of the brain, epilepsy, or any other diseases where the brain may also be affected. Furthermore, it may be related to focal cerebral disease.[38]

In 1944, Hill reported the posterior slow wave phenomenon recorded in electroencephalographic tracings that was correlated to psychopathic behavior, and which was confirmed in a study performed in 1952, where he found a 12% prevalence in 194 nonepileptic psychopaths as compared with 2% in a normal population of 146 persons; all this was related to cerebral immaturity. These findings were corroborated by Rey et al.[39] and Aird and Gastaut,[40] whose work seemed to show that aggressive psychopaths have immature brains whose EEGs are similar to a child's EEG, and that if the brain matures, the psychopath loses his aggressiveness. However, Fenton et al.[41] replicated these studies, matching a population of patients with posterior slow wave foci and a group of patients with a normal EEG. The groups were compared with respect to a number of developmental, forensic, psychiatric, behavioral, and psychometric variables, with negative results.

Jenkins and Pacella[42] suggested that aggression but not delinquency per se was related to EEG abnormalities. In an EEG study made on 1,250 inmates in custody for crimes of aggression in and around London, abnormal EEGs were found in 65% of habitually aggressive delinquents compared to 24% in inmates who, although they had committed a major violent crime, were not habitually aggressive.[43] In a study performed by Sayed et al.[44] in 1969, 32 murderers were found to have an incidence of EEG abnormality four times that of the control group. In another study on 100 capital cases, 50% abnormal EEGs were reported by Hill and Pond.[45]

Epilepsy is often considered a possible medical defense against violent crimes in its relation to automatism and crime. Murder during posictal automatism has been reported, where the EEG had a pattern of 14 and 6 cps positive spikes.[46] On the contrary, in a study done on 32 epileptic patients who committed violent crimes, only two cases could be associated with the ictal process.[47] Furthermore, Rodin[48] did not find that patients suffering from psychomotor epilepsy were prone to aggressive behavior. In 120 cases of limbic epilepsy in childhood, aggressive activity was observed in 44 cases,[49] yet the issue of the behavioral characteristics of psychomotor epilepsy is still controversial.[50]

Temporal lobe epilepsy (TLE) has drawn the attention of psychiatrists because it could cast some light on an understanding of the neurological basis of behavior, primarily because the temporal lobes of the brain are related to behavioral changes, as previously indicated in this chapter. This particular group of patients present diverse symptomatology, such as *sensorial* (taste, olfaction, hearing), *mental* (*déjà vu*, cloudiness, hallucinations, anger, fear), or *motor* ([focal] clonic or tonic contraction, speech impairment, etc.).[51] Additional evidence has been provided by Penfield[52] and Lennox[53] among others. The latter proposed the term TLE because it was associated with the pathology of this region. Furthermore, Gastaut described three anatomical variations of TLE with special clinical and EEG patterns as follows: (1) temporal, (2) hippocampal, and (3) diencephalic.

Kligman and Goldberg[54] have made an excellent review of TLE and aggression, and have concluded that TLE is too heterogenous and ill-defined and human aggression is too complex to allow correlations of both at present.

Minimal brain dysfunction in young adults may be associated with impulsive-destructive behavior, EEG abnormalities, and soft behavioral organic signs.[55]

Neurological syndromes are sometimes accompanied by aggressive symptoms, primarily when there is focal brain disease, for instance, in neoplasms of the hypothalamus[56] or of the septum pellucidum, both usually characterized by excitability, restlessness, and irritability,[57] and also in tumors of the limbic system; the cerebral region is intimately engaged in emotional regulatory activity.[58] Moreover, hydrocephalus with normal pressure may yield aggressive symptoms and dementia.[59]

A syndrome characterized by loss of control leading to physical attack on individuals and/or destruction of property has been described by Menninger.[60] This syndrome was extensively reviewed by

Bach-Y-Rita et al.,[61] who found a high incidence of violence and alcoholism in patients' family backgrounds. The same authors viewed violence as an interplay of psychogenic and organic disturbance, grouping these patients under an episodic dyscontrol of explosive behavior. This syndrome was further studied and corroborated by other investigators.[62,63]

Fear may be the cause of a deadly attack where there is no participation of anger.

Alcohol has a potent action in modifying behavior, and violence may be induced by drinking a rather large dose. However, some persons having a low threshold for alcohol tolerance may respond with much less quantity. A low tolerance for alcohol may be due to various biological circumstances, not all of them known. Alcohol intake is usually followed by a hyperglycemic response, and then by a hypoglycemic response, as the result of glucose utilization in its metabolism, which also requires vitamins of the B complex, such as thiamine, niacin, and pyridoxine; and both acute and chronic cases of alcoholism may cause depletion or a vitamin deficiency. This deficiency would partly account for the neuropsychiatric syndrome observed in alcoholism. In other words, the brain clinical symptoms and pathology observed in alcoholics are not always from a direct action of alcohol on cerebral tissues, but from an indirect action by nutritional deficiencies. Moreover, alcohol use is contraindicated in certain diseases of the brain, mostly in convulsive disorders because it may precipitate an epileptic attack. Therefore, it is not surprising that alcohol is related to aggressive behavior, not only by causing a psychological disinhibition but by altering cerebral physiology and biochemistry.

As a matter of fact, it has been found that 60% of all homicides are perpetrated by persons under the influence of alcohol and some 55% of the arrests made in the U.S. are due to alcoholic intoxication. Furthermore, volatile solvents used by drug addicts resemble alcohol in their behavioral effect.[64] However, pathological alcoholic intoxication may not produce EEG changes in persons with normal EEGs[61] or precipitate seizures in epileptic patients.[65] Furthermore, alcohol is also related to delinquency and violence, even if the primary diagnosis is not alcoholism (e.g., schizophrenia with secondary alcoholism).

For many years, glucose disturbance has been linked to mental pathology, and it has been statistically so confirmed.[66] Functional hypoglycemia is known to be a causative factor for explosive rage.[67] It may activate EEG abnormalities in patients with temporal lobe epilepsy,[68] and it may be present during the premenstrual period in violent prisoners.[69] In patients suffering from labile diabetes or diabetes mellitus, EEG abnormalities and psychological changes, including temper tantrums, have been described.[70,71]

A syndrome characterized by aggressive and/or assaultive behavior, glucose disturbance, and brain dysrhythmia has been described by Yaryura-Tobias,[72] and it has been hypothesized that it could be caused by a disturbance of tryptophane metabolism.[73,74] The main clinical characteristic of this syndrome is that patients come for consultation because of untractable violent behavior. A need to rule out this syndrome before contemplating the possibilities of psychosurgery is a must.

Hormonal participation in rage reactions and its relationship to neurogenic mechanisms also should be considered. Basically, the physical characteristics of rage comprise increased muscular tone, tachycardia, vasodilation of muscular vessels, and visceral constriction. There is also an increase of hormonal output, primarily of the adrenal group, its release being regulated by sympathetic mechanisms. Glucose metabolism also appears modified, and a hypoglycemic phase probably precedes a compensatory hyperglycemic phase caused by glycogenolysis. In addition, sex hormones also are involved in the mechanism of violent behavior, where male hormones are related to the precipitation of aggression.

The increase of the drive by testosterone administration and its decrease by stilbestrol explain why males are more aggressive than females.[75] Plasma testosterone levels in fighting and verbal aggression in prison and past criminal behavior did not show a correlation or differ from those in nonfighting individuals.[76] However, another study showed a higher significant level of plasma testosterone in an aggressive group as compared with a nonaggressive group.[77,78]

In a study carried out in 111 women killers, 7% showed organic brain disease and 18% psychoses.[79] The social implication of menstruation includes emotional and behavioral changes in women. It is well recognized that irritability, aggressive behavior, depression, and some form of periodic psychosis are related to the menstrual cycle. A study of 386 newly committed women prisoners showed that half of all crimes were perpetrated in the premenstrum or during menstruation. Yet, aggression or violence was not necessarily involved.[80]

Aggressive and violent behavior is also common in children and can be found independently or accompanying varient forms of mental disorders, such as mental retardation, psychosis, or hyperkinesia. It has been reported that a triad characterized by enuresis, firesetting, and cruelty to animals can be predictive of adult criminality.[81] Those symptoms may be a reflection of psychological or organic factors or a combination of both, as a cause for anti-social behavior. In Finland, Pitkanen[82] has compared a population of extremely aggressive eight-year-old boys and one of extroverted, well-controlled boys; stimulation exercises for constructive behavior (alternatives to cope with aggressive behavior) yielded positive results. At times homicidal aggression in juveniles can be foreseen by psychological or physical signs that may or may not be related to the act of homicide, where homicide is committed to save one's self.[83]

During the eighteenth century, Lombroso, in Italy, put forward the hypothesis that criminality was related to physical characteristics; however, this theory was never confirmed.

The contribution of genetic factors in criminality was described by Galton.[84] It has been emphasized that a 47, XYY karyotype is associated with criminal behavior (as reported in the review by Kessler and Moos, 1969). This male pattern is characterized by high stature, soft neurological types, EEG abnormalities, dermatoglyphic alterations, and testicular changes, including at times cardiac anomalies and, of course, short temper and limited intelligence. The issue is still controversial,[85-87] and the relationship between the extra Y chromosome and aggressive behavior is questionable. So far, the prediction of dangerousness in mentally ill criminals is related mainly to social factors, while psychological and biological parameters require further studies.[88]

The use of addictive drugs, stimulants, and alcohol is not unusual in a delinquent population, and such use may precipitate the individual to commit a violent act. Amphetamines and cocaine may cause assaultive or aggressive behavior, probably because they impair judgment and increase the degree of self-confidence and courage. In children, barbiturates in high doses may increase aggression.[89] The same may occur with the use of anticonvulsants.[90]

It seems that marijuana use is not a pharmacological cause of aggressive behavior, and the same could be said of opiates, where only their strong physical and psychological dependence may force the addict to commit crimes in order to obtain the drugs.[91] Psychosis and violent behavior, followed by homicide, have been reported from use of LSD.[92,93] This can be explained on the grounds that hallucinogenics may cause aggressive behavior including murder if paranoid symptomatology is involved.[94,95] Psychiatric disorders such as sociopathy, alcoholism, and drug addiction are associated with adult criminality where schizophrenia is not increased in the criminal population.[96]

TREATMENT OF VIOLENT BEHAVIOR

At the present time, current medical treatment of aggressive and violent behavior includes the use of minor and major tranquilizers, anticonvulsants and vitamins, primarily those of group B. A low carbohydrate, high protein diet where functional hypoglycemia is diagnosed is also helpful to control aggressiveness. Furthermore, fasting and the habit of skipping meals should be avoided in order to maintain a satisfactory glucose plasma level. In intractable cases, psychosurgery is recommended.

Medical research perspectives should include the following:

1. To distinguish violent mentally ill individuals from violent individuals without mental illness.
2. To operate research programs unbiased; and, if funded by Federal or state institutions, not to compromise oneself in socio-political schemes.
3. To be extremely careful in the selection of violent patients who have a clearly defined medical cause for their violence from those whose violence is the result of socio-politico-economic reasons.[97]
4. To study the incidence of nutrition effects in criminal behavior.
5. To study the action of vitamins that are known to participate in the biochemistry of brain physiology.
6. To study other organs besides the brain, in order to look for primary medical causes of aggressive behavior.

In the meantime, world hierarchies should be asked to refrain from causing wars and to improve the living conditions of human beings. Violence must not be sold as a consumer good. It seems naive and offensive to engage oneself in research studies about aggression and violence, while others stimulate in an unparalleled manner any imaginable form of aggression and violence, ultimately to profit from the pain and the loneliness of the individual.

References

1. Dollard, J., Doob, L., Miller, N., Mowrer, O., and Sears, R., *Frustration and Aggression*, Yale University Press, New Haven, 1939.
2. Bandura, A., and Walters, R. H., Social learning and personality development, Holt, Rinehart & Winston, New York, 1963.
3. Neziroglu, F., Sillman, E., and Horai, J., The labeling of aggression, submitted to *J. of Applied Personality*, 1977.
4. Benedict, R., Anthropology and the abnormal, *Readings in Anthropology*, Fried, M. H., ed., Thomas Y. Crowell, New York, 2:801, 1968.
5. Selye, H., A syndrome produced by diverse noxious agents. *Nature (Lond.)* 138:32, 1936.
6. Laborit H., Bases biologiques generales de la reaction a l'agression, *Agressologie* 13(1):1–53, 1972.
7. Tarchalska, B., Kostowski, W., Markowska, L., and Markiewicz, L., On the role of serotonin in aggressive behaviour of ants genus *Formica*, *Pol. J. Pharmacol. Pharm.* 27:237–239, 1975.
8. Lorenz, K., *On Aggression*, Harcourt Brace Jovanovich, New York, 1966.
9. Kluver, H., and Bucy, P. C., Preliminary analysis of function of temporal lobes in monkeys, *Arch. Neurol. Psychiat.* 42:979–1000, 1939.
10. Watts, G. O., *Dynamic Neuroscience*, Harper & Row, New York, 1975.
11. Roberts, W. W., and Kiess, H. O., Motivational properties of hypothalamic aggression in cats, *J. Comp. Physiol. Psychol.* 58:187–193, 1964.
12. Horovitz, Z. P., Relationship of the amygdala to the mechanism of actin of two types of antidepressants (thiazenone and imipramine), *Recent Adv. Biol. Psychiat.* 8:21–31, 1965.
13. Delgado, J. M. R., Cerebral and behavioral effects on the monkey of CAPP, *Arch. Int. Pharmacodyn.* 133:163–172, 1961a.
14. Cannon, W. B., *Bodily Changes in Pain, Hunger, Fear and Rage*. Harper & Row, New York, 1963 (originally pub. in 1915).
15. Haley, T. J., Intercerebral injection of psycholomemetic and psychotherapeutic drugs into conscious mice, *Acta Pharmacol. Toxicol.* 13:107–112, 1957.
16. Herman, Z., A study of some psychotropic drugs with the Burn-Hobbs test. *Arch. Immunol. Terapii Doswiadczalnej* 9:543–549, 1961.
17. Schwarz, B., Wakim, K. G., Bickford, R. G., and Lichtenheld, F. R., Behavioral and electroencephalographic effects of hallucinogenic drugs, changes in cats on intraventricular injections, *A.M.A. Arch. Neurol. Psychiat.* 75:83–90, 1956.
18. Consolo, S., Garattini, S., and Valzelli, L., Amphetamine toxicity in aggressive mice, *J. Pharm. Pharmacol.* 17:53–54, 1965a.
19. Melander, B., Psychopharmacodynamic effects of diethylpropion (tylinal), *Acta Pharmacol. Toxicol.* 17:182–190, 1960.
20. Valzelli, L., Drugs and aggressiveness, *Advances of Pharmacology*, Garattini, S., and Shore, P. A., eds., Academic Press, New York, 1967.

21. Kreiskott, H., and Hofmann, H. P., Stimulation of a specific drive (predatory behavior) by *p*-chloropheneylalanine (*p*CPA) in the rat, *Pharmakopsychiatrie Neuro-Psychopharmakologie* 8:136–140, 1975.
22. Jones, A. B., Barchas, J. D., and Eichelman, B., Taming effects of *p*-chlorophenylalanine on the aggressive behavior of septal rats, *Pharmacol. Biochem. Behav.* 4:397–400, 1976.
23. Eichelman, B. S., Jr., Thoa, N. B., Ng, K. Y., Facilitated aggression in the rat following 6-hydroxydopamine administration, *Physiol. Behav.* 8:1–3, 1972.
24. Senault, B., Amantadine: Effet agressogene propre; Effet sur l'agressivite induite par l'apomorphine chez le rat, *Psychopharmacologia* 46:167–168, 1976.
25. Allikmets, L. H., Vahing, V. A., and Lapin, I. P., Dissimilar influences of imipramine, benactyzine and promazine on effects of microinjections of noradrenaline, acetylcholine and serotonine into the amygdala in the cat, *Psychopharmacologia* 15:392–403, 1969.
26. Bergstrom, R. M., Johansson, G. G., and Niskanen, H., Responses elicited by intraventricular injection of carbachol in the kitten, *Acta Physiol. Scand.* 88:287–288, 1973.
27. Allikmets, L. H., Cholinergic mechanisms in aggressive behavior, *Med. Biol.* 52:19–30, 1974.
28. Johansson, G., Relation of biogenic amines to aggressive behavior, *Med. Biol.* 52:189–192, 1974.
29. Rose, R. B., Holaday, J. W., and Bernstein, I. S., Plasma testosterone, dominance rank and aggressive behavior in male rhesus monkeys. *Nature* 231:366–368, 1971.
30. Bernard, B. K., Testosterone manipulations: Effects on ranacide aggression and brain, monoamines in the adult female rat. *Pharmacol. Biochem. Behav.* 4:59–65, 1976.
31. Orenberg, E. K., Renson, J., Elliott, G. R., Barchas, J. D., and Kessler, S., Genetic determination of aggressive behavior and brain cyclic AMP, *Psychopharmacol. Commun.* 1 (1):99–107, 1975.
32. Resnick, O., Proteins and aggressiveness, *Barbados Advocate-News*, April 14, 1974.
33. Frankova, S., Effect of protein-calorie malnutrition on the development of social behavior in rats, *Develop. Psychobiol.* 6:33–43, 1973.
34. Randt, C. T., Blizard, D. A., and Friedman, E., Early life undernutrition and aggression in two mouse strains, *Develop. Psychobiol.* 8 (3):275–279, 1975.
35. Yen, C. Y., Stanger, L., and Millman, N., Ataractic suppression of isolation-induced aggressive behavior, *Arch. Int. Pharmacodyn.* 123:179–185, 1959.
36. Clark, L. D., in *The Roots of Behavior*, E. Bliss, ed., Harper & Row, New York, 1962a, p. 179.
37. Kinzel, A. F., Body-buffer zone in violent prisoners, *Am. J. Psychiat.* 127(1):99–104, 1970.
38. Sweet, W. H., Ervin, F., and Mark, V. C., The relationship of violent behavior to focal cerebral disease, *Proceedings of the International Symposium on the Biology of Aggressive Behavior*, held at instituto di ricerche farmacologiche "Mario Negri," Garattini, S., Sigg, E. B., eds., Milan, 1968.

39. Rey, J. H., Pond, D. A., and Evans, C. C., Clinical and electroencephalographic studies of temporal lobe function, Proc. Roy. Soc. Med. 42:891–904, 1949.
40. Aird, R. B., and Gastaut, Y. Occipital and posterior electroencephalographic rhythms, *Electroenceph. Clin. Neurophysiol.* 11:637–656, 1959.
41. Fenton, G. W., Tennent, T. G., Fenwick, P. B. C., and Rattray, N., The EEG in antisocial behavior: A study of posterior temporal slow activity in special hospital patients, *Psychol. Med.* 4(2):181–186, 1974.
42. Jenkins, R. L., and Pacella, B. L., Electroencephalographic studies of delinquent boys, *Am. J. Orthopsychiat.* 13:107–120, 1943.
43. Williams, D., Neural factors related to habitual aggression, *Brain* 92:503–520, 1969.
44. Sayed, Z. A., Lewis, S. A., and Brittain, R. P., An electroencephalographic and psychiatric study of thirty-two insane murders, *Brit. J. Psychiat.* 115:1115–1124, 1969.
45. Hill, D., and Pond, D. A., Reflections on one hundred capital cases submitted to electroencephalography, *J. Ment. Sci.* 98:23–43, 1952.
46. Walker, A. E., Murder or epilepsy? *J. Nerv. Ment. Dis.* 133:430–437, 1961.
47. Gunn, J., and Fenton, G., Epilepsy, automatism, and crime, *Lancet* (June 5):1173–1176, 1971.
48. Rodin, E. A., Psychomotor epilepsy and aggressive behavior, *Arch. Gen. Psychiat.* 28:210–213, 1973.
49. Glaser, G. H., Limbic epilepsy in childhood, *J. Nerv. Ment. Dis.* 144(5):391–397, 1967.
50. Small, J. G., Milstein, V., and Stevens, J., Are psychomotor epileptics different? A controlled study, *Arch. Neurol.* 7:187–194, 1962; Small, J. G., Small, I. F., and Hayden, M., Further psychiatric investigation of patients with temporal and non-temporal lobe epilepsy, *Am. J. Psychiat.* 123(3):303–310, 1966.
51. Gastaut, H., So-called "psychomotor" and "temporal" epilepsy: A critical study, *Epilepsia* 2:59–96, 1953.
52. Penfield, W., and Jasper, H., *Epilepsy and the Functional Anatomy of the Human Brain*, Little, Brown, Boston, 1954.
53. Lennox, W. G., Phenomena and correlates of the psychomotor triad, *Neurology* 1:357–371, 1951.
54. Kligman, D., and Goldberg, D. A., Temporal lobe epilepsy and aggression, *J. Nerv. Ment. Dis.* 160:324–341, 1975.
55. Quitkin, F., and Klein, D. F., Two behavioral syndromes in young adults related to possible minimal brain dysfunction, *J. Psychiat. Res.* 7:131–142, 1969.
56. Reeves, A. G., and Plum, F., Hyperphagia, rage and dementia accompanying a ventromedial hypothalamic neoplasm, *Arch. Neurol.* 20:616–624, 1969.
57. Zeman, W., and King, F. Tumors of the septum pellucidium and adjacent structure with abnormal effective behavior: An anterior midline structure syndrome, *J. Nerv. Ment. Dis.* 127:490–502, 1958.
58. Malamud, N., Psychiatric disorder with intracranial tumors of limbic system, *Arch. Neurol.* 17:113–123, 1967.
59. Crowell, R. B., Tew, J. J., Jr., and Mark, V. H., Aggressive dementia associated with normal pressure hydrocephalus, *Neurology* 23:461–464, 1973.

60. Menninger, K., *The Vital Balance*, Viking Press, New York, 1963.
61. Bach-Y-Rita, G., Lion, J. R., Climent, C. E., and Ervin, F. R., Episodic dyscontrol: Study of 130 violent patients, *Am. J. Psychiat.* 127(11):1473-1478, 1971.
62. Maletzky, B. M., The episodic dyscontrol syndrome, *Dis. Nerv. Syst.* 34:178-185, 1973.
63. Elliott, F. A., The neurology of explosive rage: The dyscontrol syndrome, *Practitioner* 217:51-60, 1976.
64. Vista Hill Psychiatric Foundation, *Drug Abuse and Alcoholism Newsletter* 2:3, 1973.
65. Giove, G., and Gastaut, H., Epilepsie alcoolique et declenchement alcoolique des crises chez les epileptiques, *Rev. Neurol. (Paris)* 113:347-357, 1965.
66. Yaryura-Tobias, J. A., and Neziroglu, F. A., Psychosis and disturbance of glucose metabolism, *J. Prevent. Med.* 3:38-45, 1975.
67. Wilder, J., Sugar Metabolism and Its Relation to Criminology, in *Handbook of Correctional Psychology*, Linder, R., and Slieger, R., eds., Philosophical Library, New York, 1947.
68. Green, J. B., The activation of electroencephalographic abnormalities by tolbutamide-induced hypoglycemia, *Neurology* 13:192-200, 1963.
69. Morton, H. H., Addison, H., Addison, R. G., Hunt, L., and Sullivan, C., Clinical study of premenstrual tension, *Am. J. Obstet. Gynec.* 65:1182-1191, 1953.
70. Fabrykant, M., and Pacella, B., Labile diabetes: Electroencephalographic status and effect of anticonvulsive therapy, *Ann. Intern. Med.* 29:860-877, 1948.
71. Wilson, D. R., Electroencephalographic studies in diabetes mellitus, *Canad. Med. Assoc. J.* 65:462-465, 1951.
72. Yaryura-Tobias, J. A., Behavioral-gluco-dysrhythmic triad, *Am. J. Psychiat.* 130 (7):825, 1973.
73. Yaryura-Tobias, J. A., and Neziroglu, F. A., Violent behavior, brain dysrhythmia and glucose dysfunction: A new syndrome, Presented at 3rd meeting of Academy of Orthomolecular Psychiatry, San Francisco, May 4-6, 1973.
74. Yaryura-Tobias, J. A., and Neziroglu, F. A., Violent behavior, brain dysrhythmia and glucose dysfunction: A new syndrome, *J. Orthomolecular Psychiatry* 4:182-188, 1975.
75. Beach, F. L. A., *Hormones and Behavior*, Hoeber, New York, 1948.
76. Kreuz, L. E., and Rose, R. B., Assessment of aggressive behavior and plasma testosterone in a young criminal population, *Psychosomat. Med.* 34 (4):321-332, 1972.
77. Ehrenkranz, J., Bliss, E., and Sheard, M. H., Plasma testosterone: Correlation with aggressive behavior and social dominance in man, *Psychosomat. Med.* 36 (6):469-475, 1974.
78. Persky, H., Smith, K. D., and Basu, G. K., Relation of psychologic measures of aggression and hostility to testosterone production in man, *Psychosomat. Med.* 33 (3):265-277, 1971.
79. Cole, K. E., Fisher, G., and Cole, S. S., Women who kill, *Arch. Gen. Psychiat.* 19:1-8, 1968.
80. Dalton, K., Menstruation and crime, *Brit. Med. J.* (Dec. 30):1752-1753, 1961.

81. Hellman, D. S., and Blackman, N., Enuresis, firesetting and cruelty to animals: A triad predictive of adult crime, *Brief Communications*, 1431-1435, 1966.
82. Pitkanen, L., The effect of simulation exercises on the control of aggressive behavior in children, *Scand. J. Psychol.* 15:169-177, 1974.
83. Malmquist, C. P., Premonitory signs of homicidal aggression in juveniles, *Am. J. Psychiat.* 128 (4):461-465, 1971.
84. Kessler, S., and Moos, R. H., The XYY karyotype and criminality: A review, *J. Psychiat. Res.* 7:153-170, 1970.
85. Rainer, J. D., Abdullah, S., and Jarvik, L. S., XYY karyotype in a pair of monozygotic twins: A 17-year life-history study, *Brit. J. Psychiat.* 120 (558): 543-548, 1972.
86. Owen, D. R., The 47, XYY male: A review, *Psychol. Bull.* 78 (3):209-233, 1972.
87. Jarvik, L. F., Klodin, V., and Matsuyama, S. S., Human aggression and the extra Y chromosome, *Am. Psychologist* 28 (8):674-682, 1973.
88. Rubin B., Prediction of dangerousness in mentally ill criminals, *Arch. Gen. Psychiat.* 27:397-407, 1972.
89. Eisenberg, L., and Connors, C. K., Psychopharmacology in childhood, *Behavioral Science in Pediatric Medicine*, Talbott, N. B., and Kagan, J., eds., W. B. Saunders, Philadelphia, 1971, pp. 397-423.
90. Millichap, G., Anticonvulsant drugs in the management of epilepsy, *Mod. Treat.* 6:1217-1232, 1969.
91. Kozel, N. J., DuPont, R. B., and Brown, B. S., Narcotics and crime: A study of narcotic involvement in an offender population. *Int. J. Addictions* 7 (3):443-450, 1972.
92. Barter, J. T., and Reite, M., Crime and LSD: The insanity plea, *Am. J. Psychiat.* 126 (4):113-119, 1969.
93. Reich, P., and Hepps, R., Homicide during a psychosis induced by LSD, *J.A.M.A.* 217:7, 1972.
94. National Commission on Marijuana and Drug Abuse, 2nd Report, *Drug Use in America: Problem in Perspective*, March 1973.
95. Neustatter, W. L., The state of mind in murder, Lancet 1:861-863, 1965.
96. Guze, S. B., Woodruff, R. A., Jr., and Clayton, P. J., Psychiatric disorders and criminality, *J.A.M.A.* 227:6, 1974.
97. Coleman, L. S., Perspectives on the medical research of violence, *Am. J. Orthopsychiatry* 44 (5):675-687, 1974.

Chapter 9

Some Effects of Nicotinic and Ascorbic Acids on the Behavior of Institutionalized Juvenile Delinquents

M. Ellis Ware, M.S.
Staff Psychologist
Mobile Psychiatric Clinic
Bon Air, Virginia

RATIONALE FOR THE PRESENT STUDY

One of today's most pressing problems is effective treatment of the acting-out, asocial child. Within the Training School System, Commonwealth of Virginia, there are two specific problems: inadequate staff and inadequate treatment time. Even with all positions filled, there are seldom more than two full-time psychologists per training school. In addition, the average length of detention, and therefore treatment, is from six to eight months. The System includes eight Training Schools with an average total population of 1,400 children. It is obvious that there is neither sufficient time nor personnel for effective counseling and therapy. Therefore, there is a constant search for new and effective treatment approaches that are simple, inexpensive, and do not require extensive personnel for administration.

In May, 1969, Dr. Ruth Harrell, Portsmouth psychologist and then a member of the faculty of Old Dominion University, Norfolk, Virginia, wrote a letter to the father of an emotionally disturbed youth, describing the Hoffer Osmond Diagnostic Test (HOD) and pointing out that Drs. Hoffer and Osmond strongly advise persons who score high on this test to supplement their diet with two nutrients, vitamin C (ascorbic acid) and vitamin B-3 (niacinamide) in large daily amounts of 3 grams of each vitamin. Dr. Harrell wrote:

> Theirs is a new—that is, new to us—theory of abnormal behavior. They state that high scorers on the HOD test will also exhibit the "pink spot" in the urine when it is analyzed carefully enough. The pink spot indicates, they write, that the subject is out of balance biochemically, is manufacturing LSD unfortunately, and is exhibiting odd, senseless, impulsive behavior of which he seems unaware.
>
> Dr. Hoffer and Dr. Osmond surveyed the arrested youth in their province in Canada, finding about half of them high scorers on the HOD test. The government offered these high scorers the daily vitamins suggested by these psychiatrists. A few refused, they report. Most of them accepted the free supplement.
>
> The Detention Home authorities are very enthusiastic about the response these young persons made. One of their reports states that after five years none has since had a brush with the law, that all are back in school or at work successfully, and that most impressive was their quick—within a few days—response. They report "noticeably improved behavior." Their enthusiasm is echoed by the school authorities in Canada.

In a personal communication, dated June 16, 1969, Dr. Harrell called attention to the work of Dr. Hoffer with malvarians in trouble with the law, and also to the work of Dr. Russell Smith. Dr. Harrell stated that in a Michigan Youth Correctional Institution of which Dr. Smith is the director, a group of delinquents was HOD-tested. Thirty-five percent of those tested showed perceptual distortions. Dr. Smith, she said, reported that "those willing to try B-3 showed marked behavioral improvement."

On the basis of this information, it was felt that this area demanded investigation, and preliminary research was undertaken. The Director of Clinical Services, Division of Youth Services, Virginia Department of Welfare and Institutions, commented:

> Although I tend to be skeptical of bright promises and quick, easy solutions to disturbed and delinquent behavior, I also find that we cannot afford to ignore any possible avenue of help and information. Therefore, I am recommending this research project to attempt to verify some of these claims in a controlled study on subjects in our population.

It can be said that the rationale for this study was a purely pragmatic one. There had been several claims (Hoffer and Osmond, Smith, and later Harrell) alleging that megavitamin therapy was beneficial to delinquent youth. However, it was impossible to find any controlled, statistically analyzed studies on populations comparable to that of the Division of Youth Services. It was felt that a critical study using subjects from this population was the only way in which it could be ascertained whether or not these claims were valid. If so, we would have a method of treatment whose properties of safety, cheapness, ease of administration, and rapid effectiveness would be an invaluable addition to our limited therapeutic methods.

Biochemical Factors in Schizophrenia

In 1951, Drs. Abram Hoffer and Humphry Osmond began an exploration of certain ideas formulated earlier by Osmond and Dr. John Smythies, then in England. Their thesis was that schizophrenia might be caused by the production of a metabolite of adrenaline, whose psychological effect would resemble effects of mescaline or LSD-25.

According to Hoffer and Osmond[1] these ideas seemed promising because there are certain resemblances between the chemical formulas of adrenaline and mescaline, as well as the psychological effects of mescaline and some of the symptoms of schizophrenia. These ideas later became known as the adrenaline metabolite theory of schizophrenia. According to this theory, schizophrenia is due to a disturbance in adrenaline metabolism, resulting in a toxic substance that subtly changes the workings of the brain. Just how this occurs was and still is subject to question. It was felt, however, that anything which prevented the formation of adrenaline or relieved the effects of the hypothetical metabolites would probably be proven therapeutic. It was suggested that niacin, an acceptor of methyl groups, might compete with noradrenaline and so reduce adrenaline formation. Ascorbic acid seemed another promising substance, since it also serves as an adrenolution inhibitor and further potentiates the action of niacin.

Hoffer writes:

> One evening when we were discussing the possible mechanisms by which deep insulin treatment might work and comparing it with the popular histamine shock, we asked ourselves what would be an ideal treatment supposing our ideas were correct. A treat-

ment should be safe, easy to administer, continuous, cheap, and as little empirical as possible, i.e., it should be aimed at some psychophysiological process. If our adrenaline metabolite theory was correct, then anything which reduced the production of adrenaline might help. Nicotinic acid was mentioned as something which might compete for methyl groups. At that time, nicotinic acid had been used in what was then considered large doses of deliria and also we discovered later for depression.[1]

Nicotinic acid (niacin) was discovered to be a vitamin many years after it was synthesized by Huber in 1867. In 1937, Elvehjem et al.[2] reported that both nicotinic acid and its amide cured black tongue in dogs. By the early 1940s nicotinic acid was incorporated into white flour, with the result that pellagra was virtually eliminated in North America. This later fact gave considerable impetus to the study of nicotinic acid as a factor in psychological disturbances, since the clinical symptoms of pellagra and some psychoses are very similar. These symptoms include perceptual changes (hallucinations, disturbances of body image), changes in thought (blocking, delusion, confusion, disorientation), and severe changes in mood. In the past these were diagnosed as toxic psychoses if disorientation and confusion were predominant. If not, they were diagnosed as schizophrenia.

Work on the role of biochemical factors in mental and character disorders has taken many directions over the intervening years, with the most prolific work having been done in the field of schizophrenia. More recently, investigators have applied biochemical theories to such problems as hypoglycemia, alcoholism, drug addiction, and various character disorders, including juvenile delinquency. Some researchers active in this field are Hawkins,[3] Smith,[4] Cott,[5] Downing,[6] and Ward.[7] The references cited are only a fractional listing of the vast reservoir of biochemical studies and literature on subjects related to biochemical factors in schizophrenia and other emotional as well as physical disorders.

In the study presented in this chapter, the development and results of some of the more prominent theories will be surveyed. Emphasis will be on the possible causes and effects of perceptual distortion, as the purpose here is to test the theory that biochemical imbalance leads to perceptual distortion and thus inappropriate, bizarre, and antisocial behavior.

General Problem Area and Purpose of Study

The general problem area under evaluation concerns the possible results of chemical imbalance upon the asocial behavior of institutionalized delinquent youth and the response of such behavior to megavitamin therapy as originated by Hoffer and Osmond.

In this study, we propose to determine if there are significant perceptual and behavioral differences in youth receiving vitamin therapy, youth receiving placebo, and youth receiving no specific treatment at all.

Since the major emphasis is the concept of perceptual distortion, it should be noted that the HOD was developed basically as a test of perceptual changes. Kelm[8] writes: "Convinced by research workers, clinical experience, autobiographies of schizophrenic patients, and experiences with various psychoto-mimetic substances, that perceptual changes are important in schizophrenia, Hoffer and Osmond developed a test called the Hoffer-Osmond Diagnostic Test (HOD), designed to record these changes." Hoffer and Osmond[9] report on a study by Andrew McGhie and James Chapman in England. McGhie and Chapman collected descriptions from various schizophrenic patients on how the disease affected them. They found that disturbance in areas of perception and attention is primary in this disease. El-Meligi notes that the HOD "taps dimensions pertinent to the phenomenal world" and that it "focuses on sensory alterations and distortions."[10] As discussed in the review of the literature, LSD-25 and various toxins known to cause perceptual distortion produce marked increases in HOD scores.[11]

Hoffer and Osmond write:

> Our basic assumption is that the biochemical changes somehow interfere with normal perception. As a result the external world is seen, heard, etc., in an unusual or distorted way. The subject is unaware the change has occurred in him and believes it has occurred in the environment. He therefore reacts appropriately to what he perceives in the new world, but to the observed his actions are inappropriate.[9]

Hoffer and Osmond also observe that perceptual changes are present in the majority of schizophrenic patients and that any psychiatrist wishing to corroborate this needs only to take a careful history of all the possible perceptual changes in schizophrenic patients. They suggest the HOD as a useful guide in assessing such changes, and state that "this test is based to a large degree on the presence of perceptual changes."[9]

In addition to the measure of perceptual distortion as shown on the HOD, it was felt that some assessment of observable behavior was needed. The requirements were relative simplicity and ease of scoring and behavioral traits applicable to this study that could be reliably rated, rather than more generalized attributes requiring sophisticated interpretation. A copy was obtained of the Symptomatic Behavior Rating Scale, an adaptation of the Quay-Cutler Classification System, and this scale was found to meet most of the requirements stated above. The SBR Scale is a simple rating scale measuring behavioral traits that are relatively easy to observe and interpret. The scale consists of 66 items designed to measure such traits as deceitfulness, neurotic factors, organic-psychotic factors, immaturity-dependency, distractability, passivity, aggressive acting-out, values, and personality and conduct problems.

Originally a three-point scale, it was expanded to five points in an effort to increase validity. The range was from "no problem at all" to "so serious as to be among the worst you have ever observed." In addition, the test, while remaining essentially unchanged, was rewritten in an effort to clarify and simplify the behavioral descriptions for the benefit of less sophisticated raters.

The SBR was adopted with a definite measurement problem in mind: changes in observable behavior of subjects in the three study groups. The selection of any test for this purpose was necessarily restricted by the testing situation. Raters varied widely in interpretive skills, and it was assumed that there would be wide divergences in the amount of personal involvement on the part of different raters. However, for the sake of increased reliability, evaluations from four different raters were obtained. In this study, the evaluators were a caseworker, a house-parent, and two teachers. Since it was felt that the teachers would have far less intimate knowledge of the boys than would either caseworkers or house-parents, different statistical analyses were made on the median scores of all four raters and on those of the caseworkers and house-parents alone. The results were substantially the same.

Hypothesis

The hypothesis is that in combination niacinamide and ascorbic acid administered in doses of 3 grams each per day will create significant differences in perception and behavior between treatment, placebo, and control groups with the treatment group showing improvement in perception as measured by the HOD and improvement in observable behavior as rated on the Symptomatic Behavior Rating Scale.

REVIEW OF THE LITERATURE

Adrenochrome and Adrenolution Changes in Infrahuman and Human Subjects

The adrenochrome-adrenolution hypothesis was first presented by Hoffer and Osmond in 1952. By 1966, Hoffer and Osmond[12] were able to state that adrenaline can turn into a very toxic and changeable hormone known as adrenochrome, a substance which has been frequently produced in the laboratory. According to Hoffer and Osmond, there is substantial evidence, both direct and indirect, that adrenochrome is also produced in the body.

Operating on this assumption, Hoffer and Osmond[9] postulate that adrenochrome as produced in the body as in the test tube, can evolve into two new compounds. One of these is 5, 6-dihydroxy-N-methylindole, called dihydroxyindole, a harmless substitute. The other substance is the highly poisonous adrenolution. Large amounts of dihydroxyindole have been administered to animals and men[9] with only beneficial effects. Hoffer and Osmond feel that this compound may work against adrenolution to maintain a balance, preventing a person from becoming too tense or anxious.

The process from adrenaline to adrenochrome to dihydroxyindole or adrenolution is the foundation of the adrenochrome-adrenolutin theory of schizophrenia. As early as 1954, Hoffer and Osmond suggested that the normal pathway of these changes is from A to B to C, but in schizophrenics, for unknown reasons, the pathway is from A to B to D, thus interfering with normal chemical reactions in the brain, and instituting the process of perceptual distortions and schizophrenia.

The first human studies with adrenochrome were conducted by

Hoffer and Osmond in 1952. This reversed the usual process of preliminary animal experimentation but, as Hoffer comments, "no animals were then available, and we were."[9] In an informal, two-man study, Osmond was the chief subject. Approximately ten minutes after taking adrenochrome, he reported some of the following symptoms; changes in colors; change in color and intensity of lights; preoccupation with inanimate objects, and indifference and hostility to people; suspicion; detachment and an inability to relate distance and time. A number of additional volunteers were administered the substance and all reported similar experiences. The most striking changes were noted as personality changes, continuing in some volunteers for up to two weeks. These volunteers continued to show such uncharacteristic behavior as violent temper outbursts, delusions, suspiciousness, and other traits typical of schizophrenia. Based on this highly informal, but pioneering, study, Hoffer and Osmond concluded that in humans adrenochrome or adrenolution produces the following changes:

1. Changes in perception: these are subtle, but no less serious, when small doses are used. With 30 mg or more placed under the tongue, visual hallucinations are produced, which may be as clear and distinct as those experienced with LSD.
2. Changes in thought: these are also similar to those found in schizophrenia.
3. Changes in mood: in most cases, the subjects were depressed but sometimes they were too relaxed or too flat.

The Hoffer and Osmond studies of the effects of adrenolution and adrenochrome upon humans also were largely confirmed by a series of infrahuman studies. These studies all seemed to confirm that adrenochrome and adrenolutin are active in animals and humans. They are now generally included among the family of compounds known as hallucinogens, compounds capable of producing profound psychological changes in man.

The Malvarian Factor

Research on the adrenochrome-adrenolution theory of schizophrenia has led to the discovery of a condition known as "malvaria," which is an operational diagnostic term for patients showing a "mauve" spot in the urine.

Hoffer and Osmond[13] first isolated and demonstrated this substance in the urine of schizophrenic and psychotic patients. In a purified approach, Irvine[14] also isolated chemical substances from the urine of schizophrenic patients, and showed that they were present more frequently in psychotic patients than in nonpsychotic controls. Irvine's approach was used by Hoffer and Mahon[15] as a standard for comparison studies. They found that approximately 27 of 33 schizophrenic patients (about 80%) had these unknown substances in their urine when ill. Of 57 urine assays performed on patients when ill, 41 were positive. Only 26 of 57 urine assays on patients classified as "well" or "much improved" were positive. The possibility that this is a chance finding is less than 1 in 1,000 (chi square for 1 df = 15).

Hoffer[16] examined 26 children considered mentally retarded. Eleven of these children had the same substance in the urine as that found by Hoffer and Mahon[15] in a majority of adult schizophrenic patients. These substances did not appear in any of the six children who appeared to be physically abnormal or who had evidence of brain damage. On the basis of these studies, Hoffer felt it was reasonable to conclude that many psychiatric patients who suffer disturbances of mood, thinking, and perception also excrete abnormal chemical substances in their urine. Further, he stated that these unknown substances could be the end product of toxins which impede the working parts of the brain, perhaps those which govern stability and perception. Veech[18] also found adrenolutin-like adrenochrome in the urine of schizophrenic subjects.

O'Reilly et al.,[19] in an evaluation of the mauve factor, conducted a study based on 200 consecutive admissions to a psychiatric unit of a general hospital. Their study demonstrated that 44.5% of these patients excrete a chemical in their urine which gives rise to what is called the "mauve factor." They found that this factor cuts across diagnostic categories and is not confined to schizophrenia. They consider this contraindicative to the findings of Hoffer and Osmond, but I feel that they have misinterpreted the Hoffer and Osmond data. Hoffer and Osmond specifically state that the mauve factor did appear in other psychotics, and even in certain normals under stress conditions.

Hoffer,[20] in a study on malvaria and the law, reported on 14 court referrals guilty of various crimes. He pointed out that in court cases there is often controversy over whether a particular person had a psychiatric disease which prevented him from functioning in an appropriate manner and which then led to criminal behavior. In this study, Hoffer tested 740 subjects for malvaria. Fourteen of these subjects were charged with some criminal offense. Of these 14, who were later used in a study, 10 were malvarians, 4 were not. Hoffer concluded that malvaria produces a kind of disorder of judgment which leads to criminal behavior. However, he warned that the proportion of criminals found to be malvarian will undoubtedly be much smaller when larger groups are tested.

The significance of malvaria for the present study can be seen by examining the results of a large-scale study reported by Hoffer and Osmond.[21] Comparing 104 malvarians with subjects who did not have malvaria, drawn at random from 150 nonmalvarians, Hoffer and Osmond concluded that malvarians differ clinically from nonmalvarians. A summary of some of these conclusions follows.

Whatever the psychiatric diagnosis, patients having the mauve factor more closely resembled each other than they resembled those who did not have it. Even nonmalvarians who were schizophrenic seldom had the vivid perceptual changes of schizophrenics who also had malvaria. In general, it was found that malvarians have a much higher incidence of perceptual changes, disturbances in thought content, and distrubed thinking processes. They show much more inappropriate mood changes much more frequently, and also bizarre and unusual changes in behavior. When examined on the HOD, malvarians scored nearly twice as high as controls. They also scored higher on the Minnesota Multiphasic Personality Inventory. When examined with certain visual tests that measure constancy of perception, they showed more rigidity. The differences were large and statistically significant. Examinations of certain changes in brain wave patterns also showed malvarians had more abnormality than nonmalvarians. Hoffer and Osmond also report that ordinary psychiatric treatment produced different results in the two groups. In general, patients with malvaria (whether neurotic or psychotic) did not respond as well to treatment, remained hospitalized longer, and needed to be readmitted more often after discharge. When nicotinic acid was included in the treatment, malvarians began to recover much sooner and in larger numbers than nonmalvarians. This included all diagnostic groups, including mentally retarded, adolescent problems, anxiety neuroses, alcoholics, and schizophrenics.

The Hoffer-Osmond Diagnostic Test (HOD)

The HOD is a simple card-sort test.[22,23] In its original form, the test consists of 145 cards describing various perceptual disturbances; disturbances of thought, time, smell, taste, hearing, and touch, social relationships, and mood. The test includes four scales: perception, paranoid, depression, and a scale for thought changes, which is made up of a number of items related to reasoning.

In spite of its relative crudity, the test differentiates schizophrenia from most other psychiatric groups.[21,24,11] Hawkins[3] found "considerable agreement" between the HOD and the Organic Integrity Test (OIT) in the diagnosis of schizophrenia. In the same study, he showed that the extent of the agreement between the diagnosis on the basis of HOD given at admission and final clinical diagnosis is more than that between clinical diagnosis on admission and final clinical diagnosis. Hawkins's findings suggest that the HOD is valuable both as a diagnostic and a prognostic instrument.

The relationship between the HOD and the biochemical test for malvaria has been found to be highly significant.[25] The HOD has also been reported to show the effects produced by LSD-25 in normal subjects[9] and by trifluperidol and trifluoperazine in acute schizophrenic patients.[26]

Hoffer and Osmond[13] compared the HOD test scores of a group of 50 subjects who did not show the mauve factor with a group of 37 subjects who did. An item analysis was made for each one of the 145 cards. Of this number, 81 cards discriminated between the groups at a significant level ($P = .01$). The HOD scores of subjects who were malvarian were the same whether or not they had been classed as schizophrenic or had been given some other diagnosis. The HOD scores of nonmalvarian subjects were also the same whether or not they had been diagnosed schizophrenic. The group showing malvaria scored higher.

Hoffer and Osmond[23] report a further study on the relationship of HOD scores and urine tests. The subjects were 60 psychiatric patients, none of whom was included in the first test. The association between the results of the two tests (HOD and test for malvaria), as reported in 1961, was again found. Hoffer and Osmond stated that the results of statistical analysis and the establishment of homogeneous groups in respect to HOD scores and malvaria were virtually the same for both series. They concluded that the abnormalities encountered in both these tests were expressions of one illness.

These findings were corroborated by a number of other studies.[25,14,22] The general conclusion is that patients positive on the biochemical test for malvaria tend to obtain higher HOD scores than those who are nonmalvarian. The correlation between the tests is so high that Osmond, co-originator of both tests, feels that either may be substituted for the other with no loss of diagnostic validity (personal communications, 1970).

Nicotinamide and Ascorbic Acid as a Treatment Approach

Nicotinic acid and nicotinamide are both methyl acceptors. As such, they were first considered by Hoffer and Osmond as a possible cure for schizophrenia, assuming that their adrenochrome-adrenolutin theory was correct. Methyl groups are chemical groups, which are necessary here in converting noradrenaline into adrenaline. Since nicotinic acid is capable of absorbing such groups, it was postulated that large amounts of the vitamin would prevent the formation of excessive amounts of adrenaline and thus slow down the production of the toxic adrenochrome and adrenolutin. As noted previously, nicotinic acid already had been used with great success in the treatment of several delirious diseases, including pellagra. It had also been used for treating bromide-induced deliria, some organic brain diseases, and depressions.[1] Doses used at that time were very small as compared to the megavitamin approach of today. In attacking schizophrenia, Hoffer and Osmond decided to use more massive doses. The first case reported was a 17-year-old acute schizophrenic who was successfully treated with 5 grams of niacin and 5 grams of ascorbic acid divided into five daily doses. Hoffer and Osmond[1] suggest an apparently lasting cure in this case. The success led to continuing research and treatment with nicotinic acid and its amide, nicotinamide, in combination with ascorbic acid. Ascorbic acid is used in conjunction with nicotinic acid for several reasons. One, ascorbic acid may restore proper epinephrine metabolism by inhibiting the oxidation of epinephrine to adrenochrome.[27] It changes adrenochrome to leuco adrenochrome (dihydroxyindole), which is not psychotomimetic.[28] Also, decreased levels of ascorbic acid are probably detrimental and are not always dietetically determined. Urbach et al.,[29] using normal controls on adequate diets, found marked variations in plasma ascorbic levels. They suggest that almost any disturbance of body or mind, especially emotional stress, can alter ascorbic acid levels. Most conclusively it has been shown that schizophrenics can consume huge quantities of ascorbic acid before normal quantitites begin to be excreted in the urine.[21] The biochemical basis for this fact is admitted to be unknown, but the findings suggest that it is beneficial for them to receive large doses of this vitamin.

In 1952, Hoffer and Osmond gave large doses of niacin (from 1 to 5 grams per day) to eight schizophrenic patients at the Saskatchewan Hospital, Weyburn, Canada. All eight recovered sufficiently to be released from the hospital[30].

Denson[31] compared nicotinamide and placebo as adjuncts to the therapy of schizophrenia in a blind trial. The sample consisted of male schizophrenic patients entering the hospital and requiring ECT. The nicotinamide group, comprising 17 patients, spent a total of 1,810 days in the hospital (mean: 106.4 days per patient). Van der Waerden's X-Test, applied to the individual totals, indicated significance at the 5% level. Twenty-one weeks after admission, one patient from the treatment group of 17 and 8 patients from the placebo group of 19 remained in the hospital. For these figures, chi square was 4.51, again demonstrating significance at the 5% level. Denson concluded that nicotinamide therapy shortened the length of stay in the hospital for schizophrenic patients.

Denson's findings supported an earlier conclusion by Hoffer et al.[32] that treatment with nicotinic acid appreciably shortens the length of hospitalization for schizophrenic patients. Studying a group of 171 patients, they found that for the nicotinic acid treatment group of 73, the mean days in a mental hospital were 234, while for the comparison group (no treatment with nicotinic acid or its amide) the mean days in a mental hospital were 319. In addition, there were no suicides in the treatment group of 73, but four suicides in the nontreatment group of 98. A few conclusions from the series of previously mentioned Saskatchewan studies, summarized by Hoffer,[30] are:

1. Early cases of schizophrenia respond better than chronic cases.
2. Long treatment prevents relapse more effectively than short treatment. The ten-year cure rate is over 75% compared to the control rate of 35%. (A ten-year cure is a patient who has been free of schizophrenic symptoms and has not required hospital treatment for the schizophrenia during those ten years.) Several patients began to recover after five to seven years of continuous nicotinic acid therapy.
3. Nicotinic acid is more effective than nicotinamide for chronic schizophrenia.
4. Nicotinic acid potentiates the action of barbiturates, anticonvulsants, and tranquilizers.
5. Nicotinic acid is remarkably safe and easy to administer. In over 400 cases in Saskatchewan, there have been no cases of toxicity.

Some fairly recent work of great interest has developed in the field of alcoholism and with hallucinogenic drugs. D. R. Hawkins, of the North Nassau Mental Health Center, has been a pioneer in the field of alcoholism and B-3 (niacin) therapy. This is a large out-patient psychiatric clinic with a high percentage of alcoholics and schizophrenics.

Hawkins[3] reported the results of treatment on a series of 315 consecutive adult schizophrenic patients applying for treatment. He states that the Center began using the megavitamin approach in 1966, in order to "derive clinical experience and data to help the individual patient by using, as a base, a biochemically-oriented treatment program." About 22% of the patients were alcoholic as well as schizophrenic. Patients were put on the following medication: (a) niacin or niacinamide, with minimum daily doses of 3 grams and maximum of 12 grams; (b) ascorbic acid, 4 grams per day; (c) phenothiazine; and (d) pyridoxine, 0.2 gram per day. A majority were placed on a hypoglycemic (high protein, low sugar) diet. Hawkins found a "surprisingly high" degree of patient cooperation and acceptance. He reports that the majority of the patients improved significantly and progressively. Those in whom the illness began in adulthood showed the most dramatic response, with the grown-up childhood schizophrenics accounting for most of the treatment failures. The overall improvement rate for the 315 patients was 71%, including moderately improved, much improved, and recovered. This study has been considered at such length because it involves three apparently interactive diseases, schizophrenia, hypoglycemia, and alcoholism, which I consider a promising field for further research.

Hawkins reports that niacin or niacinamide was also given to numerous alcoholics who had not tested schizoid but were suffering depression, tension, insomnia, anxiety, and exhaustion. Hawkins has not conducted any formal study, but states that "because of our satisfactory experience with it, we are planning to continue using it indefinitely."[3]

Downing[6] suggested that "freak-outs," terrifying LSD experiences, can be counteracted by vitamin B-3. Downing, who has been experimenting with LSD for the past ten years, called B-3 the "perfect antidote." He reported that the San Francisco Health Department in cooperation with the YMCA distributed large amounts of B-3 in the city's Haight-Asbury district.

Downing's observations support those of Hoffer and Osmond[32] and Hoffer and Callbeck[32] in their extensive study of drug-induced schizophrenia. Hoffer and Osmond[21] found niacin highly effective in controlling the most severe symptoms and helping to "phase out" hallucinogenic experiences induced by both LSD-25 and adrenolutin.

They noted that the effects of these two substances were similar and that both responded to niacin and, less swiftly, to niacinamide medication.

Hoffer, in his previously mentioned study of 14 criminal cases, also used nicotinic acid, 3 grams daily, as a treatment. He reports that 8 of these made good recoveries, which he attributed to niacin therapy. One recovered without niacin, and one was a failure.

Similar Studies

One of the reasons for the present study is that there have been no truly comparable studies that have been both properly controlled and submitted to statistical analysis.

Two informal studies are of interest, one in which Hoffer and Osmond treated arrested youth in their Canadian province, who showed high HOD scores, with niacinamide and vitamin C. Hoffer and Osmond[21] reported "noticeable improved behavior" and stated that none of the youths so treated had been in trouble with the law over a follow-up period of five years. Also similar was the work of Smith, who HOD-tested a group of delinquent youth and administered B-3 therapy to the 35% showing perceptual distortion. Smith reported that those willing to try the treatment showed marked behavioral improvement. In a special publication on B-3 therapy, Smith[4] noted that a research project in depth would be undertaken to test these findings. I was unable to find any literature on the subject and contacted Smith personally. He stated that the study was being carried out but had been forced to take second place to a study concerning alcoholism. Smith (again in personal communication, 1971) stated that no data on his study of delinquent youth had been statistically analyzed and that he had no firm findings to report. It would thus appear that controlled, statistically analyzed studies of delinquent youth are at a premium, if not virtually unavailable, and that further research in this area is strongly suggested.

EXPERIMENTAL DESIGN

Subjects

The subjects used in this study were 45 male youths, aged 16 to 18 years, committed by the courts to the State Department of Welfare and Institutions and placed at Beaumont School for Boys. Subjects were randomly selected by an impartial selector from a group of approximately 100 boys with significantly high scores on the HOD, i.e., 50 or above as indicated by Hoffer and Osmond as the cutoff point for those under 21 years. The sample was limited by the fact that the study was postponed for nearly three months, and of the more than 400 boys originally tested, only about 100 would remain institutionalized long enough to complete even an abbreviated study. All subjects were required to have letters of permission from their parents or guardians allowing them to participate in the study. A reading level at or above grade 5.5 was considered necessary for proper execution of the HOD test. These latter factors further limited the population.

Initially, 60 boys were selected and assigned on a random basis, 20 to each group, Treatment, Placebo, and Control. Throughout this study, only one person held the code to the composition of groups, and this was not broken until all evaluations were complete. Fifteen subjects were lost during the course of the study, with nine leaving before termination of medication and six turning in obviously invalid final HOD tests.

Testing Procedure

All boys were group tested on the HOD. To facilitate this, permission was requested and received from Dr. Humphry Osmond, co-author of the test, to randomize the statements from the HOD cards and reproduce them in printed form. Use of the printed form permitted testing large groups simultaneously. Boys were generally tested in groups of 60, with 20 to a group and three monitors present in each group to answer questions and tally papers. One counselor explained the test to all groups, giving the following directions:

> This is a simple test to find out how you feel about things. First, read the statement on the right. See how well it describes how you feel or what is happening to you. If you think the statement describes you, check the column marked TRUE. If you do not feel it describes you, check the column marked FALSE. If you are not sure, check the column that comes closest to describing the way you feel. Please answer each question as honestly as you can. Do not skip *any* questions. Now, there are a few statements in this test that do not apply directly to you. An example is the first statement. When you come to

a statement like this, simply check whether you think it is TRUE or FALSE. Don't discuss this with your friends. If there are any statements you don't understand, raise your hand and one of us will help you. Now write your name at the top of the paper and begin.

Scoring was done by the standard manual method. All boys scoring over the cutoff of 50 on the Total Score were assigned to the list of prospective subjects.

Medication

Niacinamide and ascorbic acid combined in tablets containing 1 gram of each and identical sugar pill placeboes were especially manufactured for the study. Each boy in the Treatment group received one pill at each daily meal, totaling 3 grams per day of niacinamide and ascorbic acid each. Boys in the Placebo group received their tablets at the same time and in the same way. Tablets were administered by counselors who would have no part in evaluating the boys. The Control group received nothing.

The medication period was approximately six weeks. During this time, none of the boys received any special therapy or were allowed to deviate from their usual routine. In order to see that these precautions were carried out, as well as to secure evaluations, the study was explained in a very broad sense to the caseworkers, house-parents, project supervisors, and teachers of the boys in the groups. They were told that some of the boys would be receiving an ordinary non-prescription vitamin and were given a list of all boys in the study. Expectations were not discussed. They were told not to pay the boys any more attention than they would ordinarily, but to report immediately to the Intake Counselor any unusual behavior or special punishments or rewards. Direct medical supervision was provided by the school doctor, two registered nurses at the school infirmary, and indirectly by a consulting psychiatrist assigned to the study. The infirmary was given a master list of all boys in the study and asked to report immediately any physical symptoms or complaints to the Intake Counselor. It was also necessary to give the boys some explanation of why they were singled out to receive special medication. The Treatment and Placebo groups were told that they had been selected at random to receive an ordinary vitamin in order to see if it would make them feel better.

Evaluation Procedures

Besides the qualifying HOD test, boys were retested on the HOD at the termination of the medication period. In addition, caseworkers, house-parents, project supervisors, and teachers were asked to evaluate each boy in the group on the Symptomatic Behavior Rating Scale. They were asked to complete a scale on each boy before medication, midway through the medication period, and after termination of the medication.

It should be noted here that the laboratory test for malvaria was not performed. It was deemed impracticable from a standpoint of time and available funds and facilities. Dr. Osmond was personally contacted about this. He stated that the correlation between HOD scores and the test for malvaria were so high that the latter could safely be omitted without affecting the validity of the study.

RESULTS

Statistical analysis (Table 9-1) indicates that vitamin therapy significantly affected the HOD scores of the three groups, with the Treatment group showing significant improvement over the Placebo group at the .05 (t = 1.999) level of confidence and the Treatment group showing significant improvement over the Control group at the .01 (t = 2.617) level of confidence. There were no significant differences in the Placebo and Control groups. The hypothesis that vitamin

TABLE 9-1 Comparisons Between Adjusted Treatment Means of HOD Scores

Comparison	Mean	Adjusted mean	df	t
Treatment	67.067	61.066		
vs.			41	1.999*
Placebo	80.412	83.833		
Treatment	67.067	61.066		
vs.			41	2.617**
Control	90.538	92.990		
Placebo	80.412	83.833		
vs.			41	.77
Control	90.538	92.990		

*.05 level of significance.
**.01 level of significance.

TABLE 9-2 A Kruskal-Wallis Solution for Differences Between Behavior in Three Groups

	Sum of ranks treatment $N-15$	Sum of ranks treatment $N-17$	Sum of ranks treatment $N-13$	df	H
Before treatment	349.5	441.5	244.0	2	2.055
Midpoint treatment	272.0	439.5	323.5	2	2.955
After treatment	253.0	437.5	344.5	2	4.756

therapy would significantly improve the HOD scores of the Treatment group is confirmed.

On the Symptomatic Behavior Rating Scale (Table 9-2), statistical analysis shows no significant difference between the three groups at any rating point—initial, midpoint, or final. The hypothesis that vitamin therapy would significantly improve the observable behavior of the Treatment group as measured by the SBR Scale is rejected.

A more detailed analysis of the data will show that there was some degree of improvement in HOD scores in all groups. Also, further analysis of the data for the SBR Scale shows a definite trend towards improvement in the Treatment group with no corresponding trend in the Control group. However, there was a trend towards improvement in the Placebo group.

DISCUSSION

Before proceeding with this discussion, it is important to note that this experiment was actually designed and carried out as the pilot run for a much larger, longer, and more comprehensive study. It was originally planned to use 180 boys, with 60 subjects each in Treatment, Placebo, and Control groups. The length of the treatment period was set at three months. It was hoped that the pilot study would provide the opportunity to improve the experimental design and solve the anticipated, but then undefined, problems of conducting a large research project within the framework of a state-administered youth institution.

This proposed plan was rendered impossible through the intervention of a local psychiatrist, who expressed misgivings as to the safety of the study. To allay his concern, more than a dozen eminent physicians, biochemists, and other researchers who had safely used the treatment for many years were contacted. A full report of their findings was made to the psychiatrist in question. He was advised that if he had no further objections the study would proceed. After a considerable delay, costing a number of prospective subjects, the pilot study was begun. This study was not quite complete when the consulting psychiatrist to the study was asked to appear before the Ethics Committee of the Virginia Medical Association. The request was met. The Committee reported that they could not approve of the study unless laboratory tests for liver functioning were performed periodically on all boys in the study. It was pointed out that liver function tests were not valid (Boyle, personal communication, 1970) with subjects in niacinamide treatment, and that no cases of liver damage had ever been reported from any of the many thousands of patients receiving this treatment. The Committee insisted that the conditions be met. Since there were neither facilities nor funds for liver function tests, and since several months and many subjects had already been lost because of the described proceedings, the initial proposed plan was temporarily abandoned and results were assessed from the pilot study.

The overall results would seem to support the many confirmatory findings on the effect of nicotinic acid and niacinamide as a treatment approach to perceptual disorders. The significant differences in improvement in the HOD scores of the Treatment group, and the lack of any significant difference in the Placebo and Control groups, can only suggest that niacinamide therapy does indeed improve perception, as it is measured on the HOD.

For the purpose of this study, it might be well to ask what, precisely, is perceptual distortion, and how does it effect asocial behavior in youth? Since the nature of man's "experiential" world, particularly that of the adolescent, is the subject of so much speculation and so many conflicting theories, any answer to this question would have to be presented within a theoretical framework. The best psychological-physiological models would seem to be reports of recovered schizophrenic or other hallucinatory patients,[9] the reports of researchers having undergone self-induced drug psychoses,[1] and the reports of those who have used hallucinogenic drugs.[6] All of these groups report striking changes in one or more of the following areas: the ability to evaluate time and distance; the ability to maintain a stable mood; vision, taste, touch, and smell; irrational anxiety; and indifference or hostility to others. Perceptual distortion, then, can be defined as any significant deviation from the norm in sensory and time perception, usually accompanied by mood and personality disturbance.

Thus, a youth with perceptual distortion could be said to live in a different world. Since he perceives the world differently, he reacts differently. He perceives, judges, and evaluates according to his "own" world, and thus behaves in a manner that most often differs significantly from that of so-called normals. The possibilities for difficulty in his relationships with his family, the law, and society become obvious.

As reported in this study, the success of megavitamin therapy in alleviating perceptual distortion does not, of course, offer any confirmation for any particular biochemical theory concerning the source. It does, however, tend to confirm that there is, at least in part, a biochemical basis for such a condition.

It can be noted in Table 9-3 that there was some improvement in the HOD scores of the majority of boys within each group. This improvement might be assumed to be a function of time. Most boys are HOD-tested soon after they arrive, at which time they are generally new to the institution and often apprehensive, depressed, and confused. The majority apparently make some adjustment within the first few weeks of institutionalization. This study should provide meaningful data and perhaps open new avenues for research that will eventually prove useful to juvenile institutions such as Beaumont.

The fact that there were no significant differences in the statistical tests for the Symptomatic Behavior Rating Scale should be considered in more detail. This scale was frankly a makeshift affair, originally intended for use by teachers and adopted to our needs for efforts to increase reliability, as described earlier. However, the instrument could not really be considered reliable despite these efforts. It suffered from all the well-documented drawbacks of rating scales in general, as well as the peculiar difficulties encountered in obtaining this type of information from a large, heterogenous group of untrained and uninvolved raters. In this case, almost all the raters had difficulty with the

TABLE 9-3   A Comparison of Average HOD Scores Before and After Megavitamin Therapy

Groups	Before treatment	After treatment	Points improved
Treatment	100.4	67.7	32.4
Placebo	95.2	80.6	14.6
Control	90.5	82.8	7.7

imprecision of behavioral definitions. Many were suspicious of the project itself; some appeared to feel threatened by the task, and others to resent the time and paperwork involved. As a result, the forms were often carelessly and/or incompletely filled in or simply not turned in at all. Differing treatment philosophies and individual rater bias toward certain subjects became increasingly noticeable. In short, we simply found no way to obtain any accurate data from the SBR Scale, and the study would have been scientifically more sound if it had been omitted completely. However, since it was included and despite its lack of reliability, it did show some interesting trends; these will be discussed further. As noted in the report on results there were definite trends in these tests in the direction of statistically significant differences in the three rating stages.

In the first series of tests, analysis was made on the basis of four raters per subject, i.e., caseworker, house-parent, and two teachers. If we examine Table 9-4, we find a midpoint improvement in the Treatment group of 10.35; a worsening in the Placebo group of 2.49; and a worsening in the Control group of 4.26. Between midpoint and final ratings, the Treatment group rose slightly, by .5; Placebo improved by 4.18; and Control continued to become worse, with a rise of 3.37. Ignoring the midpoint ratings, and considering the treatment period as a whole, the Treatment group shows a test score improvement of 9.85 points, Placebo improved by 1.69 points, and Control became worse by 7.63 points.

Much the same trend can be found in the second series of tests, based on two raters, caseworker and house-parent (Table 9-5). There is steady improvement in the scores of the Treatment group, while

TABLE 9-4 Average Median Scores of Three Ratings* on the Symptomatic Behavior Rating Scale**

Groups	Rating I	Rating II	Diff.	Rating III	Diff.	Total treatment diff.
Treatment	27.65	17.30	−10.35	17.80	+.5	−9.85
Placebo	33.14	35.63	+2.49	31.45	−4.18	−1.69
Control	28.05	32.31	+4.26	35.68	+3.37	+7.63

*Based on four raters.
**Decreases in scores indicate improvement.

TABLE 9-5 Average Median Scores on Three Ratings* on
the Symptomatic Behavior Rating Scale**

Groups	Rating I	Rating II	Diff.	Rating III	Diff.	Total treatment diff.
Treatment	40.43	26.50	−13.93	23.47	−3.03	−16.96
Placebo	47.32	42.08	−5.24	43.77	+1.69	−3.55
Control	31.19	37.19	+6.00	41.15	+3.69	+9.96

*Based on two raters.
**Decreases in scores indicate improvement.

Placebo shows slight improvement, and Control becomes worse. An analysis of the raw scores of the Behavior Rating Scale yields much the same results.

The evaluations of house-parents and caseworkers for each boy were compared; a summary of the raw score differences is given in Table 9-6. Again, the trend clearly shows the Treatment group with a steady improvement, with Placebo improving less sharply, and Control continuing to worsen.

Despite the lack of statistical significance, the picture is that of one group of boys, randomly selected from their fellow students and treated with vitamins B-3 and C, showing marked improvement in observed behavior, while in two similar but untreated groups Placebo showed minor improvement, and Control a continuing tendency to less acceptable behavior. The improvement in Placebo, particularly marked in the analysis of raw scores, might be attributed to the psychological effects of extra attention and to suggestibility, a commodity relatively rare in institutional life.

The fact that statistical significance was not obtained in this in-

TABLE 9-6 Average Raw Scores of Three Ratings in SBR*

Groups	Rating I	Rating II	Diff.	Rating III	Total diff.
Treatment	40.43	26.80	−13.6	20.8	−19.60
Placebo	47.32	42.08	−5.2	34.9	−12.38
Control	31.19	37.19	+6.0	39.2	+8.0

*Based on two raters.
Note: Decrease indicates improvement.

stance, despite the strong trend towards improvement on the part of the Treatment group, could be attributed to a number of factors cited earlier. Another assumption would be that the number of subjects was too small and the length of medication too short. A larger group of subjects, plus a longer term of treatment would at least provide more time for treatment effects to be translated into observable behavioral changes. Obviously, a much more reliable rating system would also be required.

Ideally, the study should have included testing for malvaria, as described earlier, which would at least provide a purely physiological correlate to the HOD, and would be more in line with earlier research. Also, since this paper hypothesizes that perceptual dysfunction may be the basis for the thinking and affect disorder found in schizophrenia, a well-designed study should include testing for such dysfunctions.

Also, Dr. David Hawkins (personal communication) reports that of some 1,400 juvenile delinquents studied, approximately 60% suffered from hypoglycemia, or low blood sugar. Dr. Hawkins reports success in treating these youth with a combination of niacin and a high protein diet. This suggests that the six-hour glucose tolerance test for hypoglycemia also would be useful in a study of this type.

As pointed out earlier, experimentally controlled and statistically analyzed studies of the effects of megavitamin treatment on institutionalized juveniles are not readily available, if they are available at all. In the course of this study, none were found in the literature; neither was there any reference to any study of this type. Therefore, despite its many shortcomings, the results of this pilot study may have a small contribution to make in an area of biochemical research that seems to have been relatively neglected.

While the results of this study are far from conclusive, they strongly suggest that further research in this area is well warranted. In particular, they confirm the hypothesis that at least some juvenile delinquents suffer from perceptual distortion as measured by the HOD, and that this condition apparently responds to megavitamin therapy. There are also corresponding trends towards improvement in observable behavior, which suggest that some forms of behavior may correlate with perceptual distortion. While not statistically significant, they are evident enough to interest the researcher who is receptive to the challenge of the possible answer.

References

1. Hoffer, A., and Osmond, H., Some psychological consequences of perceptual disorder and schizophrenia, *Int. J. Neuropsychiat.* 2:1–19, 1966.
2. Elvehjem, C. A., Madden, R. J., Strong, S. M., and Wooley, D. W., *J. Am. Chem. Soc.* 59:1767, 1937.
3. Hawkins, D. R., Treatment of Schizophrenia based on the medical model, *J. Schizophrenia* 2:3–9, 1968.
4. Smith, R., Vitamin B-3 therapy, ed. by Bill W., Oyster Bay, N. Y., 1968.
5. Cott, A. A., Treatment of chronic ambulant schizophrenics with vitamin B-3 and relative hypoglycemic diets, Brunswick Hospital Center Conference on Concepts and Treatment of Schizophrenia, January 21–22, 1967.
6. Downing, J., *San Jose Mercury*, San Jose, California, April 22, 1967.
7. Ward, J. L., Treatment of neurotics and schizophrenics using clinical and HOD criteria, *J. Schizophrenia*, 13:140–149, 1966.
8. Kelm, H., Reliability of the Hoffer-Osmond Diagnostic Test, *J. Clin. Psychol.* 23:380–382, 1967.
9. Hoffer, A., and Osmond, H., The Kovish story. *J. Ment. Sci.* 104:302–325, 1958.
10. El-Meligi, A. M., The HOD test: A review, from the HOD and the EWI—A new concept in psychological testing. *J. Schizophrenia*, in press.
11. Kelm, H., Hoffer, A., and Hall, R. W., Reliability of the Hoffer-Osmond Diagnostic Test, *J. Clin. Psychol.* 22:120–122, 1966.
12. Hoffer, A., and Osmond, H., A perceptual hypothesis of schizophrenia, *Psychiatry Digest* 28:47–53, 1967.
13. Hoffer, A., and Osmond, H., *The Chemical Basis of Clinical Psychiatry*, Charles C. Thomas, Springfield, Ill., 1960.
14. Irvine, D. G., Mauve factor and 6-sulfactoxy skatole: Two biochemical abnormalities associated with specific measures of psychiatric disease, *J. Clin. Chem.* 9:444, 1963.
15. Hoffer, A., and Mahon, M., The presence of unidentified substances in the urine of psychiatric patients, *J. Neuropsychiat.* 2:331–362, 1961.
16. Hoffer, A., Treatment of organic psychosis with nicotinic acid, *Dis. Nerv. Syst.* 26:358–360, 1965.
17. Hoffer, A., The effect of nicotinic acid on the frequency and duration of rehospitalization of schizophrenic patients: A controlled comparison study, *Int. J. Neuropsychiat.* 2:234–240, 1966.
18. Veech, R. L., *Arch. Gen. Psychiat.* 5:127, 1961.
19. O'Reilly, P. O., Hughes, G., Russell S., and Ernest, M., The mauve factor: An evaluation, *Dis. Nerv. Syst.* 26:562–588, 1965.
20. Hoffer, A., Malvaria and the law, *Psychosomatics* 7:303–310, 1966.
21. Hoffer, A., and Osmond, H., Treatment of schizophrenia with nicotinic acid (a ten year follow-up), *Acta Psychiat. Scand.* 40:171–189, 1964.
22. Kelm, H., Hoffer, A., and Osmond, H., *Hoffer-Osmond Diagnostic Test Manual*, Saskatoon, Sask.: Modern Press, 1967.
23. Hoffer, A., and Osmond, H., A card sorting test helpful in making psychiatric diagnosis, *J. Neuropsychiat.* 1:306–330, 1961.

24. Hoffer, A., and Osmond, H., Some schizophrenic recoveries, *Dis. Nerv. Syst.* 23:204–210, 1962.
25. Hoffer, A., Malvaria, schizophrenia and the HOD test, *Int. J. Neuropsychiat.* 2: 175–178, 1966.
26. Sugarman, A. A., and Williams, B. H., Trifluperidol and trifluoperazine in acute schizophrenic patients, *J. New Drugs* 5:318–326, 1965.
27. Angel, C., Leach, B. E., Martens, S., Cohen, M., and Heath, R. G., Serum oxidation tests in schizophrenic and normal subjects, *A.M.A. Arch. Neurol. Psychiat.* 78:500–504, 1957.
28. Melander, B., and Martens, S., The mode of action of taraxein and LSD. *Dis. Nerv. Syst.* 19:478, 1958.
29. Urbach, C., Hickman, K., and Harris, P. L., Effect of individual vitamins, A, C, E and carotine administered at high levels on their concentration in the blood, *Exp. Med. Surg.* 10:7–20, 1952.
30. Hoffer, A., A comparison of psychiatric inpatients and outpatients and malvaria, *Int. J. Neuropsychiat.* 1:430–432, 1965.
31. Denson, R., Nicotinamide in treatment of schizophrenia, *Dis. Nerv. Syst.* 23: 167–172, 1962.
32. Hoffer, A., Osmond, H., Callbeck, M., and Kahan, I., Treatment of schizophrenia with nicotinic acid and nicotinamide, *J. Clin. Exp. Psychopathol.* 18:131, 1957.

Section III
ECOLOGIC-BIOCHEMICAL APPROACHES TO DIAGNOSIS AND TREATMENT

INTRODUCTION

As earlier indicated, the orthomolecular approach to "antisocial" forms of behavior is of quite recent origin. Nevertheless, a considerable array of diagnostic tools has been developed for those who would like to become involved with this approach to the problem. Also, a highly effective group of treatment methods has been devised. The authors in this section review the specifics of many of these various tools and techniques.

In the first paper, Drs. Bonnet and Pfeiffer give an extensive overview of the application of a number of important diagnostic categories and techniques used in the orthomolecular approach. A number of these techniques have been developed as a result of their clinical and research work at the New Jersey Neuro-Psychiatric Institute and at the Brain Bio Center.

Then, Dr. Cott reviews from his extensive experience with children who have learning and behavioral disorders some of the more effective treatment methods he has used. He stresses the importance of megavitamin therapy and dietary control with these children, and the need to consider the possible role of trace mineral deficiencies and toxic metals in their treatment.

Dr. Wunderlich, in the next paper, focuses on the role of neuroallergies as a contributing factor in the development of antisocial forms of behavior. He explains the many diagnostic signs that he has observed in his extensive practice with these children, and he outlines his approach to treatment—with illustrative case histories—for which he has become nationally recognized. Dr. Wunderlich stresses that neuroallergy as a contributing factor to learning disorders, school failure, and delinquency should be more widely recognized and treated.

Next, Turkel and Nusbaum discuss the problem of the slow learner. Not only is mental retardation a serious problem among the general population, but it is an extensive problem among delinquent and criminal institutional populations. The authors suggest that the mildly retarded adolescent or adult (IQ 60–85) is more likely to be led into antisocial acts than are persons of higher intelligence. Further, few antisocial persons who enter the criminal justice system have progressed near to their level of academic potential, probably because of their untreated physical and psychosocial liabilities. Thus, correctional institutional staff face many special problems and challenges in managing and treating these groups. Most institutions, unfortunately, do not have trained staff for dealing with these persons. Even among trained staff, there has been a lag in knowledge development and use among the mentally retarded. Turkel and Nusbaum introduce orthomolecular approaches to the treatment of a wide range of mentally retarded persons. But they stress, more particularly, the need for treatment of the mildly retarded, since these persons are more apt to be part of institutionalized delinquent and criminal groups and because the probability of success with this group is good. The suggested megavitamin and dietary treatment of these persons certainly would be an important supplement to any other institutional programs now in use.

Dr. Green then speaks to the problem of the treatment of penitentiary inmates, many of whom might be considered incorrigible or untreatable. His discovery that many of these inmates are suffering from subclinical pellagra, or some related nutritional deficiency or dependency, has been voiced by other psychiatrists consulting in similar institutional settings. Because of the ascendency of current psychiatric nomenclature, however, many of these prisoners are classified as psychopaths (or sociopaths). And psychopaths, using classical psychiatric methods, largely are not responsive. With the subclinical diagnostic label, however, and with use of appropriate megavitamin and dietary treatment, behavioral improvement often can be accomplished. Dr. Green, however, suggests that we not wait for treatment until the criminal reaches the penitentiary stage, but that children before the age of 10 be diagnosed and treated as a means of preventing the development of criminal careers!

In the final paper of this section, Dr. Smith discusses procedures of diagnosis and treatment of alcoholism. He says that alcoholism is a great masquerader because no one sees it as a disease. Orthomolecular medicine, on the contrary, identifies alcoholism as a vitamin-mineral deficiency disease, which typically also is complicated by a pattern of poor general nutrition. The treatment approach thus utilizes megavitamin and nutritional therapy, supplemented by supportive psychosocial programs to assist the alcoholic to deal with problems that arise secondary to his alcoholism disease. This new approach to this widespread societal problem—also a large contributor to the crime problem—offers new hope to those who today are largely unsuccessful in dealing with the problem of alcoholism.

Chapter 10 | Biochemical Diagnosis for Delinquent Behavior

Philip L. Bonnet, M.D., Psychiatrist
Carl C. Pfeiffer, Ph.D., M.D., Director
Brain Bio Center
Princeton, New Jersey

INTRODUCTION

It has been popular to blame delinquent behavior on socioeconomic factors, which contribute to the decompensation of the family structure. It is now known that various biochemical disorders (hypoglycemia, food allergies, heavy metal poisoning, and so on) may be the underlying cause. This chapter is a guide to various diagnostic methods to evaluate and treat such disorders.

INITIAL PROCEDURES

A careful case history is essential for diagnosis. Significant areas include behavioral problems, school problems, physical illnesses, psychiatric symptoms, diet, allergies, drug and alcohol use, and family history. A patient demonstrating delinquent or aberrant behavior usually has disrupted his or her family or school enough to cause referral. Tactful questioning should be used to gain a specific description of this disruptive behavior—is it characterized by temper tantrums, abusive language, suicide attempts, physical violence, irritability, or provocation? Does it occur at home, at school, or in social situations? Is it associated with any mental or physical symptoms or eating patterns? Ask the patient about school problems—does she or he have trouble concentrating, reading, understanding? Does the patient have trouble sitting still or completing assignments? Different views of problem behavior may be revealing; behavior a parent describes as rebellious might be viewed by the patient as a reaction to feelings of fear, loss of control, irritability, or physical discomfort. A patient who is disturbed by his own actions may be more willing to discuss them in detail. Behavioral and school problems are significant to the degree that they interfere with normal growth and development.

Physical illnesses and chronic conditions may affect delinquent behavior. A patient who has been unusually vulnerable to childhood sicknesses, colds, or recurrent infections may have biochemical imbalances. Delinquent behavior may be a continuation of childhood hyperactivity. A history of injury causing accidents may indicate poor muscular coordination, high impulsivity, low self-image, or a neurological condition like epilepsy. Injuries and illness aggravate social and personal problems.

A detailed account of eating habits is important. The interviewer might begin by asking the patient what he ate yesterday, then proceed to a discussion of favorite foods. Inquire further about special or highly restricted diets; few daily meals; excessive use of coffee, coke, or tea; food cravings; food binges; indifference to or preoccupation with food. With obviously anorectic patients, ask about forced vomiting and laxative use. Heavy consumption of soda, cake, candy, and high carbohydrate snack foods may indicate hypoglycemia, while food cravings suggest hidden food allergies. Americans seem to feel more guilty about diet than about sex, so try to distinguish between self-blame and fact. Someone who drives two miles at midnight for a half-gallon of ice cream probably has a food craving, while someone who nibbles leftovers does not. Food allergies may cause dizziness, weakness, irritability, rage, or depression after certain foods are eaten. Dietary information provides a basis for testing, as blood tests for trace metals may pinpoint nutritional deficiencies, while provocative food testing may reveal food allergies.

While asking about known allergies, inquire about severe side effects of prescription drugs. Use these questions to lead to inquiries about drug use and drinking, which are often implicated in delinquent behavior. Ask the patient which street drugs (pot, cocaine, LSD, STP, heroin, hashish, amphetamines, downers, and so forth) he or she has used. Ask about frequency, doses, and reactions. Adolescents may use drugs and alcohol to relieve severe anxiety, mind racing, disordered thoughts, depression, or hallucinations. If the patient says he feels wonderful on drugs, ask how he feels when off them. If he reports frighteningly bad trips, get the details. Determine if the drug reaction intensifies his usual feelings or is completely different from them. Besides flashbacks and frank psychosis, prolonged drug use, especially amphetamine use, sometimes causes nutritional deficiencies, hypoglycemia, and/or personality changes. Heavy or steady drinking has a similar effect. Either alcoholism or poor tolerance for alcohol may indicate hypoglycemia. Drugs and alcohol intensify the delinquent's other problems; the younger he is, the more destructive their effects are.

Inquire about mental or physical illnesses in the patient's family. Mental disorders that indicate biochemical disturbances include schizophrenia, depression, manic-depression, and postpartum psychosis. Try to get as specific information as possible; recollection of an uncle who was "odd" or had a "nervous breakdown" is not helpful. Physical illnesses with metabolic bases include thyroid problems, diabetes, allergies, and high blood pressure.

After asking more routine questions, ask about psychiatric symptoms. Adolescents tend to be more willing to admit to them if they are explained as disperceptions that can be experienced by anyone under conditions of stress, fatigue, illness, drugs, or allergies. Does the patient feel anxious or depressed? Does he have thought disorder, phobias, compulsions, rituals, or mind racing? How are his memory and concentration? Is he paranoid or suspicious? How does he react to the interview? Determine how intense and disabling the symptoms are. Inquire about psychiatric hospitalizations, especially the presenting symptoms, length of stay, drug or shock therapy.

A thorough case history should include queries about conditions or incidents in the patient's life that may be contributing to his behavior. Stress is hard on everyone; to a teen-ager who cannot see a way out of a bad situation, it may be intolerable. A useful case history is a detailed account of the patient's life, habits, symptoms, and illnesses, which provides clues for further psychological and biochemical tests.

GENERAL STUDIES

Anyone whose behavior is sufficiently dysfunctional to warrant the term delinquent clearly deserves the benefit of a routine medical evaluation, which would include a history and physical and standard laboratory determinations. The standard laboratory determinations should include analysis of urine for sugar, protein, ketone bodies, and kryptopyrrole, a complete blood count, and a blood chemistry profile, which should include tests for zinc, copper, lead, histamine, and spermine, as well as the standard determinations.

Urine is an easily obtained sample from which much information can be gleaned. Any abnormal color or cloudiness may indicate the presence of significant disease. Urine that turns the color of burgundy wine on standing indicates the presence of porphyria, a biochemical abnormality responsible for madness in the good King George III. More commonly, sugar or ketone bodies indicate the presence of uncontrolled diabetes, which unfortunately even now is confused with drunkenness because the sufferer has confusion together with the sweetish-aldehyde odor to the breath that is frequently mistaken for alcohol. Much publicity has been given to situations in which diabetics have been arrested for drunken and disorderly behavior or drunken driving and confined to jail rather than given vital medical treatment. Protein in the urine may be a sign of serious kidney pathology, but more frequently it is indicative of food allergy or vitamin B-6 deficiency. With commercially available dipsticks, nonmedical personnel at negligible cost can obtain all this information in less than a minute.

A complete blood count yields a wealth of information, also, at nominal expense. The total number of white cells is normally between 4.8 and 8.10 thousand, with elevation of the white cells indicative of infection. An abnormally low number of white cells is frequently found in the food-allergic patient. Hemoglobin is normally between 12 and 16 grams in females and between 14 and 18 grams in males. Abnormally low levels of hemoglobin (anemia) may indicate any of a variety of nutritional deficiency states: B-6 deficiency, folic acid deficiency, zinc deficiency, iron deficiency, or a specific toxic reaction such as lead poisoning. An elevation in the hemoglobin (polycythemia) may indicate carbon monoxide poisoning. Chronic carbon monoxide poisoning is notorious for causing behavioral abnormalities including delinquent behavior. A differential count, in which one makes a smear of the blood and stains the white cells to determine the percentage of the various types of white cells, can also shed light on the biochemical status of a person being evaluated. An elevation in the eosinophils, for example, may indicate presence of allergies, deficiency of vitamin B-6, or the presence of intestinal parasites. The absolute basophil count is a simple and relatively practical method of determining blood histamine (see below).

With the advent of automated laboratory equipment, the blood chemical profile has become inexpensive; tests that previously, with the determinations done individually by hand, would have cost hundreds of dollars now are available from commercial labs for $5–10. The standard screening studies, the normal values, and significance of abnormalities are summarized in the Table 10-1.

TABLE 10-1   Standard Screening Studies

Low	High
COPPER 80–120 mcg%	
Wilson's disease	Birth control pill, estrogens
Total parenteral feeding	Depression, arthritis,
Premature infants	migraine, pregnancy
	Hypertension
ZINC 90–120 mcg%	
Pyroluria	B-6 deficiency
Malnutrition, burns	Starvation
Puberty, acne	
Psoriasis	
IRON 50–130 mcg%	
Anemia, uremia	Depression
Hemorrhage	Siderosis
Rheumatoid arthritis	Hemachromatosis
Pregnancy	Thalassemia
CALCIUM 8.4–10.8 mg%	
Hypoparathyroid	Hyperparathyroid
Pancreatitis	Hyperthyroid
Vitamin D deficiency	Excess vitamin D
Low albumen	Thiazides, tumors
INOR. PHOS. 2.5–4.8 mg%	
Rickets	
Hyperparathyroid	Hypoparathyroid
Hypokalemia	Hemolysis
Cirrhosis	Diabetic acidosis

TABLE 10-1 (*Continued*)

Low	High
	GLUCOSE
	75–125 mg%
Hypoglycemia	Diabetes mellitus
Insulin	Thiazides
Addison's disease	Birth control pill
Myxedema	Liver damage
	BLOOD UREA NITROGEN
	6–24 mg%
Liver failure	Dehydration
Pregnancy	Renal disease
Starvation	Hypertension
	URIC ACID
	2.5–8.0 mg%
Allopurinol	Gout, thiazides
Benemide	Steroids, leukemia
Cortisone	Psoriasis, polycythemia
Wilson's disease	Pernicious anemia, hypothyroid
	CHOLESTEROL
	150–280 mg%
Hyperthyroid	Hypothyroid
Infection	Diabetes, pancreatitis
Inanition	Pregnancy
	TOTAL PROTEIN
	5.7–8.0 gm%
Nephrosis	Dehydration myeloma
Burns	Collagen disease
Inanition, dermatitis	Hepatic disease
	ALBUMEN
	3.5–5.3 gm%
Overhydration	Dehydration
Malnutrition	
Nephrosis	
	TOTAL BILIRUBIN
	0.2–1.2 mg%
	Liver disease, hemolysis
	ALK. PHOSPHATASE
	15–240 mu/ml
Hypophosphatasia	Bone growth
Pernicious anemia	Hyperparathyroidism
Hypothyroidism	Pregnancy

TABLE 10-1 (*Continued*)

Low	High
	LACTIC DEHYDROGENASE
	50–225 mu/ml
Clofibrate therapy	Heart disease
	Hemol. anemia
	Nicotinic acid
	Sprue, hemolysis
	SGOT
	10–50 mu/ml
	Heart or liver disease
	Pancreatitis
	Hemolytic anemia
	Anticoagulants
	SGPT
	6–50 mu/ml
	Heart or liver disease
	Pancreatitis
	TRIGLYCERIDES
	30–150 mg%
Starvation	Recent meal, type IV
	SODIUM
	135–145 meq/liter
Diuretics (may be abused by drug-dependent people trying to control it)	Starvation
	POTASSIUM
	3.5–5.5 meq/liter
Diuretics	Potassium poisoning
Dietary: no vegetables, fruits	
	CHLORIDE
	96–107 meq/liter
Diuretics	Dehydration
Heat stroke	
	CO_2
	24–30 meq/liter
Hyperventilation	Alkalosis

TRACE METALS

All trace metals are usually measured by spectral analysis. There is some controversy about whether trace metals should be determined in the hair, blood, urine, nails, skin, or other tissue. Brain tissue would be most interesting when behavior is the phenomenon under study, but this is seldom a possibility. Urine and feces yield very useful data when one is studying trace metals. Hair has the obvious advantage of being an easy tissue to sample. Hair can be linked to previous points in time—the newest hair is closest to the scalp. Hair can be analyzed segmentally to establish temporal pointers. One patient we studied at the Brain Bio Center had a history of two psychotic episodes resulting in hospitalization separated by three years of apparent normalcy. When her hair was traced back to the time of the psychotic episodes, there was a marked increase in the copper content of the hair. There are two main disadvantages of hair analysis. Hair is quite prone to environmental conditions; shampoos, hair conditioners, dyes, bleaches, and process solutions all affect the analysis. Even exposure to automobile exhaust may alter the lead content of hair. The second disadvantage of hair is that it is several steps removed from the area of greatest interest, the brain, and the results are often difficult to interpret. Blood is only one step removed, and the results reflect the situation at a given point in time. There are some known temporal variations of the trace metals in blood; zinc diminishes from morning to evening, while copper increases during the latter half of the menstrual cycle.

Lead is a toxic heavy metal; lead poisoning can produce a variety of psychological symptoms that mimic hyperactivity and schizophrenia. Lead is a pollutant in the human body, although blood lead levels up to 20 ppm are considered normal in adults; in children, the lead blood level should not exceed the child's age. Sources of lead contamination include gasoline, paint, newsprint, water pipes, and industrial exhaust. Although recently lead in paints has been reduced or eliminated, children may become poisoned by eating paint chips from old buildings. Leaded gasolines are the widest source of lead pollution; since the introduction of tetraethyl lead in 1924, the lead content of the Arctic ice cap has risen annually, indicating that the entire Northern hemisphere has been polluted by lead. Children in urban areas are especially vulnerable to lead poisoning because the lead in automobile exhaust settles near the ground. Food grown near heavily traveled roads may contain dangerous quantities of lead.

Lead can be measured directly in blood and urine by atomic absorption spectrophotometry. Recently, Dr. A. A. Lamola and his colleagues at the Bell Laboratories in New Jersey have devised a simple inexpensive diagnostic screening test for lead poisoning. Zinc protoporphyrin, a fluorescent compound, accumulates in the red blood cells of people with lead poisoning as a result of lead interference with heme (red blood pigment) synthesis. The researchers at Bell Laboratories have designed a fluorometer to measure the zinc protoporphyrin accurately, thereby monitoring the blood lead levels.

HISTAMINE STUDIES

Measuring histamine is a difficult laboratory procedure requiring column chromatography, which must be performed by highly trained chemists or laboratory technicians. A technician can do only a few histamine determinations in a working day, thus the test is quite expensive. The absolute basophil count, on the other hand, is a relatively simple test, which is performed by placing a blood sample in a given volume of staining solution, then counting the stained basophils. Since the introduction of larger and more accurate counting chambers, the correlation between absolute basophil count and histamine level is close enough to be clinically useful.

Histamine is thought to be a neurotransmitter of the hippocampus, the part of the brain in which personality resides, activating an inhibitory system. Deficiency of histamine is associated with an overstimulated brain, causing a hyperideational paranoid state in which the person has an exaggerated sense of danger. Conversely, an excessive amount of histamine leads to blank mind depressions. The quantitative electroencephalogram (EEG) reflects an overaroused brain in both high and low histamine states, but the high-histamine person will have neither thoughts nor mental pictures.

Spermidine is a polyamine that increases with rapid cell division. It is elevated in conditions in which cells are dividing rapidly, such as ulcerative colitis, regenerating liver, leukemia, and cancer, and is known to be low in vitamin B-6 deficiency and malnutrition. Barbara D'Asaro reported in the Morristown jail study that a low spermidine level may be correlated with crimes of violence. We reexamined our schiozophrenic population and did not find a correlation between low spermidine and violent behavior. Spermidine clearly warrants further investigation in a nonschizoprenic population.

Spermine is a diagnostically useful polyamine, whose normal range is 1.10–2.00 ug/ml. It is usually slightly higher in males (average 1.5) than in females (average 1.3). Spermine is the polyamine that bridges RNA molecules in the brain where recent memory is stored, and is correlated with recent memory storage and retrieval. Dr. Pfeiffer has called it the closest thing to a chemical IQ test. Levels of spermine are very low (often around 0.5) in cases of senility. Generally a spermine level below 1.0 suggests hypoglycemia. This test has an obvious advantage over the GTT in that it uses a single sample of blood and does not require the consumption of large quantities of sugar. Deficiency of vitamin B-6, as well as deficiency of zinc and manganese, is associated with low spermine. While addition of B-6, zinc, and manganese will raise spermine levels in cases where they are deficient, they will not raise spermine in cases of hypoglycemia or senility. An increase of spermine is associated with a favorable prognosis in these conditions.

The routine clinical EEG is generally not a useful tool in evaluating a person with deviant behavior. Most seizure discords are not associated with aberrant behavior. The exception, of course, is temporal lobe epilepsy, in which abnormal firing of neurons in the temporal lobe of the brain can cause violent, destructive, and irrational behavior. The majority of temporal lobe epileptics will have normal EEGs. Special nasopharyngeal or sphenoidal electrodes increase the chances of finding an abnormality, although the diagnosis depends mainly on a good history and careful evaluation of the signs and symptoms.

The quantitative EEG, which mesures both the mean electrical activity of the brain and variability of that electrical activity, is presently a research tool. Since the quantitative EEG gives an objective measure of the arousal level of the brain, it may enjoy a wider clinical application.

PSYCHOLOGICAL TESTING

One psychological test, the Experiential World Inventory test, devised by A. Moneim El-Meligi and Humphry Osmond, is a useful method of determining sensory disperceptions, as well as affective, ideational, and volitional disturbances. It is designed to describe the experience of disturbed adolescents and adults. The patient who takes the EWI reveals how he experiences himself and the world by answering true or false to a series of statements. The EWI consists of 400 statements divided into two parts, describing perception of senses, time, body, self, and others. It also includes descriptions of abnormal ideation, depression, and impulsivity. For each part of the test, a normal score would be 2 to 3 on each scale.

Sensory disperception, Scale 1, includes visual, auditory, olfactory, taste, muscular, tactile, balance, pain, and space orientation, measuring a range from mild changes to gross distortions. It also measures sensory overloading, increased or decreased sensory acuity, overall perceptual disorganization, loss of perceptual constancy, and synthesthesia. Scale 1, in effect, measures the patient's perception of the physical world. Time perception, Scale 2, described perceptions of subjective time, including fluctuations of personal time, dissonance between one's lived time and social time, temporal discontinuity, time orientation, and experimental age. Body perception, Scale 3, covers emotions about one's body, hypochondriacal complaints, and disperceptions about one's body in relation to the world. Self perception, Scale 4, includes expressions of self-esteem and identity problems. Perception of others, Scale 5, describes the social groups, social roles, cultural institutions, animals, and inanimate objects that are imbued with personal and cultural meanings. Types of deviant perception include dehumanization of people, attribution of unusual powers to people, and anthropomorphic views of animals. The scale also indicates suspicion, paranoia, and ideas of reference about people. Feelings of change about people, for example, "People smile strangely at me," are described; they emphasize meanings that the patient ascribes to other people. The whole scale samples a wide spectrum of emotions about others. Ideation, Scale 6, focuses on disturbed thinking, including defective thinking processes, thought disintegration, intellectual omnipotence, and bizarre ideas. Scale 6 also measures experienced change in rate of thinking, thought habits, ideology, or intellectual preoccupations. Scale 7, depression, measures somatic, emotional, and intellectual levels of dysphoria, as well as death wishes and self-destructive tendencies. Scale 8, impulsivity, reflects the experience of losing control over one's thoughts, or actions, whether or not this is associated with behavioral acting out. It includes hypertonicity, restlessness, and excitability in reaction to internal or external stimulation, as well as asocial, antisocial, or bizarre impulses. Impulsivity also covers defective volition, indecisiveness, compulsivity, and apathy.

EWI scores can be used to confirm diagnostic information from other sources. As far as validity is concerned, El-Meligi and Osmond assume that the patient is telling the truth unless proven otherwise. They do admit that some patients may deny symptoms—such patients include paranoids, those being considered for hospitalization, and those being treated against their will. Schizophrenics in remission may also produce unusually low scores. They define a low score on one part of the test as having all scales below 25 with a raw score of one or zero on at least two scales. Delinquents who feel that they may be labeled crazy probably will produce unusually low scores; a frank explanation of the purpose of the test might reduce this reaction. Total scores, while not definitive, give a rough indication of the patient's burden of perceptual anomalies. At the Brain Bio Center, the scores for one part of the test were categorized as: 10–20 = normal level, 20–50 = employed outpatient, 50–100 = unemployed outpatient, and 100–200 = hospitalized patient. These scores indicate the effect of disperceptions on functioning, and are not a guide to normalcy or relative sanity. Occasionally a patient with a high score functions well, but usually multiple disperceptions amount to a crippling degree of stress.

In addition to using the total score, test profiles can be variously classified. El-Meligi and Osmond suggest sorting on the basis of which score (or combination of scores) is the highest point in the profile, on which is the lowest point in the profile, and on the specific relationships between individual scales or combinations of scales. They further suggest some tentative EWI profile configurations. High Dysphoria and Self Perception scales with other scales low indicate neurotic trends. Dysphoria, Scale 7, is the most frequent high point in profiles of depressed patients. Time Perception and Ideation are the most frequent high points in the profiles of hallucinogenic subjects who developed psychosis prior to hallucinogen abuse. Scores of 35 or above on five scales and at least one standard deviation higher than the Dysphoria scale indicate schizophrenia. If, in addition, Sensory Perception and Perception of Others are conspicuous peaks, paranoid schizophrenia is likely. Paranoids with delusions about the body frequently produce elevated profiles with Body Perception and Perception of Others as the highest points. Central nervous dysfunction is a possibility if Sensory Perception and Ideation are the highest points, especially if the items marked indicate deficit or impairment rather than distortion. The Body Perception scale is also prominent. In intracranial dysfunction resulting from trauma or sudden illness like encephalitis, Time Perception and Dysphoria scores are elevated, reflecting the disorientation and distress the patient is suffering. In female patients, prominent Body

Perception, Sensory Perception, and Dysphoria scores suggest depression with an endocrine or neurohormonal basis.

Violence and drug abuse play major roles in delinquency. Osmond and El-Meligi administered the EWI test to prison inmates with histories, respectively, of violence and drug abuse. In the EWI profiles of 100 prison inmates with histories of serious violence committed against individuals, the most frequent high points were Perceptions of Others and Sensory Perceptions, while the least frequent high points were Body Perception and Impulse Regulation the most frequent low points. The authors believe that in their small test groups "sensory changes and distorted perception of people are closely connected to assaultive behavior, especially if the body is experienced as essentially intact." They comment that these assaultive prisoners viewed themselves as in command of their bodies and actions. Violent people evidently regard violence as an acceptable mode of handling situations.

The 60 prison inmates with histories of drug abuse produced EWI profiles with Ideation and Perception of Others as high points. Body Perception and Self Perception are the least frequent high points.

Although they emphasize that their samples are too small to be conclusive, El-Meligi and Osmond note that drug addicts and violent subjects apparently share a paranoid view of life, reflected in notably high scores in Perception of Others. Perceptual anomalies are more prominent in profiles of violent inmates, while ideational features are more prominent in profiles of drug abusers. These results may indicate psychological bases for delinquency and should be considered in the interpretation of EWI scores of delinquents.

The EWI may be used to confirm possible perceptual anomalies aggravating delinquency. Probably depression and poor self-image contribute to acting-out behavior, destructive accidents, suicide attempts, and cycles of failure. The EWI may indicate whether delusions, sensory overstimulation, and poor impulse control are playing a role in destructive, bizarre, or delinquent behavior. A careful check of items marked true, of course, provides the most precise information on the patient's symptoms; combined with other information, they may suggest either the method of treatment or further tests. Retesting the patient after two to four months of orthomolecular treatment provides an indication of the patient's progress and biochemical status.

HYPOGLYCEMIA

Hypoglycemia may be a contributing factor in delinquency. In affected individuals, it may cause irritability, depression, rage, mood swings, and aggression. The condition is aggravated by the refined carbohydrate, high sugar, low protein, junk food diet popular among adolescents. Often cravings for candy, tobacco, caffeine, or alcohol are symptoms of the condition, which may be further intensified by food allergies. Understanding hypoglycemia and its varied symptoms is a necessary part of effective treatment.

Hypoglycemia or low blood sugar is a chemical change in the body due to a drop in readily available glucose, a change which occurs several times daily as part of the complex process of glucose metabolism. Hypoglycemia usually refers to chronic low blood sugar due to defective regulation of blood glucose levels. Glucose, the fuel that provides energy for all the body cells, is manufactured from food protein and carbohydrates by enzyme systems in the small intestine. Carbohydrates are converted to glucose most rapidly.

Shortly after a meal, glucose absorbed in the small intestine enters the bloodstream. Cells in the hypothalamus of the brain detect the raised blood sugar and signal the pancreas to release insulin. The hormone insulin promotes rapid absorption of glucose from the blood by the body cells and facilitates the transport of glucose into the liver cells; the liver converts glucose into glycogen for storage. When the blood sugar drops enough, the hypothalamus signals the pituitary to stimulate the adrenal gland to release adrenaline and the glucocorticoid hormones which antagonize insulin activity. These hormones also stimulate the pancreas to secrete glucagon, which converts glycogen to glucose in the liver. The glucose is then released into the bloodstream. Glucose metabolism is affected by vitamin C, B complex vitamins, calcium, potassium, magnesium, zinc, and phosphorus. Essential to insulin function is the recently discovered glucose tolerance factor (GTF) containing nicotinic acid, chromium, and three amino acids. If imbalance in blood glucose regulation produces too much insulin and/or too few insulin antagonists, chronic hypoglycemia or low blood sugar results.

When the blood sugar level is too low to refuel the cells, they become starved. Since the brain cannot store glucose and requires a continuous supply, hypoglycemia affects the central nervous system. During hypoglycemia, the brain cannot efficiently use oxygen, nor can it effectively direct vital processes; thus physical and emotional behavior are disrupted. Symptoms of hypoglycemia vary according to the intensity of the condition, the individual, and contributing factors. Fatigue, irritability, anxiety, depression, crying spells, dizziness, faintness, insomnia, confusion, poor concentration, headaches, and disperceptions are common hypoglycemic symptoms. Some hypoglycemics also suffer from phobias, destructive outbursts, heart palpitations, muscle cramps, convulsions, low sex drive, and blurred vision. Lowered body temperature (hypothermia) is a frequent symptom. These signs, of course, occur in many disorders. However, if they are episodic, occurring at regular intervals, they strongly indicate hypoglycemia. Physical and emotional stress may aggravate hypoglycemic symptoms.

GLUCOSE TOLERANCE TEST

The glucose tolerance test is the standard diagnostic method of establishing the diagnosis of hypoglycemia. In this test the person is instructed to eat a carbohydrate-rich diet (at least 250 to 300 grams carbohydrate) for three days and report to the lab on the morning of the fourth day in a fasted state. At the lab fasted blood and urine samples are obtained, and the person drinks a flavored solution containing 100 grams of glucose. Blood samples are collected at intervals of $\frac{1}{2}$, 1, 2, 3, 4, 5, and 6 hours after he has drunk the solution. Also a sample should be taken at any time the person experiences any symptoms. All urine voided during the test is checked for sugar. The blood samples are analyzed for glucose.

There are three types of glucose tolerance curves encountered clinically (Figure 10-1). The typical curve in the hypoglycemic patient shows a drop of 20 mg% or more below the initial value. The prediabetic curve goes much higher and drops 60 mg% or more in the third and fourth hours. The flat type of curve still indicates hypoglycemia. Other factors to be considered seriously are typical symptoms occurring during the test, such as sweating, disperceptions, nausea, and tremor. Relief of symptoms with a low starch and sugar diet also indicates functional hypoglycemia. These patients have a return of their initial symptoms when they eat sugar.

There are many problems with the test: (1) The test is traumatic; it is never a good idea to consume so large an amount of glucose with no supporting nutrients, trace metals, or vitamins. (2) The test is ex-

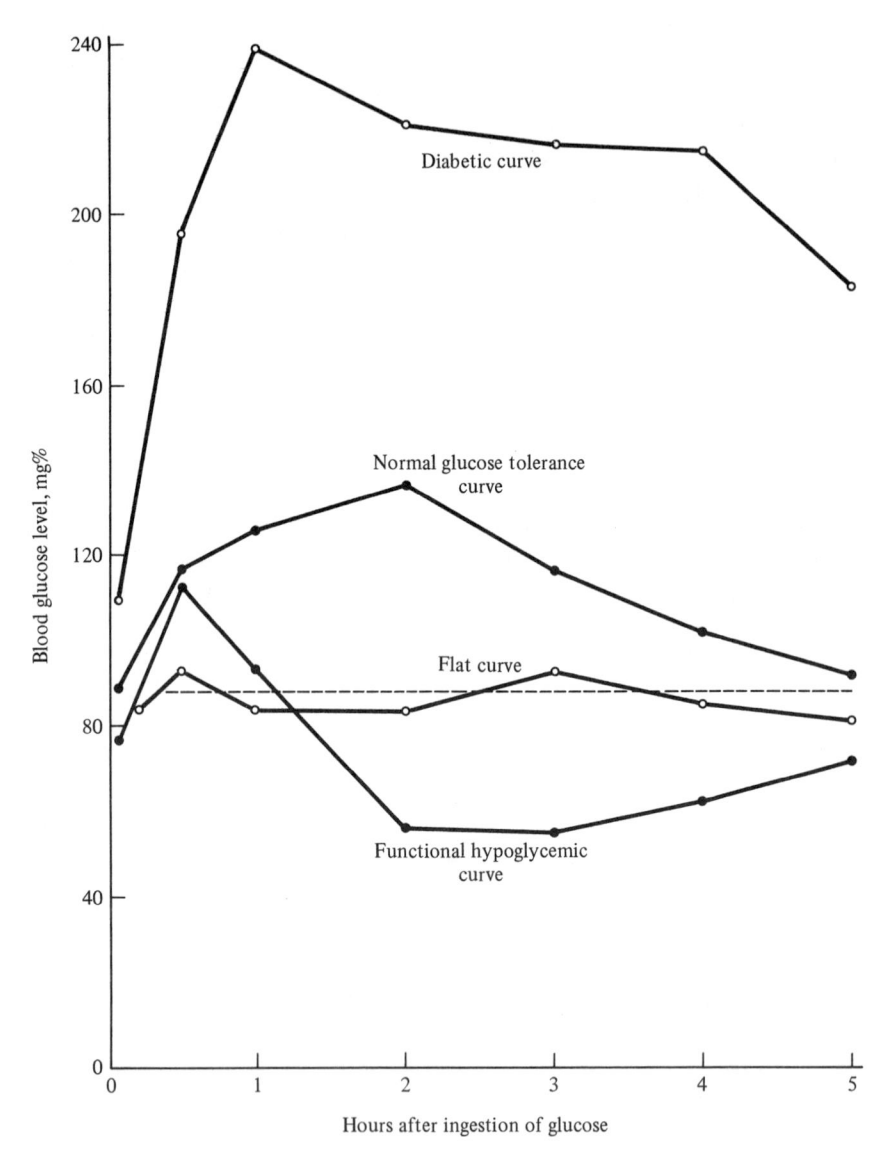

Figure 10-1. Typical glucose tolerance curves.

pensive (frequently over $100, double that if insulin as well as glucose is measured). (3) The test frequently is inconclusive; many people with a hypoglycemia history whose symptoms are relieved by dietary avoidance of refined carbohydrates will have fairly normal glucose tolerance curves. In clinical practice the test's greatest value is in persuading the dubious patient that eating refined carbohydrates leads to a faster drop in his blood sugar, during which time he will feel bad.

ALLERGIES

Food allergy is a disorder that has only recently gained general recognition as a causitive factor in many cases of psychopathology. Various authors have indicated that between 10% and 90% of schizophrenic patients have a difficulty on the basis of sensitization to foods ordinarily in their diet. Food allergy has also been found to be responsible for a host of chronic ailments: everything from the hyperactive child with learning disabilities to the arthritic patient.

Pioneering workers, such as Dr. Theron Randolph, have for decades been reporting to the medical profession the cure of such conditons by dietary adjustment, but only recently has much recognition taken place. Part of the problem lies in poorly understood biochemical mechanisms and the absence of simple diagnostic tests. Ordinarily when one thinks of allergies, one thinks of the itchy eyes, runny nose, and sneezing of the hayfever sufferer. The symptoms of food allergy are frequently vague, and to further complicate matters, the person will frequently feel better after eating a food to which he is sensitized, a feeling that can lead to cravings and addiction. These cravings are frequently the best diagnostic clue, but to properly evaluate cravings it is necessary to have a thorough understanding of the concept of hidden foods. For example, craving for ice cream most obviously might indicate a sensitization to milk, but it might also indicate a sensitization to corn. To further complicate matters there are two forms of food allergy, fixed and cyclic. Fixed food allergy, though less frequent, is the more generally recognized form because the person will be sensitized to a food and have a reaction each and every time he has eaten it. Cyclic food allergies are vastly more prevalent but less likely to be diagnosed because the reactions are often delayed and a function of recent dietary exposure.

Much investigative work is presently underway to elucidate more clearly the biochemical mechanism of cyclic food allergy and our understanding of this disorder from its origins. There is mounting evidence that part of the problem is a lack of competency of the gut and that the gut allows protein fragments to be absorbed into the bloodstream, where they can cause systemic reactions. It has been known for some time that the non-breast-fed infant is more likely than the breast-fed one to have food allergy, which manifests itself in infancy as colic and later in childhood as hyperactivity, perhaps with learning disabilities. It is now known that the breast-fed infant receives from his mother's milk antibodies that line the gut and prevent the absorption of these protein molecules. It is also known that alcohol is likely to trigger food allergy, not only as a source of allergen from the substance from which it is made (wheat, corn, and so on), but also as a dispersing agent because it increases the solubility of various antigens and thus inhances its absorption across the gut. There are many other factors involved. The food-allergic patient often has a family history positive for allergies.

None of the diagnostic tests for food allergies is absolutely reliable. In the classic test, elimination provocation, a suspected food is eliminated from the diet for four days, then eaten. The patient is observed for specific symptoms. If the person is allergic to the food, he will suffer withdrawal symptoms of depression and irritability during the elimination period. On the day of the provocative feeding, the patient's pulse should be measured before and after his eating the suspected food. Eliminating a specific food may not result in complete disappearnce of symptoms, as food allergies are usually multiple. The patient continues to eat other foods to which he may be sensitive although his symptoms may not be acute. It is quite difficult completely to eliminate certain foods.

At the Brain Bio Center we struggled with this method for a year and a half to discover that it was a rare patient who could discipline himself to read all food labels and completely avoid specific substances. One compulsive patient, an engineer, had rages that were destroying his marriage and threatening his career. His strong cravings suggested that wheat might be the offending allergen. He accordingly spent three months repeatedly eliminating it from his diet and attempting provocation. He kept charts of his moods, including lulls in his depression and irritability, concentration, and confusion.

Our nutritionist and psychiatrist read his records, yet we could find no signs of sensitivity to wheat. After reviewing all his menus and reading the food labels in his big bound notebook, we detected no flaws in his method. Finally, he casually remarked "There wouldn't be any wheat in beer, would there?" Beer is loaded with wheat! Similarly, corn—as oil, sugar, and starch—is a universal ingredient in processed foods. We have yet to encounter a patient who has successfully eliminated corn from his diet except by total fasting—even postage stamps have corn glue. Because it is so widely used, corn is the most common source of food allergy, followed by wheat, milk, and eggs.

Other provocative tests have been devised to circumvent the problems of food elimination. In the sublingual mood, a solution of food allergen concentrate is placed under the patient's tongue; then his symptoms are noted. Sublingual testing can be dramatic, since the allergen may provoke immediate psychosis or depression, which can be stopped by a neutralizing dose. The allergen can be injected intradermally providing a skin wheal as an objective reaction besides the subjective symptoms of provocation. Symptoms produced by intradermal testing can be relieved by neutralization.

There are a few laboratory tests for allergies. Cytotoxic studies use white cells from a blood sample. Different aliquots are mixed with various antigens, then added to the cell solution; the cells are then observed under a microscope. In the most intense reaction (+4), the cells will evacuate and burst, leaving ghost cells. In a less intense reaction (+1), the cells will lose mobility. Cytotoxic tests require specially trained technicians, hence are expensive. The tests are about 80% accurate with both false positive and false negatives. The RAST test, which measures specific immunoglobulin antigens, has been used. However, food allergies are nonmediated by immunoglobulin E, and thus the test is often negative in people with food allergies. Other laboratory methods continue to be developed.

OTHER DIAGNOSTIC AREAS

Pyroluria is a condition in which an abnormal product of pyrrole metabolism (kryptopyrrole) complexes with pyridoxal phosphate (the active form of vitamin B-6) and zinc, creating deficiencies in these substances. It is now known that pyroluria is the etiology agent in a third of the people diagnosed as schizophrenic, and it is also known to exist in 10% of the so-called normal population. These symptoms of pyroluria are all related to deficiency of either zinc or vitamin B-6. The signs of zinc deficiency include white spots on the fingernails and a tendency to form stretch marks. Without use of sequestered agents in food processing and with a tendency not to replace zinc in the soils in which our foods are grown, zinc deficiency has become so widespread that borderline zinc deficiency is, in fact, the norm of the general population so that stretch marks with pregnancy are the norm rather than the exception.

The most frequent symptoms of vitamin B-6 deficiency are a poor tolerance to stress, tendency not to recall dreaming, sensitivity to sunlight with a tendency to burn first before tanning, and a pain in the left upper part of the abdomen. It does exist in children, and may be responsible for hyperactivity and learning disabilities in them; but usually it has its onset in adolescence. In a typical history the onset of difficulties occurs at times of stress; not uncommonly the schizophrenic patient will report that his first psychotic break occurred during his freshman year at college. When away from the stabilizing influence of the home, he subjected himself to unwise amounts of stress and eventually decompensated.

Frequently, sufferers of pyroluria will have cyclic or periodic depressions. A careful reconstruction of events will reveal that during the depressed phase the stress is low, the person cares about little, and zinc and B-6 stores are thus repleted. As the depression tends to lift, the person begins to resume his normal activities; and as the stress increases, once again the stores of B-6 and zinc are depleted, the person's functioning fails, he may or may not have psychotic symptoms, but eventually he cannot continue functioning and again becomes depressed. Adolescents with this condition are prone to suicide.

Diagnostic methods include analysis of the urine for kryptopyrrole and determination of blood zinc. Not uncommonly the initial blood zinc may be elevated owing to the deficiency of vitamin B-6; the body is incapable of getting the zinc from the serum into the zinc-deficient tissues. Also, the initial urine or kryptopyrrole may be normal. If the person is badly deficient in vitamin B-6, he has difficulty in making pyrroles, including kryptopyrrole. Therefore, it is necessary to begin treatment with vitamin B-6 in dosages sufficient to cause recall of dreaming. Not uncommonly in the schizophrenic patient the dosages are as high as 1 to 3 grams of B-6, while usually 30 to 60 mg of zinc as gluconate is sufficient, followed by redetermination of the kryptopyrrole. Kryptopyrrole will fluctuate widely with stress, so that repeat determinations are frequently necessary.

Three biochemical syndromes account for most of the schizophrenias. Based on test results, as well as physical and psychological symptoms, these syndromes are histapenia, histadelia, and pyroluria. Histapenic patients with abnormally low blood and brain histamine levels account for 50% of the schizophrenias. Histapenics demonstrate a typical cluster of biochemical results. Their blood histamine is below the normal range of 40–70 mg/ml, while their serum copper levels are abnormally high, well above the normal level of 100 mcg%. Histapenics may be low in serum folic acid but high in creatine phosphokinase (CPK). They are also low in mean energy content of the alpha waves in their EEG. A few histapenics may be sensitive to wheat gluten. Histapenics have low basophil counts. Characteristic mental symptoms include thought disorder, overarousal, grandiosity, paranoia, hallucinations, insomnia, ideas of reference, and mania. Copper, a brain stimulant which destroys histamine, probably causes many of the symptoms, including the histapenia. The Brain Bio Center treats histapenia with vitamin C, niacin, B-12, and folic acid, as well as with antipsychotic drugs when indicated.

Histadelia is a schizophrenic syndrome with high levels of blood histamine. Histadelia patients have normal to low copper levels, high basophil counts (often above 1%), and high MEC levels in their EEGs. Typical mental symptoms include severe depression, overarousal, thought disorder, compulsions, insomnia, and obsessions. Histadelics often suffer from blank minds and severe headaches. Effective treatment for histadelics consists of Dilantin, calcium, and methionine to lower their blood and tissue histamine levels. Supplements of zinc and manganese also help reduce symptoms.

Pyroluria, the above-described condition in which the urine contains kryptopyrrole (mauve factor), accounts for many schizophrenic symptoms. The mauve factor, identified by Dr. Arthur Sohler of the Brain Bio Center as 2,4-dimethyl-3-ethylpyrrole, occurs more frequently in schizophrenics than in normals. It is called mauve factor because urine extracts containing it, when combined with reagents, turn a bright magenta. Kryptopyrrole is measured in a spectrophotmeter against a standard kryptopyrrole solution. Normal subjects may have a kryptopyrrole of 20 mg%, while pyroluric patients may excrete free kryptopyrrole at levels above 20 mg%. Pyrolurics have normal histamine, basophil, and copper levels. Their zinc levels are usually low, as the kryptopyrrole depletes them of both B-6 and zinc. Pyrolurics may have any or several of the classic schizophrenic symptoms, but they have better affect. They have abnormal EEGs with occasional slow waves and isolated high voltage spikes. Patients characteristically cannot recall their dreams. Other symptoms, some discussed above under zinc and B-6 deficiency, include white spots on the fingernails, sweetish aldehyde breath odor, and occasional abdominal pain in the upper left quadrant, as well as constipation, morning nausea, cutaneous striae, inability to tan, itching in sunlight, and malformation of knee cartilage, with joint pain occurring frequently. In addition, patients may suffer from anemia and muscle spasms.

REFERENCES

D'Asaro, B., Groesbeck, C., and Nigro, C., Diet program for jail inmates, *J. Orthomolecular Psychiatry* 4 (3):212–221, 1975.

D'Asaro, B., Groesbeck, C., and Nigro, C., Polyamine levels in jail inmates, *J. Orthomolecular Psychiatry* 4 (2):149–152, 1975.

El-Meligi, A. M., and Osmond, H., *Manual for the Clinical Use of the Experimental World Inventory*, Mens Sana Publishing, New York, 1970.

Finberg, L., Fast foods for adolescents, *Am. J. Disturbed Child.* 130, 1976.

Hawkins, D., Diagnosing the schizophrenias, *J. Orthomolecular Psychiatry* 6 (1):18–25, 1977.

Heald, F. P., Adolescent nutrition, *Med. Clin. N. Am.* 59 (6):1329–1336, 1975.

Hudgens, R. W., Adolescence: Sick is never normal, *Psychiatry* 79–80, 1971.

Human Ecology Research Foundation, *Bulletin of the Human Ecology Research Foundation*, Chicago, n.d.

Kanwar, A. J., Pasricha, J. S., and Malaviya, A. M., Reassessment of the significance of delayed blanch phenomenon and serum IgE levels of atopic disorders, *Ann. Allergy* 38 (4):275–277, 1977.

Klotz, S. D., Allergy screening consultation service to an inpatient psychiatric service, *Clinical Ecology*, L. D. Dickey, ed., Charles C Thomas, Springfield, Ill., 1976.

MacKarness, R., *Eating Dangerously: The Hazards of Hidden Allergies*, Harcourt Brace Jovanovich, New York, 1976.

Mandell, M., Ecologic mental illness: Cerebral and physical reactions in allergic patients, *New Dynamics of Preventive Medicine*, L. K. Pomeroy, Ed., Intercontinental Medical Book Corp., New York, 1974.

Mandell, M., and Rose, Gilbert J., May emotional reactions be precipitated by allergen? *Connecticut Med.* 32 (4):300, 1968.

Pfeiffer, C. C., *Mental and Elemental Nutrients*, Keats Publishing, Inc., New Canaan, Conn., 1975.

Rinkel, H. J., Randolph, T. G., and Zeller, M., *Food Allergy*, Charles C Thomas, Springfield, Ill., 1951, reprinted 1976, by The New England Foundation for Allergic and Environmental Disease of the Alan Mandell Center.

Rinkel, H. J. The management of clinical allergy. *Arch. Otolaryng.* 76:491–508, 1962, reprinted 1975 by R. I. Williams.

Yaryura-Tobias, J. A., and Neziroglu, F. Violent behavior, brain dysrhythmia and glucose dysfunction, a new syndrome. *J. Orthomolecular Psychiatry* 4 (3):182–188, 1975.

Chapter 11 Symptoms and Treatment of Children with Learning Disorders

Allan Cott, M.D., F.A.P.A.
New York, New York

INTRODUCTION

Learning disabilities constitute the most prevalent and urgent medical problem afflicting children not only in the United States, but in most countries of the world. The number of children involved is staggering when we consider that 5% of the nonretarded child population is affected. Physicians must be made aware that a child suffering from learning disabilities will not "outgrow it," that his condition is not "a phase he is going through." If adequate intervention is not made in these disabilities, the child's potential will never be realized, and the effects on his life will be more devastating than those of most other childhood disorders with which he might be afflicted. The earlier the diagnosis is made, the more rewarding the child's response to orthomolecular therapy or to pharmacotherapy will be, hence the more successful the results of remedial effort. Delayed diagnosis or treatment exposes the child to improper assessment by school personnel, peers, and parents, increasing the probability of permanent psychological damage.

Recent research suggests that learning disabilities are associated with minimal brain dysfunction. This term refers to certain learning or behavioral disabilities in children of near- or above-average intelligence, ranging from mild to severe, which are associated with deviations of function of the central nervous system. There is growing recognition that the hyperactive "problem child," the child with a learning disability, may indeed be suffering from a biochemical disorder. The characteristic sign most often observed is hyperactivity—the one symptom common to all children suffering from severe disorders of behavior, learning, and communication. Other symptoms may include perceptual-motor impairments, impulsive behavior, general coordination defects, inability to concentrate, short attention span, and disorders of speech. Many children with diagnosed minimal brain dysfunction seem normal or near-normal until they enter a classroom. Then, despite average or above-average intelligence, they have difficulty in one or more areas of learning, the most common being difficulty in reading (dyslexia). The resulting academic and emotional difficulties easily lead to misdiagnoses of retardation or of primary psychiatric problems.

The child who cannot perform on a level with his peers is a child who will in one way or another be destroyed and never achieve his full potential. He is improperly assessed by his parents, his teachers, and his classmates. The latter ultimately destroy the fragile threads of self-esteem he has managed to maintain when they label him a "retard." He is finally precipitated into an emotional disorder as he progresses through each school year under the mounting stress of the demands to perform beyond his capabilities. Early recognition of his difficulties by parents and teachers can help avoid disaster by early intervention into his problems.

SYMPTOMS

While the problem of most learning-disabled children becomes manifest when they enter a school and can be detected by a kindergarten teacher, it is generally not diagnosed until the child enters the first grade. Many children progress fairly well through the early grades, but their handicaps become overt when they are introduced to subjects in which abstract thinking is required.

Learning disabilities are not disorders like the usual childhood diseases with which all parents are familiar. The signs that characterize these conditions occur in groups or clusters which vary just as children vary in other respects. Some children may have difficulty in reading because they have difficulty distinguishing letters which look alike—such as *p* and *q*, *b* and *d*—or they may have word reversals and see the word *was* when *saw* was written. Many children will be seen frequently rubbing their eyes. Other children may have disturbances in the important visual functions so necessary to reading. Their eyes may not move smoothly over the printed line because they lack smooth eye muscle control; if focusing is not properly established, they may skip words in the line, lose their place, and then be unable to comprehend what they have read. Problems of this nature can often be spotted by observing a child's posture as he reads or writes, for he will often cock his head at a sharp angle, keep his book on the desk, and lower his head until it is inches away from the page. Often the child is unable to follow successive words in reading unless he moves his finger along the page under each word.

Some children show visual-motor or perceptual-motor problems in which their hands or feet cannot process the information their eyes give them. Such children cannot perform well in spots involving the need to catch a ball, bat, kick, or throw with some degree of accuracy. They will avoid sports and show interest in solitary activities rather than subject themselves to the ridicule of their peers. Other groups of children lack fine finger control—they are unable to color and keep within the outlines of the drawing they are coloring. Because they cannot hold a pencil in a proper pincer grip, their writing is awkward—letters written above and below the line, some very small, other gigantic by comparison. Lack of fine finger control manifests itself early in the inability to cut with play scissors. Coordination of the large muscles used in running and throwing is impaired in learning-disabled children in general; they are clumsy in their movements and lack the gracefulness seen in their well-coordinated siblings. Their attention span is short, and they have difficulties with memory, especially for material presented sequentially. Abstract reasoning is impossible for them, or at best is very poor and disorganized.

Many parents will miss the early presumptive signs of the child at risk for learning if that child is their first-born. Only when they have a second child do they have a basis for comparison which makes the disability overt. When their overactive infant pulls himself to his feet at six months, climbs out of the crib at eight months, and is walking at ten months parents are usually pleased and often boast of this "precocious agility." Their pride turns to dismay when these "feats" are followed by the developing tornado of hyperactivity that is so often the cardinal sign of the learning-disabled child. As the learning-disabled child grows and becomes mobile, he is into everything, rushing from one thing to another, unable to concentrate or stay at anything long enough to gain anything meaningful from the experience. His attention span is short; he is easily distractible. He touches everything and overturns almost everything he touches. He may not deliberately destroy anything, but in his uncontrollable activity he frequently breaks toys and household objects. He explores every recess of a room, fingers everything, moves anything movable. The energy he exerts in whatever he does flows from an inner source that drives him relentlessly. As he grows up, he cannot rest and be tranquil, even if he wants to, for moments of peace and silence. He frequently appears clumsy in his movements. He is a disruptive influence not only in the classroom but in his home as well. Mealtimes are a nightmare of overturned glasses, spilled food, clattering cutlery, and shouting. He is the center of emotional storms involving himself and the other members of the family. He often disrupts the relations of his family members with each other.

Bedtime, the final exhausting struggle of the day, bears no resemblance to a quiet period of being tucked into bed, listening to the bedtime story, and falling quietly to sleep as Mother tiptoes from the room. The learning-disabled child is in and out of bed, may roam around the house until the early morning hours, and falls asleep when he is overcome, not by sleep, but by utter exhaustion. Or he may fall asleep and be up in a short time to awaken his parents, repeating this pattern several times during the night so that the entire family awakens exhausted each morning.

His speech and thinking processes often reveal many defects. Just as some learning-disabled children have their greatest problems with visual perception, others cannot integrate what they hear and, therefore, cannot understand, even though they do not have a measurable hearing loss. They may hear words which merely sound alike as identical, and this inability to discriminate interferes with their comprehension of what is said in conversation or of sequential commands to carry out. If, for example, the learning-disabled child with these problems is asked to "pick up the ball and then bring the book" and he hears instead the command to "pick up the bowl," he doesn't know what he must do before he "brings the book." Often the development of speech in such a child may be delayed; when he does develop speech, his pronounciation may be so immature he can't be easily understood. He is rarely aware that his speech is not like that of his peers.

TREATMENT

Even with early intervention, many of the effects of learning disabilities cannot be overcome with the best help now available. While much emphasis has been placed on the neurogenic learning disorders, however, other important variables in the learning process have been overlooked or ignored.[1] I wish to present for consideration a most important variable—the biochemical disorders which interfere with learning—and a new adjunct to treatment which involves the use of large doses of vitamins, minerals, and the maintenance of proper nutrition to create the optimum molecular environment for the brain. Drugs are being used widely as the primary intervention for the treatment of learning disabilities and are of importance in helping many children.

In January 1971 the Office of Child Development and the Office of the Assistant Secretary for Health and Scientific Affairs, Department of Health Education and Welfare, called a conference to discuss the use of stimulant medications in the treatment of elementary-school-age children with certain behavioral disturbances. Public concern was growing over the increasing use of stimulant medications in treating so-called hyperkinetic behavior disorders. Questions were raised by concerned parents as to whether these drugs, which were widely abused by adolescents and adults, were truly safe for children. Were they properly prescribed, or were they used for children who in fact need other types of treatment? Was emphasis on prescribing medications to alleviate behavior disorders misleading?

To clarify the conditions in which these medications were beneficial or harmful to children, HEW's Office of Child Development invited a panel of 15 specialists drawn from relevant fields to meet in Washington, D.C., to review the evidence of research and experience and prepare an advisory report for professionals and the public. Their report dealt with the wide range of conditions and disabilities that can interfere with a child's learning, and highlighted such etiologic factors as social deprivation, stress at home or at school, mental retardation, childhood psychosis, and autism. Other factors included were medical conditions, such as blindness, deafness, or obvious brain dysfuction. Some cases were described as associated with specific reading or perceptual defects, and others with severe personality or emotional disturbance.

They clearly defined hyperactivity as physical activity which appears driven as if there were an "inner tornado." Thus, the activity is beyond the child's control, as compared to other children. The child is distracted, racing from one idea and interest to another, unable to focus his attention.

They continued that the fact that these dysfunctions range from mild to severe and have ill-understood causes and outcomes should *not* obscure the necessity for skilled and special interventions. Attention was drawn to the similarity of the majority of better-known diseases—from cancer and diabetes to hypertension—which have multiple or unknown causes and consequences. Their early manifestations are often not readily recognizable, yet useful treatment programs have been developed to alleviate these conditions. Uncertainty as to cause has not prevented tests of the effectivenes of available treatments while the search for clearer definitions and more effective kinds of therapy continues. The panel suggested that the same principles clearly should apply to the hyperkinetic behavior disorders.

The focus of the HEW panel's report was on issues related to the use of drugs in treating learning disabilities. They concluded that stimulant medications are beneficial in only about one-half to two-thirds of the cases in which use of the drugs is warranted. They considered the stimulant drugs to be the first and least complicated of the medicines to be tried, while other medications—the so-called tranquilizers and antidepressants—should be generally reserved for a smaller group of patients. They agreed that the medications did not "cure" the condition, but that the child might become more accessible to educational and counseling efforts. Over the short term and at a critical age, this treatment can provide the help needed for the child's development.

The panel emphasized the rights of parents and took the position that under no circumstances should any attempt be made to coerce the parents to accept any particular treatment, and that the consent of the patient and his parents or guardian must be obtained for treatment. They further added that it is proper for school personnel to inform parents of a child's behavioral problems, but members of the school staff should not directly diagnose hyperkinetic disturbance or prescribe treatment. The school should initiate contact with a physician only with the parent's consent. The report was concluded with the summary that there is a place for stimulant medications in the treatment of the hyperkinetic behavioral disturbance, but that these medications are *not* the only form of effective treatment.

I agree in essence with the conference report. Early intervention is of the utmost importance if the hyperkinetic learning-disabled child is to have an opportunity to learn and achieve. It is true in most instances that the hyperactivity will subside spontaneously by age 12 or 13, but those parents who accepted the advice that their child would "outgrow" the condition find it is then too late for him. His academic career is gone, and opportunities for work later in life are indeed limited, since there are very few jobs left which do not require a degree of literacy.

It is unfortunate that the HEW panel, while pointing out that drugs were not the only effective treatment, was not convened to report on effective alternatives to drug treatment or effective treatments for the one-third to one-half of five million children who are not helped by drugs.

There is rapidly accumulating evidence that a child's ability to learn can be improved by the use of large doses of certain vitamins, mineral supplements, and improvement of his general nutritional status through removal of "junk foods" and additives from his daily diet.

Orthomolecular treatment has been described by Dr. Linus Pauling, in his classic paper on orthomolecular psychiatry (1968), as treatment of illness by the provision of the optimum molecular composition of the brain, especially the optimum concentration of substances normally present in the human body. The implications for much-needed research in the more universal application of orthomolecular treatment are clear.

In my experience, orthomolecular intervention with the hyperkinetic learning-disabled child has been able to help more than 50% of the children treated. These statistics achieve greater significance when it is considered that many of the children treated had failed to improve with the use of Ritalin or amphetamines. In such cases, many parents were searching for an alternative to drug therapy because their children were experiencing the side effects of insomnia, loss of appetite with concomitant weight loss, reduction in rate of growth, a reaction of fatigue and sedation, or irritability and tearfulness when the drug was given in doses large enough to control the hyperactivity. Many children had been put on a regime of various psychotropic (tranquilizer) medications, which failed because they produced the paradoxical effect of overstimulation and increased the hyperactivity and disturbed behavior.

Many parents who had read of the orthomolecular approach or had spoke to other parents whose children were achieving notable improvement on the regime sought it as the primary treatment. Since the orthomolecular approach is compatible with all other substances used in the drug intervention, and since the megavitamins potentiate the action of most drugs, the treatments can be combined. This is frequently done early in treatment while the vitamin doses are gradually being raised to the optimal maintenance level and more rapid control of the hyperactivity is required. At times, tranquilizer medication is added at the request or insistence of school authorities to bring the hyperactive, disruptive behavior under more rapid control.

The large majority of children treated by the orthomolecular approach improve without the use of drugs. Fortunately, very few parents accept the clichés with which their concerns about their child's development are met by so many of their pediatricians and family physicians. They are not satisfied with such palliatives as "boys are slower than girls," "you're an anxious mother, your baby is fine," "lots of healthy children do not speak until they are four years old," or "there's nothing to worry about if your baby creeps backward or rolls from place to place." In the author's experience, the mothers most often were first to notice their child's problems; only in a very low percentage of cases was their pediatrician first to make the diagnosis. Many parents, after reading about the orthomolecular approach, instituted the recommended dietary changes and found that these changes alone brought about a dramatic reduction in hyperactivity. Other parents purchased vitamins and reported improvement when their child was given several of the vitamins used in the treatment.

During the treatment of many hundreds of psychotic children, the author noted and reported that in most cases in which parents persisted in the proper administration of the vitamins and the diet, significant improvement in many areas of functioning was achieved.

The most significant and earliest sign of improvement reported by the parents was a decrease in hyperactivity, which led to improved capacity for learning. Trials with the orthomolecular treatment were then begun in children exhibiting specific learning disabilities, the child diagnosed hyperkinetic or minimal brain dysfunction.

With orthomolecular treatment, results are frequently quick and the reduction in hyperactivity often dramatic, but in most instances several months elapse before significant changes are seen. The child exhibits, among other qualities, a willingness to cooperate with his parents and teachers. These changes are seen in the majority of children who have failed to improve with the use of the stimulant drugs or tranquilizer medications. The majority of the children the author sees have been exposed to every form of treatment and every known tranquilizer and sedative, with little or no success even in controlling the hyperactivity. Concentration and attention span increase, and the child is able to work productively for increasingly longer periods of time. He ceases to be an irritant to his teacher and classmates. Early intervention is of the utmost importance, not only for the child, but for the entire family, since the child suffering from minimal brain dysfunction is such a devastating influence on the family constellation. He is the matrix of emotional storms that envelop every member of the household and disrupt their relationships both to him and to each other.

Until orthomolecular studies were begun, most remedial specialists stressed the more peripheral aspects of a handicapped child's performance and ignored the biochemical basis of his disturbed behavior and impaired ability to learn. In this means of intervention, remedial efforts are directed toward both brain function and body chemistry. In addition to the employment of perceptual motor techniques and pharmacotherapy, attempts should be made to improve the child's biochemical balance through the use of orthomolecular techniques.[2] Improvement under the orthomolecular treatment is directing the attention of the scientific community to the central processes and causing closer scrutiny of the biochemical processes of the learning-disabled child.

MEGAVITAMINS

Based on empirical data, the application of orthomolecular principles can be successful in helping many learning-disabled children.

Positive results have been obtained when the treatment regimen consisted of the following vitamins: niacinamide (vitamin B-3) or niacin (vitamin B-3), 1 to 2 grams daily, depending on body weight; vitamin C, 1 to 2 grams daily; pyridoxine (vitamin B-6), 200 to 300 mg daily; calcium pantothenate, 200 to 400 mg, daily; B-complex, 50 mg, half a tablet. The vitamins are generally administered twice daily. Magnesium is frequently used for its calming effect on hyperactivity, and to prevent a depletion of this important mineral by the large doses of pyridoxine.

These are starting doses for children weighing 35 pounds or more. If a child weighs less than 35 pounds, one gram daily of niacinamide and one gram daily of vitamin C are used in half-gram doses administered twice daily. If the child shows no signs of intolerance after two weeks, the dose is increased to twice the amount. For a child weighing 45 pounds or more, an optimum daily maintenance level of about 3 grams of niacinamide and 3 grams of vitamin C is reached. Frequently, vitamin B-12, vitamin E, riboflavin (B-2), thiamine (B-1), folic acid, and B-15 can be valuable additions to the treatment. No serious side effects have resulted in any of the thousands of children treated with these substances. The side effects that occur infrequently are dose-related and subside with the reduction of the dose.

SIDE EFFECTS

Niacin and Niacinamide

Niacin can elevate blood glucose levels and levels of uric acid. These side effects are very infrequent, and the parameters return to normal with a reduction of the dose or with discontinuation of the niacin and the substitution of niacinamide. For two or three days after beginning its use, niacin will produce a feeling of warmth in the body, a flushing of the skin comparable to a mild sunburn, sometimes accompanied by itching. These symptoms occur 15 to 20 minutes after the medication is taken and subside in one to two hours; they recur with each succeeding dose, but with diminished intensity. This effect no longer appears after the second or third day of administration of niacin.

Niacinamide, the preferred form of vitamin B-3 for use in children, does not produce these symptoms. Headaches of the temporal variety, however, may occur and will respond to reduction of the dose. Both niacin and niacinamide may produce nausea. While this side effect occurs very infrequently, it is the most common side effect and, like other side effects of the megavitamins, responds to a reduction in dose. In the treatment of 8,000 adults, swelling of the face or ankles occurred in six patients and a brownish patchy discoloration of the skin occurred in five, but neither of these side effects occurred in the treatment of 2,000 children. The side effects cleared when niacinamide was substituted for niacin.

Vitamin C

The major side effects of vitamin C are increased frequency of urination and mild diarrhea. These occur infrequently and respond to reduction of the dose. Some children can be intolerant of vitamin C and are treated instead with sodium ascorbate, which does not produce side effects.

Pyridoxine

Dr. Paul Gyorgy, who discovered B-6, indicates that it is quite safe even at high dosage levels. In 1966, the American Academy of Pediatrics reviewed the use of B-6 and concluded that "to date there had been no report of deleterious effects associated with ingestion of large doses of vitamin B-6 (0.2–1 gram daily)."

Calcium Pantothenate

This vitamin is reported by Dr. Roger Williams, its discoverer, to be nontoxic, even in multiple gram doses. He reported monkeys to have ingested 500 times their normal intake of this vitamin with no adverse effects. He reports the life span of mice given supplements of calcium pantothenate dialy to have averaged 645 days as compared with 549 for mice treated alike but given only a good commercial laboratory mouse diet.

AVAILABILITY

The vitamins are available as tablets, capsules, or liquids. Often side effects may be produced by the fillers used in making tablets. Fillers are most often sugar, cornstarch, and a variety of chemical substances, all of which can produce side effects. Tablets are available without these fillers, however. Capsules are less likely to contain fillers, since pure vitamin powders can be used in the manufacture of capsules. Liquid vitamins are the least preferred form to use, since all liquid medicinal preparations must contain preservatives, mold retardants, and glycerine, which is used to prevent freezing in shipment. Even more harmful for the hyperactive child are the artificial colors, artificial flavors, and sweeteners used in the preparation of liquid medications. If a child cannot swallow tablets or capsules, the tablets may be crushed and stirred into juice or some other food that would make the mixture palatable. None of the children treated have ever developed a serious side effect from megavitamins.

It has been shown that proper brain function requires adequate tissue respiration, and Dr. O. Warburg,[3] Nobel laureate in biochemistry, described the importance of vitamins B-3 and C in the respiration of all body tissues in the maintenance of health and proper function.

Laboratory findings with animals have shown a direct relationship between vitamin intake and learning enhancement. It was found by some researchers that injections of vitamin B-12 markedly enhanced learning in rats.

IMPORTANCE OF DIETARY CONTROL

Control of diet is an integral part of the total treatment of a learning-disabled child, and failure to improve the nutritional status can be responsible for achieving minimal results. Greater concern must be shown for the quality of the child's internal environment in which his cells and tissues function, if we are to help him attain optimal performance. The removal of offending foods from the diet of disturbed or learning-disabled children can result in dramatic improvement in behavior, attention span, and concentration.

The role of diets deficient in essential nutrients has been well documented as the cause of vitamin deficiency diseases such as beriberi and scurvy. The former is the result of a deficiency of thiamine (vitamin B-1); the latter, a deficiency of vitamin C. The role of improper diet as a causative factor in the production of disturbed behavior became clear when the discovery was made that pellagra was produced by a diet deficient in niacin. In the late stages of the illness, which begins with a widespread skin eruption, the patient develops symptoms resembling those of schizophrenia, including perceptual distortions and a disorder in thinking and behavior. When niacin was added to the patient's diet, pellagra receded completely.

Children or adults suffering from hypoglycemia must eat a diet richest in protein foods, with moderate fat, and low in carbohydrate foods. Cane sugar and those carbohydrate foods quickly converted to glucose must be eliminated, for they exert a definite influence on brain chemistry and overstimulate the pancreas to overproduce insulin. A study at M.I.T. (March 1975) revealed the relationship in brain tissue in rats between the amounts of neurotransmitters present in the brain and the presence or absence of protein in each meal. The daily increases or decreases in the dietary intake of certain animo acids found in foods affect the production of neurotransmitters which stimulate impulses from one brain cell to the next. It was also reported that insulin apparently sequesters some amino acids.

Cane sugar and foods prepared with sugar are offending foods for all children, normal as well as disabled. The physical manifestations of conditions produced by including cane sugar in the child's diet are well documented and known to many parents. Dentists report that children with a high intake of cane sugar have more cavities. Sugar-loaded foods spoil a child's appetite for good, nutritious foods and keep him literally "addicted" to sugar in all forms: cookies, cakes, ice cream, soda pop, and the great multitude of sugar-frosted cereals that become the basic foods in his unbalanced diet. Overlooked, however, have been the equally devasting effects that such a sugar-loaded diet has on a child's *behavior*. In the treatment of children suffering from disorders of behavior or learning disabilities, I have found that a significant percentage have been dramatically improved by removing sugar and other junk foods from their diet. Those parents who have been successful in enforcing the cane sugar-free diet have achieved great success in helping their children overcome the hyperactive behavior that was interfering with learning and peer relationships. Most of the sweetened foods also contain artificial colors and artificial flavors, to which many children react with an allergy not manifested in the usual ways but by sudden outbursts of disturbed, disruptive behavior produced by a reaction in the brain.

A high percentage of children have some disturbance of glucose metabolism; in this group, the eating of sugar-laden foods produces an initial rise in blood sugar level which is normal, but this rise is followed in an hour or two by a precipitous drop in blood sugar level to a point lower than the level at the time the sugar was eaten. This drop interferes with the levels of transmitters that control sleep, mood, motivation, and learning, and results in overactive and, at times, violent disruptive behavior.[4] When a child has been following a sugar-free diet for a period of time and his behavior has improved, members of his family know when he has had sweets by the return of his previous irritability and overactivity. I have seen a number of children who reacted to the withdrawal of sugar from their diet with the personality change and physical discomfort seen during withdrawal of drugs. Wheat products and milk, which so frequently occur in foods containing sugar, are highly allergenic for many children and often produce cerebral allergies that are manifested by disturbed behavior.

Since many disturbed and learning-disabled children are found to have either hypoglycemia, hyperinsulinism, or dysinsulinism, cane sugar and rapidly absorbed carbohydrate foods should be eliminated from their diets. It has been the universal observation of those investigators who assess the nutritional status of such children that they eat a diet which is richest in sugar, candy, sweets, and foods made with sugar. The removal of these foods results in a dramatic decrease in hyperactivity. Most children do not drink milk unless it is sweetened with chocolate syrup or some other syrupy additive. All the beverages they consume every day are spiked with sugar: soda, caffeinated cola drinks, highly sweetened "fruit juice," and other concoctions which are sold to them by television commercials. The child who drinks any water at all is indeed rare.

The appalling fact about the constant consumption of these "junk foods" is the parents' belief that these foods are good for their children. Parents must realize that they litter their children's bodies by making unnatural foods available to them and incorporating them in their daily diet. Because children will not voluntarily exclude such foods from their diet, they must be helped to accomplish this; these foods should not be brought into the home. The child must learn the principles of proper nutrition and proper eating from his parents. The dissemination of this knowledge is far too important to entrust it to the writers of television commercials, whose aim is to sell, not to educate.

Dr. Jean Mayer, Professor of Nutrition at Harvard University, speaking at a 1970 symposium on hunger and malnutrition, stated that "studies at Harvard among resident physicians suggest that the average physician knows little more about nutrition than the average secretary, unless the secretary has a weight problem, and then she probably knows more than the average physician. We did find that there is a difference between older and younger physicians in relation to this problem. The older doctors do not know more about nutrition than their younger colleagues, but they are conscious of this lack. All in all, it seems that most physicians tend to be happy about this state of affairs." Dr. Mayer complained that "only a half dozen or so medical schools in the United States include a nutrition course in the curriculum. Nutrition education should be centered on foods—their size, shape, color, caloric value, etc.—we must relate such vital information to the everyday uses of all people."

I have taken many dietary histories which have revealed that the usual "nutritious" breakfast for some children consists of a glass of soda or "coke" and a portion of chocolate layer cake! For the child with hypoglycemia, such food assures a drop in blood glucose level for several hours, during which time the child's brain function is impaired so that he cannot learn well even if he does not suffer from learning disabilities. At best, the breakfast menu of the majority of learning-disabled children is poorly balanced and varies from the just-mentioned extreme by the substitution of sugar-frosted cereals. Glucose in the bloodstream is one of the most important nutrients for proper brain function, and the maintenance of a proper glucose level is essential in the creation of an optimum molecular environment for the mind.

An increasingly greater awareness of the importance of the role of nutrition in health maintenance led to more research, which revealed that, beyond malnutrition due to lack of food or proper diet, there were illnesses or conditions produced by perfectly good foods which are offending foods for the brain chemistry of many children and adults, capable of producing mental or physical symptoms. These foods may be the basic staples in the daily well-balanced diet of a hyperactive child, yet they produce disturbed, hyperactive behavior, or physical symptoms.

Many wholesome foods can be offensive for minimal-brain-dysfunction children. Their response is an allergic one, but the symptoms produced by the allergy are not the usual allergic symptoms but a *disturbance in behavior*. This response must be considered the result of a cerebral allergy. The foods most often productive of cerebral allergies are wheat, milk, eggs, corn and corn products (the latter are almost as ubiquitous as sugar), and beef. Since these foods are consumed daily and many are used several times each day, we can see dramatic changes in behavior when the offending food or foods are removed from the diet. The reduction in hyperactivity can in many cases be immediate. This can be accomplished by an elimination diet, and I have found that the foods most often responsible are those which the child eats or drinks most often and in the largest amounts. I have found few instances in which a half-gallon-a-day milk drinker was not benefited by being withdrawn completely from milk. Other liquids consumed in prodigious amounts are apple juice and soda. I have seen many children whose daily allotment of 48 ounces of soda was consumed by noon each day. These are the sodas of which Jean Mayer said that the labels listing the chemical additives, artificial colors, flavors, and preservatives read like a qualitative analysis of a water sample drawn from New York's East River.

Dr. Curtis Dohan, Professor of Medicine at the University of Pennsylvania, who conducted studies with disturbed adult schizophrenic patients hospitalized in the Veterans Administration hospital in Coatesville, Pennsylvania, reported that with a cereal-free and milk-free diet added to the daily treatment regime, patients so treated improved more rapidly than those who were continued on the usual institutional fare, which included cereal grains and milk. Dr. Dohan's original study,[5] which drew criticism, was replicated in a recent study. Schizophrenics maintained on a cereal-free and milk-free diet and receiving optimal treatment with neuroleptics showed an interruption or reversal of their therapeutic progress during a period of "blind" wheat gluten challenge. The exacerbation of the disease process was not due to variations in the drug doses. After termination of the wheat gluten challenge, the course of improvement was reinstated. The observed effects seemed to be due to a primary schizophrenia-promoting effect of wheat gluten.

Dr. Ben Feingold's work with salicylate-sensitive children and their response to the removal of artificial colors, flavors, and foods with naturally occurring salicylates is well known. This subgroup of minimal-brain-dysfunction children responds dramatically to the elimination of these additives, which occur in sodas, most frankfurters, and other luncheon meats, as well as in wholesome foods such as apples, oranges, peaches, grapes, raisins, cucumbers, pickles, and many others.

Orthomolecular treatment has many advantages that make it especially suitable for large numbers of children. Treatment can be directed by parents and paraprofessionals, reducing to a minimum the occasions upon which the child must be brought to a specialist for therapy. It is inexpensive, as it does not depend upon complex machinery or equipment, or upon the long-term use of psychotropic drugs. Of great importance is the role orthomolecular treatment could serve as a preventive as well as a therapeutic measure, because it could easily be included in prenatal and infant care programs everywhere. These are important considerations in view of the evidence that neurologically based and biochemically based learning disabilities are especially frequent among children from low-income areas. Bronfenbrenner[6] points out that a low-income mother's "exposure to nutritional deficiency, illness, fatigue, or emotional stress can be far more damaging to her child than was previously thought. The neurological disturbances thus produced persist through early childhood into the school years, where they are reflected in impaired learning capacity."

The relationship of severe infant malnutrition to infant mortality, disease, and retardation in physical development is well documented. In recent years evidence has accumulated that malnutrition has adverse effects on mental development and learning as well. Mild malnutrition can result in a child who is a "picky eater" who chronically gags when he swallows some food, or swallows it readily and then vomits. Recent studies utilized such reported differences within young twin pairs to show that subtle variations in eating habits in the first year can be related to differences in mental abilities later in life.

TRACE MINERALS

The fact that chemical substances can affect behavior has been apparent since the discovery of alcoholic fermentation and, in recent times, has been emphasized by the therapeutic use and nonmedical abuse of psychotropic and hallucinogenic drugs such as LSD. Abnormal behavior can result from dietary deficiencies of such trace minerals as copper, calcium, magnesium, manganese, and zinc. Dr. Carl Pfeiffer, Director of the Brain Bio-Center in Princeton, New Jersey, has reported clinical improvement in a subgroup of the schizophrenic population when he reestablished proper balances of copper and zinc by administering supplements of these minerals. Zinc deficiency in pregnant rats produced loss of appetite and, in the fetus, decreased levels of DNA in the brain, decreased total body and liver zinc levels, and caused retardation in growth. Cobalt, zinc, and manganese serve as cofactors for various metabolic enzymes; iron is an integral component in hemoglobin. Magnesium activates approximately 100 enzyme chains in every cell in the body. Zinc activates 60 of these chains; copper, 12; cobalt, 16; manganese, 20; iron, 30.

At the annual meeting of the American Psychiatric Association in 1976, Dr. David C. Jimerson reported that spinal fluid calcium levels are significantly correlated with symptom severity in depressed patients, although mean calcium levels did not differ from control groups. Calcium levels showed a significant negative correlation with accumulations of the dopamine metabolite homovanillic acid, suggesting a relationship between depressed calcium levels and the function of brain transmitters. Excess of copper in the tissues can lead to zinc and pyridoxine deficiencies.[7] The resulting zinc deficiency may lead to an accumulation of vitamin A in the liver and a shortage of vitamin A in blood plasma. Deficiency of pyridoxine leads to a shortage of B-3, which in turn produces a deficiency of nicotinamide adenodinucleotide, which is converted to tryptophan. There has been insufficient clinical application of research findings of the effects of trace minerals, in spite of increasing evidence that an analysis of trace metal concentrations can be diagnostically significant. Ross Seasly of the Kettering Medical Center, for example, notes that during the last ten years Kettering's clinical laboratory has never received a request for an analysis of trace metal concentrations.

Magnesium, like calcium, is a metal of considerable physiologic importance; in the mammalian organism, it is indispensable to life. Magnesium affects the activity of numerous enzyme systems; it is slowly absorbed from the gastrointestinal tract and rapidly excreted by the kidney. Therefore, ingestion of foods containing magnesium has no particular influence on the blood magnesium level. Clinically, low levels of magnesium in the blood plasma are associated with states of hyperexcitability, while high levels of magnesium have a sedative and depressant effect. Serum magnesium levels have considerable normal fluctuation, and persistently low or high magnesium values may be present without any clinical abnormality.

TOXIC METALS

Brain catecholamines, or neurotransmitters, regulate mood and behavior and influence aggressiveness and stereotyped repetitive behavior.

The environmental pollutants are often heavy metals such as lead, mercury, or cadmium. The lead pollution of our environment, and particularly our cities, has already reached a disturbingly high level. In 1967 in Manchester, England, a group of children were found to have lead levels of 30+ micrograms per 100 mg of blood. Professor D. Bryce-Smith of the University of Reading recently wrote[8] that no other chemical pollutant has accumulated in man to average levels so close to the threshold for overt clinical poisoning. Whenever lead poisoning has been diagnosed, it has always been traced to some definite source; in children it may be chewing on old paint work or toys containing lead. There has been no known case of lead poisoning, however, from the widespread general pollution to which everyone is exposed. This is why the apparently alarming situation to which Professor Bryce-Smith draws attention has caused little concern. Lead pollution does not seem to be doing any serious damage, the complacement argument runs, so why worry about it? This position, however, begins to look increasingly vulnerable in the face of mounting evidence that lead could have harmful effects at levels well below those which cause overt poisoning.

In 1964, Sir Alan Moncrieff and others at the Institute of Child Health in London found that a group of mentally retarded children had distinctly more lead in their blood than a group of normal children. In fact, nearly half of the retarded children had higher blood levels than the maximum level in the other group. It does not, of course, follow that lead was responsible for the children's mental retardation. It could well have been that their retardation made them more prone to chew on substances with a lead content. Nevertheless, the possibility that lead at levels too low to cause obvious poisoning could result in mental retardation was one that could not be ignored. The findings acted as a spur to the search for some measurable effect of low levels of lead in the human body.

In 1970, Dr. Sven Hernberg and his associates found lead affected the functioning of an enzyme, ALA dehydratase, which is involved in haem (the precursor of hemoglobin) synthesis. Furthermore, he showed that in the test tube any level of lead affected the activity of ALA dehydratase to some degree. In October 1970, a research group lead by J. A. Millar fed lead to baby rats and found that the activity of ALA dehydratase was affected not only in their blood, but in their brains as well. They wrote in their report in the *Lancet*: "The findings of decreased ALA dehydratase activity in the blood of children with lead levels falling within the normal range, and the possibility that similar biochemical changes are present in the brain also, emphasizes the danger of exposure to even very small amounts of lead during childhood and suggests that a downward revision of acceptable levels of blood lead in children is desirable." In addition to lead discharged into the atmosphere in vehicle exhaust, people also absorb lead from foods, water, and many other sources.

It is now a well-known clinical fact that susceptibility to the harmful effects of lead is highly variable. Lead in heavy concentrations in the tissues (and some of the hundreds of children I have examined have concentrations as high as 85 ppm) can interfere with metabolic reactions that activate other metals, such as copper, iron, manganese, and potassium.

In studies of the toxic metals in children's hair, I found that children show a higher concentration of lead than do adults. In adult groups, it has been reported that pregnant women show a greater susceptibility than other adult members of the population. Now that attention has been focused on the level of lead in the tissues of many middle-class Americans who may be exposed to lead by-products in gasoline exhaust fumes, many new cases of borderline lead toxicity are appearing without the usual explanation of lead ingestion. While a close correlation exists between the level of atmospheric lead and the levels of lead accumulated and stored in the body, there is a wide diversity in susceptibility, not only to symptoms, but also to accumulation of this toxic trace metal. Recent experiments again give evidence that nutritional factors, particularly dietary calcium, may be important determinants in the capacity of the body to absorb and retain lead. Animals receiving lead in their drinking water showed a greater absorption of lead when their diet was deficient in calcium. This group of animals absorbed four times as much lead compared to the group which received a normal dietary calcium intake. Lead is everywhere in our environment. Each year the average car spews out about 2 kg of lead from its exhaust. While lead is not highly toxic like cadmium, its presence in such large amounts adds to the dangers it presents. The automobile is not alone responsible for enveloping the earth in an envelope of lead. Ice borings at the polar ice cap revealed that samples of ice layers deposited decades before the advent of the internal combustion engine and leaded gasoline contained lead.

Children breathe lead and accumulate it from sucking their dirty fingers and toys, from inhaling road dust and airplane exhaust, and from many other sources. Children can absorb dangerous quantities of lead from chewing newspaper or color-printed pages in magazines. At present one quarter of several hundred thousand children tested and living in cities have blood levels at the borderline of toxicity.

Dr. Caprio and his associates[9] studied the blood levels of 5,226 children living near the congested traffic lanes of Newark and reported those children living closest to the highways had the highest levels of lead in their blood. Some had poisonous levels of lead.

While the chronic ingestion of lead has yet to be clearly associated with hyperactivity, two recently reported studies of mice and rats showed that lead produces definite changes in brain chemistry. Such changes may lead to behavioral disorders including hyperactivity.[10] At the University of Cincinnati Medical Centers, Drs. I. R. Michaelson and Mitchell U. Sauerhoff administered varying concentrations of lead solution to nursing mother rats and then measured neurochemical changes in 90 babies. They found 15 to 20% decreases in brain dopamine. At John Hopkins University, Drs. Ellen K. Silbergeld and Alan M. Goldberg[11] tested the effects of lead ingestion on mouse behavior; after administering lead solutions to nursing mothers, the investigators found the offspring were retarded in development and suffered behavior disorders. They were hyperactive and aggressive. The animals did not, however, exhibit signs of lead poisoning. It was reported that the behavioral effects were due to abnormalities in the concentration of serotonin in the brain and alterations in the metabolism of norepinephrine.

In a study reported in the *American Journal of Psychiatry*,[12] lead-chelating medication was used to treat 13 hyperkinetic school children whose blood and urine lead levels were in an elevated but "nontoxic" range. Six children with histories of etiologically relevant perinatal or developmental complications showed relatively little improvement. Seven other children with unremarkable histories, and for whom a lead etiology could thus be entertained, showed marked improvement. The authors conclude that lead may play an important role in the etiology of some cases of hyperactivity, and the medical workup of hyperactivity should include lead level measurements and careful consideration of other possible etiological factors.

Of equal importance as a pollutant and more lethal than lead is cadmium. High ratios of cadmium to zinc in the kidney have been associated with death from hypertension. Injection of a zinc chelate into cadmium-hypertensive rats resulted in a return of the hypertension to normal levels. Vitamin C is effective against cadmium-produced anemia. Recent research showed zinc and selenium to be protective against the accumulation of lethal doses of cadmium.

The accumulation of toxic metals interferes with pyruvic acid levels, thus impairing the energy supply to brain cells. In young children this would be of particular significance, since, up to age four, children experience greater oxygen demand in the brain than adults do. A Federal court recently upheld the claims of environmentalists that lead emissions are harmful, and the Environmental Protection Agency has been ordered to add the toxic metal lead to its list of air pollutants.[13] The greatest, strongest, most immovable forces blocking the improvement of our children's environment in the air we breathe, the food we eat, and the water we drink are the mammoth corporations whose activities continue to impair the environment dangerously.

A report that chronic daily ingestion of lead produced no changes in the behavioral pattern of rhesus monkeys was published by the research arm of the lead and zinc industry, despite the fact that experimental evidence favors the view that lead does produce behavioral abnormalities in animals and, more importantly, in man. Moreover, most of mankind appears to be more sensitive than rats and rhesus monkeys to lead. A report in 1960 revealed a high spontaneous abortion rate among female workers in the lead industry. The central barrier does not protect the fetus against the lead to which its mother is exposed.

CONCLUSION

A measure of the state of its civilization is any society's attitude toward its handicapped. If we are to continue to count ourselves among the leaders of the civilized world, we must gain a new perspective on the things we do for and to our most precious commodity—our children. We feed them foods containing allowable amounts of filth approved by the FDA. Included in this filth are mouse droppings and animal hair. They eat hot dogs containing allowable amounts of bone splinters and bone dust. All their luncheon meats are treated with sodium nitrite and other additives. Most of their food and beverages contain artifical colors and flavors, which produce hyperactivity in a significant percentage of their population and seriously interfere with their ability to learn. We then add to all this the lead and the stench in the air they breathe. From the billions of cigarettes we consume, we blow cadmium, another toxic metal, into their air space. We then punish them for their inability to learn. Only after due consideration of these disasters can there be understanding of the enormity of the problem our children share with us.

References

1. Cott, A., Megavitamins: The orthomolecular approach to behavioral disorders and learning disabilities, *Academic Therapy* 7(3):245–258, 1972.
2. Cott, A., Orthomolecular approach to the treatment of learning disabilities, *Schizophrenia* 3(2):95–105, 1971.
3. Warburg, O., The prime cause and prevention of cancer, 1966 Lindau Lecture, presented for the Nobel Peace Committee, 1966.
4. Yaryura-Tobias, J., and Nezioglu, B. A., Violent behavior, brain dysrhythmia and glucose dysfunction, *J. Orthomolecular Psychiatry* 4(3):182–188, 1975.
5. Dohan, F. C., Grasberger, J. C., Lowell, F. M., Johnston, H. T., and Arbegast, A. W., Relapsed schizophrenics: More rapid improvement on a milk-and-cereal diet, *Brit. J. Psychiat.* 115:522, 1969.
6. Bronfenbrenner, U., Dampening the unemployability explosion, *Saturday Review*, 1969, 4, January.
7. Pfeiffer, C. C., Observations on trace and toxic elements in hair and serum, *J. Orthomolecular Psychiatry* 3(4):259–264, 1974.
8. Bryce-Smith, D., and Waldron, H. A., Lead pollution, disease and behavior, *Community Health* 6:1968, 1974.
9. Caprio, R. J., Margulis, H. L., and Joselow, M. M., Lead absorption in children and its relationship to urban traffic densities, *Arch. Environ. Health* 28:195–197, 1974.
10. Michaelson, I. A., and Sauderhoff, M. W., Lead poisoning, *Medical World News*, September 7, 1973.
11. Silbergeld, E. K., and Goldberg, A. M., Effects of lead ingestion on mouse behavior, *Medical World News*, September 7, 1973.
12. David, O. J. et al., Lead and hyperactivity; Behavioral response to chelation, *Am. J. Psychiat.* 113(10):1155–1158, 1976.
13. *Wall Street Journal*, March 3, 1976.

Chapter 12

Neuroallergy as a Contributing Factor to Social Misfits: Diagnosis and Treatment

Ray C. Wunderlich, Jr., M.D.
St. Petersburg, Florida

INTRODUCTION

Social misfits are often found to have biological health problems. Adverse socio-cultural and biological factors often interweave to limit the development of the individual. When such is the case, I describe the situation as biosocial decline (see Figure 12-1).

It is well recognized that socio-cultural deprivation or adversity may be responsible for the making of social misfits. Less well known is the fact that biological health problems can be primary factors that underlie or lead to social difficulties such as school failure, juvenile delinquency, and crime.

Allergy is one of the most common biological health problems in our society today. Allergy of the nervous system is more common than realized. Neuroallergy is particularly devastating because it may interfere with thought, planning, reasoning, reading, learning, vision, and the ability to get along with others. Neuroallergy is a common biologic factor in retarding social development. The relationship of neuroallergy to allergy in general and to social factors is shown in Figure 12-2.

Neuroallergy has long been overlooked as a biological disorder of great importance. Only in recent years have a few pioneering

Figure 12-1

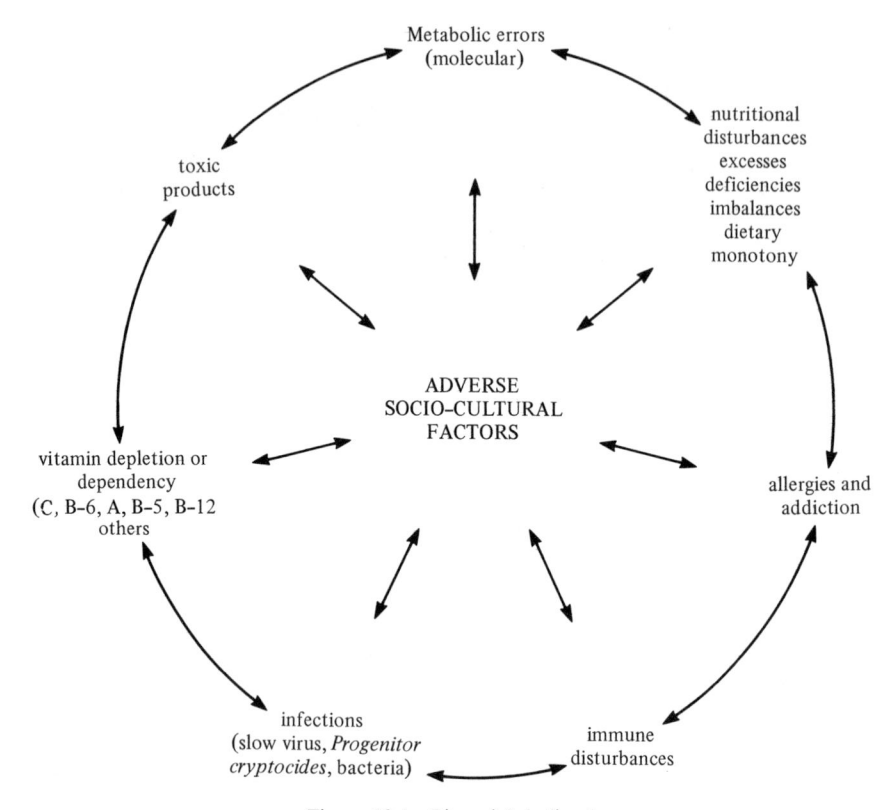

Diagram of Biosocial decline showing ADVERSE SOCIO-CULTURAL FACTORS at center with bidirectional arrows connecting to:
- Metabolic errors (molecular)
- nutritional disturbances: excesses, deficiencies, imbalances, dietary monotony
- allergies and addiction
- immune disturbances
- infections (slow virus, *Progenitor cryptocides*, bacteria)
- vitamin depletion or dependency (C, B-6, A, B-5, B-12 others)
- toxic products

Figure 12-1 Biosocial decline.*

investigators recognized the potentially devastating effect of neuroallergy on one's interpersonal transactions and social adjustment. Allergy of the nervous system strikes a hearty blow at favorable adaptation.

In this paper I will first devote considerable discussion to a description of successful and unsuccessful citizens, and factors that determine whether an individual becomes one or the other. Then I will describe allergy and neuroallergy, and relate them to these factors. Finally, I will present therapeutic methods that can be responsible for preventing and treating neuroallergy and its associated social maladjustment.

*The concept of biosocial decline was first elaborated in *Allergy, Brains, and Children Coping*.[1]
Figure 12-1 was used in *Neuroallergy: An Overlooked Cause of Neuromental Dysfunction*, edited by Pattabi Raman and to be published by Greylock Publishers, Stamford, Conn. It is used with permission of the editor and the publisher.

Neuroallergy as a Contributing Factor to Social Misfits 231

```
              ALLERGIC REACTIONS
              in the brain and other
                parts of the body
```

SYSTEMIC SYMPTOMS
Pale color
Circles under eyes
Nasal congestion and other
respiratory symptoms
Abdominal pain and other
digestive symptoms
Aching in legs and other muscles
Urinary symptoms, etc.

A →

NERVOUS SYSTEM SYMPTOMS
Headache
Fatigue
Drowsiness
Slowness in thinking
Inability to concentrate
Short attention span
Irritability
Hyperactivity
Perceptual blurring

← B

A person with disagreeable personality traits who doesn't feel well or perform well in school, on the job, or in the home

C → LOSS OF SELF ESTEEM AND FEELING OF INSECURITY

PSYCHIC SYMPTOMS: Depression, Anxiety, Agitation, Paranoia, etc.

← D

CRITICISM AND REJECTION BY
teacher
parent
sibling
spouse
boss

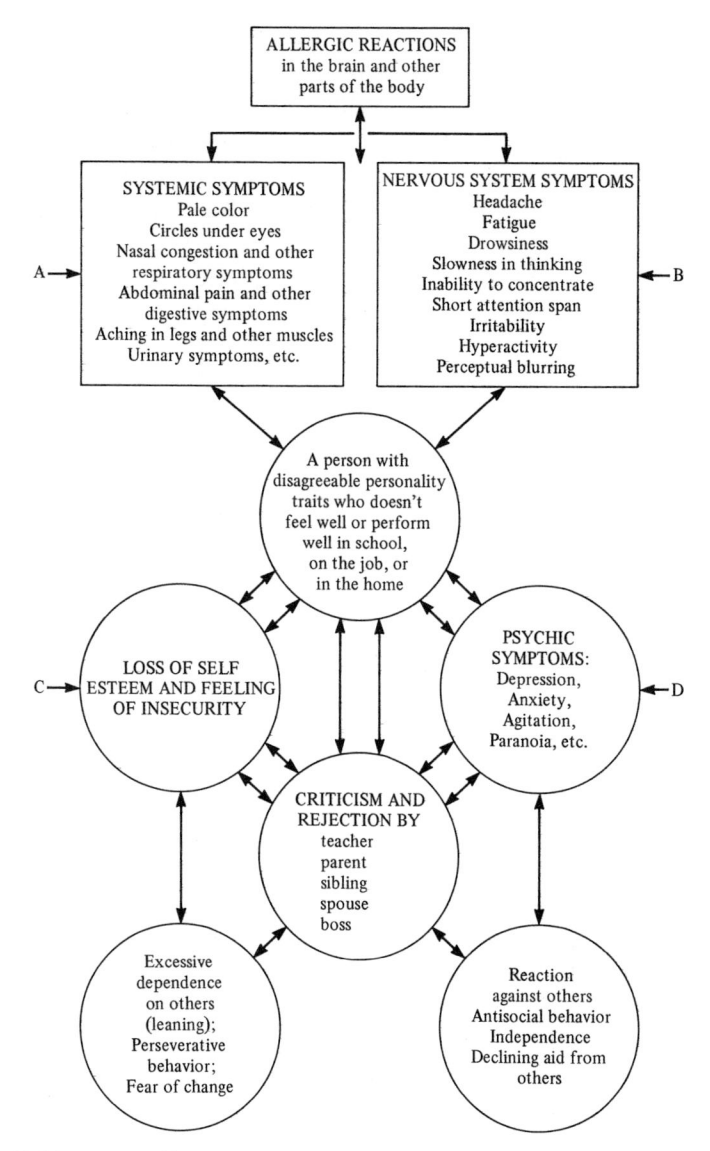

Excessive dependence on others (leaning); Perseverative behavior; Fear of change

Reaction against others
Antisocial behavior
Independence
Declining aid from others

Figure 12-2* The relationship between systemic and nervous system allergy, life factors, emotional behavior, personality development, social behavior, and learning problems

*Figure 12-2 is based on a figure in the book *Can Your Child Read? Is He Hyperactive?* by William G. Crook, M.D., Pedicenter Press, 1975, Jackson, Tenn. The diagram with considerable alterations was used in *Neuroallergy: An Overlooked Cause of Neuromental Dysfunction*, edited by Pattabi Raman and to be published by Greylock Publishers, Stamford, Conn. The diagram is here used with the permission of all of the above.

Health or social disturbance may have varied origins. An infection, for example, may precipitate disturbance of the immune system, resulting in an allergy with subsequently impoverished nourishment, dimished enzyme function, production of toxic products, and socio-cultural adversity. On the other hand, disturbed social relationships may precipitate biological malfunction on many levels. Commonly, monotonous dietary habits and the consumption of inferior-quality food lead to nutrient depletion, immune dysfunction, infection, unsatisfactory lifestyle, and so on.

Our modern culture, with its increasingly chemicalized, fabricated food supply, subjects most of us to nutritional and toxic stress on a daily basis.

Once adversity is established, the effectiveness of the individual to cope with developmental problems, job, family, and the many disadvantages of our modern corporate society is compromised. Increasing dependence on society occurs (doctors, tranquilizers, antidepressants, caffeine, nicotine, vitamins, minerals, counselors, therapists, and so forth), or withdrawal from the mainstream of society takes place (school failure, juvenile delinquency, crime).

Notice in Figure 12-2 that an individual may commence with disability in any circle and proceed to develop the problems listed in the other circles. For example, a low-grade allergy that is not interfering with a child's progress may become clinically disabling in the face of undue criticism and rejection.

The arrows at A, B, C, and D indicate primary causes other than allergy that may serve as inciting events to precipitate neuroallergy. For example, at A, nutritional depletion may give rise to the characteristics listed, as well as to neuroallergy. At B, an infection might produce the nervous symptoms indicated and trigger neuroallergy. At C and D, a situational life event could give rise to the symptoms listed and set off neuroallergy.

TWO KINDS OF CITIZENS

Individuals who live together in communities on the face of the earth may be described as successful or unsuccessful citizens. The successful citizen has joined ranks with his fellow human beings and lives in basic harmony with them. The unsuccessful citizen has failed to develop this bond of mutual getting-along. He thrives, parasitelike, by swearing allegiance to a small, negatively-oriented subculture that harasses the larger group of successful citizens.

Anything that interferes with interpersonal communication, the development of pride and self-accomplishment, and the recognition of the need to live positively with others will encourage delinquency and criminal behavior.

The person whose biological development is compromised is often a vulnerable individual. He is vulnerable to imperfect parents, teachers, and social systems, as well as bacteria, viruses, allergens, and other sources of adverse stress. When a person is not adequately strong in biological characteristics, he may be exquisitely sensitive and susceptible to his environment. When his social environment is disorganized, random, and without effective loving structure, then a doubly handicapped individual results. He is biologically weak and socially inadequate.

Frequently, biosocial handicaps are found in several members of a family, often appearing in parent(s) and child. These may be hereditary traits, but maladaptive behavior is also commonly learned.

The nonsuccessful citizen is, or becomes, the delinquent and the criminal. The unsuccessful citizen radiates anger, frustration, and tension. He does not consider the rights of his fellow citizens. He sees them as objects to be manipulated for his own selfish purposes. Fame (actually infame) and notoriety spring from the actions of the unsuccessful citizen. He makes "waves" and headlines by attracting and stealing from his fellow men. He obtains stimulation (excitement), importance, and a sense of self-accomplishment by infringing on the rights, properties, and territories of those around him. He often becomes enamored with himself because of his successful exploits at the expense of others.

For the nonsuccessful citizen, society and all that it stands for has become a foundation against which he reacts. The delinquent and the criminal, for one reason or another, have failed to take the positive act of merging with society. Unsuccessful citizens remain caught in the backwash of society's wake. They are unable to generate energy in the direction that will enable them to catch on, to become participants and passengers in society's voyage. The nonsuccessful citizen wallows in his successful irritation of society, and is usually unable to lift himself out of the waters of antisocial behavior.

The successful citizen, on the other hand, has "caught the boat" at an early age. He is, at the same time, a worker and a passenger on society's vessel. He contributes to the work necessary to move along, but at the same time enjoys the ride. The successful citizen sees nonsuccessful citizens, awash in the wake of society's boat, and strives to "reach" them by various means. He hopes to bring them aboard so they too can participate in the work and the pleasures of the voyage instead of living a life of torment, ferment, and turbulence. The successful citizen is a good sailor. He is an acculturated individual who enjoys the exercise of self-control for his own welfare, as well as that of others.

The successful citizen is the bulwark of society, as a general rule. The good that he does does not ordinarily make "waves" or headlines. He takes care of his own needs and respects the rights, belongings, and territories of those with whom he shares living space. The successful citizen positively adapts. He lives with others and likes it. He is not overcome by sharing space, time, and feelings. He has sufficient life energy to do for himself and to tolerate the peculiarities of others who are different from himself. His viewpoint is basically one of *acceptance*, not one of rejection. He has positive mental health instead of negative, narrow, or fragmented mental outlooks.

In family, city, state, and nation, the positively adapted citizen acquires and preserves personal belongings and territory, but he also shares for the common good. He invests prominently in himself. He builds wealth and personal strength without stealing from or diminishing that of others. He recycles his resources with an eye to improving himself and his family. He sees to his own survival needs in a calm and orderly fashion, yet, at the same time, he may contribute something for the guy on the other side of town who is less fortunate than he. He generally shows largesse to others if he feels that he is not being victimized or "taken." The successful citizen uses his strengths to bob back from adversity rather than becoming caught up in a stream of negative endeavors.

The successful citizen combines a necessary degree of selfishness with altruism. He is appropriately aggressive and combative when his citizen-rights are threatened. However, he does not go out of his way to assert his power, and he does not attain stimulation and status primarily at the expense of others.

The successful citizen is a busy person. He is a worker. He is like an ant or a bee, busily involved in work that is compatible with community interests. He does not find the time to interfere with the rights of others. Unlike the ant or the bee, however, the successful citizen obtains individual recognition and reward in one form or another for his efforts.

Within his community, the successful, involved citizen interrelates with others in one way or another. The citizen recognizes the interdependence of one citizen upon another, and does not rebel or lash out against the fact that he needs others to further his own goals.

The successful citizen is involved in socially acceptable, positive ways that enhance his image of himself as an important person, a "good" person, and a contributing member of society. He receives stimulation, recognition, and security from his activities at home, job, or play, and he feels that he is improving himself and his family by his activities. He employs his considerable energies in organizational ways (clubs, groups, politics, sports, etc.), or by influencing others around him toward his own viewpoints. He may exert considerable effect upon others around him, but his efforts are directed at building rather than tearing down.

An overall sense of common good is characteristic of the successful citizen. He pays reasonable taxes, generally waits at the stoplight, doesn't litter very much, volunteers at the hospital, runs for office, coaches Little League, and may help out in an emergency. He speeds a little when the cop isn't looking, but pays his fine when caught and is more careful the next time.

The successful citizen is part of a system—the community—and derives much of his positive feeling and well-being from that belonging. He works within the system to correct inequities and to improve the rules and conditions under which he lives.

The unsuccessful citizen, the delinquent, or the criminal, is busily engaged in fights with humanity, stealing from others in one way or another, and often protesting his lot to the fullest. Out of the mainstream of positive social development, he thrusts against the system and grows increasingly different. He likes to believe that he needs no one, but in reality, he is highly dependent upon the existence of successful citizens. If they did not exist, he would have no one to prey upon and act against. The maladapting individual says to himself, "By doing wrong, I can experience success! I have power. I exist. I can exert a significant effect on others."

Early in his life, boredom may have threatened dissolution. Anticivil acts provide stimulation and excitement to feed a negatively adapting ego. Soon these acts become a way of life, and they are repeated for their shock effect on the world and the stimulation that they provide. His personal contacts grow among a group of less-than-desirable associates. Soon these contacts are the only ones available. They feed the budding misfit's need for human interaction, but encourage further anticivil behavior.

BEHAVIORAL DETERMINANTS

Many factors combine to determine whether an individual becomes a successful or a nonsuccessful citizen. The prenatal and postnatal environments of the child are crucial areas of influence.

The individual may have suffered maltreatment early in life, which can serve as a model of behavior to be copied or reacted against. Either way, an unsuccessful citizen may result. For every physically battered child there are large numbers of children who are socially or emotionally battered.

The mother's state of health is eminently related to the status of the infant within her womb. The nourishment of the mother is the nutrient lifeline that feeds the developing fetus. If the mother is malnourished, the fetus may not obtain an adequate supply of nutrients, or he may so drain the mother of vital elements that she will be in a weakened state after birth and serve inadequately in her mothering capacity.

From the earliest days in the crib a person is programmed and shaped to react in certain ways to environmental stimuli, objects, situations, or events. Behavior modification can alter behavior after the fact because behavioral interaction is such an important variable in determining behavior in the first place, before the fact.

The parent(s) who has a neuroallergic disorder is often beside herself, or himself, with worries, irritability, poor management, disorganization, fuzzy thinking, lack of follow-through, and associated other physical health problems. Such a parent(s) does not usually mold, shape, or program a child in ways that lead to positive adaptive social behavior. The child may continually be tampered with and fussed at, he may be unsupervised and left alone to his own machinations, or he may be showered with bursts of attention followed by drought periods when parental love, guidance, and supervision are dreadfully absent.

Many developmental deviations coalesce to produce the picture of a noncapable child. Some nonsuccessful citizens have had a reading problem, some visual disability, and others, allergy or poor nutrition; many have had suboptimal parenting. As such children venture into society, they frequently stay in need of extra assistance. Speech therapy, reading instruction, tutoring, special schools, medication, physical therapy, glasses, and so on, serve as crutches for the Johns and Janes who cannot, or will not, grow in independence. Because they need help, they see themselves as dependent. Because they see themselves as dependent, they may remain behind in development of self-worth and self-reliance. One illness after another often occurs, reinforcing the concept that these children are weak and in need of extra investigation and therapy. When opportunities are available for "goofing off," skipping school, acting out, or participating in antisocial behavior, the child is likely to find the temptations too great.

Parents come in all varieties. The majority do not have any special training for rearing children. Very often they come up against problems of child rearing for which they are not prepared. Young adults, the ones who have the children, often have not "found" themselves. Trying to solve their own problems of adjusting to young adult life, they are suddenly faced with the strange business of child rearing. It's hard enough with a healthy, bouncing baby, but much more challenging, indeed, with a congenital hyperactive; a child with recurrent infections; an infant who fails to thrive; a child with visual, auditory, or learning difficulty; and it's especially difficult with a child who has neuroallergy.

The life style of parents, siblings, or neighbors may provide a model of negative, antisocial behavior for the child to emulate. In other cases, living in a "home" is so oppressive that a child seeks the company of an asocial gang to strike back at the powers that be.

Faced with considerable tasks in bearing and then rearing a challenging child, the imperfect or vulnerable parent may not provide a suitable environment. For numerous reasons, the parent(s) may be absent from the home at critical times when the child needs the support and structure that a warm, loving adult can provide. Future unsuccessful citizens often grow up in a vacuum, or in a random environment without close human contacts, without loving touch, without caring words, without constructive guidance, and without an opportunity to be important to someone. What we do, when we do it, and how we do it, are crucial variables in developing future citizens. Neuroallergy in supervising adults intimately affects their acts and deeds, and rarely improves their quality.

There is no question that the behavior of persons in a child's environment is a major variable in determining whether he becomes a successful citizen or a social misfit. There is also no question that the behavior of the child is a major variable in determining the behavior of his adult associates and peers. Some children have such incorrigible behavior that the persons around them can only serve as watchdogs and policemen, guarding the rights of others. Such treacherously negative behavior brings out the imperfections and inadequacies of adults who live with and around them.

Deviant behavior in children may derive from chronic neuroallergy. Unfortunately, at this time, this disorder is not often recognized; hence important therapeutic efforts may not be directed at the underlying problem.

THE NEUROALLERGY FACTOR

Allergy is an unusual or excessive reaction of the body to a foreign substance. The immune system of the body is involved in classical allergic conditions; the system includes the lymph organs of the body (lymph nodes, tonsils, adenoids, thymus, and intestinal Peyer's patches), circulating blood lymphocytes, mast cells and basophils, and antibodies. The antibody associated with allergic conditions is known as immunoglobulin E (IgE).

In a classical immune allergic condition such as hay fever, a substance, foreign to the body, pollen, elicits a response from the immune system. An outpouring of cells and antibodies occurs, directed against the foreign pollen in the nose, eyes, and sinuses, and chemical mediators released from cells give rise to the classical symptoms of the disorder. Sneezing, red itchy eyes, sinus ache, nasal discharges, and so on, are recognized as hay fever.

When classical immune allergic reactions such as hay fever, asthma, eczema, hives, and so forth, occur, it is possible for a person's nervous system to be involved. The individual might feel dull and sluggish, and be unable to perform mental activities which he might otherwise do easily. This is one form of neuroallergy. The actual mechanism underlying that neuro-mental dysfunction is not known. Possibilities include a pollen overload in the body (toxicity), immune reaction in the nervous system, pH shift in fluids irrigating the brain, alterations in neuroactive chemicals, mechanical changes in facial tissues draining to the brain (venous congestion), and so on.

A somewhat similar form of nasal and sinus involvement occurs in perennial allergic rhinitis. In this condition, nasal allergy is chronic all year long, not periodic or seasonal as it is in classical hay fever. Symptoms of stuffy nose, headache, and so forth, may abound, but also may be entirely absent. As in the acute allergic disorder, neuromental dysfunction may be prominent. At times, it may be the only presenting symptom. The individual may be mentally sluggish (brain fog), unable to read or figure, or he may be markedly irritable, fatigued, or depressed. Hyperemotionality, hyperaggressiveness, hyperactivity, and violent behavior may all be allergically based.

Neuroallergy may be a concomitant of allergy in the body as a whole (hypersensitivity disorders), it may be a component of respiratory tract allergy, it may be a sequel to gastrointestinal allergy, or it may be the direct result of immune system disturbance in the nervous system. Klotz has written an excellent summary of neuroallergy and its manifestations.[2]

The individual with neuroallergy thus has it as an accompaniment of allergy elsewhere in the body, or as a direct involvement of the nervous system.

Philpott, Randolph, and others[3] have called attention to allergylike conditions that are termed maladaptive reactions. They are thought to involve a change in body pH and to occur in the patient with nutritional deficiencies. A lack of vitamin B-6 is believed to be a key factor in the production of these maladaptive reactions, because B-6 is such an important agent in their treatment.

In other persons who do not have any known nutritional deficiency, certain foods may exert a neuroallergic or maladaptive reaction. Some individuals find that the use of foods of animal origin is followed by lethargy, muddled thinking, irritability, and so forth.

The neuroallergic individual may show a host of neuromental symptoms, or he may be plagued with only one. In the Allergic-Tension-Fatigue Syndrome[4] he is unduly tired and/or anxious. The individual may be predominantly fatigued, excited, tense, tired, hyperactive, irritable, weepy, hyperaggressive, or depressed. Almost any neuromental dysfunction may be associated with allergy or allergylike disorders.[5]

Neuroallergy may be acute or chronic. An individual may become acutely ill, for example, when exposed to certain environmental chemicals. Befuddled thinking or an acute episode of mental illness may occur upon exposure to petroleum fumes, carbon tetrachloride, the fumes of a gas range, or the odor of a Magic Marker. In the acute case the neuromental disorder may be correctly attributed to the chemical exposure, but it is surprising how often it is not. In chronic cases it is much more difficult to ferret out the cause of the chronic brain syndrome. Mandell has described sensitivities to elements in the environment and the illnesses that they may bring on.[6]

A common origin of neuroallergy is a diet lacking in variety. When a susceptible individual (one with a family history of allergy) eats certain foods in large amounts, in a chronic repetitive pattern, neuroallergy often results. The person who lives in a disorganized home and who has little interest in nutrition often develops a monotonously regular diet composed of less-than-desirable foods. Food cravings and food addictions appear as malnutrition and neuroallergy develop.

Neuroallergic reactions to foods or food additives may not involve immune dysfunction (true allergy as we presently know it), but may be maladaptive or allergylike reactions.

The substances commonly implicated in food neuroallergy are, first of all, the various chemicals that are added to foods. Since refined white sugar is devoid of all nutrients except naked calories, it is considered the prime food additive of modern society. Refined sugar is probably the single factor responsible for the most neuroallergic reactions. This matter has been extensively discussed.[7,8]

Artificial colors, flavors, and other food additives may also be the source of unwanted behavior.[9] In a controlled double-blind experiment, Conners et al. recently found support for the Kaiser-Permanente Diet that is based on Dr. Ben Feingold's observations of hyperactivity due to food additives.[10]

The foods commonly implicated in neuroallergy are cow's milk, wheat, corn, chocolate, citrus, and eggs. The greater the quantity of a food eaten, and the more frequently it is consumed, the more likely it is to be the cause of allergy in a susceptible individual.

The concept of food addiction explains the food cravings that individuals have when they are experiencing maladaptive reactions. Eating the offending food temporarily relieves unpleasant feelings or adverse physiological states that come about due to eating the food at a prior date. The sequence of eat–hurt–eat–relieve becomes a part of daily existence. Soon hurt (symptomatic or physiologic) is not realized because the food is taken so frequently. Usually the offending food is not suspected as a culprit in the origin of neuroallergy.

It is likely that drug addiction and alcoholism are similar craving-addictive disorders, frequently related to food sensitivities and disturbances of blood sugar levels. There is growing awareness that maladaptive reactions to foods may be associated with significant deviations in blood sugar levels (hypoglycemia or hyperglycemia).[11]

A mother who is unduly fatigued and irritable because of excessive sugar in the diet will not be the kind of parent who can flexibly respond to the demands of child rearing. A parent who is lethargic and depressed because of a maladaptive reaction to cow's milk will not be likely to radiate enthusiasm and love with his child. The teacher who is not thinking clearly owing to wheat in the diet will not be able to organize the classroom, meet the needs of vulnerable children, and manage wiggly kids with calm.

The father who is sleepier than he should be because of the mental torpor associated with allergy will not be available to share precious moments with his child. Baseball, walks, and man-talk just don't make it into his day. Furthermore, the man of the house who is ill has difficulty supporting and satisfying his wife. Most of his energy goes into the work day. Home is for his recovery.[12]

For the neuroallergic adult it is easier to let a child stay the way he is and to let him have his way, than to invest time and energy in the difficult project of objectively meeting his needs and providing guidance. Communication often suffers in the home of the neuroallergic. When one is biologically ill, he is not adept at managing the tricky business of child rearing, and he is not very skillful at successful citizen making.

The sibling who is hyperaggressive and violent because of milk allergy, makes home a living hell. Chaos reigns. Survival and beat-a-retreat displace cooperation in such a home. The teenager with asocial behavior due to corn in the diet can disrupt the best of families.

Because allergies can seriously interfere with the integrity of the respiratory mucous membranes, infections of the nose, ears, sinuses, throat, and bronchial tubes are common. The condition RURD, recurrent upper respiratory disorder, is due to allergy. One respiratory infection after another plagues the allergic individual with RURD.

When one is infected, he is not apt to function at his best. He may not feel well, and he may be short-tempered. Evident, but more often low-grade infections further add to the stress load of the neuroallergic person and impede his effectiveness as a positive influencer of youth. Mom's chronic bad breath is usually due to low-level allergic-infectious sinus inflammation, not a "sour stomach." Dad's postnasal drip and headaches may be due to insidious allergy-infection rather than working too hard.

Some children, seriously neuroallergic, appear to be "born mean." Such children may be the product of malnutrition or allergy in the mother during pregnancy. They exist by virtue of negative friction with their environment. The efforts of ordinary adults to contain them are ineffective. Dietary manipulations, allergic management, and understanding behavior modification in an environment of caring (love) may break the back of such negative disposition. A lifetime of irritability, poor concentration, and not feeling well may change within a few days, or weeks, when appropriate management is carried out. Often, however, a longer treatment effort is required. The combination of allergy management, nutritional improvement; and psychological guidance are particularly important, but not often enough invoked.

IDENTIFICATION

How can one be sure that neuroallergy is the cause of a patient's problem? Sometimes one cannot be certain. A therapeutic trial of allergy treatment may be needed before the diagnosis becomes clear in retrospect. More often, however, neuroallergy can be diagnosed, if it is thought about. Professionals who treat nervous and mental disorders have generally been unaware or have failed to recognize the importance of the NeuroAllergic Syndrome.

A high index of suspicion for the presence of neuroallergy needs to be developed in those who care for individuals with states of neuromental dysfunction. Learning disorder, hyperactivity, attentional disorders (poor mental concentration), character disturbances, undue anxiety and depression, schizophrenia, and social misfit should be considered to be neuroallergic problems until proven otherwise. If the family history is positive for such disorders as asthma, hay fever, eczema, food allergy, drug allergy, hives, and emphysema, the case for neuroallergy is strengthened.

One of the first tests that a physician desires on any patient is the white blood cell count. The white count, along with the differential analysis of white cell types* gives indications about the presence of infection, the type of infection (bacterial vs. viral), nutritive status, and the adequacy of the bone marrow and lymph system in producing white blood cells.

---

*The differential analysis is performed by microscopic viewing of the stained blood smear. The presence and number of each variety of white blood cell is reported in percentage of the total.

I have found that a slight lowering of the white blood cell count is often seen in the allergic patient. The normal level is usually given as 5,000 to 10,000 cells per cubic millimeter of blood. Levels from 4,000 to 5,000 may provide a clue to the presence of an allergic condition. The white blood cell count may also be lowered because of nutritional depletion associated with allergic conditions.

A strong clue to the presence of allergy may be obtained when attention is paid to the percentage and absolute number of eosinophils, a type of white blood cell.

Eosinophils may be termed "allergy cells." They are characteristically increased in the presence of allergic condition. A lack of eosinophil increase, however, does not exclude allergy by any means. An elevation of eosinophils may occur in conditions other than allergy, but from a practical standpoint the nonallergic causes are not very common.* The presence of an elevated level of eosinophils in the blood or in the nasal mucus is excellent evidence of the presence of an ongoing allergic process, even in the absence of symptoms referable to the blood or nose. The normal level of eosinophils is usually given as 0%–4% of the total white blood cells.

Allergy has been the "stepchild" of medicine, considered by some to be a "pseudoscience." Hence, elevations of eosinophils in blood counts have often been dismissed as trivial, of a transient nature, or of no significance. At times, much energy is directed toward identifying rarer causes of eosinophil increase, and the more common allergy to foods or environmental substances is overlooked.

I recall one patient who had been shuttled from child guidance clinic to psychiatrist, to neurologist, to hospital, and who was treated with many drugs to no avail. At times when she was not taking drugs, her eosinophil blood levels were greatly increased. This eosinophil increase was usually ignored or overlooked. The reason? Most physicians charged with the responsibility of managing neuromental disorders are not trained in the identification and treatment of allergy. Furthermore, they are generally unaware of the possible production of neuromental dysfunction by allergy and allergylike maladaptive reactions.

My writing, along with that of Dr. William Crook,[13] has called attention to the prevalence of neuroallergy. Dr. Ben Feingold's empha-

---

*The presence of intestinal parasites may produce a rise in eosinophil levels. In semitropical Florida, over the past 15 years, all patients with eosinophil increases in my practice have been carefully examined for worms. They have almost never been found.

sis on food additives as a cause of hyperactivity and attentional disorder is a step in the right direction.[14]

Many times neuroallergy is suspected because of the company that it keeps. Neuromental dysfunction may be a concomitant of allergy that is active in parts of the body other than the brain (see Figure 12-3). The person tired and irritable because of neuroallergy may, for example, have allergic respiratory disorder with postnasal drip, sinusitis, bad

A: Dark circles (allergic shiners) under the eyes; blonde hair; puffiness at the sides of the nose; and a tendency to shortening of the tissue between the nose and the upper lip.

B: Allergic circles; pallid nose; shortened upper lip. Paranasal puffiness on the patient's right side is particularly evident. The girl's sad expression is a manifestation of her chronic condition and is commonly encountered.

C: Head tilt (neck muscle weakness); blonde hair; puffiness over the cheekbones (infraorbital edema); open mouth; shortened upper lip; and swelling at the sides of the nose. Puffiness over the cheekbones is especially notable. The boy's saddened and somewhat anxious gaping look is frequently encountered. It denotes the adverse stress that accompanies chronic allergy, as well as the difficulty in carrying out ordinary nasal breathing.

D: Boggy skin of the nose and surrounding tissues; paranasal puffiness; allergic circles (particularly on the subject's left side); and shortened upper lip. Long silky eyelashes may also be noted. A transverse crease is evident near the tip of the nose. The transverse nasal crease is one of the most valuable signs of chronic allergy.

E: Geographic tongue. The white coating of the tongue sets off several circular areas of rash.

F: Severely white complexion. This pseudoanemia is frequent in the neuroallergic individual. (The extra-white appearance of the skin can be better appreciated in color photos.) This girl's serious expression is a characteristic finding in patients with chronic allergy, especially those with neuroallergy.

G: Open mouth; shortened upper lip; white nose; paranasal puffiness; allergic circles; and puffiness of lower eyelids. Lack of humor and vivacity is an indication of the serious nature of the chronic allergic condition.

H: Narrow, thin chest with grooves below the nipples; prominent breastbone (xiphoid) and clavicles. The individual with chronic allergy may have underdeveloped breathing capacity due to nasal obstruction, nutritional deficiencies, bronchial narrowing, constricted chest bellows, and poor diaphragmatic movement. Many chronic allergy patients expend much of their energy in breathing and still are underventilated. A poorly nourished appearance is a common feature of the individual with chronic allergy.

Figure 12-3 Some physical characteristics of the individual with chronic allergy.

breath, and so forth. Other allergic manifestations include failure to thrive, nosebleeds, deafness, fluid collection in the ears, vertigo, bowel disturbance, rash, swollen glands, recurrent respiratory infections, stomach aches, joint symptoms, and catarrh.

Examination of the patient may provide considerable evidence for the presence of allergy. In some patients, many stigmata of allergy are found in the absence of symptoms referable to the allergy. Symptoms may, however, be subtle or chronic, or become evident only in future years, in future generations, or when life factors become adverse (see Figure 12-2).

Physical findings indicative of allergy include: pale, boggy, nasal mucous membranes; dark circles under the eyes (allergic shiners); extra wrinkles around the eyes; a transverse nasal crease; white nose (the Wunderlich Sign*); paranasal puffiness; eczematous rash in the flexural creases of the extremities and behind the neck; puffiness around the eyes and over the cheekbones (infraorbital edema); cobblestone, swollen, or reddened inner membranes of the eyelids (allergic conjunctivitis); torus tubarius;** microeczema;† and geographic tongue.‡ Many highly allergic individuals have blonde hair, possibly due to nutrient or hormonal dysfunction.

Identification of allergy is assisted when there is a seasonal fluctuation in symptoms. The child whose schoolwork declines in the spring and fall may have neuroallergy as the cause of his problem. He may not be able to think as clearly in certain seasons of the year. Other individuals with foggy thinking may show no seasonal variation. For them, neuroallergy is unremitting unless someone thinks of the condition, investigates it, and treats it.

Finding allergic antibodies may be helpful in establishing the presence of an allergic condition. A blood test for immunoglobulin E (IgE) may be obtained. When the level of this allergic antibody is elevated, the presence of the immune form of allergy is usually indicated.

---

*White nose (the Wunderlich Sign): Pallor of the skin of the nose when the skin of the surrounding face is nonpallid.
**Torus Tubarius: A bony overgrowth of the midportion of the hard palate jutting into the mouth just underneath the nasal cavity. It is seen in patients with chronic allergy of the nose.
†Microeczema: A word that I have coined to describe multiple small white patches on the skin of the face, neck, upper trunk, and upper arms. It is seen in some chronically allergic individuals.
‡Geographic Tongue: Smooth patches on the tongue that change in location from time to time; a major sign of chronic allergy.

Elevated levels of histamine in the blood are indicative of allergy. Histamine is liberated by certain cells when an allergic reaction takes place.

Tests for food allergy may be carried out by eliminating suspected foods from the diet, performing skin tests, inducing symptoms or pulse change by provocation (sublingual or subcutaneous techniques), or referring the patient's blood to specialized laboratories for the RAST test or the cytotoxic test. The RAST (RadioAllergoSorbent Test) is an immunological assay for antibodies present in the patient's blood against specific test antigens. The cytotoxic test is made by mixing the patient's white blood cells with specific food antigens and looking for morphological changes in the cells.

Allergy to inhalants, as well as to foods, may be responsible for neuroallergy. Frequently, food and inhalant sensitivities coexist and appear to worsen one another. Currently, allergy investigation for plant-derived inhalant substances is limited to the pollens of plants, but in the future, testing with leaves and chemical substances from the plant (odors, terpenes, and so forth) may be possible.

Skin tests using commercially available extracts of plant pollens, as well as dust preparations and air molds, are quite helpful in determining an individual's sensitivity to these substances. Scratching the skin, or introduction of test substances into the outer layers of the skin (intradermal testing), can be used. Skin reactions are looked for, and the results are correlated with the patient's history. Treatment with a series of desensitizing allergy injections may be carried out. The treatment vaccine is composed of substances to which the person is hypersensitive. I discussed this form of testing and treatment in a recent paper.[15]

Mucus in the urine is perhaps the most characteristic physical sign of neuroallergy. The "nervous" allergic person is most apt to show urinary mucus. Foods or chemical additives in the diet may be responsible for this finding. The absence of mucus does not exclude neuroallergy. When a patient is treated and improves, mucus in the urine generally lessens and disappears.

At times, the presence of protein in the urine may indicate an allergic condition. When the amount of protein is slight, it is often associated with mucus. When it is greater, it may be due to allergic involvement of the kidneys (hypersensitivity nephritis). The most severe form of protein in the urine is seen in the Nephrotic Syndrome. This condition may be an allergic disorder accompanied by body swelling (edema), mental instability, fluctuations in body chemistry, and so on.

TREATMENT

It may be necessary to use treatment as a diagnostic aid in order to establish that an allergy or maladaptive reaction is at the root of a neuro-mental problem. A therapeutic trial is worthwhile, considering the results that may be obtained. Usually, however, treatment is carried out as a logical sequence to identification of allergy.

Food eliminations require the will to avoid particular foods or dietary chemicals, a capable supervisory adult, and a controlled source of dietary supply. The social misfit finds food elimination difficult to carry out by himself. It is important that families, homes, and institutions realize the great importance of dietary details in assisting such treatment programs.

One or more foods can be eliminated from the diet at the same time. Supervisory guidance should always be obtained so that nutritive deficiencies are not produced. A three-week avoidance period is necessary, followed by a one-at-a-time challenge with the individual foods that were eliminated. One looks for improvement in symptoms, behavior, or function during the elimination period and relapse when the food(s) is reinstituted in the diet.

Although any food may be the source of neuromental disorder, most commonly implicated are sugar, artificial colors and flavors, cow's milk, chocolate, wheat, corn, citrus, and eggs. Refined sugar, chocolate, and artificial colors and flavors add little or nothing to one's nutritive supply. Therefore, they should be automatically eliminated from the diet as a group. Milk, wheat, corn, citrus, and eggs can then be eliminated individually or in groups.

The elimination of all food for a period of four days, the four-day fast, can rapidly relieve symptoms. Addition of foods, one at a time, when breaking the fast, can indicate food sensitivities. Longer fasts may also be used as treatment, but they require careful supervision.[16,17]

When elimination of offending foods is difficult or impossible, the use of desensitizing food drops or injections may be helpful.

Improvement of body chemistry and reduction of adverse stress can assist in ameliorating neuroallergy. Psychological counseling; correct educational placement; visual therapy; vitamin, mineral, and digestive supplements; exercise programs; and dietary alteration may be important tools in management.

Desensitizing allergy injections may be the most valuable tool of all for improving the patient. Matters of dosage, strength of extract, and timing of injections may spell success or failure with this method. For this reason, the qualities of the therapist and his treatment regimen assume great significance.

The treatment of neuroallergy due to ecological factors is a matter of growing importance, as man is exposed to an increasing number of chemicals foreign to his nature.

CASE HISTORIES ILLUSTRATING SUCCESSFUL TREATMENT

A five-year-old child was unable successfully to paste cut-outs in a book. She seemed unable to match a cut-out with its place in the book. When her mother stopped her from licking the glue on the back of the cut-out, she performed quite well.

A 16-year-old girl became so sleepy in the afternoons that she could not do her school work. A sublingual provocative test revealed strong sensitivity to petroleum products. Questioning revealed that she had a chemistry class in the late morning, and that she was exposed to several petroleum-derived chemicals. When the girl discontinued chemistry, she was no longer sleepy.

A 30-year-old female clerk in a pharmacy experienced intermittent blurring of vision and decreased mental alertness. When she transferred to an outdoor job, her symptoms disappeared. When she returned to work in the pharmacy, her symptoms returned. A sensitivity to cigarette smoke is believed to be the cause of her problems, because challenge with cigarette smoke has reproduced her visual and mental deficit.

A seven-year-old boy was chronically unhappy. He was described as angry, very irritable, unsatisfied, and plagued with recurrent cough and stuffy nose. He was known for his "flash temper" and his aggressive assaults on companions and siblings. Violence and anger with destruction of toys and possessions had been noted since early infancy. He received a whipping from his parents five to seven days out of a week.

Examination of the blood revealed an eosinophil level of 10% (normal up to 3% or 4%). In the urinalysis a very large amount of mucus (4+ on a scale of 0 to 4) was noted.

Skin testing revealed extremely large reactions to inhalent pollens. Treatment with a vaccine containing pollens was instituted. Within a few months the parents reported that the boy was cooperative, manageable, and happy. His "flash temper" appeared only when his allergy injection was overdue or missed. At these times he was described as mean and intolerable, and he argued with everyone, giving "15 different reasons" why he shouldn't cooperate with his parents. Now the administration of the boy's allergy vaccine was used to control the boy, instead of a whipping. Within a minute or two after the allergy injection, the boy became cooperative and pleasant. A trial with placebo injection (sterile saline) failed to influence his behavior.

There is no question that psychological problems existed in this family. The point is that sometimes allergy treatment is needed instead of, or along with, psychological management. Appropriate antiallergic therapy can be a specific need for which there may be no apparent substitute.

T. J., a 14-year-old boy, was seen because of antisocial behavior. He had episodes in which he would steal possessions from others, exhibit hostility, destroy property, throw tantrums, and cry. His concentration for school work was poor, and he was known as a clumsy, uncoordinated boy. He had been characterized as hyperactive since infancy. His IQ was normal, but he was two years behind in school. T. J. was well known to police authorities and various social agencies.

He and his family had received psychotherapy and behavioral guidance from several different psychiatric sources over many years. Court-appointed counselors and psychologists had worked with him and his family on numerous occasions. Many medications had been tried, including Ritalin, amphetamines, Mellaril, Tofranil, and lithium. No treatment was helpful. Hospitalization in a psychiatric ward for several months resulted in no change in his behavior, but a marked gain in weight occurred. T. J. was placed in foster homes, but the same episodic hostility, stealing, property destruction, and hyperemotional behavior continued.

He was known to sneeze, cough, and wheeze around dust. He was a chronic mouth breather and breathed noisily at night.

T. J. was markedly obese and was noticed to trip over various objects around him. He barely lifted his feet from the floor when he walked (gravity-bound). He sniffed every few seconds and exhibited dark circles under the eyes, paranasal puffiness, white nose, bunny nose,* torus tubarius, and open mouth.

He fidgeted constantly and scratched his nose or the skin of his body every few seconds. In the interior of his nose, glistening, white, swollen nasal tissues were characteristic of chronic nasal allergy.

T. J.'s diet consisted of sweetened cereals, Cokes, an assortment of refined carbohydrates, and a few other foods.

A glucose tolerance test was performed using the boy's usual breakfast (Figure 12-4); it yielded a flat curve with a decline at 2 and 6 hours. In the figure, the blood sugar values before and after breakfast are indicated by the connected line; the blood insulin values are shown by the broken line.

The blood sugar curve is essentially a flat curve, although declines in blood sugar levels occur at 2 and 6 hours. The significance of the flat curve has been greatly debated; it is seen in a large number of social misfits. Many orthomolecular physicians believe it to be one form of relative hypoglycemia.[7] The flat curve may denote poor glucose absorption from the gut, hypothyroidism, adrenocortical insufficiency, or lack of nutrients.

In this boy the flat curve is associated with hyperinsulinism. The blood insulin shows a marked rise at one-half hour. The hyperinsulinism may be of genetic origin, but it often indicates a "hair-trigger" (hypersensitive) pancreas that is primed by prior dietary exposures to react (secrete insulin) with a bang! Repeated consumption of sweets and refined carbohydrates (lacking minerals needed for metabolism) leads to such a picture.

The decline of blood sugar at 6 hours in this patient suggests a deficit in counter-regulatory factors and could indicate liver dysfunction.[7]

Sublingual testing** for food sensitivities was carried out. Interestingly enough, all tests were negative except for cane sugar. T. J. showed a marked sensitivity reaction to an extremely high dilution of cane sugar. His pulse bounded and raced, his nose filled up with mucus, and a staring look came into his eyes.

---

*Bunny nose: Wiggling and wrinkling of the nose carried out by the patient with chronic nasal allergy in an attempt to alleviate nasal obstruction and itching.
**Sublingual food testing: Introduction of diluted food drops under the tongue. Reactions to foods may produce various symptoms or a change in pulse rate or volume.

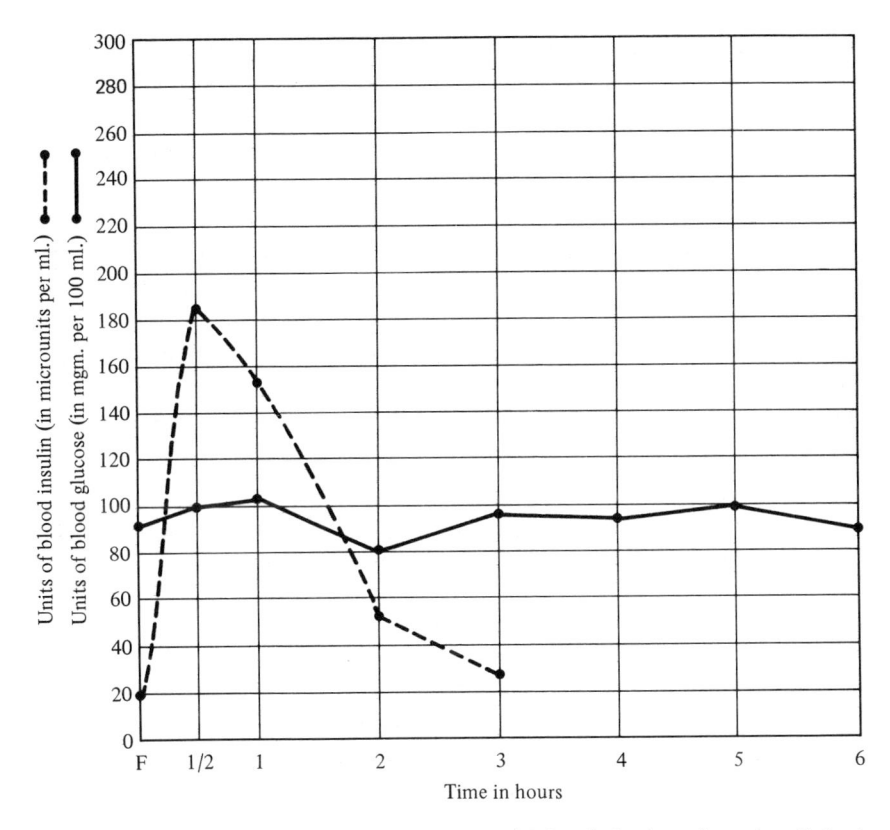

Fig. 12-4 Results of 6-hour glucose tolerance test with insulin levels performed on T. J., the 14-year-old social misfit. The boy's usual breakfast was used instead of the standard loading dose of glucose. His breakfast consisted of pancakes, syrup, butter, sausage, and eggs.

It is likely that blood insulin tests done at that time would have shown hyperinsulinism, and blood sugar tests might have shown distinct hypoglycemia.

Skin testing for inhalant allergens showed many strongly positive reactions including dust. A blood test for allergic antibody (immunoglobulin E) was markedly elevated.

Treatment with an allergy-desensitizing vaccine and elimination of sugar and reduction of refined carbohydrates in the diet resulted in a drastic, prompt improvement. All antisocial behavior ceased, and he became more and more interested in helping himself with the passage of each month. He became able to sit still without scratching and fidgeting. He lost weight and began to lift his feet and legs when walking.

Improvement in coordination and lengthening of attention span occurred. In school he began to make up academic work that he could not previously accomplish.

This boy was a chronic allergic child with school failure and chronic antisocial behavior. His glucose tolerance test was flat, with hyperinsulinism. He was markedly sensitive (allergic) to sugar and inhalants. In the parlance of some, he was a functional hypoglycemic.[7] The exact relationship of allergy to hypoglycemia is not yet clear. It is probable that allergy is a cause of hypoglycemia in some cases.

Although T. J. had been extensively investigated and treated by general physicians, pediatricians, neurologists, and psychiatrists, his biologic problem—neuroallergy—was not detected and treated. Removal from his home as a last-ditch effort to help had failed. Removal of sugar and treatment with other allergens succeeded.

Management of neuroallergy was successful in retrieving this boy from juvenile delinquency and a probable life of crime.

CONCLUSIONS

Not every social misfit has neuroallergy. Not every neuroallergic person can be helped with present methods of therapy. Nevertheless, there are a large number of neuroallergic social misfits who can be changed for the better through biological treatments that permit them to make new efforts at becoming successful citizens.

The link between learning disorders and social misfits has been established. Failure in school portends failure in society as a general rule.[18]

Neuroallergy in the child or family is one important factor in learning and juvenile disorders, and it can often be successfully treated.

It is hoped that this writing will help educators, physicians, students, and others to recognize neuroallergy and the importance of appropriate therapy for it.

Treatment of neuroallergy provides an additional therapeutic modality to supplement other social and orthomolecular approaches to the prevention, management, and rehabilitation of the unsuccessful citizen.

References

1. Wunderlich, Ray C., Jr., *Allergy, Brains, and Children Coping*, Johnny Reads, Inc., St. Petersburg, Fla., 1973.

2. Klotz, S. D., The immune diseases of the nervous system, Chapter XLVIII in *Immunoalergia Clinica*, Clinicas de Alergia, S. A., in press.
3. Dickey, Lawrence, D., ed., *Clinical Ecology*, Charles C. Thomas, Springfield, Ill., 1976.
4. Crook, W. G., The Allergic-Tension-Fatigue Syndrome, The Allergic Child, Speer, F., ed., Hoeber, New York, 1963.
5. Wunderlich, Ray C., Jr., *Kids, Brains, and Learning*, Johnny Reads, Inc., St. Petersburg, Fla., 1970.
6. Mandell, Marshall, Ecologic mental illness: Cerebral and physical reactions in allergic patients, *New Dynamics of Preventive Medicine*, Pomeroy, Leon R., ed., International Medical Book Corp., New York, 1974.
7. Wunderlich, Ray C., Jr., *Sugar and Your Health*, Johnny Reads, Inc., St. Petersburg, Fla., in press.
8. Wunderlich, Ray C., Jr., *Improving Your Diet*, Johnny Reads, Inc., St. Petersburg, Fla., 1976.
9. Feingold, B. F., *Introduction to Clinical Allergy*, Charles C. Thomas, Springfield, Ill., 1973.
10. Conners, C. Keith, Goyette, Charles H., Southwick, Debora A., Lees, James M., and Andrulonis, Paul A., Food additives and hyperkinesis: A controlled double-blind experiment, *Pediatrics*, 59 (2):1976.
11. Philpott, William, Physiology of violence: The role of cerebral hypersensitive reaction in aggression, audiotape from conference Crime, malnutrition, and the orthomolecular approach, Huxley Institute for Biosocial Research of Ohio, Inc., Defiance, Ohio, April 1976.
12. Wunderlich, Ray C., Jr., *Fatigue*, Johnny Reads, Inc., St. Petersburg, Fla., 1976.
13. Crook, William G., *Can Your Child Read? Is He Hyperactive?* Pedicenter Press, Jackson, Tenn., 1975.
14. Feingold, Ben F., *Why Your Child is Hyperactive*, Random House, New York, 1975.
15. Wunderlich, Ray C., Jr., Desensitizing allergy injections: A biological and psychological tool for behavior change, *Orthomolecular Psychiatry*, 5 (2):138-147, 1976.
16. Cott, Allan, *Fasting: The Ultimate Diet*, Bantam Books, New York, 1975.
17. Shelton, Herbert M., *Fasting for Renewal of Life*, Natural Hygiene Press, Chicago, 1974.
18. Find LD major factor in delinquency; Schools far from meeting LD needs, *ACLD Newsletter* No. 109, Association for Children with Learning Disabilities, Pittsburgh, Pa., July/August 1976.

Chapter 13 | Treatment of the "Slow Learner"

Henry Turkel, M.D.
Ilse Nusbaum, M.A.
Southfield, Michigan

DISTRIBUTION OF INTELLIGENCE

A glance at the bell-shaped curve of the distribution of intelligence shows that almost a quarter of the population have IQs below 85. In the United States this means that approximately 40 million people who are not officially classified as being mentally retarded (IQ below approximately 70) may still be academically handicapped, with environmental stress, abnormal metabolism of epinephrine, and resultant violence. Another 5.5 million are classified as mildly retarded (IQ 52–67). The moderately, severely, and profoundly retarded (IQ below 50) number about 600,000.[1] In fact, however, the "slow learner" with an IQ between 70 and 85 shares many of the social problems of the mildly retarded person. The classification of borderline (IQ 60–85)[2] acknowledges these similarities. In this paper the term "slow learner" designates persons in the IQ range 60–85.

GENETICS: CRIME AND THE SLOW LEARNER

The mildly retarded adolescent or adult is more likely than persons with higher IQs to be led into antisocial behavior, for both environment and biochemical reasons. Among mentally retarded boys, "these are likely to be aggressions against property or the community; in the girls, sexual acting out. . . . Once the mildly retarded person is out of school, finding and keeping a job becomes a problem. . . ."[3] Social problems, especially criminal behavior, associated with the slow learner make medical treatment, when available, urgent. The retarded comprise about 3% of the total population but comprise 15-20% of those in juvenile detention homes and probably adult prisons.[4] Most of these 15-20% come from the upper range of the mildly retarded. Though the moderately, severely, and profoundly retarded drain the fiscal resources of society, especially if institutionalized, they are not the overt threat posed by the mildly retarded, who are "easily led into unlawful acts."[5] Many forms of mental retardation are caused by a genetic defect, a biochemical error.

Any genetic error, whether inherited or acquired (mutational, *de novo*), produces metabolic accumulations of a substrate that remains unmetabolized by the defective enzyme, as well as a deficiency of the end product or products. Although some accumulated metabolites and their alternate products injure or irritate the brain, sometimes it is the mere *presence* of the metabolites that interferes with the circulation of nutrients and removal of wastes, and results in slow physical and mental development. At other times the lack of end products causes the retardation. In either case, alteration of the biochemical environment—administration of drugs that "bind to the metabolite and [are] excreted from the body"[6]—may ameliorate the problem.

For example, cretinism, associated with a defective thyroid gland and its products, is a serious form of physical and mental retardation. If early treatment with thyroid substances is instituted, the infant can develop very nearly normally. A different disease (in which accumulations and alternate metabolites cause the mental abnormalities) is phenylketonuria, or PKU. One of the factors (in the liver) of the enzyme phenylalanine hydroxylase is defective.[7] Therefore the essential amino acid phenylalanine cannot be completely metabolized into tyrosine. It accumulates, and alternate metabolic pathways produce brain-irritating phenylpyruvates, which also accumulate. By restricting the intake of phenylalanine, the physician can control the fluid levels of phenylalanine; and if the deficient product, tyrosine, which is present in foods, is supplemented, development can proceed more normally even though the patient remains phenylketonuric. The fact that PKU remains incurable becomes significant if the treated and apparently normal phenylketonuric patient becomes pregnant. Even her fetus who is not affected by PKU genetically can be severely injured by her abnormal biochemistry.[8]

All genetic and, of course chromosomal, disorders are associated with metabolic accumulations. Metabolic accumulations take up space required for delivery of nutrients and elimination of wastes. This can clearly be seen in arteriosclerosis, in which diseased blood vessels eventually become so clogged with lipid and mineral accumulations that insufficient oxygen reaches the heart or brain. Death can occur, due to compensating high blood pressure and ruptured blood vessels of the brain, or to heart attack.

Undernutrition and deficit of oxygen can cause brain damage at any age (e.g., arteriosclerosis) and/or mental retardation at an early age. Malnutrition at critical ages reduces DNA, RNA, and protein, all needed for mitosis, thus reducing the number of brain cells. However, the critical developmental age may differ from the norm if a chromosomal disorder is involved. Malnutrition results not only from the absence of food from the diet but also from the body's inability to utilize ingested foods. One of the most severe forms of genetically induced malnutrition associated with mental retardation is Down's syndrome (mongolism). This disease is presently not considered amenable to treatment.[9] The reason for the pessimism about a disease that has been treated for some 30 years is that, unlike PKU or other "treatable" incurable genetic diseases, this disorder involves a whole or partial extra chromosome of the G group (by convention designated #21). Since the entire body is affected in all or many cells, treatment must be directed to the entire body.

DOWN'S SYNDROME (MONGOLISM) AND THE SLOW LEARNER

It has been estimated that some 5,000 new mongoloids are born each year, costing society an additional $1.25 to $1.7 billion or more in custodial costs annually.[10,11] However, it is entirely possible that many of the slow learners and mildly retarded who are frustrated because of an inability to find and keep jobs are mild mosaic mongoloids who can be treated with present methods. Others who are classified as idiopathic retarded (no diagnosed etiology) may suffer from other genetic disorders associated with metabolic accumulations and treated by similar methods. Several of my own patients who were taken from one diagnostician to another without any established diagnosis or reason given for their mental retardation were treated *as if* they were mongoloids and improved more rapidly and more permanently than those with the established diagnosis.

It was not until 1956 that an accurate count of human chromosomes was made[12] and found to be 46—with 22 pairs of autosomes and two sex chromosomes. Each chromosome contains probably thousands of different genes. If a person has three rather than the normal two of a specific chromosome, severe biochemical imbalances result.

Abnormal cell division can occur in several ways to produce a trisomic or mosaic embryo. During meiosis the gametes divide into the haploid number. If a pair of chromosomes fails to separate during reduction division, one of the cells has 24 chromosomes, the other has 22. If the cell containing 24 chromosomes is fertilized by a normal gamete, the resulting zygote will have 47 chromosomes. A 45-chromosome zygote is usually not viable, but if born is severely retarded.[13] When the 47th chromosome is the #21, the trisomic zygote is mongoloid. In this standard trisomy and in translocation Down's syndrome, all cells are affected.

The major source of chromosomal abnormalities pertinent to this discussion is nondisjunction during mitosis, after conception. If the error is immediate, all cells will be trisomic (the 45-chromosome cell at this stage of development presumably dies out). However, this accident can occur during later embryonic or fetal development. In this case, the individual is "mosaic" with some normal, some monosomic, and some trisomic cell lines.

Chromosome patterns vary considerably, and the phenotypic effects vary also. The mosaic mongoloid can be phenotypically normal or be clinically indistinguishable from the trisomy or translocation types. The later the error occurs, the fewer the number of trisomic, monosomic, or other abnormal cells. Obviously, if the abnormal cell line exists only in unexamined tissues, diagnosis on the basis of karyotyping will be in error. If the patient is also within the normal range of physical development—and there is no single characteristic of Down's syndrome that is not found in persons without this diagnosis—then the mental retardation, especially if mild, will be attributed to other or unknown causes. Ordinarily, if the person's IQ is normal or above normal, chromosome studies are not made.

Mosaicism is considered to be relatively rare, but the chances for nondisjunction during any specific division of cells makes it likely that this is a fairly common but undiagnosed form of Down's syndrome and therefore of idiopathic mental retardation. If this, in fact, is the case, it helps to explain why mentally retarded children require more nutrition than do normal children.[14] Down's syndrome children have starved tissues because of the faulty circulation of nutrients, and because cells are clogged with accumulations.[15] These retarded children would naturally have higher nutritional requirements than children without metabolic accumulations.

Whether the person with Down's syndrome is affected in all cells or only a few, there are extra genes, extra enzymes, extra products that cannot be further metabolized because sufficient consecutive enzymes are lacking on the normal diploid chromosomes. From the moment of the error, only two-thirds of the products of the genes controlled by chromosome #21 are metabolized. No single product signals the maternal excretory system prenatally that the substrate is abnormal in quality because the extra chromosome is normal. Moreover, because there are numerous extra products, each of which is two-thirds metabolized, no *single* chemical accumulates in massive quantities (as in PKU): thus the maternal excretory system is not signaled prenatally than an abnormal quantity of a specific substrate must be removed to protect the fetus. Because thousands of genes are in excess, the total number of unmetabolized substrates is massive, clogging all systems (circulatory, excretory) prenatally as well as postnatally, so that the infant is at birth already retarded. These accumulations "produce an imbalance" that "results in the developmental and metabolic abnormalities."[16] The lag in development of excretory organs leads to secondary accumulations of wastes[17] that further retard development without destroying fetal cells.[18] Because all endocrine and exocrine glands are also developmentally retarded, the body develops at a rate that is chronologically slower than normal. Undernutrition therefore apparently does not injure during what are usually critical periods for brain and other structural development. This finding contrasts with the reduced cell growth pattern of marasmic children, who in some cases had 60% fewer brain cells than normal and also reduced lipid content, with a poor prognosis for making up this deficiency afterwards.[19] In Down's syndrome the cells remain undifferentiated, according to the findings of Stephens and Menkes, and therefore ready to develop into brain cells at a much later chronological age than normal—if the metabolic accumulations are removed.

Some chemicals, e.g., uric acid, are in the range of high or high normal; others are in the range of low normal to below normal (e.g., serotonin) because the accumulations take up space. Adding more of the deficient chemicals, as Dr. Mary Bazelon Coleman in her experiments with serotonin discovered, does not help.[20] However, if metabolic accumulations were removed by medication, then metabolites in the range below normal in the fluids could exit the tissues where stored, be excreted, and provide more space for circulation of supplemented nutrients and elimination of wastes. Then organs and tissues, including the brain, could develop normally, and the gap between developmental age and chronological age could be narrowed. This is exactly what happens in Down's syndrome.[21,22]

When we turn our attention to the mildly retarded without the diagnosis of Down's syndrome, we must recall that all genetic disorders, whether diagnosed as such or not, result in metabolic accumulations that retard, injure, or irritate the brain and other structures, and that the mosaic form of Down's syndrome may remain undiagnosed.

The group of medications and nutrients described in Table 13-1,

Table 13-1 Contents of Medication Comprising the "U" Series of Drugs

UMORPHOID-A	(BREAKFAST)	Diastase	3.3 mg
Thyroid Globulin	66 mg	Ketocholanic Acid	66 mg
Organic Iodine	66 mg	Desoxycholic Acid	66 mg
UMORPHOID-B	(BREAKFAST)	UPNEOID-A	
Vitamin A	25,000 Units	(BREAKFAST, LUNCH, DINNER)	
Vitamin E	10 mg	Phenylpropanolamine	
UNOID-A		Hydrochloride	20 mg
(BREAKFAST, LUNCH, DINNER)		Pyrilamine Maleate	25 mg
Pentylene Tetrazole	50 mg	Rutin	20 mg
Glutamic Acid	200 mg	Ascorbic Acid	100 mg
Nicotinic Acid	50 mg	Aminophylline Magnesium	
UPEPTOID-A		Glycinate	100 mg
(BREAKFAST, DINNER)		UPNEOID-B	(AT BEDTIME)
Betaine-Choline Tartrate	100 mg	is Upneoid A but Enteric Coated	
Choline-Methionine Tartrate	100 mg	UPNEOID-C	(PRN)
Inositol	50 mg	Naphazoline Hydrochloride	0.05%
Unsaturated Fatty Acids	100 mg	Pyrilamine Maleate	0.50%
Liver Dessicated	75 mg	Chlorpheniramine Maleate	0.25%
UPEPTOID-B	(DINNER)	Methyl Paraben	0.01%
Betaine Hydrochloride	66 mg	Propyl Paraben	0.02%
Papain	66 mg	UTROPHOID-B	(LUNCH)
Pepsin	66 mg	Thiamine Mononitrate (B-1)	20 mg
Pancreatin	66 mg	Riboflavin (B-2)	20 mg

(*Continued*)

Table 13-1 *(Continued)*

Calcium Pantothenate	20 mg	Iodine	0.15 mg
Para Aminobenzoic Acid	20 mg	Iron	10 mg
Pyridoxine (B-6)	20 mg	Magnesium	1 mg
Niacin	20 mg	Manganese	1.25 mg
UTROPHOID-C	(DINNER)	Molybdenum	0.1 mg
Folic Acid	5 mg	Zinc	1 mg
Cyanocobalamin (B-12)	25 mcg	Bone Meal (BREAKFAST,	
Calcium	30 mg	LUNCH, DINNER)	200 mg
Cobalt	0.1 mg	Glutamic Acid (BREAKFAST,	
Copper	1 mg	LUNCH, DINNER)	200 mg

DO NOT ADD ANY VITAMIN "D" AS A SUPPLEMENT—IT IS CONTRAINDICATED TO THE "U" SERIES DRUG

SUGGESTED STARTING DOSAGES

3 mos. to 2 yrs. $\frac{1}{6}$ to $\frac{1}{3}$ of full dosage
2 yrs. to 6 yrs. $\frac{1}{3}$ to $\frac{1}{2}$ of full dosage
6 yrs. to 10 yrs. $\frac{1}{2}$ to full dosage
10 yrs. and over   Full dosage

If the patient's age indicates a dosage size which would be intermediate between those available, it is suggested that the patient be placed on the larger size, since the dosages are figured on the minimal level.

SUGGESTED SUPPLEMENTARY MEDICATION

1. All patients may receive, at the physician's discretion L. Triiodo-Thyronine as follows:

3 mos. to 2 yrs.   5 mcg daily with breakfast
2 yrs. to 6 yrs.   10 mcg daily with breakfast
6 yrs. to 10 yrs. 12.5 mcg daily with breakfast
10 yrs. and over   25 mcg daily with breakfast

2. Edematous patients *must* receive a potent diuretic for two consecutive days each week during the entire course of the treatment as follows:

2 mos. to 2 yrs. $\frac{1}{6}$ to $\frac{1}{4}$ size dosage
2 yrs. to 6 yrs. $\frac{1}{4}$ to $\frac{1}{2}$ size dosage
6 yrs. to 10 yrs. $\frac{1}{2}$ to $\frac{3}{4}$ size dosage
10 yrs. and over $\frac{3}{4}$ to full size dosage

Nonedematous patients in whom excessive calcification or indication of accumulation of mineral deposits is seen on X-rays should receive similar dosages of diuretics as above at the physician's discretion.

3. Patient's diet shall consist of unbleached flour products, 1–2 glasses of milk daily, butter, cereals, lean meats, fish, eggs, fruits, vegetables, soft drinks *other* than cola products. *Avoid the use* of bleached flour products, greasy fried foods, pork and peanut products, cola drinks.

Additional supplements depend on the individual condition: Calcium Pantothenate, Pyridoxine HCl, Pangamic Acid, Vitamin C and E.

called the "U" Series, was developed during the 1930s and 1940s as a means of removing metabolic accumulations associated with such diverse diseases as diabetes, allergies, and arteriosclerosis. To treat Down's syndrome, all three groups of the original series (that is, medications to remove water-soluble substances, fat-soluble substances, and minerals) were combined, and to these were added digestive enzymes, vitamins, and minerals. This series of drugs and nutrients has been modified with some success by the National Institute of Mental Health in Japan, a medical doctor in Texas, and a parent in Maryland (*National Mongoloid Digest*, July 1976).

TREATMENT OF SLOW LEARNERS WITH THE "U" SERIES

The "U" Series has benefited a number of slow learners with certain characteristics of Down's syndrome.[23] The "U" Series was prescribed to these patients because of the difficulty of establishing a correct diagnosis for a mosaic patient. It should be pointed out that the rationale of the "U" Series is not primarily as a nutritional supplement of megavitamins. Down's syndrome patients are not, as far as is known, vitamin-dependent, nor do megavitamins alone seem to benefit them. The rationale of the "U" Series is based on the knowledge that there are metabolic accumulations due to the extra chromosome in Down's syndrome, and that before the nutritional supplements can be utilized these accumulations of fat- and water-soluble substances and minerals must be removed.

Patient R. S., who exhibited the clinical characteristics of Down's syndrome, illustrates the difficulty of establishing a correct diagnosis for a mosaic patient. Her father first corresponded with me March 4, 1964. By that time chromosome studies were routinely required before a new patient was accepted, so I advised Mr. S. to have the study made. Eight years later he wrote again:

> You will recall, the first time I contacted you, was about seven year ago when I wrote and said that I was not sure whether my little baby was mongoloid or not. I could not get the Children's Hospital in Los Angeles, the Kaiser Medical Group of which I was a member, nor even the UCLA Medical Center to arrive at any conclusive proof as to what was her problem. All they could tell me was that she was retarded. As she had had a head injury

when she was nine weeks old in an automobile accident, we were not sure whether the accident was responsible. She also had some traits of Down's syndrome.

Please read copies of reports from different doctors and different hospitals I have taken her to (5 copies). The Children's Hospital in Los Angeles, under the guidance of Dr. Koch—specialist in retarded children—stated she was a Mosaic child. His explanation to me at that time was that she required three different blood tests at different times. Out of 51 cells tested she has 17 cells which showed the trisomic chromosome #21. She also had normal cells and therefore she was what they call a mosaic child. That nothing could be done for her. That she would be mentally retarded. . . . (10/29/71)

A chromosome study made at UCLA (later) showed all cells trisomic, and the prognosis again was that nothing could be done "to correct the problem, if it really exists." (9/13/71)

The first two tests were negative, no trisomic cells, and only because of some clinical characteristics, together with the father's persistence, was the study repeated for the third time. Typically, if one chromosome study is negative, it may be repeated once. It would be all the more true in an ambiguous case like R. S.'s: she had suffered a head injury at age nine weeks. Her X-ray study was also not diagnostic of mongolism. It was only because Mr. S. believed that I would not accept R. as a patient without a diagnosis of Down's syndrome based on a trisomic karyotype that the study was repeated for the third time. It is entirely possible that even after the third study the trisomic cell line would not have been found. Moreover, abnormal cells of a mosaic trisomic syndrome have been known to disappear spontaneously.[24-27]

Therefore, to say that mongolism has not been diagnosed is only to say that the extra chromosome has not been found in examined cells. In addition to the thousands of diagnosed mongoloids, there are millions of persons without any etiological diagnosis. Cultural deprivation is apparently not a factor. Therefore, some may have a specific, undiagnosed genetic disease or metabolic imbalance; others may be mosaic mongoloids. The latter diagnosis is not considered because the implication, when one speaks of mongolism, is that the patient is severely retarded.[28] This is a common misconception, repeated even in current literature. The fact is that the typical mongoloid is often moderately to mildly retarded during his early years, especially when reared at home. The IQ ordinarily drops with age,[29] but if the child is treated with the "U" Series (or even the modified "U" Series tested in Japan) the IQ does not drop but may rise.[22] Benda has also suggested that a child who is not mentally retarded not be given the diagnosis of Down's syndrome regardless of clinical findings.

Wendy's Case

These improvements are even more evident in the patient without the diagnosis of Down's syndrome, especially if some of the clinical characteristics are present. This patient may be mosaic, or else the chromosome may have disappeared. Wendy, for example, was not a slow learner. She was moderately retarded, with an IQ of 44 ± 15, according to the University Hospitals of Cleveland, where she was examined in May 1967, a month before her fourth birthday. She was found to be hyperactive and infantile in behavior, as well as physically and mentally retarded. Her bone age at 4 years was 2½ years. Blood chemistry and urine were within normal limits, which is a usual finding in Down's syndrome also.[30] Her karyogram was normal. No specific syndrome was identified at the University Hospitals, and the prognosis was that she would not develop beyond the range of moderate retardation.

On February 14, 1969, Wendy was brought to Detroit for treatment with the "U" Series. There was significant underdevelopment of the general growth pattern. Ossification centers in the wrists corresponded to 3 to 3½ years. Diaphyseal lengths of the femur and tibia corresponded to a bone age of 3½ to 4 years. Marrow of the skull had already partly ossified, at age 5¼, corresponding to adult development. Thus, Wendy was both retarded in bone age and prematurely ossified, a condition characteristic of Down's syndrome. She also had characteristics of the hip bone compatible with Down's syndrome, hypermotile joints, protruding abdomen, narrow arched palate, and strabismus. According to her parents, her attention span was never more than 10–15 seconds.

Within three months of treatment her attention span increased from several seconds to a few minutes. She slept better. Fluid and other accumulations were removed from her tissues, and she was noticeably less edematous. She began to speak in occasional complete sentences. Most importantly, her IQ rose significantly. By August 12, 1969, her IQ was 72 ± 10, with a performance score of 83 and a verbal score of 67. At this point her father urged the school to reexamine Wendy because she was reading at the third grade level in kindergarten. Therefore, he objected to her placement in a trainable or educable special education class (TMR or EMR) on the basis of the original prognosis. Her school's psychologist tested her May 18, 1971, and found that she had an IQ of 64 (Stanford-Binet form L-M).

She was reexamined June 14, 1971. Her bone age was 5.9 years at chronological age 8 years; her skull showed marrow where it had previously been ossified. Her IQ was 85 with a verbal score of 89 (WISC)—a significant improvement, even assuming some error, and no overlap with the original IQ of 44. Wendy passed the fifth grade in June 1976, with average and above average grades, not in a TMR or EMR class, but in a regular fifth grade classroom with other normal children.

Steven's Case

Steven, born July 9, 1944, was referred to as a slow learner. His IQ was about 85 when he started treatment October 1, 1957. This was before the advent of chromosome studies. His bone age was 11 years at a chronological age of 13 years, 3 months. His height was $53\frac{1}{4}$ inches, weight 85 pounds. After a year's treatment there was a "slight advance in the progress of ossification," closing the gap between bone age and chronological age. There was equivalent advance, according to parental report, in educability. After two years of treatment, his grades were still average to below average, but two months later, he suddenly began to improve in academics. The following month treatment ended, but thereafter he improved steadily until he graduated from high school (with high honors despite previous low grades). The Columbus College of Art and Design awarded him a scholarship. After art school he worked as illustrator for a commercial art company, then joined the army, reached the rank of SP5, was honorably discharged, and although he had worked in the army as a master plumber, returned to work in civilian life as a commercial artist on a trial basis. After six months he was promoted to an executive position, director in charge of ten illustrators.

There is no way to predict, of course, what would have happened to Steven had he not been treated. He might have developed as well, but with an IQ of 85, his height below normal, and his abilities severely restricted, he could instead have become a frustrated and angry young man typical of those slow learners easily led into violent behavior.

In addition to financial and emotional problems that accompany chronic unemployment and its attendant stresses (boredom, frustration, anxiety, hostility), stress per se creates a severe imbalance in the metabolism of epinephrine. There are several forms of hormonal imbalance causing hard-to-control behavior. An excess of norephedrine, a precursor of epinephrine, creates a tendency to violent behavior. Any deviation in the normal metabolic pathway of epinephrine can lead to aberrant behavior through the production of hallucinogenic chemicals via alternate pathways.[31] Steven's various academic, social, and economic achievements helped eliminate many of the stresses that alter these metabolic pathways. Such achievement alone helps normalize behavior and reduce violence and crime. The correlation between crime and illiteracy is no accident.

Donna's Case

Donna was born November 26, 1935, an only child. When she was first examined by me (July 1956), she retained few mongoloid stigmata, although she had been diagnosed as a mongoloid when younger. She was 62 inches tall, weighed 116 pounds. She had a fissured tongue, rough skin, coarse hair, and strabismus. She was so myopic that she was considered legally blind. Radiographic examination revealed an elongated heart but no other abnormalities. She had attended classes for the mentally retarded until she was in the sixth grade, without participating in activities, and then entered the Institute for the Blind.

Six years later she started the "U" Series, and two months after that she first become involved in social activities. There was little physical change except that she began to take pride in her appearance. After two months of treatment, the "U" Series was withheld for two weeks. The reversal was immediate. She once again became solitary and apathetic, and lost interest in her looks. At that point she resumed treatment with the "U" Series, until June 1958.

Gradual changes in Donna's facial expression and appearance became more evident. Her hair grow softer and thicker. Her vision improved, and at the end of only six months of treatment, she refused to return to the Institute for the Blind but instead, with the help of a social worker, moved to another city. Social services found a room for her and a job as a seamstress. She earned her own living expenses and even sent money home to her mother.

At the Institute for the Blind she had met a man who was also partially blind. Ten months after Donna started treatment, she married that young man and discontinued all medication. She continued to work while keeping house for her husband and herself. She has two normal children who are doing well. Donna was probably not a potential criminal, but as an inmate of a public institution she would still have been a drain on society, which was avoided by means of medical intervention.

Mary's Case

Mary's problem included an intractable weight disorder. She was a slow learner and a very unhappy young woman who, her parents feared, might act out her emotional difficulties in antisocial ways. She had been sent to health farms and weight clinics, and was eventually referred to me with the clinical diagnosis of Down's syndrome on the basis of epicanthal folds and Brushfield spots. Her physical improvement was accompanied by equivalent improvement in mental attitude and ability. She now earns her own living and leads an active, happy social life.

Despite the lack of specific diagnosis and etiology for their disorders, Wendy, Steven, Donna, and Mary were retarded because of a biochemical imbalance due to either an unknown genetic disease or mosaic mongolism. Despite the lack of diagnosis, their improvements reveal that an alteration of the biochemical environment— the removal of metabolic accumulations and supplementation of nutrients—accelerated mental development. It may be that forms of functional mental retardation caused by environmental, familial, or cultural deprivation are more prevalent than retardation caused by an undiagnosed primary genetic disorder. However, even environmental deprivation, such as undernutrition or unstable family life, is associated with biochemical changes that alter the metabolism of epinephrine. These too may be ameliorated to some degree by means of medical intervention.

SUMMARY AND CONCLUSIONS

An increased incidence of violence and antisocial behavior is associated with borderline and mild mental retardation in the IQ range of 60-85. Many of these slow learners present no apparent cause for their mental retardation, which is labeled idiopathic. Some of these persons may have a biochemical disorder caused by an unknown genetic disease or undiagnosed Down's syndrome. Others may have a biochemical imbalance because of the many stresses suffered by their being illiterate, therefore virtually unemployable, members of our highly structured society. In either case, medical intervention is possible and beneficial. Slow learners who presented characteristics typical of Down's syndrome have been treated with the "U" Series. These patients have improved both mentally and physically, thereby aiding their entry into the normal world of school and jobs.

References

1. *The Problem of Mental Retardation*, HEW (OHD) 75-22003(6)75, 1975, p. 2.
2. Carter, C. H., *Handbook of Mental Retardation Syndromes*, Charles C. Thomas, Springfield, Ill., p. 7, 1975.
3. Committee on Mental Retardation, Mild mental retardation—A growing challenge to the physician, *Group for the Advancement of Psychiatry* 7:605, 1967.
4. Ibid., p. 635.
5. President's Committee on Mental Retardation Report, A friend in Washington, *Mental Retardation* 74 DHEW (OHD) 75-21010 22, 1975.
6. Bartalos, M., Medical genetics: A partner in health care, *Med. Ann. D.C.* 36:655-657, 1967.
7. Hsia, D., *Inborn Errors of Metabolism*, Yearbook, Chicago, 1959, p. 109.
8. Fisch, Robert, et al., Maternal phenylketonuria—Detrimental effects on ebryogenesis and fetal development, *Am. J. Dis. Child.* 118:847, 1969.
9. Pines, Maya, *The New Human Genetics*, NIGMS-DHEW (NIH) 76-662, p. 16, 1976.
10. *What are the Facts about Genetic Disease?* NIGMS-DHEW (NIH) 75-370, p. 27, 1975.
11. Friedman, J., Legal aspects of amniocentesis, *U. of Penna. Law Rev.* 123:141, 1974.

12. Tjio and Lavan, The chromosome number of man, *Hereditas* 42:1, 1956.
13. Holmes, L., et al., *Mental Retardation. An Atlas of Diseases With Associated Physical Abnormalities*, Macmillan, New York, 1972.
14. Nutritional needs of retarded children, *Medical World News*, December 6, 1974.
15. Baron, D. N., Down with plasma! Intracellular chemical pathology studies by analysis of cells of solid tissues, erythrocytes and leukocytes. *Proc. Roy. Soc. Med.* 62:16, 1969.
16. Tan, Y. H., et al., Human chromosome 21 dosage: Effect on the expression of the interferon induced antiviral state, *Science* 186:61-63, 1974.
17. Goodman, H. O., et al., Serum uric acid levels in mongolism, *Am. J. Ment. Def.* 71:437-446, 1966.
18. Stephens, M. C., and Menkes, J. H., Cerebral lipids in Down's syndrome. *Dev. Med. Child Neur.* 11:346-352, 1969.
19. Brenton, M., How do hunger and nourishment affect the developing brain? An interview with Myron Winick, *Mod. Med.* 44:66-70, 1976.
20. Coleman, Mary, The use of 5-hydroxytryptophan in patients with Down's syndrome, in Koch, R., and DeLaCruz, F., *Down's Syndrome (Mongolism): Research, Prevention & Management*, Brunner/Mazel, New York, 1975, pp. 111-115.
21. Turkel, H., Medical amelioration of Down's syndrome incorporating the orthomolecular approach, *J. Orthomolecular Psychiatry* 4:102-115, 1975.
22. Iida, M., and Kurita, I., *Investigational Studies of Nutritional and Medical Treatment of Down's Syndrome Children (Modified "U" Series)—Especially its Influence on Development of Mental Function*, National Institute of Mental Health and National Hospital in Monodae, Japan.
23. Turkel, H., and Nusbaum, I., *Update—New Hope for the Mentally Retarded*, US for DS, Los Angeles, 1976.
24. Hook, E. B., and Yunis, J. J., Trisomy-18 syndrome in a patient with normal karyotype, *J.A.M.A.* 193:184, 1965.
25. La Marche, P. H., et al., Disappearing mosaicism—Suggested mechanism is growth advantage of normal over abnormal cell populations, *R.I. Med. J.* 184-189, 1967.
26. Neu, R. L., et al., Disappearance of a 47, XX C+ leucocyte cell line in an infant who had previously exhibited 46, XX/47, XX, C+ mosaicism, *Pediatrics* 43:624, 1969.
27. Porter, I. H., et al., Evidence of selection in mosaicism. *J. Med. Genetics* 6:310-313, 1969.
28. Friedman, J., Legal aspects of amniocentesis, p. 100.
29. Benda, C. E., *Down's Syndrome. Mongolism and its Management*, Grune and Stratton, New York, 1969, p. 68.
30. Nelson, W., *Textbook of Pediatrics*, W. B. Saunders, Philadelphia, 1964, p. 1237.
31. Turkel, H., *New Hope for the Mentally Retarded*, Vantage, New York, 1972, pp. 201-214.

Chapter 14 | Treatment of Penitentiary Inmates

R. Glen Green, M.D., C.M.
Orthomolecular Family Physician
Prince Albert, Saskatchewan, Canada

INTRODUCTION

Subclinical pellagra is a central nervous system (CNS) allergy characterized by perceptual dysfunction involving all the senses. It is due to an allergic response of the brain previously sensitized by highly refined carbohydrates, flour, sugar, and starch. Megadoses of niacin quickly relieve special sense dysperception, while kinesthetic sense changes are more slowly corrected by dietary measures. In 1969, when I first named the condition, I thought only vitamin B-3-niacin was required to correct the complaints; hence the name subclinical pellagra.[1-3]

For seven years I attended "sick parade" at the Prince Albert Penitentiary, a maximum security institution. From 1964 to late 1969 the prisoners were able to keep me guessing about the validity of their complaints. Often this meant X-ray and laboratory tests were needed, which meant a trip downtown to a local hospital. Every weekday morning any prisoner who thought himself ill enough, could attend sick parade at the prison hospital, a euphemism to be sure, but a hospital none the less. The number on "parade" varied with the weather, the work to be done, and the state of their health, in that order. It was a con game where the patient contrived to convince the physician he was ill. The doctor had to decide in the short time at his disposal whether the man was sick or did not want to plant potatoes. An experienced physician can within two minutes decide whether to investigate further, to medicate, or to bundle the man off to work. If the doctor was concerned, the duty nurse was advised to check later on. The system was and is humane, simple, and effective. Ninety-five percent of the requests boiled down to demands for sleeping pills, pain pills, or tranquilizers. Each prisoner was examined on admission and would likely be seen at least once in the course of a year. Some men, however, were on parade every week, and this group formed the bulk of the work. The number varied from 15 to 40, averaging about 22.

I discovered subclinical pellagra early in 1969. At this time I also held sick parade at the Prince Albert Indian Residential School. This group of children, from grades one to eight, were seen at 8 A.M. so that a decision regarding their daily activity could be made. They would go to school, stay in a dormitory, or be admitted to the sick bay. We would have about 20 children whose complaints were the same as those of the penitentiary inmates: sore throat, sore back, nausea, headache, joint pains, etc., etc. While doing the physical examination I would ask, "Do words move when you read?" "Do you hear someone calling your name?" "Does the ground go up and down when you walk?" "Does your face change shape in the mirror?" Frequently the child would answer "Yes" to these questions, which meant he had perceptual dysfunction. It was the real reason for his coming to sick parade. The child knew something was wrong. Pain dysperception is a major part of the syndrome. Special sense changes were never admitted as a complaint. Unless the doctor asks specific questions about words moving he will never find out if they do. The cure for these children was megadoses of niacinamide, 1.5 to 3 grams. Cure was taken to mean that the child would no longer appear on parade.

Starting the school year in September 1970, there were 20 to 25 children to be seen. By May 1971 the average on parade was two. Obviously something had happened. The first thing was that I had worked myself out of a job. The second was that the children no longer complained, and, from all accounts, the administration, which was under the Anglican Church at that time, was very pleased. These conclusions could not be drawn for the penitentiary group.

By the fall of 1970 my recognition of perceptual changes was more astute. I could outwit the con artists at their own game, not by out-conning them, as had been necessary previously, but by actually diagnosing the cause of their complaints. This was done without ordering X-rays or laboratory tests, which meant they no longer were transferred to the local hospitals for outpatient work-up. The highlight of the "pen pals" day was to get "outside" for even so short a time. I was naive enough to feel the men would appreciate knowing why they were complaining and would be anxious for relief. They would not require tranquilizers and pain pills, but merely some vitamins and diet modifications.

Sick parades at the penitentiary got bigger during the same period, that the children's clinic decreased markedly. Most of these men had no desire whatsoever to improve their health. The prisoners drafted a petition, which was accepted by the administration and by my partners. I was forced out of the penitentiary and later resigned from my group, and set up once again in solo practice. Sadder, but wiser, I now knew the patient himself must want to get well. I also learned those in authority must want the improvement also, and must make an effort toward that end. If they do not, the prisoners will continue to demand more and more in the name of comfort, while the administration must give up more authority and accede to the prisoners' demands. It is strange how people say one thing, do another, and mean something else again.

PREVENTION OF CRIME

A subtitle for this chapter could be "From the Cradle to the Penitentiary in 16 Years." Central nervous system allergy, or subclinical pellagra, begins as soon as the patient loses his tolerance to foods. This is especially true of milk in the baby. Once the body's ability to cope has been impaired, signs of allergy will develop. In the baby, it is usually diarrhea, skin rashes, or sleeping and behavior problems. Later on, one sees asthma, joint pains, bed-wetting, headache and fatigue, and so on. By this time, words move and objects change shape, but these complaints are not admitted unless asked for specifically.

Hyperactivity, rough play, lying, and stealing are apt to appear when the child starts school. Parents try to buy good behavior with coke and candy, which is what the child craves, and is precisely what he should not get. If corrective measures are not instituted at this stage, a large percentage of these children start trying quicker methods to relieve the withdrawal symptoms. After coke and coffee came cigarettes and beer, then marijuana and LSD. Next come barbiturates and amphetamines or a combination of all these things, which sooner or later leads to conflict between society's rights and the addict's desires. Robbery and mayhem lead to jails and penitentiaries, and many of the prisoners are less than 16 years of age. Thirty-three percent of the prisoners I saw on sick parade could be classified as having subclinical pellagra. The percentage is likely higher now because of the greater number of juvenile offenders being sentenced to the penitentiary, and with good reason.

The diagnosis of subclinical pellagra is very easy to establish in youngsters because they frequently have distortions of special senses and are not afraid to admit to these when asked. As the child gets older, the visual and auditory illusions disappear and are replaced increasingly by complaints of a somatic nature. They have complaints of pain in every conceivable joint or organ, often flitting from one spot to another. The pain is real to the patient because he feels it. His problem is that the doctor cannot find any physical explanation for this pain. By a process of elimination, often very expensive and time-consuming, the prisoner eventually is labeled "neurotic." He frequently gets tranquilizers or pain killers to keep him quiet. Until doctors recognize this concept of perceptual dysfunction, we will continue to have "crisis medicine" and all it entails.

The preventive aspect of medicine, so dear to the hearts of all governments and all levels of administration, can never be achieved until this concept of perceptual dysfunction is accepted and practiced. It is unfortunate that new concepts, particularly in medicine, require 20 to 50 years for general acceptance and application.

When a prisoner is admitted to a penitentiary in Canada, he is interviewed by a classification officer and a psychiatric social worker. An attempt is made to establish the prisoner's ability and desire in regard to rehabilitation and work he can do in the institution. If the Hoffer-Osmond Diagnostic test, the Experiential Word Inventory, and Green's Perceptual Dysfunction Test were part of the initial work-up, much time and energy could be saved in about one-third of the admissions. If a prisoner admits to hearing voices or to seeing words moving about, he is liable to be unable to work or to cooperate until these aberrations are corrected. These tests help make a diagnosis and give a base line on which progress can be measured. Prisoners with high scores come to sick parade with great regularity and varied complaints. It is disconcerting if the floors and walls move; the patient realizes it isn't so, yet it makes him dizzy, so he complains of dizziness or headache. Unless the doctor asks about perceptual changes, he will never discover the cause of his dizziness, in spite of all the sophisticated laboratory tests yet devised. By looking at the HOD and the PDT scores, the doctor can know immediately where the problem is coming from. If the perception score is high, there is special sense distortion. This will respond within 48 hours to intravenous administration of vitamin B-1, B-3, B-12, C, or a combination thereof. Oral megavitamin therapy takes weeks to get the same result. If there are many physical complaints and little else, a retrospective HOD can be a great help. Perceptual distortions come and go, but if the patient ever had any, you can relate them to his present aches and pains. His brain is playing tricks due to improper diet, allergy, and the need for megavitamins.

The use of drugs in CNS allergic patients frequently increases distortion because of chemical sensitivity. Modern drugs are derived from petrochemicals. Their effects may be the opposite to what is desired. If we continue treating symptoms rather than causes, the use of drugs will continue to expand. So long as a patient complains, a succession of drugs is used until the patient stops complaining, or is so "stoned" he cannot complain. In either event, administration is happy, and this, frequently, is the criterion for treatment.

Once a patient has gone so far down the road that he is a prisoner in a penitentiary, our therapeutic success rate is not impressive; it is in fact abysmal. As mentioned earlier, just when I was getting to the point where I could help these men to help themselves, they refused, and I became a sacrificial goat. This refusal is part of the disease process. These people rationalize any and every act, like alcoholics or drug addicts, which many of them are. They want some miracle drug or program to make them better. If they have to deny themselves the least little thing, they are not interested in treatment. There isn't one of us who does not feel the same way. If we could push a button and stay healthy, we would do it. Fortunately, most of us know that we ourselves must strive to maintain our own measure of health, by watching our diets, by exercising, and by denying ourselves the dubious pleasures of alcohol, cigarettes, and stimulants, whether they be coffee, coke, or hashish. It is only by self-denial and self-regimentation that we can maintain a degree of good health.

Life in an institution should make self-discipline easy. The army in wartime is an excellent example of this. Here, for the common good, personal freedom is relinquished, and a program of hard physical exercise and strict discipline soon melds a group of individuals into a unified fighting force with a common purpose. If some of this spirit were introduced into the penitentiary service, we would see much benefit from incarceration. The rate of recidivism is steadily increasing, as is the number of prisoners, and why not? They do what they like, eat what they like, refuse to accept any responsibility, and make ever increasing demands, which are acceded to by an ever decreasing authority. Prisoners feel they are correct, and in their irrational approach to life, they are. The time has come to put a stop to this foolishness, and bring both administration and prisoners to their senses.

What brings about this strange set of circumstances? Why do prisoners become prisoners? What leads them into criminality, and why do they repeat their mistakes? The answer lies in CNS allergy—subclinical pellagra for a start, then schizophrenia and finally the psychopathic personality, just like the hero's in *One Flew Over the Cuckoo's Nest*.

You cannot cure an alcoholic; he must cure himself by stopping alcohol, thereby decreasing the allergic load on the brain, so it can function better. Then the alcoholic person may begin to reason clearly and decide for himself that alcohol is to him a poison to be avoided. What of the carboholic, the coffeeholic, the milkaholic, the cokeaholic? All these people suffer from food addiction and from perceptual dysfunction in some degree, because of their CNS allergy, brought on by food. Very often these people are sensitive to dust, molds, danders, and petrochemicals, as well, so they go along in the world only half awake. When this state is present all the time, it is considered normal by the person. If he doesn't drink coffee or smoke a cigarette, withdrawal symptoms begin. It isn't long before a combination of things is needed to allow the patient to remain free of withdrawal symptoms. Then because of headache he takes a drug "222" with his coffee and cigarette, or perhaps a bit of wine, it's quicker to act.

These people never count the cost to themselves or their friends. Self-satisfaction is the trademark of every one of them. This self-satisfaction is an example of fallacious thinking. It is recognized for what it is only by those not so diseased. Immediate gratification, brooking no denial, is a sure sign of CNS allergy-induced disturbed behavior. Many such responses become learned responses; like the Pavlovian concept, they become trained in. For a full therapeutic recovery they must be trained out, and this can be accomplished only by setting up a proper milieu—of diet, vitamins, exercise, and discipline. Dr. William H. Philpott has done some splendid work along these lines, in conjunction with the Rev. George VonHiltsheimer, at the Green Valley School in Florida. These men took failures from every imaginable treatment regimen and made them responsible citizens, which was a most remarkable achievement. It was so remarkable the school was closed down. More proof, if more was needed, that the power structure would sooner pay for failure than support a new positive, and effective, approach, which was more efficient and less expensive.

It should be obvious that prevention is better than treatment. If we can stop children from developing subclinical pellagra, we can do a great deal to prevent behavior problems, school problems, petty thievery, lying, promiscuity, and so forth, which lead straight to other problems. The pattern is there for all to see, and the time to break the pattern is before it becomes set. We must recognize CNS allergy in the very young—before 10 to 12 years of age to have the best chance of treating the individual successfully. The very allergic children may never know what a clear mind is like. The less allergic children gradually become accustomed to a twilight zone, which becomes their normal, unless someone can break the cycle and show them the difference. This can be done in several ways. The best, and the quickest, is by complete fast.

Fasting has been a method of self-treatment for centuries. A complete fast, using only distilled or pure water, will clear toxic products from the body and the brain within four to seven days. Daily tap water enemas are given throughout this period. Intravenous vitamins may be used for symptom relief in the first two days, after which their use is necessary. Fasting revitalizes body enzymes and gets rid of all toxic matter at the cellular level. By the third day hunger is not experienced, and the patient feels much better. By the fourth to the seventh day the brain has regained its equilibrium and the patient is able to think clearly and positively. It is this stage where the patient is able to look back and consider himself through a clear, clean mind. Should he decide he prefers being clear-headed, the causes of his problems can be ascertained by provocative food testing. He is given one food at a meal to see if that food evokes any of his previous complaints or actions. The usual schizophrenic patient reacts to about ten different foods. One also tests for chemical and other pollutants the same way. Once the offending foods and chemicals have been recognized, a program of avoidance and rotation of other foods is designed for the patient. By dint of self-denial, self-discipline, megavitamins, and hard work, recovery can soon be achieved. This clear state remains as long as the program is followed. Eventually, some degree of tolerance is developed for the offending foods, and they too may be worked back into the diet on a rotating basis.

The allergy pattern often begins in early childhood. Frequently the baby is a feeding problem, or colicky, or turns night into day. The next step may well be skin changes, hives, eczema, photosensitivity. Then these symptoms may clear. Then some minor learning difficulties appear. The child may fail a grade or be put in special classes, even though he should be in the top 10%. Then come behavior problems, hyperactivity, fighting, and smart-aleck behavior, which teachers abhor. Then follow skipping classes and lying about it, being unable to tell the truth, then vandalism, trying alcohol, cigarettes, and drugs. At every stage you have social workers, teachers, parents, preachers, and other interested people trying to get the child to follow the straight and narrow. The child will not listen to reason. His mind and his ability to reason are clouded and replaced by narcissism. Everyone but the patient recognizes this situation for what it is; yet no one can do anything about it. The next step is breaking the law and eventually being sent to prison to be rehabilitated. What a hope, because in prison now, things are the same as on the outside, except the patient, now a prisoner, gets everything for free and all he loses is his freedom, which he didn't want in the first place!

INMATE TREATMENT

What happens on admission to the penitentiary? The inmate is subjected to numerous psychological and sociological tests to find for what he is best fitted. Most of them have already been this route via school psychologists, welfare workers, psychiatrists, and so on, know the answers to give, and couldn't care less. They are classified as to what line of endeavor they shall follow—mechanics, school, woodworking, cooking, and the like. Education is "big" right now. They can sit in class and never learn, but the slot is filled and the administration is satisfied. Knowledge is wonderful!

What really happens is quite different. There is very little compulsory active exercise, so the body gets out of shape. There are too many hands and too little work, so sloth is the rule, not the exception. There is no strict discipline, so the prisoners keep pushing more and more in search of some limit. They rarely find one. When they do, administration apologizes for the inconvenience. Administration is so confused that murder is no longer an offense against the state, only against the victim. There is no corporal punishment, which is the only thing these persons comprehend. A severely schizophrenic, completely disoriented, person will stop if he is punished physically, because it hurts. Many of these prisoners are suicidal and haven't the guts to kill themselves, so they arrange a battle with the police. We are seeing more of this every month. Publicity given to these gunbattles encourages others to take the same route.

In my opinion, we need capital and corporal punishment more now than ever before, because more people are getting into this mindless state where life means nothing. We seem unable in our present state of knowledge to help them. Keeping a psychopath in prison for 25 years will stimulate him to do anything to get out—including killing in the penitentiary. Hijacking and political kidnapping would stop overnight if the death penalty was used, as it should be. The leaders in society have taken it upon themselves to play God, to think they can treat psychopaths. Since we cannot, we should reread our history and do what must be done.

The meals in our penitentiaries would make even the well-to-do green with envy. Each and every meal is planned to give a balanced diet—meats in abundance, vegetables and fruits, fresh, frozen or preserved; everything has been considered, except to make an attractive plate. There is dessert twice a day. I've seen men pass up beef stew in favor of white bread, pie, and a pint of coffee. They take as much bread as wanted, often six to ten slices at a meal and they throw leftovers on the floor. They can purchase chocolate bars, pop, and candy to the limit of their budget, and many of them do. One of the reasons for limits on fresh fruits and vegetables is that the inmates find them useful in making home brew! A never ending game of hide-and-seek goes on.

There are parallels between the modern home and our penitentiaries. Mealtime is considered a nuisance, something to be gotten over with as quickly as possible, and with the least amount of effort. Consequently, highly refined carbohydrates are used to excess—bread, chips, pastry, macaroni, and pizzas. Very few homemakers now think about the day's menu and make some effort for a balanced diet. Far too few think a day ahead and gets something out of the freezer to thaw, or make beef stock, or marinate a tough cut of meat for a day. Such planning is a cheap way to feed a family, and the best, but no one teaches rich or poor anything about diet.

In Canada at present, we eat one meal in three away from home. Within ten years, statistics suggest, we will eat every second meal outside the home. As a consequence, our children and the "pen pals" eat too much flour, sugar, and starch, thereby burning up their allergy resistance at a rapid rate. The parent who throws a TV dinner in the oven has no time to teach love and respect, to discipline, to make rules that inculcate thoughtfulness and consideration in the child. In school the same laxity appears, with no multiplication table to learn, no firm discipline, no hard work; just keep out of trouble and you can pass twelfth grade without learning to read, write, or do arithmetic. It is little wonder that the present generation is demanding, self-centered, and uncaring. The cycle is vicious! The more carbohydrates you eat, the more narcissistic you become, whether at home or in the penitentiary. Instant gratification has become acceptable. Loss of mores, lying, cheating, whoring, and boozing are the "in" thing now, and why not? The government encourages this by overtaxing the hard-working, and by making ever more government jobs. They throw good money after bad. This encourages illegal strikes: unions demand and get exhorbitant settlements. Welfare is a way of life. Why work? Why try?

Why did this sad chain of events happen now and not 50 years ago? In my opinion, we can link the entire degenerative process of our bodies and our society to the excessive use of flour, sugar, and starch. Those of us past 45 years of age had very little of refined carbohydrates, other than white bread, until about 1950. By that time we could and did start buying more whiskey, coffee, and cigarettes. Before that, no one could afford them! Since 1950, we have had 25 years to deplete our ability to handle carbohydrates—to get arteriosclerosis, coronary disease, diabetes, depression, tension, anxiety, fatigue, and insomnia. When you are in this state, your mind functions at perhaps 50% capacity, and you become less careful and less caring. Those under 45 years of age have had greater access to sugar, flour, and starch, to coke, chips, and chocolate, to pop, coffee, and alcohol. Now marijuana is the added attraction. The children of today are beaten before they start. Dr. Ben Feingold has shown an increase in hyperkinesis and learning difficulty among school-age children, rising in 10 years from 2 to 25%; in some areas it involves up to 40% of the school population! He points out the exact parallel in dollar value of the production of artificial flavors to the increase in the learning-disabled. He uses a salicylate-free diet in his clinic to help correct the problem.

We don't need to worry now about communism taking over the world. We are now getting the Russians to drink Pepsi Cola. What a masterful stroke! What we should stop to consider is the Chinese. I have seen only two Chinese children with minimal perceptual problems and no adults, except for a few aged, who have lived in Canada for many, many years.

What can the state do to help us help ourselves? Since we are talking about penitentiaries, let's start there:

1. Strict discipline, with strict rules and regulations for inmates and custodial staff, should be enforced, with swift punishment for any transgressions. The Warden would have to regain much of his discretionary power, which has been taken from him over the past 10 years.
2. Corporal punishment is a must. There is nothing like a good tanning to make a trouble-maker think twice.
3. Capital punishment should be reinstituted. We cannot cure these people in our present state of knowledge, and they refuse to try to help themselves. Let us stop kidding ourselves.
4. The four-day, rotary, diversified diet should be instituted immediately across the nation, and the use of sweets should be strictly curtailed.
5. Coffee, tea, cocoa, pop, and other stimulants should be used sparingly, if at all.
6. More physical labor is necessary, even if it is nonproductive.
7. A two hours per day physical training program for inmates and custodial staff should be established.
8. Smoking should be restricted to certain areas at certain times.

What can parents do to stop this tide of woe? We can and must start by education in the proper way to eat. We can rebuild ourselves and our children and rise like a phoenix from the ashes, if we will prepare food in the fashion of the Chinese. They have variety, minimal cooking, fresh greens, sprouts, and rice, which produce less allergy than wheat. They take minimal amounts of stimulants, alcoholic or otherwise. Using the four-day, rotary, diversified diet we could reduce food allergy to a minimum. The judicious use of vitamins, in megadoses for the sick and normal amounts for the symptom-free, would do much to alleviate problems already extant and to prevent disease. By a program of strict discipline from the cradle to the grave, first parental, then self-administered, we could become a proud and healthy nation. Parents and children must be made responsible for their actions. Children or convicts should restore or pay for in some way, by virtue of their own efforts, damage done to people and property. An extensive exercise program, also from the cradle to the grave, would aid immeasurably in the hygiene of the nation.

SUMMARY AND CONCLUSION

What I am proposing is a very simple program of prevention through early recognition of subclinical pellagra and early treatment by diet, exercise, vaccines, and vitamins. If the child is diagnosed before age 10, the probability of his ending up in jail or the penitentiary is minimal.

The schools of this nation, from the ivory tower to the basement nursery, must begin an educational program in the proper way to eat, which is a rotation-type diet with a minimal amount of refined carbohydrates and a good variety of vegetables and fruits. We should eat less meat, once a day is sufficient, and we should eat most foods raw, or nearly so. A copy of the four-day, rotary, diversified diet is listed below as an appendix.

Penitentiary inmates have a golden opportunity to improve their health by simple, inexpensive means. Good foods are less expensive than junk foods. Raw food takes less preparation time than cooked, yet it contains more vitamins and minerals. Chewing is a forgotten exercise, yet the gastrointestinal tract works best when it is required to digest raw foods. The rotation diet works for most degenerative diseases—diabetes, asthma, high blood pressure, to name a few—which is reasonable because degenerative diseases have a common root in poor food habits. Prisoners and custodial staff, too, would benefit from the program outlined. We do not need to build more institutions; we need to run the present ones properly. We need dietary control, more exercise, fewer drugs, and more minerals and vitamins as required. Swift punishment of transgressions, tempered with justice and mercy, and a set of rules of conduct would benefit everyone concerned.

APPENDIX

The Four-Day, Rotary, Diversified Diet

This diet is intended to rotate foods so that no food is eaten more than one day in four. Only the foods on the diet of the day can be eaten that day. Milk is on day 1; therefore milk and milk products can only be eaten on day 1, then day 5, day 9, day 13, and so on. Rare exceptions are allowed, if the doctor agrees. You can choose any food of the day; it is not advisable to have snacks; it is not advisable to eat any food more than once on that day if you have marked allergy symptoms. Note the following:

1. If you are allergic to the meat of the day, be it pork, beef, fowl, or fish, you may substitute: Mollusks—abalone, squid, clam, mussel, oyster, scallop; or Crustaceans—crab, crayfish, lobster, prawn, shrimp. You may also substitute game animals, which are available at times, such as caribou, deer, elk, moose, antelope; also rabbit, turtle, pigeon, squirrel, bear, horse. The four-day rotation still applies.
2. Sweeteners are to be avoided if at all possible. Some may be used in cooking. Honey is a sugar refined by a bee.
3. A carbohydrate counter is a good investment if you have a weight problem. They are available at any health food store and many drug stores.
4. Gelatin is very good to whip into various desserts using fruit and fruit juices. Prepared jello has a high quantity of sugar. Buy Knox gelatin and flavor your own desserts, using fruit or vegetables. Gelatin should be used to flavor beef.
5. Soups: Most commercial soups are flavored with sugar and thickened with wheat or corn starch. You should make soup stock by boiling bones from the meat of the day.
6. In growing children it may be allowable to eat whole grain bread once a day if the doctor agrees.
7. Juices may be made from any fruits or vegetables listed, which are used without adding sweeteners. Combinations are neither necessary or desirable.
8. It is preferable to buy your meat from a butcher who makes his own sausage.

THE FOUR-DAY, ROTARY, DIVERSIFIED DIET

Day 1, 5, 9, 13, etc.

Protein: Beef—veal, lamb, sheep, goat, venison, deer, moose, etc.

Beef products—beef weiners, beef bacon, corned beef, beef tongue, beef liver.

Milk (unpasteurized milk, from a clean herd, is best)—whole, 2%, skim, powdered.

Cheese—all types—cheddar, creme, cottage, goat, rennet, etc.

Grass: wheat, barley, rye, malt, maltose. Use only whole grain for cereals and breads.

Vegetables: Group #1—Celery, carrots, parsnips, dill, parsley, caraway.

Group #2—Beet, swiss chard, spinach.

Group #3—Onion, garlic, asparagus, leek, shallot, chives.

Group #4—Mushrooms, baker's yeast, brewer's yeast, wine vinegar.

Fruits: Group #1—Bananas, plantain, arrowroot (musa).

Group #2—Boysenberry, raspberry, strawberry, loganberry.

Group #3—Coconut, dates.

Fat: Butter, coconut oil, cottonseed oil, flaxseed oil.

Nuts: Brazil nuts, hazel nuts, filberts.

Herbs: Basil, savory, sage, oregano, thyme, marjoram, lemon balm.

Tea: Comfry, fennel.

Day 2, 6, 10, 14, etc.

Protein: Pork and pork products—Bacon, ham, sausage, liverwurst, headcheese, liver, pigsfeet, lard, pork gelatin, scrapple.

Grass: Corn—Mature: corn meal, grits, hominy, popcorn, cornstarch.

Green: tinned corn, creamed corn, corn on the cob.

Vegetables: #1—Cabbage, radish, brussel sprouts, cauliflower, rutabaga, turnip, mustard, sauerkraut, broccoli, horseradish, chinese cabbage, collards, kale, mustard greens, rape, watercress.

#2—Sweet potato.

Fruits: #1—Apple, pear, vinegar.

#2—Pineapple.

#3—Rhubarb, buckwheat.

Fat: Corn oil, corn oil margarine, rapeseed oil.

Nuts: Almonds.

Herbs: Avocado, cinnamon, bay leaf, sassafras, cassia buds or bark.

Tea: Sassafras tea or papaya leaf tea, mate tea.

Day 3, 7, 11, 15, etc.

Protein: Birds—Chicken, turkey, eggs, all fowl and game birds: duck, goose, wild fowl, and their eggs.

Grass: Rice—brown preferred at all times because of minerals and vitamins.

Vegetables: #1—Soybeans, peanuts, peas, lentils, beans—lima, navy, string, kidney—bean sprouts, peanut butter (unsweetened), carob, garbanzo, fresh alfalfa.

#2—Squash, zucchini, cucumbers, canteloupe, watermelon, honeydew, any other melon, pumpkin, acorn squash.

#3—Yam, chinese.

Fruit: #1—Apricot, cherry, peach, plum, prune.

#2—Grapes, raisins, currants, gooseberry.

Fat: Bird fat—fat of any bird listed, chicken fat, peanut oil, soybean oil.

Nuts: Macadamia nuts, litchi nuts, cashews, pistachio, mango.

Herbs: Nutmeg, mace.

Tea: Alfalfa tea, fenugreek.

Day 4, 8, 12, 16, etc.

Protein: Fish—all fresh or salt water fish, cod, haddock, tuna, whitefish, herring, salmon, sole, turbot, sardine, trout, bass, mackerel, sturgeon, perch, smelt, pike, pickerel.
Grass: Oats, millet, bamboo shoots.
Vegetables: White and red potato, tomato, eggplant, peppers—green and red, chili pepper, paprika, cayenne, olives. Lettuce, endive, escarole, artichoke, dandelion, sunflower seeds.
Fat: Olive oil.
Fruit: #1—Orange, grapefruit, lemon, lime, tangerine, kumquat.
  #2—Blueberry, cranberry, gooseberry, figs, breadfruit.
Nuts: Sesame, chestnut, English walnut, black walnut, hickory nut, butternut, pecan.
Herbs: Black and white pepper, peppercorn, tarragon, paprika, cayenne.
Tea: Kaffir, lemon verbena tea, lemonade.

References

1. Green, Glen, Subclinical pellagra—Its diagnosis and treatment, *Schizophrenia*, Vol. 2 & 3, 1970, p. 70.
2. Hawkins, D., and Pauling, L., *Orthomolecular Psychiatry, A Treatment for Schizophrenia*, W. H. Freeman, San Francisco, 1974, pp. 411–433.
3. Hoffer, A., and Osmond, H., *The Hoffer-Osmond Diagnostic Test*, Kreiger Publishing Co., Huntington, N.Y.

Chapter 15
Diagnosis and Treatment of Alcoholism

Russell F. Smith, M.D.
W. J. Maxey School for Boys
Whitmore Lake, Michigan

INTRODUCTION

Since alcoholism, as presently understood, has as one of its causes the use of our society's condoned approved recreational drug, this disease has tended to become obscured by layers of folklore over the centuries. Alcohol's importance to the survival of our way of life also adds layers of institutionalized rationalizations, further hindering objective study of its effects. No one can really discuss alcohol and alcoholism without becoming emotionally involved. Very few of us can be found who are not related to, or do not know, an alcoholic. This all-pervasive general ambivalence has fostered mass denial of the health, safety, and criminal problems arising from alcohol's presence in our society.

The recent realization that the alcoholism syndrome can be caused, maintained, or abstinence-syndrome-precipitated by other sedatives may help to divest alcoholism of some of its obscuring mysticism. Current evidence is quite convincing that general anesthetics, barbiturates, and the majority of present-day "minor tranquilizers" and nonbarbiturate hypnotics can easily replace alcohol as the chemical trigger of alcoholism. The use of some of the minor tranquilizers for sedative maintenance therapy, which has become widespread practice, cannot be condoned. The factor being overlooked is that the sedativist or the alcoholic is most dangerous to himself and others when under the influence.

Because of a social and traditional need for mass denial of alcoholism, we have for centuries been doing with this disease what we have done with mental illness, tuberculosis, and epilepsy. We have dictated that the disease be diagnosed and perhaps treated only in the terminal stages. The skid-row model of the derelict who has lost health, human resources, and economic resources has been used by our society historically to exempt the vast majority of seriously ill alcoholics from confronting their disease. Even the historically established and general used Jellenek scale and British Valley chart, which can be obtained at any alcoholism information center, make the diagnosis conclusively at alcoholic blackouts. It is a shame that the alcoholic is forced to wait for diagnosis until the first signs of brain damage from the disease. Vastly improved case-finding methods and techniques of external benevolent coercion have been developed recently. Numbers of early-stage alcoholics are being referred for treatment. It is in this population that we are beginning to see a recognizable, reliable pattern of symptoms that antedates the more traditional syndrome representing more advanced stages of the disease.

DIAGNOSTIC CRITERIA

The most recent updating of diagnostic criteria was published in 1972 and was carried out by a panel of experts sponsored by the National Council of Alcoholism. These criteria were broken down into physical symptoms and behavioral symptoms. This breakdown has proved useful, since meaningful symptoms that can be used by persons from a variety of professional disciplines are provided. We will attempt to provide here enough of the currently available information to permit the reader to understand the dynamics underlying the symptoms published at that time. By gaining some understanding of the physiological and psychological dynamics of alcoholism, we can not only master presently available concepts but sensibly evaluate future contributions.

The earliest physical symptoms of alcoholism relate to the mechanism of tolerance of sedative substances. Many experts believe, and a growing research literature indicates, that the biogenic amines serotonin, dopamine, and noradrenaline play the central role in alcohol tolerance, alcoholism, and alcohol's interaction with other drugs. Older textbooks of physiology suggest that as the blood levels of alcohol or other sedatives increase, symptoms of progressive intoxication occur. Because of alterations in levels of dopamine and serotonin, subjects become progressively more drowsy and eventually go into a deep anesthetic sleep or "pass out." During this process, altered levels of noradrenaline reduce alertness and impair coordinated motion. Most persons find this experience subjectively very unpleasant and even frightening. If this is the individual's response to alcohol, he generally establishes a limit of impairment beyond which he will seldom go voluntarily. The vast majority of drinkers will state the number of drinks they limit their intake to on any occasion. The presence of such a definite drinking limit all but rules out the alcoholic disease.

The nonalcoholic also experiences the earliest hangovers. Once he is asleep, blood alcohol levels drop at a predictable one ounce of alcohol per hour in a 150-pound person, and brain biochemistry begins to return to normal. Predictably, as serotonin levels return to those compatible with the wakeful state, the nonalcoholic awakens. Return to consciousness, however, does not occur at zero blood alcohol, but ordinarily short of this level. The nonalcoholic then experiences the dull headache, sluggish reflexes, and foggy sensorium of the sedative hangover, if drinking the evening before has been carried to anesthetic levels. This occurrence tends to reinforce moderate drinking and the establishment of a fixed limit of alcohol intake. Thus, the lack of tolerance to sedatives, a fixed limit of intake established by long experience of unpleasant effects, the early onset of unpleasant levels of impairment, and sedative hangovers all signal the absence of alcoholism. In fact, these symptoms may clearly rule out the possibility of future alcoholism or at least indicate a very low risk.

The alcoholic on the other hand is able to alter biogenic amine metabolism to accommodate higher and higher levels of sedation. The alcoholic seldom reaches a point of impairment that is recognizable as true intoxication. In fact, alcoholics do not enjoy being impaired any more than nonalcoholics do. The absence of an easily definable drinking limit and the ability to drink one's companions under the table is hardly cause to seek medical attention. When the level of sedation is kept constant, the alcoholic's central nervous system can adapt to that environment. Thus alcoholics can "drink themselves sober" and function quite well on a fifth of whiskey a day. Again, the ability to use large quantities of alcohol or sedatives without apparent ill effects is not considered a problem and seldom prompts one to seek professional attention.

The moment of truth occurs when the alcoholic stops the intake of sedatives. There is a noticeable and progressively more painful lag in the return of brain biochemistry to normal. It is the presence of the unopposed catacholamines that is responsible for the characteristic physical abstinence syndrome seen in alcoholics. This phase of the alcoholic disease process gives ample proof of how ecumenical drug use can be.

It is at this point that the most serious interactions with other recreational drugs occur. The brain chemistry picture during alcohol withdrawal is identical to that seen when a person is under the acute influence of a hallucinogenic drug like LSD (lysergic acid diethylamide) and a stimulant such as methamphetamine, cocaine, or strychnine. LSD alters brain levels of seratonin and dopamine in such a way that there is progressive distortion of perception. In mild withdrawal the alcoholic commonly experiences heightened perception of sound, light, and temperature. The drinker who complains that the flies are stamping their feet on the velvet draperies beside the bed is nearly identical to the LSD user hearing augmented sound at a rock concert. More severe alcohol withdrawal with its nightmares, "night terrors," or organized hallucincations is the result of brain chemistry identical to that in the LSD "trip." Severe alcohol withdrawal, with its toxic delerium, is identical to the LSD drug psychosis. It is during true alcohol withdrawal that serious unexpected potentiation of hallucinogens can and does occur. Even a mild hallucinogen like cannabis can produce startling and unexpected effects.

LSD, THC (tetrahydrocannabinol, the most active ingredient in cannabis), and other hallucinogens also effect the digestive tract, through altering body serotonin levels. Alcohol withdrawal affects serontonin levels in similar fashion. In mild withdrawals loss of appetite occurs, followed in a day or so by the onset of a ravenous appetite. This is seen in much abbreviated form with smoking cannabis. In more serious sedative withdrawals, any type of intestinal upset can occur. In its severest form, total gut paralysis is possible. The effect of serotonin on sleep is well established. With hallucinogenic drugs, insomnia is pronounced during acute use, followed by some drowsiness in compensation afterward. With alcohol withdrawal, insomnia is marked for several days and can persist for weeks. The effect of this configuration of biogenic amines on the extraocular muscles has long been known and described. Blurred, double, or fixed paralysis of vision is commonly seen with sedative withdrawals of various intensities.

The high levels of noradrenaline accumulated to offset the sedative effect of alcohol trigger a far more dangerous and life-threatening constellation of withdrawal symptoms when the sedative is removed. Adrenaline functions in our bodies to prepare us in every possible way to meet crisis situations. This body substance can immediately prepare us to fight for our lives or flee like the wind. It would be natural to expect that in even slightly elevated levels the person would become wary, hyperactive, and perhaps a bit paranoid. In higher levels progressive hypertension, rapid pulse, muscle tremor, and eventually seizures occur.

Very early in the alcoholic disease we can, if we look, find unmistakable physical signs of the disease. Unfortunately, because of our tendency to deny the problem as a society, these symptoms and their implications are either largely ignored by health professionals or treated symptomatically. It is not uncommon at alcoholic treatment centers to be able to discontinue unneeded tranquilizers, cardiac medications, hypertensives, anticonvulsants, and antipsychotic medications. Alcoholism is today's great masquerader simply because we and our health professionals refuse to see the disease even when its presence is obvious. Avoidance of the diagnosis appears even more deliberate when the above abstinence symptoms occur with gastritis, ulcer disease, chemical hepatitis, fatty liver change, pancreatitis, and toxic brain syndrome. At this stage alcoholism and sedativism are obvious, but all changes, although serious and dramatic, are totally reversible. It seems almost inexcusable that we still see gastrectomies, scarring of the liver, intestinal bleeding, organic brain syndrome, and cardiac collapse due to advanced alcoholism even today.

The foregoing symptoms of alcoholism, of necessity, require health professionals to detect and interpret them. For those with other backgrounds the behavioral symptoms of alcoholism provide a reliable alternative. Despite the fact that no consistent pattern of mental health precedes, accompanies, or follows alcoholism, alcoholics do tend to behave in a similar fashion. This common behavior stems from the fact that all alcoholics find themselves in the same dilemma. Caught with physical symptoms that are increasingly more difficult to ignore, the culturally established need to deny alcoholism, and the inability to stop drinking, the alcoholic behaves as any of us would in similar circumstances. Intermediate between physiological and behavioral symptoms of alcoholism is another group of symptoms, related to persisting distortion of brain biochemistry set in motion by the acute stages of the disease.

In those alcoholics who have repeated severe withdrawals, predictable and rhythmic swings of the brain catacholamines are set in motion. Since serotonin, dopamine, and noradrenaline are the brain transmitters responsible for our expression of mood, corresponding painful extremes of mood occur. Just as withdrawal from stimulants is followed by physical and psychological depression, alcohol withdrawal—being the same physiological state—is followed by a similar state of depression. Current research evidence is pointing to the fact that in severe and extreme cases rhythmic rises and falls in catacholamines can persist long after the last acute episode and its withdrawal. Accompanying corresponding changes in mood can be troublesome or even on occasion life-threatening. Many indicators suggest that such mood swings may actually trigger future drinking.

The moderately severe manifestations of this prolonged biochemical hangover are rhythmic cycles of excitement and depression that can mimic true manic-depressive psychosis. The intermittent insomnia, loss of appetite, depression, and excitement can be troublesome. Occasionally, these symptoms simply prompt drinking, which at least temporarily relieves the symptoms. In a misguided attempt to manage the problem medically, some health professionals are led to playing tranquilizer and antidepressant roulette. All is well while the person is in the excited state and taking a sedative tranquilizer; but when brain biochemistry swings to the depressed state, these drugs can heighten the depression to perhaps suicidal levels. Similarly, antidepressants appropriate for a depressed state can heighten the excitation phases.

In the severest form of this prolonged biochemical hangover from acute alcoholism, drinking is nearly inevitable. Even several years after acute drinking, a minor event like the death of a pet can be superimposed in time on a cyclic depression and prompt suicidal thinking or even suicide. Many single-car fatal accidents in known recovering alcoholics are felt by many highway safety experts to represent this type of suicide. Any alcoholic knows that in his case alcohol is a potent antidepressant. Very likely drinking under these circumstances might actually be life-saving. Excitement superimposed on the antidepressant swing of neurohormones can precipitate high blood pressure, rapid heart rate, tremor, and seizures. The presence of symptoms identical to withdrawal can be relied on at least to suggest drinking as a relief measure, since it has proved effective before.

It has also been observed and reported in the popular media that some alcoholics remain in the hyperirritable state, and anticonvulsants have appeared to be pragmatically effective in some of these cases. Altered carbohydrate metabolism is seen, and when not explained on the basis of altered liver metabolism, may be interpreted on the basis of the alcoholic's chronic high intake of pure calories. A can of beer has the caloric value of a glass of milk; a shot of whiskey that of a handful of peanuts. These metabolic problems persist into the early years of abstinence for the alcoholic, pointing out the advisability of carefully planned total nutrition for the recovering alcoholic.

The behavioral manifestations of alcoholism turn on three major dynamic factors. The first we have already discussed, the physical. Basically, the more an alcoholic drinks in volume or over time, the sicker he gets at withdrawal. The more drinking episodes there are, the more likely the more traditional chronic liver, brain, and heart changes to appear. In the alcoholic it is predictable that the longer the acute stages of the disease exist, the more difficult it will be to deny its presence. Second, all persons in our society have programmed into our brains a battery of ideas, attitudes, and values concerning alcoholism, carefully contrived to make us all feel that alcoholism is a moral and character problem. Needless to say, this social picture of alcoholism is unacceptable to us and particularly to the alcoholic. This hideous distortion of the facts, made in an ill-fated attempt to prevent alcoholism, kills the majority of alcoholics through neurotic pathological denial on the part of the alcoholics, meaningful persons in their lives, and the society in which they function. Finally, alcoholic, and for that matter nonalcoholic, human beings have to be taught to drink.

It is well known that "dumb" animals don't voluntarily consume alcohol. Human beings learn to drink as well. This learning process occurs in recognizable stages. Experimental drinking often begins in the early teens, and determines whether future drinking will occur. Social drinking follows, from midteens throughout life, if alcoholism doesn't occur. During this phase alcohol is closely associated with the best times, best people, and best things that happen to the drinker. In a society conditioned for years by mass advertising to be intolerant of any minor psychological or physical discomfort, we have all become magical thinkers. This thinking leads to the use of alcohol to make a sale, get through a difficult situation, or ask the boss for a raise. The alcoholic adds two additional learning stages. As withdrawals become unpleasantly symptomatic and the symptoms are relieved by restoring the blood alcohol, alcohol becomes medicine. During the medicinal stages of alcoholism, the alcoholic is drinking to get well. Finally, as drinking all day long is necessary to remain asymptomatic, or relatively so, the alcoholic rationalizes this fact away on the basis of the problems he has. Thus the alcoholic's entire experience with alcohol is subjectively positive, and intake is reinforced by the total weight of past experience. The alcoholic, caught between these three mechanisms over which he has little control, reacts as most of us would caught in a similar dilemma.

Contrary to common belief, alcoholics do not have trouble stopping drinking. In fact, alcoholics are experts in quitting, since they are the only persons who have reason to quit. Alcoholics experience difficulty in maintaining abstinence, but not in starting it. Even early in alcoholism alcoholics begin to sense they are different because they are always closing down the bars and driving the group home; the thought that they might be alcoholic comes into consciousness. The need to deny this frightening identification is overriding—almost anything will do to support sagging denial. The common magazine quiz that diagnoses alcoholism is a favorite at this stage. It may appear these quizzes are poorly conceived and unscientific, until one realizes that left to their own decisions it is only the alcoholics who take them. Nonalcoholics simply aren't worried about their drinking. It is taking the quiz that is diagnostic, not passing or failing it. Reassured, the fighting alcoholic can return to drink, and the physical aspects of alcoholism progress. Later, other people begin to suggest pathological drinking. Problems at home, work, and with the law suggest a drinking problem.

Here the alcoholic searches for a credible professional—a physician, psychiatrist, social worker, or sometimes A.A.—to diagnose him as nonalcoholic. Usually a credible expert can be found, and this chapter is closed. Later, severe withdrawals, loss of jobs, loss of driving privileges, and property repossession clearly indicate serious problems. Marriages totter and break; the alcoholic loses his financial, personal, and human resources. At this stage primitive mechanisms are used not so much to deny but to avoid confronting the alcoholic diagnosis. Hostility sufficient to drive everyone away, alibis, secret drinking, accusing others—all are employed. Inevitably the physical progression breaks through these defenses, and the alcoholic has no way of avoiding the diagnosis. Treatment, commitment, death, or suicide are the only alternatives at this stage.

INTERVENTION AND TREATMENT

With increasing skill at recognizing the earlier stages of the physical and psychological processes of alcoholism, earlier intervention is possible. With newly gained information that indicates that alcoholics have historically considered death a plausible alternative, and that abandonment by loved ones whose presence makes them guilty anyway only provides the privacy and reason to continue drinking, more powerful motivations for treatment are being sought. The driving privilege and the job seem to be potent sources of "benevolent coercion." This is felt to be true, since most of us identify ourselves by what we do, and how well we do it by what we drive. Today it is possible to force the alcoholic to "volunteer" for treatment at earlier stages of the disease. In fact many treatment centers agree that in today's rehabilitation climate, where financial, personal, and human resources are intact, simple rehabilitation to a sedative-free existence is required.

Detoxification of the sedative-dependent person is an acute medical emergency with significant incidence of death and complications. Withdrawal is usually managed by reinstituting sedation, then slowly tapering the subject off sedation. Depressing the biogenic amine levels is also possible, in conjunction with tapering off sedative doses, or alone in less severe withdrawals. In the more frequent milder withdrawals resulting from earlier intervention, nomedical detoxification is not only possible but practical.

Following acute withdrawal it is then necessary to replace the external factors that prompted treatment with more reliable personal motivation. This has been found to be basically an educational process, which permits the alcoholics to understand themselves, the disease, and the alternatives. Currently it is estimated that for every ten alcoholics in this country there is less than one bed available to treat alcoholism. This means that currently nine out of ten alcoholics will die of cirrhosis, heart disease, or pancreatitis, or be committed for irreversible brain damage, without ever knowing what they had.

Rehabilitation of the alcoholic has long been an area of controversy divided along disciplinary lines. The more traditional school, operating on the premise that alcoholism is a symptom of an underlying basically emotional problem, provides primarily lifestyle modification services. Physicians restore physical health; psychiatrists and psychologists restore mental health; legal, budget, marital, and vocational counselors attempt to establish a lifestyle that no rational person would turn in for a drink. Unfortunately, in this context little or nothing is said about alcohol and drinking. The alcoholic, after a short period of apparent control, generally relapses. Most treatment programs close, and the alcoholics are labeled sociopathic because they have failed to respond to this treatment.

At the same period in history that the traditional approach developed, a few treatment centers scattered about the country approached the problem by attempting to alter the alcoholic's values about alcohol and drinking. Unfortunately, these facilities in the 1940s and 1950s did not enjoy the confidence of the health insurance industry and were very-low-budget operations. The alcoholic was taught to seek a non-chemical drug-free existence, but few resources were available to improve physical or mental health. So many problems beset the alcoholic after release that relapse was very common. Present-day comprehensive treatment centers provide both lifestyle and value system rehabilitation services, vastly increasing treatment success.

Alcoholism as seen today is a life-long chronic relapsing disease. Long-term aftercare is a necessary part of treatment. Current research indicates that persisting symptoms can be moderated by the use of lithium and nicotinic acid. Lithium chemically slows biogenic amine production. Nicotinic acid is a product of biogenic amine production, and it is suspected that it can in high doses accomplish the same end. Recent symposiums on the use of lithium in the treatment of alcoholism suggest that it is a far too toxic and dangerous substance to be put in the hands of magical thinkers. In the outpatient setting, most therapists report spending nearly all of their time treating lithium-poisoning rather than alcoholism. This is to be expected in a group that believes if one drink is good, two is better. Nicotinic acid, or vitamin B-3, therapy is slower and perhaps safer, although there are real and serious contraindications to its use. If one can overcome the alcoholic's impatience and intolerance of mildly unpleasant side effects, B-3 can be a valuable adjunct to alcoholism therapy, especially in cases of multiple severe withdrawals followed by symptomatic mood, sleep, and appetite changes related to brain biogenic amines. Some experts feel that in the rare cases of residual hyperirritability hydantoin-type anticonvulsants can be useful. Along with these possible long-term components of medical aftercare, treatment of diagnosed liver, brain, heart, and digestive residuals is necessary.

Various types of professional counseling and mental health services may be indicated to help the alcoholic deal with problems that arise secondary to alcoholism. With today's earlier intervention into alcoholism, the need for formal professional aftercare is lessening. This is a tremendous step forward, since all professional services are becoming increasingly costly and eventually could be beyond the reach of our personal financial resources or tax dollars.

Less formal and expensive aftercare is a must. The alcoholic has demonstrated many needs over the years. First, the alcoholic needs a method of remaining under control. Since drinking is a learned phenonemom, the majority of experts feel it must be unlearned. Since alcoholism is a chronic relapsing disease, it requires that the alcoholics treat the disease largely by themselves. A self-care system needs to be provided. Finally, several general rehabilitation services also need to be provided.

A variety of techniques have emerged to help the alcoholic "unlearn" how to drink. Various unpleasant experiences, such as emesis and electrocution, have been associated with drinking, with some short-term success. Unfortunately there is an established need to reinforce these experiences periodically to keep the process operable. Decades of experience strongly suggest low patient acceptance of periodic electrocution or emesis. They eventually miss reinforcing experiences and end up drinking again. Alcoholics Anonymous in a way represents the same type of experience. At weekly intervals several alcoholics congregate to remind each other that they are alcoholics and cannot drink. Such experiences may be occasionally dull, but, by comparison to harsher methods, the A.A. experience can be considered benevolent aversion.

Reality therapy, meditation, transactional analysis, and an endless procession of self-actualization systems have all been proposed as part of the alcoholic's aftercare plan. Certainly these systems are useful, particularly in cases where selective indications exist. On the other hand, such therapeutic systems are expensive and not specifically designed to adjust an alcoholic to a sedative-free existence.

Certain general needs are common to all recovering alcoholics. Because of the guilt generated by acceptance of all or part of the social model of alcoholism, alcoholics are alienated personally and spiritually. Because of preoccupation with hoarding and consuming alcohol in secret, alcoholics also have lost a great number of social skills through lack of use. Because of constant fabrication of systems of denial, intellectual honesty also suffers. Most important is the fact that alcoholics eventually come to use alcohol as their single coping mechanism, and lose most other coping skills through lack of use.

Certainly, established techniques for dealing with these problems are needed. To deal with all of them simultaneously, however, would require a number of resources in most cases. Again, Alcoholics Anonymous and its companion movements, Alanon and Alateen have an impact on all of these problems at one place. A.A. provides a milieu where, among other alcoholics, the alcoholic feels normal instead of different. A.A. philosophy deals directly with spiritual alienation. Alanon and Alateen, along with A.A., work to reduce personal alienation from family and children.

Empathetic knowledgeable confrontation on the part of other nondrinking alcoholics tends to restore intellectual honesty and a more conventional value system. The A.A. group provides a safe, comfortable, benevolent social laboratory in which the alcoholic learns to trust, make friends, and develop social skills. By constant exposure to other alcoholics who have solved similar problems, the alcoholic early in his recovery maintains the hope and self-confidence necessary to carry on a sustained effort to develop his own coping skills.

The majority of experts in the field of alcoholism therapy understandably feel that Alcoholics Anonymous should form the central core of any alcoholic aftercare program. Certainly more in-depth professional help may be required even in the use of A.A. itself, but A.A. does provide the most comprehensive armamentarium of services for the alcoholic. When this fact is coupled with A.A.'s general availability, its low cost, its freedom from inherent ill effects, its patient acceptance over long periods of time, and its confirmed effectiveness, it appears that confidence in and widespread use of A.A. is justified.

CONCLUSION

With our current degree of knowledge regarding alcoholism, we have the following capabilities: (1) diagnosis of the disease far earlier than was before considered possible; (2) comprehension of alcoholism's basic pharmacology, physiology, and psychodynamics; (3) early external motivation of treatment; (4) safe and humane management of sedative detoxification; (5) techniques necessary to manage physiological residuals of alcoholism, either in existence or being developed; (6) practical methods of generating individual personal motivation; (7) an adequate comprehension of rehabilitation needs, which is necessary to facilitate effective comprehensive treatment planning; (8) knowledge of aftercare and follow-up needs, and recognition that a tried and tested central aftercare resource, Alcoholics Anonymous, already exists. If our society simply would mobilize the knowledge and resources it already has, serious inroads into its alcoholism and alcohol problem could be made. With early treatment of alcoholism and restructuring of social values toward more responsible use of its recreational drug, alcohol, our society could drastically reduce or eliminate the tremendous costs in life, health, crime, productivity, and dollars we now collectively pay.

Section IV

PREVENTION-INTERVENTION APPROACHES TO DELINQUENCY AND CRIME

INTRODUCTION

Our greatest opportunity for crime reduction in the immediate future lies in early intervention and prevention of crime-producing behaviors. As the authors of this volume have indicated, once the behavior develops and continues unchecked, the likelihood of its advancing to the point of being labeled delinquent is very good. Thus, very great efforts must be made in infancy and early childhood to identify and correct what appear to be maladaptive behavior tendencies and patterns. This effort should be aimed primarily at the parents and schools.

A secondary but still very important point of remedial possibility exists at the point when behavior first is identified as delinquent. This behavior may be seen in school in the form of assault, truancy, running away, stealing, vandalism, gang activity involving crimes, or drug or alcohol abuse. Or, the behavior may involve some minor or major criminal act for which a police investigation and/or arrest is involved. The youngster may be brought into juvenile court and possibly placed in a detention home.

At any of these points, early detection, intervention, and effective treatment are a possibility. Effective resolution of the problem at the point of school–police–court can avoid the delinquency label and association with other delinquent-prone persons in confinement. This is important not only for purposes of treatment, but to avoid the real and severe social penalties that such labels place on the future lives of the persons involved.

The authors of this section stress the importance of prevention-intervention strategies. Dr. Rosenberg begins by pointing to the great importance of improving basic dietary habits at the family level. He emphasizes the need for better maternal and infant nutrition, and indicates how these early nutritional patterns, if inadequate, can lead to a host of later health and behavioral problems, including crime.

Dr. Rees points to the many contemporary contributing factors in childhood disorders. She reviews the common types of childhood problems that she has experienced in treating children brought by parents or referred by the schools. Dr. Rees stresses that many of these problems have a malnutrition base. Unless detected early and treated, she says, many of these children will develop learning and behavioral disorders, which may develop into problems of delinquency.

The paper by Blanchard and Mannarino is concerned with perceptual deficiencies and their relation to poor academic performance of juvenile delinquents. They hypothesize that juveniles may in part be delinquent because of poor academic performance, and that this poor performance is related to visual and perceptual abnormalities. Their study of delinquents in a Florida detention center tends to support this hypothesis, and they recommend adoption of diagnostic and treatment procedures in this area of remediation with all detained juveniles, as a necessary adjunct to current practices.

The paper by Bachara and Lamb indicates the results of two contrasting approaches to intervention with delinquents: present and future. They first review the typical limited approaches used currently in most juvenile courts. Then they report on the results of a comprehensive medical/psychiatric intervention program developed for use with a juvenile court in Virginia. The approach used is illustrative of the new orthomolecular concepts. The procedures not only uncovered a high incidence of biochemistry-related deficiencies and disorders among the delinquents, but their treatment results suggest that this comprehensive biochemical-psychiatric approach shows great promise of effectiveness in reducing delinquency-types of behavioral problems.

The final paper of the section, by Dr. Hippchen, attempts to synthesize the knowledge presented in this book into a model set of concepts and principles for operating a community program for antisocial persons. This program would be designed to deal with the many forms of maladaptive behavior typical of antisocial persons. Although emphasizing early intervention at the level of school–police–courts, the program also would involve preventive efforts with mothers, infants, and children. Dr. Hippchen suggests seven basic assumptions as important to the new treatment model, the most important of which probably is the one calling for an understanding and correctional approach rather than a nonunderstanding and punitive approach to antisocial persons. He also outlines and discusses 14 principles that he considers important to the successful operation of an intervention effort.

The thrust of all of the papers in this section is toward a new approach to the delinquency-crime problem. They emphasize that the new ecologic-biochemical knowledge presented in this book is vital to our improved effectiveness in dealing with the crime problem. They further stress the great need for very early intervention and treatment, and, more importantly, for preventive efforts at the pre- and postnatal periods.

Chapter 16

Family Planning, Nutrition, and Crime

Harold Rosenberg, M.D.
Orthomolecular Practitioner, New York City

THE PROBLEM

Nutrition has been the stepchild of medicine since time immemorial. What held for the past still prevails today. Few institutions of health education have incorporated formal nutrition courses. Consequently, physicians, dentists, and associated paramedicals are virtually ignorant in the application and recommendation of nutritional guidance. Further, no more than $2 million from Federal sources has gone into nutritional research per year. With so little emphasis placed upon nutritional requirements, it is no small wonder that the public is lacking in nutritional awareness.

Senator Schweiker, a member of the Senate Committee on Nutrition and Human Needs, has said that skipping breakfast is the great American pastime; no longer is it skipping school. Dr. Jean Mayer, formerly of the Harvard School of Public Health, former Chairman of the White House Conference on Nutrition, as well as the Seventh National Nutritional Policy Planning Conference Chairman, is credited with stating that a secretary knows as much about nutrition as a physician, except when she has a weight problem, and then she knows more.[1]

A great deal of a family's leisure time is spent watching television. Most of the morning hours, especially on Saturday, are devoted to children-oriented programs. And, of course, since this orientation is drawing a youthful market, the sponsors are developing it.

Senator George McGovern, the Chairman of the Senate Hearings, stated before the Senate Committee on Nutrition and Human Needs of the United States Senate, on March 5, 1973:

> There is increasing concern, evidenced by professionals and laymen alike, about the quality of the American diet. Both Department of Agriculture surveys as well as the Ten-State Nutritional Survey by the Department of Health, Education and Welfare, indicate a disturbing decline in some very important parts of the traditional American diet. This decline is accompanied, on the other hand, by a striking increase in the consumption of an array of nontraditional kinds of snack foods.[2]

He went on to say:

> In its investigation of this issue, the committee has become aware of the special importance that TV now plays in influencing the Nation's nutritional habits. The TV advertising of food products now exerts an enormous new influence on the Nation's children. The committee has been told that moderate TV viewing by children today amounts to 5000 commercials a year and, theoretically, 80,000 commercials by the time a child reaches the age of 16. A heavy proportion of these commercials deal with food products and predominately with breakfast and snack products.[3]

Dr. Jean Mayer, Professor of Nutrition, Harvard School of Public Health, Boston, Massachusetts stated:

> I think it's legitimate to try to classify foods in perhaps four groups of decreasing usefulness.
>   Group One would have fruits and vegetables and would have animal products such as milk, fish, eggs, meat and cheese.
>   Group Two would have such useful foods as bread, potatoes, macaroni products, some of the better breakfast cereals, soups, particularly the better ones.
>   Group Three, and we are beginning to go down considerably, would have such foods as the sugar-coated breakfast cereals, most of the snack foods, many of the cake mixes.
>   Finally, Group Four, the empty calories group, would have candy and soft drinks and, at the chance of being thought guilty of a horrible pun, we might perhaps have alcoholic beverages as a fifth group.[4]

He continued:

> Now, it's fairly obvious to any even casual television viewer that national advertising expenditures are in reverse order to the useful-

ness of the foods. Group one, the fruits and vegetables and such things as fish, eggs, and meat receive very little advertising. Advertising for potatoes, macaroni and so on is also limited.

By contrast, if you go to soft drinks, alcoholic beverages and so on, advertising is an extraordinarily large item. Now, I do not subscribe to a "devil theory" of advertising. I could not think that the advertising profession is made up of people who have set out to deliberately pervert the food habits of the American population; but, the effect in many cases, is just the same. I think the reason for this is fairly plain. The foods in group one—the foods produced by farmers, basically, and which are consumed almost directly by the population—are not branded. They are produced by a very large number of farmers who don't have any advertising resources at their disposal.

By contrast, foods in group three and group four are produced by a very small number of manufacturers who have very well established brands of snack foods, candy and soft drinks, and who have enormous resources available for advertising. So that we end up with the fact that the structure of our food industry—in spite of the undeniable good will and excellent intentions of many of its leaders . . . resulted in a very strong endorsement by leaders of the food industry of the concept of nutritional education at the White House Conference. In spite of all this, the structure of the industry and advertising industry end up with the whole weight of enormous resources of advertising going far toward the destruction of our food habits.[5]

He further stated:

I think television is a very striking phenomenon for small children, equating goodness with sweetness, selling food on the basis of anything except nutrition, on the basis of the fact that it is sweet, that the box is attractive, that you can get a green monster if you buy this one or that cereal. It becomes very difficult, all of a sudden at the age of six, to revert the whole process and explain to them that the first reason we eat is to get the necessary nutrients.[6]

Dr. Mayer also said:

I think the consumption of sugar in England was only about six pounds of sugar per-person-per-year in 1830—it is now 125 pounds per-person-per year. Sugar is thus a new good and it is one with which the human system, at least many people, are not equipped to live.[7]

At the same hearings, on March 6, 1973, Mr. Robert B. Choate, Jr., President of the Council on Children, Media and Merchandising, Washington, D.C., discussed poor food values in American breakfasts, naming many well-known products as examples.

Dr. Roger J. Williams stated that a person would get as much value from the box surrounding the breakfast cereals as he gets from the products contained therein.

In this chapter I will attempt to review the latest information concerning nutritional inadequacies, additives, molecular awareness, and biochemical individuality; and to discuss the disruptive effects on family, persons, and institutions of our lack of nutritional awareness.

THE BASICS OF NUTRITION

Food, water, and air are essential to the maintenance of life. Any disruption of these elements promotes deterioration, degenerative illness, and eventually death. Further, a healthy mind needs a healthy body—*Mens sana in corpore sano*. Interference with any of the three basics handicaps normal emotional as well as physical performance.

Where does one start with nutritional guidance? Is it too early to start *in utero* (with the fetus within the uterus), or is the logical step to start at birth? This is like asking "Which comes first, the chicken or the egg?" No chicken, no egg; no egg, no chicken. In truth, life starts upon the acceptance by the ovum of the sperm. This combination goes through various stages of growth, finally culminating in the infant. The fertilized ovum acquires its nutrients from the mother—in effect, this is parasitism. All living creatures, plants as well as animals, in order to sustain life are parasites; the small amoeba and the human, a much higher and more complex organism, are both parasites.

The 1969 WHO (World Health Organization) panel found that there was no nutritional policy on maternal health and nutrition. In essence, the WHO panel stated:

> There must be a national affirmation that every woman has the right to high quality and high standard health care. This includes a food intake that will prepare her for, and carry her through, a healthy

pregnancy and childbirth and permit her infant to flourish. It affirms that the right to adequate nutrition is an inseparable part of the basic right to health care, and that women require and are entitled to sufficient amounts of nutritional foods.[8]

Let us consider now the scientific axiom that matter can neither be created nor destroyed. I translate this to mean that all the molecules that are existing today were present in some form at the outset. We are living examples of borrowed molecules. In fact all things (living as well as inert) are composed of "compounds" of molecules, which came together under appropriate conditions to produce life. Temperature, climate, molecules, and opportunity all joined at an optimal level, thereby inducing life.

In the scheme of nature, it has taken millions of years for these transitions to take place. *Homo sapiens* (the human) is the highest organism on the phylogenetic scale, but, like all other organisms, it must be continually in harmonious relationship with its environment in order to survive. It appears that a continued exchange of like molecules is central to the maintenance of cellular vitality. Dr. Claude Bernard, a nineteenth century French physiologist, referred to this equilibrium as the balance between the *milieu exterieur* and the *milieu interieur*; we refer to it as homeostasis. Sound health is the maintenance of naturally composed molecules and compounds that are freely able to replace equal amounts of molecular components which constitute life. This is, in essence, what sound health is based upon, the homeostatic balance of cellular vitality by the maintenance of like molecular components.

FAMILY NUTRITION NEEDS

Nutrition and health of infants was considered by two panels at the 1965 White House Conference (WHC), chaired by Jean Mayer. The great majority of the recommendations focused upon the pregnant female and the family, not upon the child. Two recommendations by the WHC were as follows:

Family as Distributive Unit: One important recommendation of Panel 11-1 concerned the family as the distributive unit for nutrition and health programs. The panel expressed its opposition to the design and implementation of special programs that make food available solely for pregnant women and infants. Because the logic of the recommendations is apparent, it is distressing to note that the major new food assistance programs (Welfare for Infants and Children) are oriented not toward the family, but toward particular individuals—pregnant or lactating women, infants and preschool children.

Maternal and Child Health Programs: Another recommendation of Panel 11-1 concerned major expansion of facilities, manpower, and programs for maternal and child health care. In fact, little expansion has occurred, and, in a number of states, programs have been curtailed.[9]

A summary of five years of WHC on food, nutrition, and health, stated that food assistance should involve the family, not specific subgroups of the family (e.g., pregnant female, infants), as well as expansion of day care facilities and introduction of prevention of dental cavities, obesity, and iron deficiency.

Maternal nutrition affects fetal growth. Senator Hubert Humphrey, in the preface to "To Save the Children, Nutritional Intervention Through Supplemental Feeding," prepared by the staff of the Select Committee on Nutrition and Human Needs, U.S. Senate, January 1974, pp. V, VII, quoted Dr. Myron Winick:

1. An association exists between the amount of weight gained during pregnancies, and birth weight in all types of population.
2. An association exists between maternal nutritional status prior to pregnancy and birth weight in poor populations.
3. The difference in birth weight between rich and poor actually accounts for the difference in mortality between rich and poor.
4. The larger the number of smaller infants the greater the chance of mental retardation.
5. Malnutrition retards infant growth, producing smaller infants and organ growth, producing smaller brains.
6. In animals, malnutrition results in behavioral abnormalities, which may persist throughout life. In humans, early malnutrition results in similar abnormalities. *This can be a major cause of criminal behavior, as well as under achieving.* (emphasis added)
7. Feeding a better diet during pregnancy increases maternal weight gain, birth weight, and therefore should decrease mortality and the incidence of retardation.

There are at least 300,000 premature infants born each year. The cost of sustaining the survivors is staggering, let alone the pressure on the parents. Over 150,000 mentally retarded are born each year.

As the population continues to explode, so too does the number of mentally retarded and premature infants. Senator Hubert Humphrey goes on to state the fact, most obvious by now, that protein deficiency "may well play a crucial role in the causes of mental retardation." The cost of protein supplementation is $10–20 per pregnancy. Thus, the total cost of a city's supplementation is less than the estimated public expense necessary to care for only a few retarded infants over their lifetime. The cost to correct anemia is also low—approximately $2–5 per pregnancy. Fetal brain development is dependent on the oxygen-carrying capacity of the maternal blood, and iron. An anemic mother faces the threat of bearing a mentally retarded baby. Thus the seeds of future delinquencies are integrally related to the maintenance of an unhealthy climate within the maternal subject.

Senator Marlow W. Cooke was equally impressed by poor nutrition and its effect upon maternal and infant vitality. He commented that preventive efforts are far less expensive and far more effective than those after-the-fact services." He further stated that "sound maternal and infant nutrition is a key element of physical and mental development, and one way in which we can assist in the prevention of problems later in life."

Pregnancy is nutritional stress. The homeostatic maintenance during pregnancy is forced to its highest plane by the demands of the growing fetus, an *in utero* parasite. It is a critical state of life and death. There is evidence to show that a (maternal) diet poor in good-quality protein, plus the utilization of drugs as well as liquor and nicotine, has a fearsome effect on the fetus. It is also apparent that in the zest to maintain maternal low weight, small babies are born. These babies are frequently handicapped by smaller brain growth. The diet of the mother, for that matter of all humans, has to be realistic. Again, I must emphasize, we are naught but borrowed molecules, and with our demise all does not really end, but only goes back into the mainstream of the molecular pool. The molecules unceasingly go on into other forms or groupings, known as compounds in that endless support of vitality.

EFFECTS OF EARLY FEEDING

As critical as the maternal organism is, so too is that which develops after the birth of the infant. No longer sustained by an umbilical cord which facilitated the deposit of nutrients and removal of wastes, the infant has total external dependence upon the external environment, for food, air, and water. It is believed by some that the fullest development of the infant brain takes place within the latter months of pregnancy and the first two weeks to a month after birth. Other information indicates that the brain of a child reaches its fullest development by its second year. In any case, it is apparent that maximal attainment of cerebral development is related to the intake of nutrients, which includes proteins, fats, carbohydrates, vitamins, and minerals.

Hans Selye, in response to a question about the stages of man, stated:

> The period of childhood is characterized by low resistance and excessive responses to stimuli. Adulthood is the period during which we adapt to most commonly encountered agents and increase our resistance. And, finally, during senility, irreversible loss of adaptability and eventual exhaustion occurs, ending with death. The puzzling thing is that during the resistance stage food intake is normal. So, you would think that once adaptation has occurred, and enough energy is available, resistance should go on indefinitely. But, just as any inanimate machine gradually wears out, even if it has enough fuel, so does the human machine, sooner or later, become the victim of constant wear and tear.[10]

Although death is an eventuality, as certain as taxes, vitality can be promoted and, with it, adaptability to stress or the maintenance of homeostasis, by basic nutrition. Later, I will review the concept of biochemical individuality. This concept states that, unlike the goose and gander, not all is good for all of us. Or, as Lucretius long ago stated, "What is one man's meat, is another man's poison." Dr. Roger J. Williams, professor in chemistry at the University of Texas, has been hammering away at this individuality for years. This concept will be discussed further in this chapter with consideration of vitamins and minerals.

As stated above, nutrition two weeks to a month postpartum has a significant influence upon the fetal brain. Drs. Jensen, Shockley, and their followers would have us believe that blacks are inherently less intelligent than whites, and also less intelligent than Orientals and American Indians. There is supposed to be a fundamental genetic inferiority of people of African descent. Not so! It is more likely that the foolhardiness of negligent ghetto diets, malnourished nursing mothers, plus the poverty of good nutrition as well as economic poverty, contribute to impaired cerebral development. Any black child from an environment that supports sound health practices will equal any other ethnic group child in intelligence. Numerous American and African blacks have come under my care. I have not found any instances of lowered intelligence, except where malnutrition and poverty have combined to undermine them. This is equally true of whites, Orientals, and other groups.[11]

After the birth of a child, it is a rare mother who breast-feeds. The Western mother, and particularly the American, has through the advent of convenience, in the guise of modernization, cast aside breast-feeding. We have been told that breast-feeding would create cosmetic problems, hanging breasts. The latter idea is related to our being a breast-conscious sexist society. I doubt that breast-feeding would create a more pendulous breast than would ensue without resorting to this method.

I mentioned molecular integrity earlier, the balance of molecules which has taken place over millions of years of slow transition. This transition, a sort of trial and error, the elimination of the weak, the incorporation of beneficial mutants, depends on the maximal exchange of molecular balanced nutrients. It is within the design of the scheme of nature to sustain natural resources. Man in his effort to improve convenience by emphasizing modernization has disparaged breast-feeding.

Dr. Derrick B. Jelliffe and E. F. Patrice Jelliffe emphasize the concept that mammalian milks are specifically tailored in composition to the particular needs of the offspring of the species, emphasizing that this concept is not new. They have indicated that human milk contains large quantities of those nutrients needed for rapid growth of the main organ that differentiates man from other mammals—the brain. It has the highest lactose content of that of any mammal, 7%. Lactose is needed in the production of galactose, which, together with cholesterol, is a main constituent of the brain.[12]

The ration of cystine/methionine in human milk is distinctly different from that in other milks, especially cow's milk. These two sulfur-containing amino acids are needed in the brain development of premature infants, when the enzyme cleaving mechanism for cystathionine is lacking. Further, evidence is provided by the two Jelliffes that the composition of polyenoic fatty acids in human milk parallels that of the tissue of the human brain, and not that of any other species. They have further shown that the levels of phenylalanine and histidine lead to hyperaminoacidemia in low-birth-weight newborns. This results in immediate maldevelopment and possibly birth defects. Another influence of cow's milk is low calcium content due to poor absorption of calcium from cow's milk. This, plus the increased obesity attendant with bottle-feeding, exacts a toll of ideal infant vitality. In breast-feeding, the infant controls its intake; the composition is virtually molecularly exact. Newer evidence, according to the two researchers, indicates that the fat content of breast milk constantly changes and may be an important influence signaling the end of that type of feeding by the infant.

The higher salt content of bottle-fed infants increases thirst, forcing increased needs for fluids. This does not occur in breast-fed infants, since breast milk has a low salt (solute) content.

Breast-feeding induces the initial colestrum, and it is believed that it contributes to increasing the infant's resistance to infection.

As a mission of mercy, formula was given to the nations of the draught-stricken sub-Sahara. Feeding a Ugandan baby now takes 30% of a laborer's salary. To stretch a penny, these people have watered down the formulas. They have been Westernized to give up breast-feeding at the expense of increased poverty plus the reduction of molecules naturally accrued from maternal milk.

Irwin Stone stated in a 1975 issue of the *Journal of the International Academy of Preventive Medicine*, in a discussion on cataracts, that (1) L-golonolactone oxidase, the human liver enzyme required for the endogenous synthesis of ascorbate from blood glucose, and (2) a-galactoskinase and b-galactose-1-phosphate uridyl transferase (GPUT), the two initial enzymes involved in the metabolism of galactose, derived from milk sugar, are missing.[13] This gives evidence of another factor that is lacking in our ability to biologically assimilate milk, in this case cow's milk. When the enzymes are missing after the age of two, they are certainly not apparent in adults, according to other sources.

The continual assertiveness of human ingenuity has not always contributed to alleviating our problems. For every gain or plus on the one hand, there must be a balancing out on the other. We seem to pay the price for convenience. I feel that we have achieved a point of no return. As we sweep away forests, destroying species of animals, plants and insects; as we gobble up and alter the molecules from the pool of molecular balance; as we encroach upon the balance of nature and its scheme—we will surely run out of enough pure water, air, and nutrients. Death will be but the banishment of life, since the human is already an endangered species.

THE INADEQUACY OF FAMILY DIETS

I have used the phrases *Mens sana in corpore sano*, molecular balance, the nature of things, the scheme of nature, over and over. I have made an effort to prove that convenience in the guise of modernization is not necessarily achievement. At this point I would like to discuss the inadequacies of our diets, the danger of additives, both medicinal as well as food, and the impact that these have upon our relationship to others. Proper performance of any living organism is based on the natural acquisition of balanced molecules, in the form of water, food, and air, in order to sustain a harmonious (homeostatic) relationship with the external environment.

In all other species of life, except for domestic creatures, a balanced diet is primarily found by parasitizing the inhabitants of the environment. A balanced diet to such a predator as an owl, a hawk, a tiger, a lion, a shark, a fluke, is the total devouring of the killed prey. To the Eskimo, raw meat eater, the devouring of the entire creature suffices to keep him healthy and strong and free of modern infirmities. Infirmities of cardiovascular disease, gall bladder, and gastrointestinal pathologies were unheard of by the Eskimo, unheard of until modern civilization encroached upon him!

To the modern Western mind, a balanced diet includes intake each day from each of the following four groups: meat, fish, and poultry; milk and dairy products; fruits and yellow and green vegetables; cereals and grains. These foods are relatively balanced in the nature of things, but, in order to reach our tables, they have to be altered in order to increase shelf life. Vitamins and minerals are removed; chemical additives are added to thicken, to emulsify, to harden, and to add and enhance flavor. Chemicals are used to increase color, as well as to ripen fruits artificially. Additives, furthermore, are used to retard sprouting, and to reduce pest infestations.

The result is to fool the nature of things. It is axiomatic: what is poisonous to a single-cell organism, a bacterium, or to an insect, is as poisonous to our cells.

Three important commodities are altered, and when one is not skipping meals, show up as an active ingredient in nearly all that is ingested: flour, oil, and sugar.

Dr. Paul Buck of Cornell University, a professor of chemistry, has described vitamins as a team, and indicated graphically that the removal of any one vitamin or group of them is similar to having a quarterback without his wide receivers. Nature in her wisdom put all the molecules together in harmonious relationships in order to support life.

NUTRITION AND BEHAVIOR

The ingestion of natural foods permits the entrance of all vitamins and minerals en masse, thus enhancing the utilization of the ingested basics. Flour that has been separated from the bran, and wheat germ of the wheat plant; oil that has been petroleum-solvent-extracted under high temperature and then bleached with caustic lime; plus white granulated sugar that has been appropriated from the sugar cane, and the beet—all leave behind vitamins and minerals and are nutritionally empty caloric intruders. They exact a demand upon the cellular chemistries, forcing their uninvited presence upon a meagerly supplied cell. The effect is similar to that of an unannounced guest showing up for dinner. The good hostess, in order to satisfy the guest, borrows from the others in the family, in the case of cells, vitamins and minerals. This does not make the situation right. It only promotes lessened vitality of already meagerly satisfied cells. The continuation of a nutritionless diet, though satisfying the criteria for the basic food components, undermines physical and mental vitality, a major cause of underachieving and fatigue. Any individual thus supplied is literally at the end of his rope. Short temper, indecisiveness, as well as poor judgment, can be a consequence of a so-called, balanced diet.

Behavior can be affected by what we eat as well as by what we fail to obtain. Dr. Benjamin F. Feingold, Chief Emeritus of the Department of Allergy at the Kaiser-Permenta Medical Center of San Francisco, has indicated that one can literally turn on and off hyperkinetic children by restricting or adding salicylates found in aldehyde-containing compounds such as apples, colorings, additives, and flavorings. He describes a case of a seven-year-old hyperkinetic boy, who was so angry and agitated he would charge oncoming cars with his bicycle. This behavior occurred when he was given foods containing these substances. He states that 80% of all the colorings and additives in foods cause emotional problems, as well as arthralgia, macroglossia, etc.

Dr. Marguerite Stemmerman, a Huntington, West Virginia, internist, found that the removal of MSG (monosodium glutamate) from the diet of a one-year-old girl ended her multiple petit mal seizures. She was given a half frankfurter, and within three hours a shuddering seizure ensued. You can imagine that if this can occur in one small child, what else can be attributed to additives: personality disorders, poor judgments, and why not crime-related problems?

Fears have developed that the nation's supermarkets are virtually warehouses of harm to this as well as the next generation. Food technology in the guise of convenience is nearly unimpeded; relentless efforts continues to create thousands of unnatural molecular compositions—compositions that are gulped down to the tune of $128 million annually by the food industry.

Additives stand accused of being suspected carcinogens, mutagens, and tetragens, and causing brain damage. CNS (central nervous system) disorders, as well as such hematological diseases as methemoglobinemia, are also attributed to additives. Each person receives approximately five pounds of unnatural molecular compounds per annum. A total of one-half billion dollars' worth is sold to food manufacturers each year. This amount is expected to rise above three quarters of a billion by 1980, and, with the additives, to increase by 40 to 100% by 1980.

The FDA (Food and Drug Administration) is charged with the control of nutrients and additives, as well as chemicals that preserve, flavor, and color foods. Their critics, such as Dr. Feingold and Dr. Samuel Epstein, a Case Western Reserve University Medical School professor or environmental health and human ecology and of pharmacology, complain about the FDA's monitoring methods and that

> the concept of matching benefit against risk has often been applied by the FDA to minimize short term benefits to the industry ... with minimal benefits and maximal risks to the consumer. The democratic process is largely absent from FDA regulatory practices. In this country, you can buy the data you require to support your case.[14]

Some of the additives under attack are the nitrates, monosodium glutamate (MSG), and food colorings. Nitrite is believed to be the most toxic chemical in the nation's food supply. Found in hot dogs, lox, bacon, ham, luncheon meats, and smoked fish, it is added to seven billion pounds of these foods each year. It preserves colors, increases flavor. It has a strong affinity for hemoglobin; this keeps ham pink, but it can cause methemoglobinemia, which blocks oxygen transport. Children under one year of age are sensitive to it—it is now no longer included in baby products.

Nitrates are considered to be the most potentially dangerous carcinogenic source. Nitrates combine with amines to form nitrosamines, which are formed in the presence of stomach acid. At 200 ppm nitrates are considered safe. One part per million is equal to about one inch in sixteen miles. Yet, the question of safety is suspect when one considers that numerous products at any one meal contain nitrates. Further, safety limits have been found to be exceeded, with spot-checking by the FDA revealing as much as 3,000 ppm in smoked salmon. Hot dog headaches also have been attributed to nitrates. How many behavioral patterns ending in crime may be due to additives, to nitrates?

Monosodium glutamate increases taste acuity. It has been associated with strange feelings of oppressiveness and emptiness, as well as pressure across the chest. It has also caused weakness of the arms and legs, a general feeling of malaise, and headache. I personally had acute abdominal seizures due to its presence in food. It originally was considered the cause of the so-called Chinese Restaurant Syndrome. Dr. John Olney, of the Washington School of Medicine, reported as far back as 1969 that subcutaneous injections of MSG damaged the central nervous system of infant mice and rats. This result was confirmed by other laboratories by using varying laboratory assay methods. Dwarfism, obesity, learning defects, behavioral disturbances, and retinal defects also were attributed to its use. In spite of Dr. Olney and Drs. Jean Mayer and Edward Arce of Harvard, Drs. Tommie Redding and Andrew Schally of Tulane, and Drs. Jerome Knittle and Fredda Ginsberg-Fellner of the Mount Sinai School of Medicine, all objecting to its use, a committee of the National Academy of Sciences concluded that its risk was small. But since they considered that the infant was unable to determine taste, they permitted its voluntary withdrawal by the baby-food manufacturers. This again indicates the limits of concern for the public when the question of industrial benefits are applied. Five of the seven members of the committee were employed or subsidized by industry.

Dyes from coal-tar derivatives are entering our foods at about four million pounds per year as complex, low-molecular-weight synthetics. Additives, as we have said, are unnatural molecular balances. Orange #1 and Orange #2 were removed in 1960 for causing internal organ damage. Red #1 was indicated for causing liver cancer. FDC Red #4, which damages the adrenal cortex in dogs, is restricted to maraschino cherries and to pills. Citrus Red #2, a weak carcinogen and a damager of internal organs, still is used to dye oranges. Yellow #1, 2, 3, and 4 have been removed for causing intestinal lesions as well as heart damage, but Yellow #5 and 6 are still used. Red #2 (amaranth) was recently removed from the composition of colorings after much consumer and scientific pressure; in 1971 the U.S.S.R. banned this dye, after indicating that it caused the impairment of reproduction and cancer in rats. FDC Violet #1 was banned after 22 years of being questioned by toxologists. It was not until the Japanese revealed it had strong carcinogenicity that it was removed.

NUTRITIONAL FALLACIES

It has been said that vitamins and minerals are supplied in abundant amounts by commonly available foods, except for persons with special medical needs, and that there is no scientific basis for recommending routine use of dietary supplements. This statement has been proposed by the FDA to be placed prominently on the label of every vitamin product, *a most misleading statement*! It is misleading because in the scheme of nature, all things being equal, a natural food must have its entire team in order to replenish the molecular regularity of the host organism.

George L. Mehren, Assistant Secretary of Agriculture, called this an "inaccurate and misleading statement" that would give a consumer who was eating unwisely "a false sense of security." Dr. Linus Pauling, twice Nobel prize winner, flatly declared, "This statement is not true!" It is a proposal of "no relevance . . . which, taken out of context, creates a false impression" declared the Chairman of the Committee on Recommended Dietary Allowances of the National Academy of Science–National Research Council, Dr. William Sebrell.

The 1973 FDA proposals were accompanied by a listing of so-called "Findings of Fact," several of which regrettably are not only fictional (being merely optional) but actually in error or self-contradictory. For example, one such "finding" states: "There is no relationship between the vitamin content of foods and the chemical composition of the soil in which they are grown." *False!* It is well known that proper content of soil does indeed relate to the vitamins and minerals in the plants grown on it! It is also common sense to know that fertile soils produce plants with higher nutrient content.

Another "Findings of Fact" statement claimed that minerals in foods are not significantly affected by storage, transportation, cooking, and other processing. *False!* The minerals in wheat and sugar cane (or sugar beets) are largely removed when the plants are processed into white patent flour and refined sugar. Nearly all the calcium, magnesium, and so on, are removed. Also, minerals are often present in foods in the form of water-soluble salts, and vegetables cooked in water can lose much of their mineral content into the cooking water. Thus the minerals frequently go down the drain.

Still another so-called fact: the term "subclinical" and similar ill-defined terms when used to define vitamin and mineral deficienies . . . are neither informative nor meaningful to customers. *False and self-contradictory!* The FDA claims to draw its scientific knowledge primarily from the works of the Food and Nutrition Board, and states that this Board's 1968 report, *Recommended Dietary Allowances* (Seventh Revised Edition), "shall be used as the source of authentic and reliable information" about nutritional matters. But, this report does state (p. 12) in dealing with a particular nutrient (linoleic acid, one of the essential fatty acids), that in some cases supplements may be necessary "to prevent a subclinical physiological deficiency. . . ." About pantothenic acid, the report states (p. 39), "biochemical defects may exist undetected for a time. . . ," which is the very meaning of "subclinical." The Food and Nutrition Board report also refers in this vein to magnesium (p. 60): "Animals fed moderately low levels of magnesium, sufficient to allow normal growth and prevent all gross signs of deficiency, often develop calcified lesions of the soft tissues and increased susceptibility to the atherogenic effects of cholesterol feeding. . . ." Severely damaging magnesium deficiencies in animals may also be "subclinical."

At the heart of all of these proposals is the intent to control vitamins and minerals, literally to create the image that these nutrients are drugs, which they are not. Drugs are alien substances that can cause irreversible damages at toxic levels; vitamins are nonalien, and the removal of any one group or any single vitamin, can lead to death by lack, rather than by abusive use. Life can do without drugs but not without vitamins and minerals. These are, in general, natural molecular compounds, which are needed to bring about chemical change.

Let us to some adding. The FDA established RDAs (Recommended Dietary Allowances) on a reference female of 22 years of age, 124 pounds, 5'4" tall, and a male 22 years of age, 154 pounds, 5'7". This fails to take into consideration the needs of the aged, the ghetto dweller, the very young. But, the FDA claims its allowances would be sufficient for nearly all "normal healthy" persons—90 to 95% of them.

Many would quarrel with this assertion, citing biochemical individuality of different persons (which often produces distinctive vitamin and mineral needs in particular individuals), the special needs for trace nutrients among the elderly (many of whom unknowingly have trace nutrients deficiency), and so on.[15]

Also, 60% of the people are estimated to be low in hydrochloric acid, and to show gluten (whole grain) sensitivity. These factors, plus additives in foods, temperament, disease states, and numerous other parameters, show the need for an individual approach to vitamin-mineral assessment.

Yet, by taking the FDA's assertion at face value, we can draw the following conclusion, using governmental statistics. Our population is 220 million, of whom 11% or 24 million are chronically ill to some degree. Add to this number at any given time, 10 million persons sick or injured—suffering from colds or other minor illnesses, broken limbs, serious infections, recuperating from surgery, and so on. The total is 34 million or more in poor health, leaving 186 million "normally healthy." Now take 5% of these "normally healthy," for whom the RDA's are alleged to be insufficient, and we obtain 9.3 million more.

Add it all up, and there are at least 43 million Americans for whom the U.S. RDAs—in vitamin-supplemented limitations based on them—would be insufficient by the FDA's (and the Food and Nutrition Board's) own estimates. For the population as a whole, the RDAs and the FDA's proposed regulations would have advocated a 20% or greater risk of malnutrition.

Fortunately, much of the pressure has been alleviated by a decision by Judge Friendly of the United States District Court for the Southern District of New York, which forces the FDA to reassess its case in relation to certain vitamin groups.

HYPOGLYCEMIA

Dr. Benjamin Feingold is one who has objected to the frequent use of hypoglycemia as the diagnostic entity by nutritionally oriented practitioners of health (including doctors of osteopathic medicine, medicine, dentistry, podiatry, psychiatry, and psychology). This objection was made during a personal interview I recently had with him in Denver, Colorado. Before responding to his objection, I recalled being on a program in which a National Institute of Health participant exclaimed that 87% of those tested for low blood sugar suffer a reaction during a glucose tolerance test. The Institute of Health participant considered this to be a normal occurrence. However, many of those in attendance who had been treating patients nutritionally believed this to be an accurate assessment of their own findings in their specific practices. Simultaneously, I had a flashback to one of the greatest criminal attorneys, Samuel Segal, who in the 1950s successfully defended a morally suspect female of a heinous crime on the basis of her suffering from hypoglycemia.

Fortified with these experiences and thoughts, I responded to Dr. Feingold by stating that were it not for hypoglycemia, for what other reason would anyone come to a physician in search of dietary education. He nodded in acknowledgment. I do not state that it does not exist; its existence is relatively commonplace, possibly affecting eight out of ten.

Considering the ill effects of nutritional inadequacies, such as skipping meals as well as the perversions of our food supply, enough ground exists to increase nutritional awareness. Adding relative as well as reactive hypoglycemia to the total, nutritional needs present a formidable problem!

Most alleged hypoglycemia sufferers exhibit underachieving, irritability, inward trembling, fatigue, headaches (migrainous), muscular weakness, crankiness, short temperedness, and depression—a virtual gamut of unpleasantries. Additionally, hyperventilation, clammy hands, and blurred vision are a few more subjective signs that are experienced.

I have noted in females considerable decrease in vitality, indecisiveness, irritability, and poor judgment menstrually. Apparently, with the decline of estrogen, there is a parallel decline of calcium as well as glucose levels. I wonder at the degree of incarcerations due to hypoglycemia as a result of the premenstrual state.

Hypoglycemia is the decline of glucose below normal functional levels for effective and efficient cerebral oxidation. In general, cortisone and insulin operate in response to the various chemical feedback mechanisms of the body in an effort to sustain appropriate levels of glucose. Insulin stores glucose as glycogen, and cortisone releases it. Where there is failure in homeostatic balance, the flight fear mechanism of adrenal activity is activated. This forces glucose out in a dramatic but shaky fashion. Inward trembling results, with the release of adrenaline-like substances. As a result, the mind, overwhelmed by this feeling, exhibits recognitions of unreal fear, and uncertainty.

It is not the province of this chapter to go into biochemistry, but a short review should suffice. Since cortisone and insulin are instrumental in balancing glucose levels, it is important also to realize that they are involved in fat metabolism and protein synthesis. To put it simply, insulin not only stores glucose as glycogen, but also it is involved in fatty acid storage and protein synthesis. Insulin enhances amino acid direction and assimilation. Cortisone slows up, borrows, or converts fatty acids and amino acids into cell fuel, as well as increasing carbohydrate production. Cortisone also is a relative of estrogen, testosterone, aldosterone, and vitamin D, all of these precursed by cholesterol. Yes, cholesterol, that much maligned, yet essential ingredient! No cholesterol, no steroids, no vitamin D. None of these . . . no life! Hence, a glucose tolerance test does go beyond the glucose levels in evaluation. It is the description of an inadequate balance of biochemical feedback between insulin and cortisone upon glucose metabolism. By perceiving the total metabolic effects of insulin and cortisone, a far greater relationship involving the chemistries, fats, proteins, and carbohydrates is acknowledged.

Diet is extremely important in the overall control of nutrients and of behavior. Dr. Carlton Fredericks in the book *Psycho-Nutrition* and Dr. Abraham Cheraskin in *Psycho-Dietetics* point out the effects of nutrients on behavior.

Hypoglycemia responds to a diet low in glucose, which alleviates the insulin-cortisone mechanism by removing free available refined carbohydrates. A great deal of the adverse reaction responds to diet, if not dramatically, at least sufficiently to reduce symptomatology.[16]

THE ADDICTIONS

Many alcoholics crave sweets, as do drug addicts. Addicts, alcoholics, or pillaholics in general respond to diets free of refined carbohydrates, refined oils, and refined flour (white). I prefer to call these unnatural molecular hordes "denuded substances."

I have accompanied alcoholics to alcoholic-sponsored meetings, only to see them guzzle down black coffee, laced with heavy amounts of sugar, and nibble on large amounts of pastry. I visited a drug halfway house, noting a pattern of care similar to the 12 steps of Alcoholics Anonymous, as well as the same unnatural imbibing of large amounts of cola beverages, sweets, pastries, cakes, and sugar.

Restriction of caffeine stimuli, the removal of white sugar, refined oils, and flour, plus the use of vitamins and minerals, as well as frequent small feedings, go a long way towards correcting the problems of these patients.

Failure comes only from the unwillingness to cooperate by the individual, from the unwillingness of the family to assist both financially and morally, and from the snobbery of one's peers. It takes at least one year, possibly two, of constant professional guidance to get one "over the hump" and on his way to nutritional balance.

Considering individual inabilities to absorb supplementation properly, use of injectible vitamins and minerals may be indicated. Considering the missing enzymes, which influence milk and milk product availability, and the decreased amount of hydrochloric acid often found, our overall proficiency in nutritional availability is suspect. Coupled with the natural devitalization of aging, the debilitation of disease plus our alteration of foods, and so on, supplementation, both orally and parenterally, is required.

THE FEEDING OF CRIMINALS

I am quite concerned over the diets administered in our institutions (see Table 16-1). It is quite difficult to liberalize one's nutrition. Our institutions, such as schools, hospitals, prisons, and the armed forces, are preparing more and more convenience foods. Already, I have in-

Table 16-1 Meal Menu Ossining Correctional Facility
(One Week)

Breakfast	Dinner	Supper
Sunday, August 15, 1976		
Rice Krispies	(1) Baked pork chop	Vegetable soup
Milk and sugar	Sage dressing/gravy	Saltine crackers
Orange juice	Buttered asparagus	(2) Slices of cheese
Bread and butter	Mashed potatoes	Mustard
Coffee	Bread	Oven brown potatoes
	Pineapple ice cream	Bread
	Cold drink	Cold drink
Monday, August 16, 1976		
Rolled oats	(1) Hamburger	(2) Seafood patties
Milk and sugar	Ketchup	Tartar sauce
Stewed prunes	Oven-fried potatoes	Boiled potatoes
Toast and butter	Peas and carrots	Buttered spinach
Coffee	(1) Soft roll	Bread and butter
	Bread	Vanilla pudding
	Cold drink	Cold drink
Tuesday, August 17, 1976		
Scrambled eggs	(1) Veal pattie	(1) Roast beef sandwich
(2) Sausage	Spaghetti with tomato	Chili sauce
Milk and sugar	sauce	Cole slaw
Grapefruit juice	3 bean salad	Macaroni salad
Bread and butter	Bread and butter	Bread
Coffee	Cold drink	Bread pudding
		Iced tea
Wednesday, August 18, 1976		
Corn flakes	(1) Slice baked liver	Green split pea soup
Milk and sugar	Onion gravy	Oyster crackers
(½) Fresh grapefruit	White rice	(2) Slices bologna
Toast and butter	Cream style corn	Mustard relish
Coffee	Bread	Potato salad
	Fruited jello	Bread
	Cold drink	Cake with icing
		Cold drink
Thursday, August 19, 1976		
Bran flakes	Beef stew with fresh	(3) Boiled franks
Milk and sugar	vegetables	Mustard
(1) Fresh banana	Tossed salad with oil	Baked navy beans
Bread and butter	and vinegar	Sauerkraut
Coffee	Bread and butter	Bread and butter
	Sherbet	Corn bread
	Cold drink	Jelly
		Cold drink

(*Continued*)

Table 16-1 (*Continued*)

(One Week)

Breakfast	Dinner	Supper
Friday, August 20, 1976		
(2) Hard-boiled eggs	(2) Fish portions	Turkey salad
Hot cereal	Ketchup	(1) Soft roll
Milk and sugar	Baked potato	Cole slaw
Orange juice	Butter and green beans	Succotash
Toast and butter	Bread and butter	Bread
Coffee	Chocolate pudding	Cold drink
	Cold drink	
Saturday, August 21, 1976		
Pep flakes	Beef chow mein	(1) Slice of grilled salami
Milk and sugar	White rice	Mustard
(1) Fresh orange	Beet and onion salad	Potato salad
Bread and butter	Bread and butter	Mixed vegetable
Coffee	Cold drink	Bread
		Cake with icing
		Cold drink

dicated that all commodities of vitaminless and mineraless nutrients are to be indicted. We have indicted additives as nutritional sources. But, we failed to mention that our meats come from cattle raised in feed lots and fed special formulations, as well as the suspected carcinogen diethylstibesterol, designed to fatten them so that at seven months they are ready for slaughter. Range-raised cattle, taking two years to mature, are tough, as well as low in fat. It is almost impossible to barbeque a healthy range-fed steer; principally, its drippings are not enough to fuel the fire.

These institutional meals are heavily endowed with refined, or, as I prefer, denuded, nutritionless commodities, such as white sugar, white flour, and solvent-extracted, caustic-lye-bleached oils; these meals also include breakfast grains, toasted free of vitamins. Furthermore, the question of frozen or concentrated juices as good sources for proper nutrient values is suspect. Freshly squeezed juices, or intact fresh fruit, hold greater values. Coffee, high in caffeine, creates untoward stimulatory as well as addictive effects. Nitrates and nitrites are found in luncheon meats, franks, hams, and so forth. Soft drinks frequently contain excessive quantities of energy due to the high concentration of sugar, as well as high amounts of unnecessary caffeine. As to white rice, a nutritionless substitute for brown rice, all the nutrient value of vitamins and minerals are absent. This puts a severe strain upon cells, containing meager supplies of vitamins and minerals for processing the empty commodities that have entered the body.

I need not dignify cake, ice cream, or pastries with comment. Remembering my years in the army, I wonder whether the potatoes are real or reconstituted. Even real potatoes are suspect, losing over half their vitamin C during the process of storage.

Fresh, frozen vegetables lose nutrient values such as vitamin E. Furthermore, the habit of throwing away the juice from our cooked vegetables is accompanied by a considerable loss of water-soluble nutrients, such as vitamins, which go down the drain.

As pluses in this diet for criminals, I would accept rolled oats, the vegetables if they are truly fresh, the bread if whole grain, eggs, butter, salad, and dressings, provided the latter are not factory-constituted. Fresh fruit and whole proteins as meat, fish, and fowl that have not been precooked, frozen, and thawed out, are acceptable.

A good diet tends to promote emotional stability, quiescence, and reduced physical as well as mental handicaps. It is important that all institutions receive critical as well as objective advice from medical nutritionists.[17] The use of straight dietetic understanding does not necessarily constitute good nutritional qualifications. A medical nutritionist, steeped in knowledge of the biochemical individuality of each person plus the biochemistry of nutrients and foods, can do a great deal toward upgrading not only institutional nutrition, but that of the family as a whole.

Chickens are pellet-fed with special fattening nutrients and are ready for market in seven weeks as opposed to natural raising, which takes fifteen weeks. Ever notice how yellow and stunted they appear? You get what you are paying for—increased fat, lower protein, and overall decreased vitality.

As yet, fish have not been pellet-fed, but in time they will be placed in special tanks and fed unnatural molecular substances.

SUMMARY AND CONCLUSIONS

Remember, unnatural molecules are not consistent with good health. The nature of things or the scheme of nature has taken millions of years of trial and error and mutations to reach the optimum molecular exchange. Man has only taken a few years to undo this balance. Our encroachment upon other beasts, the plant world, our waters, and our atmosphere is like "borrowing from Peter to pay Paul." As I stated earlier, you have to pay a price; molecules cannot be accumulated by one species at the expense of other species without endangering all of us. We humans are indeed an endangered species.

With the scientist playing around with recombinant genes and inserting them into bacteria, invisible to the naked eye, we are entering a genetic world of foolhardiness. Our continued tampering with the scheme of nature in the guise of convenience and modernization is nearing its final solution through a twilight of narrow vision, influenced by greed rather than need, approaching the finality of oblivion. Oblivion will be that of our existence but not of the universe, for molecules will remain, and perhaps renewed life, for it is axiomatic, matter can neither be created nor destroyed.

It is essential to restore balance to the basic unit of life, the cell, the family. It is essential that we pay heed to the body wisdom, the sum total of cellular wisdom.[18] The molecular onslaught of drugs and medicinals, literally thousands, only masks instincts. This masking curtains cellular vitality. Unnatural molecular compounds, foreign to the body cells, precipitate untold reactions. The use of psychedelic drugs to obtain exuberance, change moods, create socially acceptable situations, represents man's tinkering with his instincts. We, at birth, are guaranteed not only the needs for food, air, and water, we are guaranteed our instincts—instincts that protect as well as direct us, that respond to beauties of sex as well as to the mortification of sorrow. It is not possible to enjoy the companionship of others by use of drugs and consider the experience real. When one needs a psychedelic to enhance one's sexual desires, one then is operating in a dream. If conscious states of cellular wisdom and our natural instincts are turned off by another, then why turn on with a drug? It is not possible that neither person is the other's "cup of tea"?

It has taken millions of years for the right molecules to come together in harmonious relationship, to make a human. So, why delve into unnatural molecular compounds to upend the most magnificent of all gifts, natural life?

Leibe F. Cavalieri has stated:

We must ask, with Professor Chargaff, have we the right to contradict, irreversibly, the evolutionary wisdom of millions of years in order to satisfy the ambition and the curiosity of a few scientists? This world is given to us on loan, we come and we go, and after a time we leave earth and air and water to others who come after us. My generation . . . has been the first to engage, under the leadership of the exact sciences, in a destructive colonial warfare against nature. The future will curse us for it![19]

References

1. Rosenberg, H., and Feldzamen, A. N., *The Book of Vitamin Therapy*, Berkley Publishing Corp., New York, 1975, (paperback, second printing). See also Rosenberg and Feldzamen, *The Doctor's Book of Vitamin Therapy, Megavitamins for Health*, G. P. Putnam's Sons, New York, 1974.
2. *Nutrition Education 1973, Hearings Before the Select Committee on Nutrition and Human Needs of the United States Senate*, U.S. Govt. Printing Office, Washington, D.C., 1973, p. 255.
3. *Nutrition Education 1973, Hearings Before the Select Committee on Nutrition and Human Needs of the United States Senate*, Part 3, TV advertising of food to children, U.S. Govt. Printing Office, Washington, D.C., 1973, p. 256.
4. Ibid., p. 258.
5. Ibid., p. 258, 261.
6. Ibid., p. 261.
7. Ibid., p. 274.
8. Jacobson, Howard M., in *Hearings Before the Select Committee on Nutrition and Human Needs of the United States Senate, 93rd Congress, Second Session*, Part 6, Nutrition and health, U.S. Govt. Printing Office, Washington, D.C., pp. 2571–2573, 1969. Howard M. Jacobson, M.D., was formerly vice chairman of the Panel on Pregnant and Nursing Women and Young Infants, White House Conference on Food, Nutrition and Health, 1965.
9. The nutrition and health of infants and children, working draft prepared for National Nutritional Policy Conference, Select Committee on Nutrition and Human Needs of the United States Senate, by Samuel J. Forman, M.D., Department of Pediatrics, University of Iowa, *Hearings Before the Select Committee on Nutrition and Human Needs*, June 21, 1974, pp. 2576–2580.
10. An interview with Hans Selye, *Practical Psychology For Physicians*, August 1976, p. 55.
11. Rosenberg and Feldzamen, *The Doctor's Book of Vitamin Therapy*, p. 345.
12. Jelliffe, Derick B., and Jelliffe, E. F. Patrice, University of California, Los Angeles, in *Post-Graduate Medicine*, Nutrition and Human Milk, 16 (1):153–165, 1976.

13. Stone, Irwin, P. C. A., A proposed regime for cataract prevention by correcting certain enzymatic dysfunctions, *J. Int. Acad. Prevent. Med.* 4: 1975.
14. Food additives, health question awaiting an answer, *Medical World News*, September 7, 1973, pp. 73–80.
15. Williams, Roger J., *Biochemical individuality*, University of Texas Press, Austin, 1956; see also Rosenberg and Feldzamen, *The Doctor's Book of Vitamin Therapy*, 1975,
16. Fredericks, Carlton, *Low Blood Sugar and You*, Constellation International Press, New York, 1974.
17. The International Academy of Preventive Medicine, 10405 Town and Country Way, Suite 200, Houston, Texas 77024.
18. Williams, *Biochemical Individuality*, University of Texas Press: Austin, Texas, 1969.
19. Cavalieri, Leibe F., New strains of life—or death, *The New York Times Magazine*, August 22, 1976, p. 68.

Chapter 17
Early Diagnosis and Treatment of Childhood Disorders

Elizabeth Lodge Rees, M.D.
*Pediatrician and Medical Director of MineraLab, Inc.
Castro Valley, California*

The diagnosis of problem children involves a complete history of each child's background as to family diseases, his own prenatal development, birth, and infancy, followed by diet history, physical examination, and laboratory tests. Psychological evaluation and consultation with podiatrists, neurologists, and other specialists may be necessary.

Treatment should be aimed at the causes—be they malnutrition, toxic metal poisoning, allergy, enzyme defects, foci of infection, and/or superimposed physical, psychological, and educational problems. The present fad of merely giving problem children one or another form of amphetamine drug is not in any way treating the cause. Because of the increasing numbers of hyperactive and other types of problem children, society needs to take a very serious look at (1) the present food supply and how it is raised, grown, and later processed; (2) the contamination of air and water; (3) the complete lack of preparation for parenthood. Mrs. Belinda Barnes[1] of Godalming, Surrey, England, is working very hard to get her country to set up prepregnancy clinics where prospective parents could be fully evaluated as to health, nutrition, dietary habits, presence of toxic metals, and emotional state. Then, the necessary corrective measures could be taken before conception. As she told me, "We spend thousands on our stallions, but completely neglect our prospective human fathers." It is not enough to wait until the mother comes to a prenatal clinic and work with her on nutrition. Usually she is several months pregnant. The formation of fetal organs takes place in the first three months of pregnancy, and it is during that time that malformations occur.

In an ideal society there would be no childhood disorders—all children would be born to healthy forebears, both maternal and paternal. All our perfect children would be breast-fed; they and their mothers would have only natural, wholesome food to eat, clean air to breathe, and unpolluted water to drink. But, alas, such is not the case in the present civilization and probably has not been true for many, many centuries. Therefore, we have children with problems—physical, mental, and emotional. Why?

CAUSES OF CHILDHOOD DISORDERS

Changes in Food Supply

During the past four to five generations, our food supply has been tampered with in a most amazing manner; and now for those of us who want to eat pure food, there is even a campaign calling us food faddists—but are we the faddists, or are those who eat what is provided by the food manufacturers the faddists? What has happened? About 1870, the milling of grains was changed from stone-ground milling of the entire kernels to a type of fractionation leading to the most extreme white flour, which has lost part or all of the 22 vitamins and minerals that are present in the whole grain. To this flour are added four to six enrichments, which may even be made from petroleum products.

Then, after World War I, came chemical fertilization of the soil, so that we grew big, beautiful plants; but those plants were not healthy, and, according to the law of nature, insects moved in to destroy them. Again chemists went to work. Thousands of chemical sprays were added to the plants, killing not only the "bad" insects but the useful ones as well. Then the "bad" insects had the temerity actually to use the chemical sprays as part of their food chain, and again multiplied in profusion. But, meanwhile, such chemicals as DDT and others permeated the entire food chain up to man, south to the Antarctic penguins and north to the polar bears in the Arctic Ocean.

The latest insult to our generation is the rapid development and proliferation of the manufactured-food industry. To any farmer the idea of manufacturing food would be a joke—he knows that food is raised or grown. Into this manufactured food supply is added, per person per year in the U.S., 125–175 pounds of sugar, 15 pounds of salt, and 19 pounds of an array of over 3,000 chemicals.[2] A few of the chemicals are for preservation of foods for winter usage, but the overwhelming majority are for color, taste, emulsification, consistency, and other nonessential factors. Some, but not all, of the 3,000 chemicals have been tested singly for their damaging and lethal effects on rats and other experimental animals. No tests have been made giving several chemicals at the same time to animals. We receive many chemicals in just one meal.

Pollution of Water and Air

Water has been variously treated with the industrial wastes chlorine, fluorine, and other chemicals. Unless constant vigilance is maintained, all kinds of human and industrial wastes are deliberately poured into streams or onto the land, ultimately to enter into the drinking water supply. Millions of tons of chemical crop sprays eventually leach from the land into water and often into us directly or via our food supply.

Air is becoming increasingly polluted. About 10 years ago, before the regular use of jets, I flew across the United States; we flew at an average of 15,000 feet. The only visibly clear air was above the tree line of the Rocky and Sierra Nevada mountains. Now it is worse. Not only do millions of tons of lead enter the atmosphere yearly from industrial and automobile exhausts, but there are other wastes from the burning of hydrocarbons. Industry discharges myriad chemicals into the air. Patterson[3] studied lead in deep ice cores in the Antarctic and found that it had been present in a low constant amount from 1000 B.C. until the Industrial Revolution, when it started to rise steadily. Since 1920, the lead content has risen precipitously, corresponding to the use of tetraethyl lead in gasoline. The lead in ice represents fallout from the atmosphere.

Thus we are dealing today with children who are products of from three to five generations of progressive physical degeneration due to malnutrition and, more recently, toxicity, in their grandparents, their parents, and themselves. Animal[4] experiments can reproduce all forms of degeneration by malnutrition alone, and can duplicate all those degenerations which may be considered genetic in man.

After the white man's diet was introduced to their culture, Weston Price[5] documented skull, jaw, tooth, and skeletal deformities in several tribes in different parts of the world.

Physical Causes of Childhood Disorders

Sometimes there has been actual physical damage to a child's body and/or brain. Automobile and other accidents have greatly increased in this mechanical age. Although diseases have been largely conquered, there are still some like meningitis that may leave permanent brain damage.

Emotional Causes of Childhood Disorders

In addition to nutrition, emotions play a large role in determining the health of babies and children. The mother is dependent upon the father, or her mate, during the time of pregnancy. If all is not well, her entire glandular system will be unbalanced as she pours out excessive adrenaline due to fear, hate, or other negative emotion. The breakup of the extended family and the small, nuclear family that has resulted have made the marriage relationship much closer and more important. The mother's parents, aunts, sisters, and grandparents are usually not present to give her emotional and physical support during her pregnancy and child-rearing periods. Sometimes she must work, either for her own physical support or to serve the needs of the marriage. Some women with professional careers have enough money to employ household and other help, but the large majority of young mothers do not. And, as we have said, the supportive extended family usually is absent.

DIAGNOSIS OF CHILDHOOD DISORDERS

When a child with a problem is brought by the parents or sent by the school to a physician, the task is to find out the basic cause, and not merely to give him Ritalin (a drug which is in essence half-strength "speed") or another amphetamine (speed) type of drug. First, what is the problem? Is he irritable, distractible, a learning problem, destructive, quarrelsome, subject to temper tantrums? Does he disrupt the classroom, the playground, and his home? Is he daydreaming or living in another world? If a preschooler, what is he doing to cause his parents to be concerned? Then the history is taken chronologically from conception to the time of the examination.

Was the mother healthy? Was the father healthy? If not, what were their problems, and if possible their diagnosis? What chronic illnesses are there in the rest of the blood relations—grandparents, uncles, aunts, cousins—as far back as is known? During pregnancy was there morning or day-long nausea indicating vitamin B deficiencies?

When the child was born, was it a normal labor; what kind of anaesthetic was used; were there forceps or other mechanical aids? Most important, was the child fed at the breast or fed abnormally— first with glucose (sugar) water and then with a formula made from cow's milk? Colostrum, the first fluid secreted by the breast, is high in protein and immune bodies, activates the digestive enzymes, and is laxative, thus cleaning out the infant's intestinal tract, which at birth is full of cellular debris. Colostrum is the normal first fluid for all newborn mammals and is species-specific, as is the milk.

What illnesses occurred in the first year? If colic, vomiting, or diarrhea, when did each start? What type, where, and when did a skin rash occur? If there were colds, earaches, and bronchitis, were their onsets before or after solid feeding was started? Were the solid foods prepared at home or were canned baby foods used? Sugar, glutamates, and other chemicals have been put into commercial baby foods to augment their taste. Thus these foods appeal to the palate not only of the mother but of ill adults who use them in treatment of peptic ulcers and other digestion disorders. The effect of glutamates has not yet, to my knowledge, been tested on human infants, but they have been suspected of causing brain damage in baby rodents.

Diet history from the first year until the date of examination is most important. How many refined carbohydrates and processed foods are used? Ice cream, soft drinks, white bread, peeled white potatoes, white rice, cookies, cakes, potato chips?* How much milk

---

*The potatoes are first peeled, removing all the vitamins and minerals, and then fried in deep fat that has been reheated many times; reheated fats become carcinogenic.

is used? The small child should not drink over one pint of milk a day after the first year or year and a half, when the rapid growth spurt from birth has ceased and only two to four pounds yearly is gained. If he takes excessive milk, he ceases to eat other foods, does not get a balanced diet, and becomes anemic, since cow's milk contains very little iron.

Physical examination may show everything normal; more often there are signs of early physical degeneration. Ears may be misplaced, odd-shaped, or not equal in appearance. Dark circles appear under the eyes. The chin is narrowed, sometimes to a point, often with crowding of the teeth. Feet may be flat, or there are other types of foot problems that lead to a sway back, protruding abdomen, and slouched shoulders. Sometimes it is hard to describe the child other than as an F.L.K. (funny-looking kid).

Laboratory work in addition to the usual blood and urine testing may need to include an electroencephalogram if there is any suspicion of convulsions of the petit mal type (a type of epilepsy in which there are momentary blackouts but the child does not fall or appear any different unless one notices that he seems to stare off into space). Hair testing for trace and toxic metals is most valuable in determining basic nutriton and the presence of lead,[6] cadmium, mercury, or copper poisoning. Normal values have been established by extensive research.[7] There is no known purpose in the body for lead, cadmium, and mercury. Copper is essential in a limited amount—at an elevated level it is a brain irritant. While all this diagnostic work may seem involved, most of it can be done in the first hour to hour-and-a-half visit to the pediatrician, especially if the blood, urine, and hair testing results are obtained before this visit. Sometimes consultation with a neurologist, podiatrist, ophthalmologist or optometrist, and/or ear-nose-throat specialist is indicated. The podiatrist is most often used in my practice, as so many of these problem children need his services. Psychological testing is usually done by the school before consultation has been obtained—but, if not, testing is indicated.

TYPES OF PROBLEM AND TREATMENT

Each physician who works with problem children has his own way of classifying them into groups,[8] although each child is really a unique individual problem. However, it does help to use a general grouping.

Type one is relatively easy—he is from a normal family; had a normal conception, pregnancy, and birth; did not have respiratory troubles, colic, or later attacks of vomiting or diarrhea. But the diet is and has been very poor—loaded with sugar and white-flour foods, as well as commercially prepared foods and beverages which contain artificial colorings, preservatives, and other additives. Thus he is chemically poisoned and malnourished with respect to needed essential natural foods that have not only calories, protein, carbohydrates, and fat but essential vitamins, minerals, and bulk. Treatment is to put him on a diet of natural foods—meats, fowl, fish, eggs, whole grain breads, rice and cereals, fresh fruits, vegetables, nuts, and honey. His behavior will improve, he will be able to learn at school, and the entire family will benefit from his nutritious diet. Unfortunately, most of the problem children are more complicated than this.

A second type of child, again not very frequently found, is full of lead, cadmium, and/or mercury, as shown by hair testing.[9] Everything else is normal; i.e., history, physical examination, and other laboratory tests. Blood testing is often done for lead on large groups of city children. If the test result is elevated or positive, certainly there is lead poisoning; but blood misses much of the chronic poisoning that shows up on hair examination by atomic spectroscopy. Lead, cadmium, and mercury do not remain in the blood but go to the tissues, especially the nervous system. Lead also goes to the bones, and cadmium to the kidneys.

Hair testing is relatively new, having been perfected by veterinarians as a means to assay proper feeding to prevent physical defects in food animals. If there is so much as one arthritic knee, the entire animal carcass is discarded for human consumption. As much as 10% financial loss was being suffered because of this problem. Then someone remembered what grandfather always knew, that if an animal has a healthy coat of hair, he is healthy, but if the hair or fur is dull, lifeless, or mangy, the animal is not healthy. Much research followed, and the use of hair testing has now become adapted to humans. There are only eight laboratories in the U.S. licensed by HEW for interstate commerce in hair. Hair is easily and painlessly obtained, can be shipped in a simple envelope, keeps indefinitely, and, most important, more nearly reflects the mineral balance of the body than does any other easily obtainable biopsy. The normals established by scientists are for hair taken on the back of the head and neck. Pubic hair and other body hair can be used in the adult, especially if the head hair has been dyed with a lead-containing dye.

If an otherwise healthy child has toxic metal poisoning, he can be treated with large doses of vitamin C, an excellent chelating agent; homemade brown baked beans containing the sulf-hydril (S–H) radical, which is also a chelating agent; and homemade applesauce for its pectin, which removes toxic metals. Some commercial firms make chelating products that contain various vitamins, minerals, and amino acids. For very severe cases hospitalization may be necessary with EDTA (calcium ethylenediamine tetracetic acid) used intravenously. It can also be given orally to milder cases. BAL (British anti-lewiscite) is used for mercury, and penicillamine (cupramine) is used to remove mercury and excess copper. These children profit by improving diet when necessary—and it usually is necessary, as toxic metals are absorbed most readily by a malnourished body.

The third type of child is by far the most prevalent in my experience. He comes from a family background that contains in various members a great deal of allergy, diabetes, hypoglycemia, alcoholism, and obesity and often arthritis, cancer, hypertension, and other forms of arteriosclerosis—needless to say usually one or two illnesses per person. In other words, this picture includes all the chronic degenerative diseases that can be caused by progressive malnutrition due to the way we have handled our soils, foods, water, and air in the past 100 years. The child may have had a relatively normal prenatal existence and birth—but more often than not has been artificially fed. His runny nose may have started at a few days of age, after which he went on to have frequent colds, bronchitis, and sometimes eczema; and, if old enough to report one, he may complain of headache and stomachache. Theron Randolph[10] had documented with thousands of cases the progression of allergy from the respiratory system and skin to the intestinal tract. Then later it becomes brain allergy,[11] which can account for the hyperactivity of the disturbed child. Physically these children show many signs of degeneration—narrowed chins, crowded teeth, dark circles under the eyes, sometimes crossed eyes, flat feet, or other podiatry problems. Diet has been high in milk and refined carbohydrates.

Treatment is multifaceted, as some may have allergy, malnutrition, and toxic metal poisoning with superimposed learning and behavior problems. Family cooperation is most essential, as elimination diets must be used to find the offending food allergens. With the child who has had symptoms at or near birth, cow's milk and/or corn are the most likely allergens, but he may have acquired other food allergies in addition to these. Food allergy is usually multiple and is most likely to involve the foods which are used daily. Testing for foods by scratch tests, which are excellent for pollens and household inhalants, is inaccurate. There are some very complicated methods of testing for foods, but they are costly and time-consuming. Sometimes a simple elimination diet, labeled a "caveman's diet" for its psychological effect, is all that is necessary. The child can tell what may be eaten—animals, birds, fish, fruits, honey, vegetables, and nuts. Since no caveman had a cow or planted grains or sugar cane, this diet eliminates many of the common allergens—milk, grain, and manufactured foods with their added sugar and chemicals. Feingold[12] has documented the group of children who react adversely to chemical additives and colorings. In addition he has identified a special type of child allergic to the salicylates, easily identified by adverse reaction to aspirin. For these he eliminates also the salicylate-containing fruits and vegetables—orange, apple, cucumber, and so on.

There is a more complicated elimination diet by rotation, where only one animal protein, one starch, one vegetable, and one fruit are eaten all day long. Seven such different daily plans are discussed with the family and written out, so that there are seven different menus, one for each day of the week. After four weeks it will be obvious when the child is upset and when he is not. This takes time to explain, but it can be done by parents in all socioeconomic levels if they are really motivated to help the child. Toxic metals are treated as explained for the type 2 child. Malnutrition will respond when the child's allergens have been identified and removed. There are many details to be worked out with this type of child, but the results can be very rewarding.

The fourth problem type includes autistic and schizophrenic children. There are medical arguments about whether these are separate conditions or whether autism is a form of schizophrenic psychosis. Either way, these are very ill children. The autistics have little or no speech from birth, are quite incapacitated by their illness, require very special classrooms, and represent a definite type, which once recognized can be diagnosed almost upon sight. Some are the result of brain allergy; others, the enzyme defect identified by Hoffer and Osmond[13] as nicotinamide adeno-dinucleotide deficiency. Allergy is treated as for the hyperactive allergic child. The enzyme defect is treated by megavitamin therapy. Sometimes schizophrenia starts later, at age eight to ten or at adolescence. These children may or may not have been hallucinating earlier, and may "break" into active illness with the hormonal changes of puberty. Diagnosis also involves contact with the child, who will then tell about visual, auditory, olfactory, gustatory, or sensory hallucinations. Again therapy is directed to the enzyme defects and/or allergy.

The fifth type of child is the truly brain-damaged, in contradistinction to the hyperactive, (but reversible) minimally brain-damaged child. The truly brain-damaged has had trauma before, at, or after birth or infection of the central nervous system. To complicate matters he may have superimposed allergens, heavy metal toxicities, and/or malnutrition. If any or all of the superimposed problems are alleviated, he will do much better. In the past we have been taught that brain damage is permanent. However, newer work shows that actual repair of central nervous system tissues can take place. There is growth of the brain until age 18–20 in the female and 22–25 in the male. All new growth of brain will be normal if the child has been endowed genetically with a normal nervous system—and if he is fed and taught correctly. Some of these children have epilepsy either of grand mal, petit mal, or psychomotor type. Grand mal, major convulsions, is easily diagnosed. The electroencephalogram is confirmatory, especially of petit mal. Psychomotor attacks may present greater problems in that the child does bizarre things, may run away from home, etc., all in a fuguelike state and have no memory of his act. It is sad to see an epileptic child who has been loaded with anticonvulsive drugs while his nutritional status has been completely neglected. He, too, may have superimposed allergies and/or heavy metal toxicities, which also need treatment.

And last there are the truly mentally defective children who are said to represent 3% of our childhood population. They result from many types of disease, genetic defects, and malnutrition. IQs fall below 70. Usually this type of child does not present a criminal problem. Most such children are cared for at home or in institutions and have little chance for delinquency that could lead to an adult life of crime.

RESULTS OF UNCORRECTED PROBLEM CHLDREN

Childhood malnutrition starts in the U.S. and other developed and developing nations with the use of refined sugar. Sugar, a most addictive drug, is being used in larger and larger amounts so that about 125 pounds per person per year is consumed by our population. In order for the body to burn sugar, it has to provide vitamins and minerals; so in effect the sugar leeches vitamins and minerals from the body. One result is that the taste buds become less and less active, and it takes more and more sweets to stimulate them—thus a vicious cycle. Later on excess sugar and other refined carbohydrates such as white flour, white rice, and the inside of white potatoes can cause bouts of hypoglycemia. When an overload of refined carbohydrate is ingested, the blood sugar rises rapidly, and the body combats it with an outpouring of insulin; the blood sugar then drops precipitously, so that a state of hypoglycemia results with shakiness, hunger, irritability, and nervousness. In severe cases fainting occurs.

The six-hour glucose tolerance test will reproduce symptoms, usually at four to five hours, and convince the patient of the diagnosis of hypoglycemia. This test need not be used on the small child when diagnosis of his major allergic or malnutrition problem is obvious. To take the disturbed child to the laboratory for a fasting blood and urine test, have him drink a calculated amount of glucose in water, and repeat the blood and urine tests every half hour or hourly is very traumatic to all involved—child, laboratory, and parents.

In the small child compensation for hypoglycemia by hyperactivity takes place. In the older individual there is usually only restlessness and irritability, with inabilty to think and concentrate. Soon he learns that by taking more sugar he feels better—only to repeat the episode a few hours later. This can lead to drug usage to combat the feelings that result from the hypoglycemia—coke with its load of sugar and caffeine becomes a frequent source of temporary drug and sugar relief. Coke addicts may result. Coffee, tea, chocolate, and tobacco work the way coke does, by temporarily stimulating the adrenal gland to pour out adrenaline, which raises the blood sugar—it again falls and more coffee, etc., are taken. Others may turn to marijuana, LSD, or other hard drugs for their effect. Alcohol is frequently used. The social effects from the "street drugs" can be disastrous. They become more and more expensive as more and more are needed. Such drugs are not pure; they may have toxins, arsenic, and strychnine added to make the user ill and further dependent upon their use. The only way he can support his habit is to steal or sell drugs by entrapping others to their use. Girls can become prostitutes to support their habits. And all this can start from artificial feeding of the person as a baby, followed by the use of refined carbohydrates, which lead to malnutrition and hypoglycemia!

Learning problems are the second result of malnutrition and sugar usage. As the blood sugar falls, it is impossible for the child to concentrate; he does not learn to read, falls behind, and becomes a trouble maker in the class. Thus he then joins others of his kind and is all set for a life of delinquency.

Physical defects of the "funny looking child" can lead to lack of self-esteem. This may result in all sorts of behavior, delinquency, and other forms of acting-out in order for the child to obtain some type of status. Especially in girls, pretty facial features are the mark of popularity. If a girl lacks them, she may seek popularity by sexual promiscuity.

Flat feet and other forms of foot deformities, if uncorrected, often cause pain. This in turn will limit activities, especially competitive sports. Again there is no chance for success or status except by delinquency, as these children cannot excel intellectually.

It may be asked, but why do some children react adversely to a highly refined diet and others do perfectly well? The best answer is given by Roger Williams,[14] in his book *Biochemical Individuality*. He carefully documents the fact that there is a 40-fold difference in need within a species for any vitamin, mineral, or other essential nutrient. Thus if one child needs, e.g., 100 mg of vitamin C daily to prevent signs of avitaminosis C, the child on the other end of the biological curve would need 40 times as much, or 4,000 mg daily. There is no way to know with regard to all nutrients how much each child needs, or where he is on the curve. Probably the children who get into trouble nutritionally and show signs of physical degeneration are those who have the greatest needs. The Food and Drug Administration has listed the average needs for vitamins, minerals, and other nutrients that they recognize as essential. These amounts are minimal, and merely enough to prevent death from scurvy, etc. The optimal amounts for good health are not given—and how could they be if there is a 40-fold range of needs for each nutrient?

Speaking of nutrition, what is it? It can be considered the net result of what goes into the body minus what goes out or is excreted. Food and water go in through the mouth, where they are in intimate contact with the absorptive lining of the digestive tract for about four days until the unused residue is excreted from the rectum.

The liver is the most important chemical organ in the body. One of its purposes is to detoxify toxic chemicals—both those that have been absorbed and those produced by the normal bodily metabolic processes. These unusable chemicals are then excreted into the bile, which in turn is excreted via the gall bladder into the small intestine. It is absolutely essential that there be coarse fibers in the diet, which, though undigestible, absorb the toxins from both the bile and ingested food and carry them out in the stools.

The second great chemical and excretory organ is the kidney. It takes metabolic wastes and other toxins from the bloodstream and passes them out of the body via the urine. Air goes into the lungs, which are meant by nature to absorb oxygen and excrete carbon dioxide. They were never built for tobacco, marijuana, medicine, drugs, or air pollutants. Volatile compounds, e.g., the odors of garlic, onions, and alcohol, are excreted through the lungs along with carbon dioxide. The skin is both an absorptive and an excretory organ. There are recorded cases of death from absorption of chemical poisons through the skin. Sweat is about one-third-strength urine in its chemical composition. The final organs for absorption in a minor way are the mucous membranes of the eye, ear, and genital tract. They also excrete—the lacrimal gland of the eye being particularly active not only in washing the eye clean of any debris, keeping the cornea moist, but in excreting excess sodium chloride (common salt).

Schools and other institutions for children should be especially concerned with the foods they serve. There is a very early start being made to improve school lunches, which all too often contain refined carbohydrates in the form of white bread, pastries, and ice cream. Vending machines actually sell candy and soft drinks in schools. The pressures of the manufactured food industry should be vigorously combatted.

Sweets should not be given as rewards, especially in classes for emotionally or educationally handicapped children. Water and air must be kept as unpolluted as possible. Lighting must be evaluated according to the standards developed by John Ott.[15] Then the school can serve its function of education, character training, and socialization for all children.

References

1. Barnes, Belinda, Personal communication, Godalming, Surrey, England, Oct., 1976.
2. Mrak, Dean, lecture, University of California at Davis, Sacramento, Calif., 1973.
3. Patterson, C. C., Contaminated and natural lead environments of man, *Arch. Environ. Health* 11:344, 1965.
4. Pottinger, Price, Pottinger Foundation, Film: Degeneration of cats, San Diego.
5. Price, Weston. *Nutrition and Physical Degeneration*, Price, Pottinger Foundation, Santa Monica, Calif., 1945.
6. *Lead Toxicity*, Sacramento Medical Prevention Clinic, Inc., Sacramento, Dec. 1974.
7. *Literature Survey of Selected Articles on Hair Analysis*, Vol. I, Vol. II, MineraLab, Hayward, Calif., 1975, 1976.
8. Rees, E. L., Clinical observations on the treatment of schizophrenic and hyperactive children with megavitamins, *J. Orthomolecular Psychiatry* 2 (3):93–103, 1973.
9. Rees, E. L., and Campbell, J., Patterns of trace minerals in the hair and relationships to clinical states, *J. Orthomolecular Psychiatry* 4 (1):53–60, 1975.
10. Dickey, Lawrence D., ed., *Clinical Ecology*, Charles C. Thomas, Springfield, Ill., 1975.
11. Speer, Frederick, *Allergy of the Nervous System*, Charles C. Thomas, Springfield, Ill., 1970.
12. Feingold, B. F. *Introduction to Clinical Allergy*. Charles C. Thomas, Springfield, Ill., 1970; *Why Your Child is Hyperactive*, Random House, New York, 1974.
13. Hoffer, A., and Osmond, H., *How to Live with Your Schizophrenia*, University Books, Secaucus, N.J., 1974.
14. Williams, Roger, *Biochemical Individuality. Basis for the Genetotrophic Concept*, University of Texas Press, Austin, 1969.
15. Ott, John N., *Health and Light*, Devin-Adair, Old Greenwich, Conn., 1973.

Chapter 18
Academic, Perceptual, and Visual Levels of Detained Juveniles

Jeffrey B. Blanchard, O.D.
Frank Mannarino, L.M.H.
Broward County, Florida

BACKGROUND OF THE STUDY

It long has been society's prerogative to remove from itself those individuals with whom it is not comfortable. One unfortunate side effect of this cultural attitude has been the disruption of the lives of those individuals who have been affected. More troubling is the fact that as our culture becomes concentrated, as our population increases and the number of sociological problems multiplies, we have begun to isolate more children. It seems sad that so little has been done to improve these youngsters—to allow them to return to the mainstream of life or to allow them to provide those positive benefits which any human being can for his society.

Broward County, in the throes of one of the worst depressions in a generation, is having more than its share of social woes. Juvenile crime is on the rise, accounting for 80% of all law enforcement contacts.[1] There is little or no success being reported in rehabilitation for these offenders once they are detained. The local juvenile justice system is bogging down, becoming a revolving door whose only exit seems to be a state penitentiary.

One of us, working as counselor at the Pompano (Florida) Juvenile Detention Center, began to try to determine possible causative factors for nonnormative behavior patterns. He felt that if an attempt could be made to determine characteristic flaws in performance by juvenile offenders, rehabilitative programs could be instituted to improve the results of our current facilities.

We were working in a private practice dealing with learning-disabled children. We discussed the apparent absence of eye care for the detainees at the detention center. We then reasoned that there was a good possibility that learning disabilities was a problem with the delinquents, since it seemed that general eye care was lacking.

It has been noted for quite some time that there seems to be a statistical relationship between the presence of a significant learning disability and nonnormative behavior. On the K. D. Proneness checklist reported by Kvaraceus, of the items showing highest incidence, poor school performance or academic attitude occur most frequently. All of the items occurred in more than 50% of the population.[2] We reasoned with Kvaraceus that poor school performance was a precursor to disturbing adolescent behavior patterns. He had reported that low reading skill in junior high school and a poor language intelligence rating indicated that a child is a prime candidate for future nonnormative behavior.[3]

These concepts are supported by Glueck, who reported an incidence of extreme restlessness in early childhood for nearly 60% for future delinquents, whereas nondelinquents show an incidence of less than 30%.[4] Restlessness in early childhood is a significant symptom of perceptual development problems. In a National Education Association Study,[5] it was found that frustration and conflict arising from a level of aspiration higher than realistic academic potential creates serious conflicts and frustrations, which often lead to delinquent behavior patterns.

We felt that any delinquency treatment program that failed to include adequate perceptual and visual rehabilitation to increase academic potential, was handicapped in its ability to deal effectively with rehabilitation. "There are effective uses of various types of punishment that may be invoked with the delinquent. However, to overlook causative factors and to capitulate to the punishment routine will neither prevent nor control further expressions of norm violating behavior."[6]

The absence of any testing or therapy for learning-disabled juvenile delinquents had been noted locally by the author, and it was determined that a local validating study would be undertaken.

METHOD

We felt that the use of standardized testing procedures would yield the most valid and quantitatively workable results. To this end, we determined to use the following testing procedures:

Sub-Tests 4, 5, 6, 13, & 16 of the Detroit Learning Aptitude Test

The Detroit Test of Learning Aptitude is a test of learning capacity. This test has the same cultural error as the Slosson Test.

Sub-test 4. *Verbal Opposites:* This test was designed to determine a child's ability to conceptualize, limited by current vocabulary skills.

Sub-test 5. *Motor Speed:* This is a test of eye-hand coordination and spatial position recognition.

Sub-test 6. *Auditory Attention Span for Unrelated Words:* This tests the ability to remember and reproduce words heard in a noncoherent order.

Sub-test 13. *Auditory Attention Span for Related Symbols:* This test repeats the same material as sub-test 6, except in a coherent form.

Sub-test 16. *Visual Attention Span for Letters:* This tests the child's ability to recognize and recall groups of words shown to him.

Level 2 Arithmetic and Word Recognition Sub-Tests of the Wide Range Achievement Test

The three sub-tests of the Wide Range Achievement Test used in the investigation are all standardized problem-solving tasks. They have been standardized against current prevailing academic curricula for primary and elementary grades.

Slosson Test of Intelligence

The Slosson Test of Intelligence is designed to be a test of general intelligence level for ages two months to 20 years. Although it has been standardized against a large population, arguments have been put forth concerning its usefulness in testing minority and/or disadvantaged populations. There were no non–English-speaking or bilingual children involved in the sample; so possible error from language difficulties was not a factor.

Visual Testing

In order to determine which was the best method of approaching the problem of diagnosing or testing these children visually and perceptually in their current facility, we performed three distinct visual testing procedures:

1. A standard refractive examination, including a check for pathology and normal refractive results for distance and near testing.

2. A Keystone Telebinocular, as a screening and/or ancillary testing device.
3. A full battery of perceptual tests—tests of gross motor, eye motor, laterality, and visualization skills.

We felt that with these three sets of results not only could we provide information necessary to make the diagnosis, but we could also make recommendations as to whether or not simple screening would be sufficient to ensure proper diagnosis.

We adopted the most lenient range of treatment criteria currently approved by the eye-care profession. The criteria are:

1. Myopia in excess of .50 diopters.
2. Hyperopia in excess of 1.50 diopters.
3. Astigmatism in excess of .75 diopters.
4. Anisometropia in excess of 1.50 diopters.
5. Visual acuity of worse than 20/40 in one or both eyes.
6. Binocular posture in excess of 2 exo or 1 eso at distance and 8 exo or 3 eso at near.
7. A manifest near refractive result of +.75 add. or greater.

The tests were conducted on ten new arrivals at the Pompano Juvenile Detention Center during the period December 25–31, 1975.

RESULTS

Slosson Test

The chronological age range was from 13 to 17½ years. The mental age range was from 7 years 4 months to 17 years 1 month. IQ range was from 56 to 103. The mean mental age was 13 years 11 months. The IQ averages were as follows: mean 95, median 93, mode 95. In essence this is a low normal IQ range.

Wide Range Achievement Tests and Detroit Test of Learning Aptitude

The results were significant in that they indicated strong deficits in both academic aptitude and current academic skills, which were behind mental age.

Raw Data

In terms of current academic skills the showing is rather poor. The mean scores for the Wide Range Achievement Test are middle third grade for Spelling, late third grade for Word Recognition, and late fourth grade for Arithmetic.

The test results for the Detroit Aptitude Tests are as follows: Verbal Opposites—mean score late seventh grade; Motor Speed—mean score eighth grade; Auditory Attention Span for Unrelated Symbols—mean score fourth grade. If we move to the Auditory Attention Span for Related Symbols, the performances rise by almost 3½ grade levels to early seventh grade. For Visual Attention Span, mean score was mid-sixth grade. The only significance we can draw from this is that there is some variation between Motor Speed and other academic aptitudes.

Comparative Data

The results were then calculated based upon lags, the difference between the performance on the specific tests and either the average academic aptitude or the mental age. The lags were calculated on an individual basis and then averaged. The lag was not calculated as average minus average—it was calculated for each child, his mental age minus his specific skill performance; then the results were averaged. If we test the specific skill performance against the child's mental age for the Detroit Tests of Learning Aptitude, we find the following: Verbal Opposites tends to lag 22 months behind mental age. Motor Speed tends to lead mental age by 6 months. Auditory Attention Span for Unrelated Symbols falls 43 months behind the mental age or average. Auditory Attention Span for Related Symbols only falls 18 months behind the mental age. The Visual Span also falls 18 months behind.

By using the same method to discuss current academic skills, the results are: Reading levels average 45 months behind their current mental age. Spelling results average 48 months behind their current mental age. Arithmetic averages 37 months behind mental ages. The results indicate that for Reading and Spelling these children are 4 grades behind. Now if we add to this lag the difference between their mental age and their chronological age, then in terms of their relationships to their peers, they lag anywhere from 4½ to 6½ grades behind.

If, however, we calculate the lag behind their general learning aptitude, we see that their Reading, Spelling, and Arithmetic skills are not quite as bad, but still lag behind. In the case of Reading, we find that the performance lag is reduced somewhat, running, instead of in the neighborhood of 4 years, somewhere in the neighborhood of 2½ years behind.

We took these results and made normalcy determinations. Normalcy determinations can be made in one of two ways. Normal can be defined as an individual whose academic aptitude and current academic skills are up to his mental age. Or one can define normalcy as a child whose performance in school is up to or exceeding that which would be predicted by aptitude to learn. Regardless of the normalcy determination taken, the percentage of children showing abnormally poor performance is extremely high (Tables 18-1 and 18-2). Using the definition of normalcy as a lag in performance on any specific test behind the child's mental age, we find the following performance results:

77.8% of the children tested showed a significant lag in Verbal Opposites; 44.4% show a lag in Motor Speed; 77.8% show a lag in the Auditory Span for Unrelated Symbols; 77.8% show a lag in Visual Attention Span; 100% show a lag in Reading; 100% show a lag in Spelling; 100% show a lag in Arithmetic; 88.9% show an academic aptitude below their mental age; 100% show an academic performance below their mental age.

Table 18-1 Lag of Specific Skills Behind Mental Age

Test	Normal No.	Normal %	Reduced* No.	Reduced* %	Total No.	Total %
Detroit Test						
Verbal Opposites	2	22	7	77.8	9	100
Motor Speed	5	55.6	4	44.4	9	100
Auditory Attention Span (Unrelated Syllables)	2	22.2	7	77.8	9	100
Auditory Attention Span (Related Syllables)	2	22.2	7	77.8	9	100
Visual Attention Span	1	11.1	8	88.9	9	100
W.R.A.T.						
Reading	0	0	9	100	9	100
Spelling	0	0	9	100	9	100
Arithmetic	0	0	9	100	9	100
General Aptitude Average**	1	11.1	8	88.9	9	100
Academic Perf. Average***	0	0	9	100	9	100

*No. or % of children showing a disability in this skill if disability is defined as a lag behind mental age.
**Average (for each child) of all learning aptitudes.
***Average (for each child) of all academic skills.

Table 18-2 Lag of Academic Skill Behind Prediction
by Learning Aptitude

Skill	Normal No.	%	Reduced No.	%	Total No.	%
Reading	1	11.1	8	88.9	9	100
Spelling	0	0	9	100	9	100
Arithmetic	0	0	9	100	9	100

In order to determine whether or not a specific academic aptitude is reduced in the population, we must determine whether or not more than 50% of the children show a performance in that skill lower than their own average performance of all the academic aptitude skills. This only occurs for Verbal Opposites and Auditory Attention Span for Unrelated Symbols (Table 18-3). The remaining three skills: Motor Speed, Auditory Attention Span for Related Symbols, and Visual Span show performance by each individual child in less than 50% of the cases to be below their average academic aptitude. The specific results are: Verbal Opposites—55.6% reduced below average academic aptitude; Motor Speed—11.1% below average academic aptitude; Auditory Attention Span for Unrelated Symbols—77.8% below average academic aptitude; Auditory Attention Span for Related Symbols—33.3% below average academic aptitude; Visual Span—44.4% below normal average academic aptitude.

By average academic aptitude we mean the average of all areas tested for the child being tested. Those averages themselves, as

Table 18-3 Lag of Academic Skill Behind Prediction by Mental Age

Test	Normal No.	%	Reduced* No.	%	Total No.	%
Verbal Opposites	4	44.4	5	55.6	9	100
Motor Speed	8	88.9	1	11.1	9	100
Auditory Attention Span (Unrelated Syllables)	2	22.2	7	77.8	9	100
Auditory Attention Span (Related Syllables)	6	66.7	3	33.3	9	100
Visual Attention Span	5	55.6	4	44.4	9	100

*No. or % of children whose performance on this subject is below that of the average for their performance on all five tests.

we have indicated, fall significantly below norms for the general population.

Visual and Perceptual Testing

Of the individuals who failed the visual screening test (Table 18-4), 81.8% have prescribable difficulties, while 18.2% do not. Of those who passed the screening test, 50% do not have prescribable problems and 50% do. The percentage of underreferral was 13.33% (this is the number of individuals who should have been referred by the testing but were not). The number of overreferrals were also 13.33% (this is the number of children who should not have been referred). The total referral error was 26.66%. The number of children referred was 73%. The screening test, while being useful, is only about 75% effective. Of the population who are referred, 20% will have been referred for no reason; and, more significantly, of the population who pass, 50% should have been referred.

Table 18-4 Visual and Perceptual Results

Visual Failures by Percent

Refractive Examination	Number of Eyes	% of Population
Myopia	5	16.7
Hyperopia	0	0
Astigmatism	10	33.3
Anisometropia	0	0
Binocular Posture	0	13.3
Near Manifest Add	10	33.3
Visual Acuity	6	20
All Cases	20	66.7

Telebinocular

Far Vision	8	53.3
Far Binocular	3	20.0
Near Vision	1	6.7
Near Binocular Picture	2	13.3

Visual Perception	Number of Eyes	% of Population
Gross Motor Performance	2	22.2
Fine Motor Performance	2	22.2
Lateral & Body Awareness	4	44.4
All Cases	5	55.6

The results of the perceptual testing were significant in that visual failures do not run as high as auditory failures run on the Detroit Test of Learning Aptitude. The total number who failed one or more sections of the battery was 55.6% (Table 18-4). Of those who failed, 80% required standard visual help as indicated by the telebinocular and the standard optometric examination. Two showed significant astigmatism. Two showed significant myopia. One showed significant binocular problems. The specific sections failed were as follows: those who showed significant lags on gross motor performance were 2.2%. Those who showed significant failures in fine motor or eye coordination 22.2%, and those who showed poor visualization or lateral awareness were 44.4%. Lateral awareness is the most significant perceptual skill necessary for good performance in reading.

DISCUSSION

It is apparent from the data that this population has significant problems in visual and academic performance. That is not a new statement. We have endeavored, however, in a very preliminary fashion, to give some specificity to that statement. It is obvious that the children's auditory and visual attentions spans are limited. They are strongest in motor skills in learning. Their word recognition and spelling skills fall below their ability to deal with numerical problems. It is safe to say that a vast percentage of these children will not be able to do well in school simply by increasing the amount of education which they have. It is also safe to say that to place a vast majority of these children back in a normal school environment is totally unacceptable academically.

The incidence of visual problems (66.6%) is a number nearly two and one-half times greater than the commonly accepted percentage of children who should be receiving eye care at this age. One cannot allow a group in which two-thirds of the population require optometric care to receive none. If a child is not functioning adequately visually; if he cannot see the blackboard; if he cannot read comfortably for long periods of time, if he has difficulty in seeing print, or he is troubled by headaches and blurring vision when doing schoolwork, then it is highly unlikely that that child will perform adequately in an academic environment.

Therefore, the remediation of these problems through the use of spectacles or optometric therapy would be necessary for the child to deal effectively with an academic environment. It is, however, highly unlikely that the application of a pair of spectacles or visual therapy would be capable of solving all the child's problems. It should, however, be reiterated that failure to take these steps will severely limit the child's capacity to improve academically. We have also shown that using the most liberal testing criteria, the visual perception performance of these children is severely reduced.

It is unlikely that such a child currently learning and currently capable of learning in the fourth to sixth grade level would succeed academically (without a tremendous level of frustration) in a classroom with individuals his own age (grades eight through eleven). The inability of the student to understand the information passed to him by his teacher verbally, coupled with his inability to deal with current academic problems, owing to a lack of simple information-gathering skills, such as reading, would make performance impossible, his frustration level high, and, therefore, the likelihood of truancy extremely high.

RECOMMENDATIONS

We recommend that these children be tested when they enter the detention facility and that the information obtained be included in the report to the hearing judge so that they can be given intensive help in learning aptitude skills and academic skills in order to make them ready to rejoin a normal classroom.

It further is recommended that the schools determine whether or not perceptual problems exist in their children at entrance. For either economic or social reasons large percentages of children are never tested and their problems go undiagnosed.

Of the population which we tested in the facility, all would fall within the State of Florida's definition of learning-disabled children! We would not submit that the presence of a learning disability is the cause of abnormal behavior, but the incredibly high incidence of learning disability among juvenile delinquents definitely indicates that some relationship exists. We believe that one of the most severe stresses which can be placed on a developing young personality is a consistent pattern of school failure. In some cases, the continued presence of this stress can cause a severe reaction, oftentimes reflected in antisocial or delinquent behavior. Therefore, a learning-disabled child, faced with this incredible pressure may react to it through antisocial behavior. This would help to explain the extremely high incidence of learning disabilities among delinquents.

References

1. Interview with Captain Yurchuk, Former head Juvenile Division, Broward County Sheriff's Department, April 1976.
2. Kvaraceus, William C., *Dynamics of Delinquency*, Chas. Merill, Inc., Columbus, Ohio, 1966.
3. Ibid.
4. Gleuck, Sheldon and Eleanor, *Physique and Delinquency*, Harper Brothers Publishers, New York, 1970.
5. Kvaraceus, William C., et al. *Delinquent Behavior (Culture and The Individual)*, National Education Association of the United States, Washington, D.C., 1974.
6. Ibid.

Chapter 19 | Intervention with Juvenile Delinquents

Gary H. Bachara, Ph.D.
William R. Lamb, M.D.
Eastern Virginia Medical-Psychiatric Associates, Ltd.
Chesapeake, Virginia

INTRODUCTION

Many attempts have been made to work with the juvenile delinquent, utilizing such approaches as social case work, psychotherapy, group therapy, academic vocational training, social-type approaches, probation, and parole, without much success. In fact, in spite of these approaches, recidivism still soars. In dealing with juvenile delinquency, many courts have embraced the medical model, which includes diagnosing a cause before treatment. This has led to much difficulty in the past, because juvenile delinquency is a syndrome or entity which is at least multifaceted and does not appear to have just one or two causes.[1]

In dealing with this multifaceted, multifactorial type phenomenon, courts have varied in their approach to deter, correct, or rehabilitate the offender. These attempts range from very meager interviews, without much background information, to quite comprehensive investigations with specific treatment plans drawn up in attempts to deal with the rehabilitation of the juvenile offender. It is no wonder that any new program, new therapy, is immediately exploited and utilized before sufficient research and back-up empirical data have been offered to demonstrate its benefits in dealing with this vast social problem.

In the Southeastern part of the country, the approaches to juvenile delinquency seem to be similar. There is a consensus throughout the larger juvenile courts as to procedure in drawing up treatment plans.

Initially, the juvenile offender may be brought to an intake-type system or a facsimile thereof. Here, petitions are taken, and the juvenile, depending on the seriousness of the offense, is either placed in a detention home, to be detained while awaiting the next appearance or disposition, or allowed to go home, with the court appearance soon following. The initial court appearance is used to determine the seriousness of the offense and the possible steps to be taken thereafter. At this point the probation officers, court officials, and judges determine whether a social history investigation is necessary, or, in many cases, whether psychological or psychiatric evaluations would be beneficial. The determination of whether these next steps are taken is based on rather subjective decisions, either stemming from the nature of the offense (a felony, possible rape, sex-related activities) or from whether the juvenile is a repeater (a recidivistic juvenile who has made many appearances in the court in the past, with previous efforts being ineffective in helping the juvenile stay out of the court system).

Many times the probation intake officer's evaluation indicates that there is possibly some dysfunction in the family, or that something is peculiar either about circumstances of the petition or the juvenile, which may warrant a full social history investigation with another court appearance scheduled. The time can vary, but usually three weeks is allowed for a social history investigation. An investigating officer is assigned, and, depending on the nature of the case, the child may be placed in the detention home awaiting the next court appearance. Again the detaining decision is somewhat subjective, and again it is related to the offense. For example, if a child is a runaway, fugitive, or dangerous, the court may fear for society, the family, or the child, and detain the child during the investigating period.

The social history investigation, from court to court, entails obtaining the same general information. It usually involves detailed history of the family members, birth facts, jobs, place of residence, financial status, attitudes, a detailed history of the child's educational experience, past grades, teachers' comments, behavior in school, possible past psychiatric history, psychological testing, and any past evaluations, and it usually ends with some type of summary of the investigating officer's opinion regarding the juvenile offender and/or his family. In many cases, where the social history investigation is requested by a judge, an addendum is attached with specific recommendation as to disposition for the individuals, which may include anything from commitment to the State Department of Corrections, to probation with appropriate rules. There are also the situations between these two points, where juveniles are placed in foster or group homes in the same geographic area.

If, at any time during the social history investigation or in the brief period of time before the social history investigation is ordered, the judge feels it necessary for the child to be evaluated by a medical professional, psychiatrist/psychologist, such evaluation may be ordered, with the data or results to be presented to him at the next court hearing. Therefore, it is during this three-week period that the various psychological testing or psychiatric evaluations are carried out. Again, the method that determines which child receives a psychological or psychiatric evaluation is many times very haphazard, very subjective, and it differs from court to court, from probation officer to probation officer, and from judge to judge.

When the court orders a psychiatric evaluation, five major bits of information are being sought. There are statements regarding: (1) the competency of the individual to defend himself at a trial or hearing; (2) the ability of the individual to know right from wrong; (3) a mental status examination to determine possible organicity (brain damage), mental retardation, or psychosis; (4) some indication of diagnosis; and (5) a possible treatment plan with specific recommendations. If there is to be psychological testing, the resulting information varies, and the reasons for the psychological evaluations vary. Many times the court is looking for intelligence, functioning levels, possible learning problems, academic progress, and some indication of personality functioning, in order to determine abilities and inabilities with specific recommendations.

In both the psychological and psychiatric evaluations, many times secondary referrals are involved—that is, recommendations for developmental visual examinations, neurological evaluations, auditory examinations. But, usually, because of the short period of time allotted for the investigation and court appearance, many of these referrals are not conducted. This is an unfortunate situation, but occurs when the child is moved to many different locations or is being placed on probation with the referral information given to the parents or a new probation officer. Because of financial reasons, loss of information through movement, and so on, the referrals are never accomplished. These referrals may include visits to an optometrist or ophthalmologist for various visual problems detected in the testing, a psychiatrist for psychiatric evaluation, or a neurologist for a complete EEG or neurological evaluation for possible difficulties noted in the initial evaluation; or there may be various referrals made to rule out particular physical, psychological, or medical problems which may or may not be factors in the juvenile's behavior.

The judge—armed with the social history background, knowledge of previous events, possible behavior reports, etc., from the detention home, information from the parents, possible psychiatric evaluations and psychological testing—is ready to determine the appropriate treatment and disposition of the juvenile. In many states, treatment centers are limited in number, which in turn limits the courts in their type of recommendations. A 1976 GOA investigation of juvenile delinquency and learning problems in five states determined from its extensive survey of leaders of juvenile correction facilities, judges, and educators that 90% felt that particular programs and treatment plans cannot be carried out because of lack of facilities, personnel, and—the biggest factor—time of involvement with the particular juvenile.

Many factors affect treatment choice. Often the type of recommendation or action to be taken is a matter of finances. Sometimes the parents have particular insurance policies, third-party payers, or resources that they can use to place a child in possible residential care or in a needed therapeutic situation. But, because of extremely large case loads and lack of training, many probationees cannot get the counseling or help needed through the court system and need to seek attention through private agencies or community mental health centers in their area. It may be found that the child needs special education or a type of special school situation. At this point, many social service bureaus are brought into play, especially if a foster home or funding for a particular foster child is needed. A good liaison between the social service bureau and the courts is always helpful in dealing with the juvenile offender. There is much overlap between the probation officer and the social worker, with the juvenile offender being the common ground. Many times, in the case of special education, the school system is involved, either by documenting past academic history or relating various educational and academic needs, which are very much a part of the treatment plan of the offender. The child may need special attention in school or a certain type of class, as in the case of learning disability, emotional disturbance, or mental retardation. The involvement of the school system can be very much a part of the treatment plan of the youth.

In these circumstances, the most common sentence is probation with inhouse treatment, assigning the particular offender to a probation officer who sets up various rules regarding curfews, school attendance, and so forth. If the court is fortunate enough to have ample staff and time, the probationee may be required to report visibly for possible counseling or group sessions, which may also involve the family, at one of the court centers or an outreach facility. If these facilities are available to the courts, the approach may have its benefits, but all too often many of the probation officers are overloaded with high numbers of cases for investigation, and insufficient time is allowed for each offender on probation. Therefore, many of the particular recommendations for counseling and other treatments are merely placed in a folder, not to be seen again until the child is brought back to the courts, possibly for a much more serious offense.

A more comprehensive approach seems to be under way within many of the courts. They are realizing that these multifaceted problems cannot be solved by any one cure-all approach. It is because of this need for changes in the court system, and various changes in other disciplines, that many cities and court systems are looking to more physical, more objective, psychiatric approaches than the more ineffectual social or probationary methods used in the past.

PRIOR RESEARCH

The history and basic research that have been giving impetus to the biochemical and orthomolecular approach to pathological and abnormal behavior are being dealt with in other chapters of this book. Thus, only a brief review of studies utilizing biochemicals and other physical treatment approaches in dealing with juvenile offenders and criminals is presented here. In the Morris County Jail, D'Asaro et al.[2] found that a significant number of inmates have abnormal levels of blood polyamines, and average blood levels of spermidine were significantly lower than normal blood levels. Inmates having the lowest levels of spermidine committed significantly more violent crimes than inmates having normal levels of spermidine. This low spermidine level is one of several indications of relative hypoglycemia noted in these Morris County inmates. Inmates had a broad range in blood level, and antihistamine ranges found in schizophrenics. In a follow-up study a year later,[3] inmates were placed on a week-long vitamin program and the researchers found significant improvement in impaired perception, as measured by various experimental inventories, and also noted improvement in morale, mood, and self-motivated behavior, as measured by self reports and staff observations. The program they utilized included diet education, inmate balanced blood sugar levels, vitamin supplements, and high protein snacks.

Chalke has stated that at least 30% of all criminals are suffering from mental illness, and that criminal behavior and cerebral dysfunctions are linked in at least some manifestation, usually a lack of impulse control. Bolton,[4] in his study of Quolla, found a very high proportion, over 50%, of hypoglycemic adults, and found excessive aggression in this culture. Hypoglycemia may be a factor in some cases of criminal behavior in so-called civilized societies. Bolton believes that Quolla are forced into aggressive type behavior by physical condition. He is also convinced that through aggressive thought and activity, Quolla unconsciously try to raise the blood sugar level to a comfortable point. Psychologically, aggressive persons force themselves into a state of anger so that their internal organs can temporarily restore a proper bodily balance. Ross[5] stated that 58% of his aggressive psychotic patients had a low blood sugar condition, and Meyers[6] found that 70% of his schizophrenic patients and 95% of his alcoholic patients had hypoglycemia.

Many studies in past and current research draw correlations between aggressive, criminal behavior, as well as acting-out unsocialized activity, and various physical biochemical abnormalities. Also, there is rapidly accumulating evidence that a child's ability to learn, as well as cognition and perception, is heavily influenced by nutrition and biochemistry and can be improved by the use of large doses of certain vitamins and mineral supplements, and by improvement of general nutritional status through the removal of junk foods from the daily diet. Cott,[7] who has done much research on learning disabilities, feels that learning, cognition, and perception can be improved through nutritional measures.

The mention of learning leads us to a very large area of research, which has investigated correlations of various factors with delinquent behavior, and points to the effect of learning problems on academic ineffectuality and delinquent activity. Such studies as those of Mauser,[8] Dzik,[9] Mulligan,[10] Holte,[11] Hogenson,[12] Tarnopal,[13] Berman,[14] and Love and Bachara[15] have shown that anywhere from 50 to 75% of the juvenile delinquents or offenders have some type of learning or reading difficulty. These learning problems are another facet of the juvenile delinquent and another subsystem in this total syndrome.

Although cause cannot be inferred from these correlations, some studies have gone a step further in an attempt to indicate that there is a high percentage of juvenile delinquency involved with learning disabilities, demonstrating that appropriate remediation can lower recidivism. In a recent study,[16] juvenile delinquents were divided into the following groups—Group A: delinquents with learning disabilities receiving academic remediation and appropriate academic therapy for their learning problem; Group B: juvenile delinquents with learning problems not receiving any type of remediation or academic therapy or special education for their learning problem. These groups were compared after two years, and it was found that Group A had a recidivism rate of 6%, with Group B exhibiting a 42% recidivism rate. This study seems to indicate that there is a particular type of juvenile delinquent who has primary learning disability, and that recidivism can be cut down significantly through appropriate educational and academic intervention. This area of research is very much related to the orthomolecular approach, since researchers[17,18] have shown relationships among learning problems, perceptual difficulties and cerebral allergies, hypoglycemia, and nutrition problems.

A COMPREHENSIVE APPROACH TO DELINQUENCY INTERVENTION

The juvenile offender presents a formidable challenge, both in diagnosis and in treatment. Now in many courts the trend is to look at the situation in a broad, overall manner, to get a gestalt perspective of the problem. We must be prepared to expose the offender to various professionals for varied opinions and evaluations. In contrast to the previously used methods of dealing with juvenile delinquents, the more comprehensive approach entails everything from the initial psychiatric and psychological evaluation to possible hospitalization for a brief period of time. Much depends, again, upon rather subjective decisions on the part of probation officers, social workers, and judges.

This seems to be the first point of concern—the judgment of individual probation officers, who carry much power with regard to the future of the probationees and offenders they are assigned. Their particular recommendations as to cause and/or treatment are usually quite influential with the judges. The professionals in the community who act as consultants to the court should play a role in the ongoing training of these probation officers. This training may take the form of court seminars, workshops, or instruction periods, in which they introduce the probation officers to various symptoms, various behavioral aspects, things to look for which may indicate serious pathology or sufficient evidence for secondary referrals, such as medical check-ups, psychiatric evaluations, psychological testing, or educational evaluations. Because the probation officer acts as an initial screening source, this type of training is vital to the multidisciplinary approach to juvenile delinquency. This knowledge is necessary because diagnosis, intervention, and treatment go hand-in-hand, and separating one from the other is very difficult.

Once the court systems are alerted to the various symptoms and factors that may indicate physical and biochemical causes of various psychiatric and behavioral difficulties, the next step is liaison between the court and the outside professionals. If the juvenile is brought to the attention of the court and is exhibiting bizarre behavior, and during the course of the social history investigation it is determined that there are possibly poor eating habits, various mood swings, and so forth, and there is reason to believe that there may be some physical problems involved, a referral to appropriate medical/psychiatric facilities is warranted. When viewing offenders, probation officers should look not only at the family system of the juvenile delinquents but also at the school system as well as integral systems inside the body—the visual, the auditory, the metabolic, and the central nervous system. When they start looking into these areas, they need to consult members of the medical, psychiatric, psychological, educational, and allied professions to help with possible explanations and recommendations. As the courts' questions receive answers that tend to explain the nature of the delinquent behavior, more specific treatment is utilized and recidivism decreases. In a community where there is a network of professionals, in either public or private practice, who in collaboration with youth and other youth service agencies share knowledge, there is a form of cross-referral system. Thus, the juvenile delinquent can start anywhere in the system and end up comprehensively evaluated, be he found by the court, school, or social service bureau.

Many cases require placing an offender in a hospital as the mode of treatment and diagnosis. Usually decisions to hospitalize are obtained from considerations involving one or more of the following areas: (1)

the nature of the crime or offense; (2) background information (personality, social factors); (3) physical components. The first category would ferret out status offenses from truly sociopathic, psychopathic type offenses. Here, involved professionals would note the nature of the offense in light of possible explanations. Unjustified aggressive reactions may indicate possible etiological factors outside of social realms. Also, detailed background information concerning the personality of the offender may reveal certain patterns of behavior, which may be tied to certain biochemical situations. Possible cognitive problems or perceptual difficulties not evident in the past, or severe mood changes, may signify recent changes in the makeup of the individual; also physical factors noted in the individual's past history may reflect some physical malfunction. Many of these characteristics are noted in the psychological and psychiatric evaluations, and might have been otherwise overlooked.

Once hospitalization is decided upon, the range is between two and three weeks, which is the time needed to complete the evaluations, gain sufficient data from psychiatric nurse observations, and prepare a relatively comprehensive report for the court.

There is no set format for ordering particular evaluations; many times they are based on clinical inference. For example, a girl may come into the hospital through the courts, and the psychiatrist may order skull X-rays. he does not, normally, order skull X-rays on every child who comes in; but as someone who is used to looking at children, he sees a couple of black eyes, and determines that this child—who has not been heretofore recognized as psychotic or acting deranged, and suddenly behaves so—requires skull X-rays, brain scan, and EEGs to see if there is any evidence of central nervous system gross pathology. One needs to look at psychological testing and psychiatric evaluation for evidence of minimal brain dysfunction or nonbasic central nervous system pathology. In comprehensive medical screening, any one of the routine tests might be ordered; e.g., blood screening, urine screening, and, generally with children, a good evaluation of physical symptoms, which may give evidence of some systemic dysfunction, involving GI system, central nervous system, cardiovascular system, skin problems, hair problems, acne, and so on. Actually, all of these possibilities are evaluated by a physician's follow-up tests, when there is any indication of dysfunction, with problems pursued until everything is absolutely ruled out.

Generally, because teen-agers rarely come to the attention of the physician, it is important that when they are hospitalized they be given a thorough diagnosis, and at least the five-hour glucose tolerance test, SMA 20 blood chemistries, a routine urine analysis, CBC, and a physical examination. If there is clinical suspicion of visual problems, there can then be either ophthalmologic or optometric evaluation, depending on the probable nature of the difficulty. Obviously, if someone has wall eyes or strabismus, he must be sent to an ophthalmologist first, because of the need for possible surgical correction. The same is true of auditory problems; if the nurse notices either that the child has a speech defect or that the individual's language, considering environmental and cultural educational factors, is not appropriate, one may suspect that there is a hearing-speech deficit and check this out with an audiogram. If the speech indicates a stuffy head, respiratory allergies may be the problem. We may take sinus X-rays and an ENT, do throat cultures, and check the passages, adenoids, and tonsils to make sure that they are not oversized. Also, an allergy can be suspected when there is unusual acne or any kind of skin problem.

It is increasingly important to run a five-hour glucose tolerance test. This is accomplished in a hospital evaluation, but it can also be done on an outpatient status with juvenile offenders. One can turn up a number of gross and borderline diabetics, or possible relative hypoglycemics, in what appears to be rather typical acting out-behavior, seen as depression, which clinically is very difficult to detect in adolescents. Hypoglycemia is a symptom, an indicator, or warning system that some other pathology is being carried on within the body. Wilson states that hypoglycemia in its interaction with hormones is directly related to the central nervous system and brain functioning.[19] He feels that hypoglycemia is one of many diseases affecting behavior and emotional involvement that are not socially effective, but many times tied in with stress and the human body's methods of adapting to stress. A very high percentage of delinquents have been found to exhibit hypoglycemia.

These blood sugar–related problems directly influence behaviors, possibly because of their effect on perception. Perception, which takes place in the cognitive level within the central nervous system, is the interpretation of stimuli received through the senses. Therefore, misperceptions or disperceptions may cause inappropriate feedback and response behavior. Also, minimal impairments of the perceptual faculties might be at work, as in the case of the child who is having difficulty in school because of problems in misperception in the visual and auditory channels, causing him difficulty in reading and writing and learning. Those individuals who suffer from stress illnesses, learning problems, behavior difficulties (delinquency), and even the extreme of schizophrenias, are basically hypometabolic, nutrient-deficient, allergic individuals, and by being so, they are unable to adapt to their environment without becoming ill. Many times it is the body's reaction, as in the case of the response of the adrenal glands to low blood sugar levels, which causes various symptoms and behavior changes that are concomitant with the body's attempting to maintain an equilibrium.

Depressive delinquents often are immature developmentally and tend to act out because they cannot internalize their anger. They find ways that they can act it out by aggression, violent behavior, kicking, fighting, bed wetting, and so forth. Also, it seems that many of the adolescents who are placed in a detention home for psychosocial behavior pathology are simply depressed. In a 24-hour-a-day hospital setting, many of the offenders who normally would act out and have been acting crazy and bizarre, begin to act quite normal with controlled diets and organized settings. One doesn't see the hyperactivity and the aggressive behavior observed in the schools and in the streets. Many of these observations suggest the real biochemical nature of the adolescent's acting-out behavior and depression. Also, in the hospital setting many of the juvenile delinquents may be reacting to the depression or anger, and their delinquent behavior is a reflection of a nonnurturent situation, such as their family or peer group.

When the delinquents are placed in a hospital setting, even a generalized psychiatric ward, a number of things are achieved. They are on relatively neutral ground emotionally. Granted, there may be psychotic patients whom they will come in contact with, and there may be sociopaths and all kinds of other people; but as far as their own emotional involvement goes, they are uncommitted. They are not related to these people and have no emotional investments; they have come to what we call neutral ground. They have no need to act out against their environment, which in the past has been negative. They may be negative initially as a matter of habit, or in anticipation of getting the same response that they have received in other environments. But because of the training of the psychiatric nursing staff, they don't get the negative feedback. What they do get is warm—but firm—control, support, someone to talk to, someone who cares about them, a lot of nutrient love, maternal care. While they are accepted, their anger and behavior are not. Also during this time, the nursing aides and staff pick up a lot of loose ends. In fact, the individual, in terms of personality dynamics, reacts with others in the hospital, with other patients, other staff, whose personalities and values are known. Obviously, then, when the offenders become part of this system, an evaluator notices whom they avoid and whom they are attracted to, and obtains a more comprehensive picture of how they should act in a free neutral environment.

During this period of hospitalization, it is beneficial to involve the family and take a look at the family systems. Involving various disciplines at this time is useful, possibly by having one professional deal with the family and another with the probation officer. This action will provide different inputs at the time of recommendation. This interdisciplinary approach allows a multitude of inputs in the comprehensive diagnosis of the individual. At the end of the hospitalization period, these facts can be fed back to the court system, so that the judge has definite medical, psychiatric, and psychosocial information, and recommendations. For example, a delinquent may have been found to have diabetes, or a sugar condition. The medical doctors have talked to the parents and suggested that he should be on a particular kind of diet; the parents should be in educational therapy, or maybe the offender should be sent to a certain type of school; he may have a particular type of learning problem, and so on. These are things that probably would not have been recommended, had it not been for use of an extensive diagnostic procedure.

In the case of delinquent behavior that seems to overlap with more serious psychiatric pathology, such as schizophrenia or sociopathic or psychopathic tendency, the intervention of megavitamins and minerals is indicated, perhaps in conjunction with various diets and regimens.

STUDY REPORT

What follows is a report of a court system and medical/psychiatric facility that utilized a comprehensive approach to juvenile delinquency.* In this study, 112 juvenile delinquents were followed

---

*The authors would like to thank Nancy Giles, Virginia Wesleyan College, for her help in collecting and collating the study data.

through a comprehensive evaluation and testing program while involved in the court system. The delinquents' ages ranged from 9 years to 17 years 5 months. They were evaluated, and spent an average of 22 days, in a hospital setting. The average stay ranged from 16 to 47 days. During this period, the juvenile offenders (69 male and 43 female) were evaluated for the Tidewater Area Juvenile Courts. Of the 112 delinquents evaluated for a two-year period, only 16% (18) were found to have no physical problems whatsoever; 84% of the juveniles had some type of medical or physical difficulty, which would not have been discovered had they been placed in a detention home and merely disposed of through the normal systems of the court.

Table 19-1 identifies the various pathologies and abnormalities that were detected. Seventy had various visual perception problems, with seven showing various physical eye problems, such as crossed eyes, or other medically related difficulties. A large number of individuals had various blood sugar related problems. This category would include either hypo- or hyperglycemia, detected through the glucose tolerance test. Previous research has indicated a direct relationship between various mood and behavior abnormalities and mood swings and various problems with blood sugar.

Fifteen abnormal EEGs were detected, which would indicate possible epileptic seizures, and so forth. These individuals were placed on a program of chemotherapy. A smaller number of individuals were found to have allergies, and 17 showed various vitamin and mineral deficiencies. These persons were placed on a program of megavitamins and dietic intervention as a method of dealing with behavior difficulties and possible other more serious abnormal pathologies. The last column deals with 46 other symptoms, such as kidney problems, bronchitis, ulcers, undetected fractures, and so on.

Table 19-1 Types of Diagnostic Problems Uncovered
(Incidence: 94 cases)

Abnorma. EEG	Sugar Related Prob.	Eye Problems	Allergies	Vitamin & Mineral Def.	Psoriasis	Other
15	28	70	9	17	4	46

Case Histories

In taking a closer look at this type of comprehensive approach, we are going to depict two case histories in which this comprehensive, multidisciplinary team approach was applied to a juvenile delinquent coming through the courts.

Case History Number 1

Bert was referred by an area juvenile court on charges of malicious wounding and aggression with the intent to maim. Bert was a 16-year-old white male, living with his 54-year-old mother. He had been adopted at age three months. His adopted father had died four years earlier, during open heart surgery. He had one stepsister, age 23, married and out of the home. Bert was attending a private boys school and in the tenth grade, although he had been put back one year earlier because his grades were quite poor. He had had numerous suspensions in public school, which led to the private school placement.

Bert's mother described him as being a very active child, having a very bad temper, and being hard to get along with.

Early childhood developmental history was very sketchy, owing to Bert's adoption, but his mother did reveal that Bert had been very ill and almost dehydrated at age nine months. His speech was quite delayed. He had hearing-related problems. Bert walked at a very early age, but did not crawl, nor did he follow the normal progression of locomotion. Teachers had described him as extremely active, almost at an uncontrollable, hyperactivity level.

During the initial psychiatric and psychological interview, Bert was found to be very immature, with many of his verbalizations quite illogical, with much covert hostility. Bert was behaving bizarrely, and seemed to be on a self-destruction path, fantasizing and distorting reality. He seemed quite suspicious, and entertained depression and emotional irritability. A diagnosis of preschizophrenia was offered initially. Bert's full scale IQ score was 94. Although in the tenth grade, he was reading at a fifth grade level; his math was at a seventh grade level. Recommendations included hospitalization for further observation, with prognosis necessarily guarded. The recommendation was accepted by the court on a suspended commitment.

On admission to the hospital, Bert showed evidence of la belle indifference, with inability to organize and process information appropriately. There was some inappropriate affect, looseness of association, and some paranoid dillusional material in evidence.

Laboratory studies revealed normal EEGs and urinary analysis, Bert was found to be hypoglycemic via a five-hour glucose tolerance test. Initially, Bert was placed on antipsychotic tranquilizers, but low doses failed to modify his behavior. At this point, Bert was managed with dietary modification and vitamin supplementation, with a gradual improvement in his mental status. It was felt that Bert, because of his learning problems, would not be able to function well in a regular school situation; he required organization and limits. Therefore, a referral to a residential school setting was made, where he could maintain a dietary and chemotherapy program. Bert's stay at the hospital was four weeks. His stay at the residential school was nine months. Bert did extremely well in school, receiving a GED and preparing for vocational training; and he secured a job near the school. In subsequent stays at home, on weekends, Bert demonstrated a remarkable improvement in behavior, thinking process, and his approach to his family. Bert spent more time around the house, something he had never done before. Seemingly, he was not interested in the wildness and acting-out approach he had been involved with previously. He was maintaining his diet, for both the diabetic condition and the vitamin program.

It should be noted that while Bert was in the hospital, his mother was involved in a counseling situation, initially attending a group education and therapy program for parents of schizophrenics. She eventually attended once every three weeks, to deal with her new role and various other factors concerned with Bert's eventual discharge.

When Bert first came to the psychiatric facility's attention, he was bordering on being sent to an adult jail facility. He had a history of three years of various charges of assault and malicious attacks, on adults as well as other youths. He had been using his car as a means of carrying out his fantasies, and had been more or less leading the life of a gypsy, running back and forth from the beach to the city, with no regard for injury to person, place, or thing, as well as himself. He had been very run down physically. His diet had been very poor, he had been eating various junk foods and abusing himself with drugs and alcohol. Bert evidenced no controls over his behavior, and was, as stated before, very self-destructive.

The dietary program, vitamin supplementation, and hospitalization seemed to bring about change very quickly; and during the two-year period following Bert's initial contact with the courts, he had no incidences of violent flare-ups or acting-out behavior. Bert was maintained on an aftercare probationary status, with outpatient treatment.

Case History Number 2

Emma was a 16-year-old, white female brought to the attention of the juvenile courts in connection with her family and school-related problems. Emma's failing grades, extreme hostility towards those in authority, teachers and parents, and difficulty in dealing with her peers, had been impeding her growth for some time. Emma's family conflict reached a pinnacle, in her parents' eyes, when she started spending most of her time with black males. Petitions were filed by her parents, and owing to the severity of the situation and background history, a referral was made to a medical-psychiatric facility. In the process, Emma and her parents were interviewed, and it was determined that Emma's pattern of rebellion, hostility, and acting-out delinquent behavior had been going on for the past three or four years, and getting increasingly more difficult for her parents to handle.

During the initial intake interview, it was felt that an extended period of hospitalization would have merit. This determination was based upon developmental and mental history taken from the parents and clinical findings in the psychiatric evaluation of Emma. Upon her admission to the hospital, a diagnosis of preschizophrenic process was offered. During the period of hospitalization, there was extensive testing; psychological evaluations revealed perceptual difficulties, extreme hostility, extreme difficulty with her sexual identity, and learning disabilities, which appeared to be visual perceptual in nature.

As is the case with many delinquents acting out with violence, the first few days in the hospital setting were filled with rebellion against the staff, including accusations, flare-ups, and abuse. But, as was noted in the history taken from the parents, Emma had been maintaining herself on a junk food diet, and her nutrition was very poor. After five days in the hospital setting, with a well-balanced diet, definite behavior changes were noted. Emma became more open, amiable, even to the point of being receptive toward staff therapists. At this point, she seemed to indicate some insight into her particular problem; she became constructively verbal, and a more favorable prognosis was taking shape as her cold, hard-core exterior faded away. Also during the hospitalization, a minor hypoglycemic condition was noted, which seemed to be an indicator of her specific dietary problems.

After 17 days in the hospital, Emma was released, with recommendations offered to the courts that: (1) Emma be placed on firm probation with limits, and knowledge of these limits; (2) Emma and her family be involved in family counseling, as well as individual counseling for Emma; (3) the probation officer keep close contact with Emma, monitoring her involvement in school, and the medical aspects of her condition, which included dietary and nutritional considerations, curfews, and so forth.

Particular psychoeducation and psychological evaluations were carried out during the hospitalization, and specific treatment plans were drawn up to deal with Emma's educational difficulties. She was placed in a special remedial class, geared toward mathematics and remedial reading. This seemed to take the pressure of the regular classes off her, but still allowed her to progress at a level whereby she would be allowed to graduate with her regular class.

This case history indicates the facets of the multidisciplinary team approach to juvenile delinquency. In order for Emma's particular situation to be made successful and profitable, psychiatric, medical, psychological, educational, and juvenile court systems had to work hand in hand. This was true both in the diagnostic stage and in remediation. In the treatment plan, the approach called for psychiatric intervention, in the form of family counseling, individual counseling, and therapy for Emma. This approach called for a monitoring of her hypoglycemic condition, nutritional dietary measures, involvement of school systems in dealing with her in a special-education program, and awareness of the systems in that function. Also, monitoring the entire system was the juvenile court and its probation officers, who, many times, made sure all the other systems were working and keeping things in motion.

SUMMARY

The wave of new views in psychiatry, utilizing megavitamins and looking at the physical and biochemical causes of behavior changes, brings with it a new look at the psychiatric evaluation commonly used in the court systems in this country. Possibly, the traditional psychiatric evaluation will be used more as a general screening mechanism in dealing with juveniles whose cases present a particular and specific difficulty to the court systems.

No one is making a claim that biochemical-physical-medical intervention is the answer or panacea for all juvenile delinquency. What is being stated is that there is a percentage of juvenile delinquents or persons who have emotional or behavior problems who are functioning in a problem manner, not because of any deep-seated personality pathology, but are functioning with inappropriate affects and misperceptions, which are in turn reflected in inappropriate behavior. Juvenile delinquency cannot really be differentiated from any other subbehavioral disorder category. It must be considered just as any other psychiatric, psychological, and social problem is. There is no such diagnosis as juvenile delinquency in any psychiatric diagnosis manual. If any offender were diagnosed and interpreted as one who is delinquent in activity, it would be a great injustice to the offender, because in no way would this diagnosis dictate treatment or cause. It is only through operationally defining the diagnosis that specific and appropriate treatment and remediation can follow. This involves use of the many support systems described in this chapter. Many juveniles whose problems extend beyond the mere medical or biochemical also require support of services in the form of individual counseling, group counseling, family services, educational remediation, and possibly social work. Therefore, if there is to be a team effort, the various team members must listen and learn to appreciate the other team members' statements, comments, and recommendations. Viewing the offender with all these systems in mind gives the comprehensive, total picture needed for appropriate rehabilitation and treatment.

References

1. Glueck, S., and Glueck, E., *Typology of Juvenile Offenders, Implications for Therapy and Prevention*, Grune and Stratton, New York, 1970.

2. D'Asaro, B., Groesbeck, C., and Nigro, C., Diet vitamin program for jail inmates, *J. Orthomolecular Psychiatry*, 4 (3):212–222, 1975.
3. Groesbeck, C., D'Asaro, B., and Nigro, C., Polyamine levels in jail inmates, *J. Orthomolecular Psychiatry* 4 (2):149–152, 1975.
4. Bolton, R., Paper presented to the Annual Meeting of the American Anthropological Association, December 1972.
5. Ross, H., Hypoglycemia, *J. Orthomolecular Psychiatry* 3 (4):240–245, 1974.
6. Meyers, L., Relative hypoglycemia in schizophrenia, *J. Schizophrenia* 1:204–208, 1967.
7. Cott, A., Treatment of learning disabilities, *J. Orthomolecular Psychiatry* 3 (4):343–355, 1974.
8. Mauser, A., Disabilities in delinquent youths, *Academic Therapy* 9 (6):389–402.
9. Dzik, D., Visions in the juvenile delinquent, *J.A.O.A.* 39 (5):461–468, 1966.
10. Mulligan, W., Dyslexia, the specific learning disability and delinquency, *Juvenile Justice*, pp. 20–25, November 1972.
11. Holte, A., Learning disability in juvenile delinquency, *A Judge's Journal* 12:40, 1973.
12. Hogenson, E., The relationship between reading failures in juvenile delinquency, Provided for the Attorney General's Office, State of Virginia, 1970.
13. Tarnopol, L., Delinquency in minimal brain dysfunction, *J. Learning Disabilities* 3 (4):200–207, 1970.
14. Berman, A., Learning disabilities in juvenile delinquents, Paper given at the Seventh Annual Conference of The Massachusetts Association for Children with Learning Disabilities, Boston, Mass., March 1973.
15. Love, W. C., and Bachara, G. H., The diagnostic team approach for juvenile delinquents with learning disability, *Juvenile Justice* 1:27–31, 1976.
16. Bachara, G. H., and Zaba, J. N., "Learning disabilities in juvenile delinquency: Beyond the correlation, *J. Learning Disabilities*, in press.
17. Wunderlich, R., *Kids, Brains and Learning*, Johnny Reads, Inc., St. Petersburg, Fla., 1970.
18. Philpott, W., Physiology of violence: The role of cerebral hypersensitive reaction and aggression, Paper given at Crying Malnutrition Approach, Bowling Green, Ohio, April 1976.
19. General Accounting Office presentation for the International Conference for the Association for Children with Learning Disabilities, Seattle, Wash., March 1976.

Chapter 20

A Model for Community Programs Dealing with Antisocial Persons

Leonard J. Hippchen, Ph.D.
Administration of Justice & Public Safety
Virginia Commonwealth University
Richmond, Virginia

INTRODUCTION

There is a great need in the community to develop a program that will deal with antisocial persons in an understanding and effective manner. Community agencies now tend to handle these persons in a way that further complicates their problems. The school teacher, for example, sends the disruptive child or teen-ager to the principal. The principal will reprimand the person for the first one or two referrals, but then might use stiffer measures, such as corporal punishment or school dismissal, on subsequent referrals.

The methods used by other community agencies also typically are no more effective. Agencies that handle emotionally disturbed, mentally deficient, or physically handicapped youngsters, or those specializing in alcoholism or drugs, generally are not staffed to cope with the acting-out type of individual. They have been established to deal with a specific type of disorder, and they tend to have great difficulty accomplishing this task if antisocial behavior is a part of the problem. Thus, antisocial persons with any of these added special problems tend to be referred to agencies dealing with delinquents or criminals; but these agencies, reflecting the punitive attitudes of the community, tend not to approach the problem with treatment in mind. Most are punishment-oriented.

Juvenile and adult courts historically have made extensive use of training schools, reformatories, and prisons in dealing with antisocial persons. The judge, after several efforts at warning the youngster and his family, and even with attempts at use of probation, finally decides that a period of confinement in a state institution will best serve the needs of the community and "straighten out" the individual. But the court usually has provided little treatment for him. The youngster typically is met with threats in courts, and with surveillance while on probation. Little treatment is made available to the person, or to his family members, who may be an important source of his problem. Referrals to mental health or related agencies generally are not satisfactory, since the antisocial person usually does not respond well to the characteristic approaches and programs used by these agencies.

The basic problem is that the community has had a punitive attitude toward antisocial persons, and there has been little sustained attempt to understand and help them. One of the primary purposes of this volume is to correct this long-standing lack of basic understanding so that social justice can be better served.

Our understanding of "antisocial" behavior may be improved first simply by recognizing that this term is merely a social label. As a label it does not help us to understand in any way the internal and external forces that may be shaping the behavior.

People who react to other persons and social situations in a hyperactive manner, and at inappropriate times, usually are the subject of reprimand and rejection. While a person who is neutral or withdrawn in his pattern of response receives social approval or sympathy, the person who is overactive, or violent, in expressing emotions tends to be viewed negatively. Also, we tend to assume that the person has planned or premeditated his behavior, rather than recognize that the behavior may be primarily an emotional reaction difficult to control.

For example, the overactive child in the family may be labeled by his parents as a "bad" child. He may be severely reprimanded or punished for this behavior, especially if it is repeated. It is as if the child "doesn't want to" learn the appropriate response, rather than that he can't. In the school, he may be called "inattentive" or "disruptive," or a "trouble-maker." Later, these children may become "runaways," "truants," "school failures," and "school dropouts."

It is just a short step from these forms of behavior and labels to delinquent or criminal behavior. By this time, the antisocial behavior may well have some of the elements of "premeditation" as a form of revenge for earlier mishandling of the person. But it is likely even here that such thoughts are more at the unconscious level, because of the serious social strictures against such conscious thinking. The tendency of parents and school personnel to react negatively and without understanding undoubtedly has a great bearing on the continuance and severity of the later behavior of antisocial youngsters. We know that antisocial persons are not born that way, although many may have physiological or psychological tendencies to act out their behavior.

Certainly, the frustration that must be borne and coped with by children of nonunderstanding adults is very great! It probably is this frustration which leads to the formation of juvenile gangs, alcohol and drug usage, and other forms of deviant behavior by these persons. Contact with the police, courts, and detention centers, and training schools merely tends to accentuate the problem of these earlier years. Everywhere the antisocial person is met with a lack of understanding and a punitive reaction, which further establish for the person a potential rationale for the continuance of these behavioral patterns.

The ideal approach to this community problem would be prevention. The greatest efforts probably should be placed on educating parents, children, and teachers on prevention techniques. But, practically speaking, this would be our long-term goal. The community more likely at present would be supportive of intervention strategies, because there is serious concern over the increasing amounts of violence and related problems with teen-agers. Although the problem began many years earlier for these youngsters, it is only just now practical to deal with it—at its explosive point! Humans historically have not been prevention-oriented. We wait until the fire is raging before moving to put it out! Also, we have tended to resist new knowledge, especially where adults must admit that they have erred because of their ignorance.

Thus, the emphasis in this recommended community model approach to antisocial persons will be on intervention strategies. Only secondary concern will be with prevention.

BASIC ASSUMPTIONS OF THE MODEL

Following are seven basic assumptions and their rationale, which are considered imperative in development of an effective community program for antisocial persons.

1. *Antisocial behavior is understandable and treatable.*

For many centuries no attempt was made to try to understand the cause of antisocial behavior, especially that of criminals. Criminals were considered to have premeditated their acts, they were held fully responsible, and they were severely punished by the state.

During the past 100 years, however, special attention has been given to the criminal from two important sources: humanitarians and social and behavioral scientists. Humanitarians has been concerned with the cruel punishments and depraved living conditions of the criminals; they have made concerted efforts to reduce the severity of punishment and to improve the harsh conditions of prison life. The social and behavioral scientists during this period have conducted numerous studies into the causes of antisocial behavior; they have focused on a wide variety of deviant acts, but particularly on delinquent and criminal behavior. These scientists have identified a host of psychological and sociological factors related to these forms of behavior. This knowledge has been important in helping us to understand that many forces contribute to antisocial behavior in addition to the "free will" operation of the person.

Most of the scientists have concentrated on phychological and social variables in their studies of crime causation. Since 1950, however, a group of physical scientists have been studying biochemical and physiological components of antisocial and related forms of behavior. It is important to add this area of knowledge to the earlier knowledge so that we have a fuller picture of the totality of internal and external factors that can influence development of antisocial behavior. The authors of this book make an important contribution to filling this need for a greater understanding of the problem.

Because of the prevailing punitive attitudes toward delinquents and criminals, relatively few serious attempts have been made to diagnose and treat these problem types. However, even where used, our attempts to treat antisocial forms of behavior have been only partially successful. Our assumption here is that when biochemical and physiological factors are added to the present psychosocial approaches, our treatment effectiveness will be greatly improved!

2. *The punitive model of the criminal justice system should be replaced by a treatment model.*

The punishment model for antisocial persons probably was more logical at an earlier time when our knowledge of many of the specifics of offender behavior were lacking. With primitive knowledge, all that we could consider doing was punitive in nature. We did not see how social conditions influenced individual development of this behavior, and we placed all the blame on the offender. We assumed that his "free will" operated in commission of the crime, and that, therefore, he was the guilty culprit.

Today, however, we know that behavior—of child, youth, and adult—is highly conditioned by social factors. We also know now that biochemical factors and ecology can be important causative elements. Thus, the punishment approach today is quite illogical and inappropriate. Control of antisocial persons certainly is still appropriate, however; control is also needed for persons with contagious diseases. But control and incarceration for treatment are more appropriate today as a model than is control for purposes of punishment. The treatment model not only is more just in the handling of antisocial persons, but it best serves the needs of society for protection. Since most offenders, regardless of their crime, are released from prison after only a short period of time, the treatment approach offers a much better opportunity for returning the offender improved to society than does the punitive approach.

3. *Community programs for dealing with antisocial people should be developed in each county and major city throughout the United States.*

Because of the availability of new knowledge with which to treat effectively antisocial persons, we now should make a concerted effort to deal with the problem at the community rather than the state level. With local programs the offender does not have to experience the shock of removal to a state institution and return to the community. Also, many of the community resources already available for academic education, vocational training, and employment can be utilized with a local program. Further, the offender may not need to break ties for any great length of time with his family and friends, and he would be more accessible for these important contacts in a local facility.

Community programs also have the advantage of being able to work closely with local agencies, such as the schools, police, and courts, and thus to emphasize early intervention and treatment. Community programs also are needed to provide preventive educational thrusts aimed at parents of infants and young children, and for teenagers.

The development of community programs throughout the country eventually would eliminate the need for all but a few of our large adult, youth, and delinquent institutions in each state. With greater treatment effectiveness at the local level, we also could expect that our institutional populations and costs would decrease considerably, and our crime rates would be down. The length of time needed for incarceration also would decrease, further reducing costs of operation.

4. *These community programs eventually should replace the municipal and county jails and detention centers.*

As the treatment approach begins to gain ascendancy over the punitive approach in dealing with antisocial persons, less use of the present control facilities will be needed. The treatment approach also encourages greater use of bail, which would decrease the need for large holding facilities for those awaiting trial.

But the new community treatment facility should be designed so that it can handle various degrees of control, from minimum to maximum. These control facilities, however, should be more homelike and less like the punitive jail structures of today. The new community facility thus will be able to control and provide treatment services for all of those offenders now serving time in jail, as well as many of those who now are referred to state or Federal correctional institutions. Jails and detention facilities as now constituted eventually could be eliminated.

5. *All diagnostic and treatment approaches should be pragmatic and based upon the latest scientific knowledge concerning antisocial behavior.*

The essence of this assumption is that we need to discard all of our past punitive traditions and methods. We also need to examine closely the effectiveness of current treatment approaches, discarding those which do not meet the test of pragmatic utility and humane value.

Use of the latest scientific knowledge means that we need to approach diagnosis and treatment from a broad, holistic viewpoint, including biochemical, physiological, psychological, and sociological factors. Each person not only should be considered with great dignity, but with the aim of uncovering his special problems and aiding him in understanding and in correcting his antisocial patterns of behavior. Also methods should be explored with each person to aid him in further developing all of his innate potentialities and capacities.

6. *The treatment program should be supplemented by a strong program of prevention.*

The greatest possibility for crime reduction in the community relates to prevention efforts. Logically, if antisocial behavioral problems can be detected early and treated in the infant or child, there is increased likelihood that delinquency and crime can be prevented. Thus, the community program should make every effort at educating parents, teachers, and children to help them understand what they might do to prevent or reduce the effects of antisocial tendencies.

Since educational approaches tend to represent a slow process, such a program should be viewed mainly with respect to its possibilities for long-term effectiveness. Thus, it would be secondary to the main intervention-treatment program.

7. *The program should be subjected to constant research evaluation and development to assess and improve its efficiency and effectiveness.*

Few programs for antisocial persons today—even treatment programs—are adequately evaluated for efficiency and effectiveness. All operational structures, processes, and procedures periodically should be reviewed and tested for efficiency, in terms of both cost and program aspects.

Also, individuals in the program and following release should be assessed on a continuing basis to determine their response to the treatment plan and its effectiveness.

BASIC OPERATIONAL CONCEPTS FOR THE MODEL PROGRAM

This section will present and discuss 14 basic principles for operation of a model community program for antisocial persons. It is assumed that most of these persons will be delinquents or criminals, referred by the police or the courts. Some might be considered predelinquent or precriminal, referred by the police or school system, or by some other community agency. All of the principles to be enumerated have been operationally tested for effectiveness in various programs throughout the country. Most of these programs have been small-scale, demonstration-type projects. What is being suggested here, however, is the inclusion of the total group of principles in a single program, which would be unique. Also, the total impact should be much greater, and the percentage of successful correction of antisocial behavioral problems should be much higher. This is the special advantage of the proposed model.

1. *The operational program and facility should be designed to be consistent with therapeutic community concepts.*

The development of a therapeutic community facility and program for offenders involves vast changes in organization from the jails and detention centers of the present day.

In the area of facility development, an attempt should be made to organize all physical arrangements so that they are consistent with treatment goals, although some degree of security should be maintained. The institution should be basically "open," without walls, bars, or cages. If segregation or control of certain offenders is needed, they should be temporarily placed in rooms behind locked, guarded doors. The facility and its furnishings and arrangements should look more like a hospital or a group home, rather than a prison.

All staff should be selected, trained, and used for treatment rather than for punitive or merely control purposes. The assumption is that all offenders who enter the program are interested in improving their ability to function effectively on a social basis. The staff, then, must be professionally prepared to guide them in this task. Offenders who for some reason are not able or do not desire to function in this type of program would need to be referred to an appropriate state institution. Experience in dealing with offenders in this type of setting, however, suggests that the number needing to be referred would be relatively small—less than 5% of the total in the program and/or community.

The treatment program should include all of those elements needed to assist in the therapeutic goals of the institution. Extensive orientation and diagnostic processes should be developed. There should be full provision of medical, psychiatric, psychological, social therapy, academic education, vocational training, and recreation programs. Many of these services, however, could be provided with consultant staff or by other community agencies, if appropriate. Each offender should be thoroughly studied for deficiencies in each of these areas of possible problems, and specialized programs for treatment should be employed to assist him in overcoming these deficiencies.

The primary emphasis in a therapeutic community is to provide programs, processes, and procedures that will stimulate and aid the offender in developing his untapped potential human resources. An important part of the therapeutic effects of community life are the growth-stimulating interrelationships established between staff and offender and between offender and offender.

2. *Each member of the professional staff should be selected and trained to function in a treatment role and as a member of a treatment team.*

The therapeutic community staff organization does not utilize a hierarchy of staff members. All are of equal rank and value, but they perform their various specialized functions in a differential manner. Also, any merely custodial role they may play is quite secondary, since primarily all staff are treaters. This organization of staff has been shown to be more effective in operation, and morale typically stays at a high level.

It is important to screen all staff applicants, both for professional competencies and for their treatment attitudes. They should have primary dedication to treatment of offender groups and be able to function effectively as cooperative team members. Since most staff will have been exposed only to hierarchical types of organization, it will be necessary to train them in team operations, procedures, and therapeutic community functioning.

3. *Operational processes and procedures should be devised that incorporate team treatment concepts.*

Treatment teams should be devised from among the staff members, including appropriate consultants. Each team should be assigned to a specific group of 15 to 25 offenders. The teams should have at least three members, each representative of one of the following areas of human behavior: physical, psychological, and social.

Teams should be responsible for performing a thorough diagnosis and for developing and following through on an appropriate treatment plan for each offender in their group. They investigate and handle on a therapeutic basis any disciplinary problems that may arise. They ensure that all of the living and treatment needs of each offender are supplied adequately. They make changes in the treatment plan when necessary, and they maintain a close contact with each offender for this purpose.

They make a final decision and recommendation to the program director concerning changes in custody levels, disposition of disciplinary problems, and release from the program. Because of their deep involvement with each offender, they are in the best position to make recommendations related to the offender's treatment plan, his progress, and final disposition.

4. *All diagnostic and treatment approaches used should be considered within a holistic frame of reference and should include four*

dimensions of interrelated human behavior: biochemical, physiological, psychological, and social.

It is hypothesized that total functioning man cannot be sufficiently understood or corrected except through use of a holistic approach. Man appears to consist of a whole of four interrelated dimensions: the biochemical, physiological, psychological, and social. Anything that occurs in any of these dimensions which affects the harmonious functioning of the parts can affect other parts, as well as the whole man. Thus, an offender can best be understood and corrected by a thorough diagnosis of each of the interrelated parts.

Further, it is hypothesized that man is evolutionary and growth-oriented. Diagnosis then not only should include a search for genetic aspects of behavior, but should include early developmental history and future potentials for full functioning and development of the person as well. From this view criminal behavior may be seen as a deficiency in one or more of the functional parts, or as a blocking or distortion of normal developmental potentialities.

5. *An important aspect of the initial screening procedure should be the determination of the degree of custody needed for the person.*

The first phase of classification or screening should consider whether or not the offender represents a serious threat to society or himself. This can be determined through use of appropriate psychological tests combined with an analysis of past behavior in the community.

Table 20-1 defines three grades of custody based upon three degrees of violence and/or suicide proneness. It is estimated from experience that about 10% of the cases classified will fall into the severe category and that 40% will fall into the medium class. In order to protect society, the offenders in these two categories should not be considered initially for any form of release, but should be maintained in the community facility under the appropriate degree of security. In most instances this merely will mean that the offender is restricted to the immediate environs of the facility. In a few cases it will be necessary temporarily to provide more secure custody in a locked room.

Offenders classified in the minimum range of social/personal threat (about 50%) should be considered for probationary or other forms of release status while treatment progresses. This assumes that a satisfactory housing and family condition is available for each offender.

Table 20-1 Correctional Classification (Custody) and Treatment Prognosis Model

Custody basis	Custody classification	Treatment prognosis	Treatment classification
Severely violent or suicidal prone 10% cases	Maximum custody: secure wing of facility	Poor: 10% cases	1. Noncooperative 2. Severe-chronic problems 3. Inadequate personality types	Long-term: Treatment program: 2+ years
Medium range of violent–suicidal proneness 40% cases	Medium security: partially open wing of facility	Fair: 40% cases	1. Cooperative 2. Severe-chronic problems 3. Immature personality types	Medium-term: Treatment program: 1 year
Minimum social or individual threat 50% cases	Minimum security: no special type of security needed	Good: 50% cases	1. Cooperative 2. Transient behavior problems 3. Good environment conditions 4. Limited offense record	Short-term: Treatment program: 3 months

Provision should be made for the easy transition from one level of custody to another. Most offenders will be moving from maximum or medium to minimum degrees of custody as they progress in treatment. More security may be needed at times for some, if lapses in acceptable levels of social behavior occur. It also must be considered possible to refer an offender to more secure custody in a state institution, but this alternative in practice should only be needed on rare occasions.

This first phase of classification also should include consideration of the probable need for incarceration as an aid to treatment. This is primarily a matter of attitude—whether the offender has a willing and cooperative attitude toward helping himself and being helped. Treatment should not be forced on any offender. However, experience has shown that most offenders will respond to offers of help when they feel that staff members genuinely are interested in them and their welfare, and that they are capable treaters. With prolonged resistance to treatment, however, the offender should be referred to a state institution.

Offenders who might be released because they do not present a serious social/personal threat, nevertheless might be retained in custody as a means of motivating them to participate in the treatment program. This may be necessary with immature personality types. By interacting daily with team members and other offenders under treatment, they soon should develop sufficient self-discipline and self-concern to allow treatment to continue successfully while they live in the free community.

6. *A second aspect of the initial screening process should be development of a treatment prognosis and classification.*

Determination of a treatment prognosis involves a decision concerning the likelihood of treatment success. A cooperative attitude appears to be the most important factor in behavioral change. But other factors also are important, i.e., genetic defects, uncorrectable physical problems, length of time the problem has existed, repetition-like cycles of behavior, and social conditions under which the person will live while under treatment if released. Psychological and social testing can be used as an aid to this probability estimate.

The treatment classification should indicate to the staff and offender an estimate of the probable length of time needed for effective treatment. The offender should be helped to understand that length of time needed for behavior change is primarily a matter of attitude. A person who feigns cooperation while continuing to manipulate will need a longer period of time in which to change. An uncooperative attitude also delays change.

Extreme cases of immaturity and chronic antisocial behavior also can require greater lengths of time for improvements to occur. However, in the area of behavior change, even with the most uncooperative, incorrigible offender, improvements at times can be quick, dramatic, and permanent. The staff constantly should be alert to these possibilities for change.

7. *The third aspect of initial screening should involve a thorough four-dimensional diagnosis of each offender.*

Table 20-2 hypothesizes four dimensions of man with suggested approaches for each dimension: mineral-chemical, growth-developmental, intellectual-psychological, and social.

The research and practice outcomes presented in this book indicate how important can be the biochemical aspects of behavior for antisocial persons. This is knowledge heretofore unavailable to correctional personnel. It is imperative that diagnosis first consider any biochemical deficiencies or dependencies which may exist in the offender. Diagnosis also should consider the possible role that ecological agents may be playing in the internal physiology of the individual, especially those relating to brain allergies.

Diagnostic procedures would involve, for example, a glucose tolerance test, a complete blood count, a protein bound iodine test, hair analysis, and urine analysis. Specific laboratory procedures would be used as indicated, following use of appropriate paper-and-pencil screening instruments and a personal interview. The laboratory procedures need to be closely supervised by medical practitioners of the orthomolecular, or related, specialties.

The second diagnostic area involves analysis of a number of factors that indicate possible physiological impairments. The most common for which to screen include sight defects and abnormalities, hearing defects, speech pathologies, skeletal abnormalities, and endocrine system disorders. Consultant medical specialists need to be retained to perform these diagnostic studies on each offender. As is indicated by the medical authors in this book, up to 90% of the offenders can be expected to show one or more of these types of abnormalities.

Table 20-2 Correctional Classification (Diagnostic) and Treatment Model

Dimensions of man	Diagnostic approaches	Pathological signs	Treatment approaches
Mineral-chemical	Blood tests Glucose tolerance tests Hair analysis—minerals	Depression Violence tendencies Suicidal tendencies Anxiety Psychotic tendencies	Selective vitamin therapy Diet therapy Chemotherapy
Growth-developmental	Comprehensive medical examination for growth defects	Genetic defects Congenital defects Sensory deficiencies Developmental defects Impaired neurological-physiological functioning	Corrective medicine Corrective orthopedics Corrective ophthalmology Physical therapy Chiropractic treatment Nutritional therapy Chemotherapy
Intellectual functioning	Scholastic history Scholastic achievement testing Logical reasoning tests Neurological testing	Organic brain injuries Impaired neurological functioning Toxic brain disorders Circular reasoning Underachiever: school, work, marriage Limited communication skills	Nutritional therapy Chemotherapy Scholastic training Communications skills training Reality training—unblock circular reasoning
Psychosocial	Psychological tests Behavioral observations Social history taking Deviant patterns analysis Attitude testing	Low self-esteem Low achiever Hedonistic behavior Sexual deviations Poor relational ability Distrustful, suspicious Hostile, suicidal Manipulative of others Psychosomatic disorders Faking, lying, evasion	Nutritional therapy Chemotherapy Psychotherapy—reality types Social education Vocational education Creative arts training Meditation training

The third area of diagnostic inquiry should be directed toward the psychological realm. This area is manifested primarily in the expressions of intellectual functioning and self-concepts. Not only should psychological defects and blocks be detected, but potentialities for growth should be assessed. In terms of behavioral change, one of the more fruitful areas of modification can come from the unexplored and undeveloped areas of the human psyche. Thus, this area of assessment is unusually critical.

The fourth area of diagnosis relates to the offender's social skills in interpersonal relations. Typically, this is the antisocial person's greatest area of difficulty. Psychometric and sociometric testing should be utilized along with the clinical interview, to uncover problems in this area.

The four-dimensional diagnosis finally will need to be put together into a holistic picture of the offender as a living entity. This is the task of the treatment team. The diagnostic picture should clearly emphasize areas of strengths and weaknesses and the specific prospects for correction and developmental treatment. Interviews then should be conducted to discuss with each offender the specifics of the diagnostic pattern as they relate to his early developmental history and his present and future goals. The purpose of this aspect of diagnosis is to understand and to communicate to the offender a more holistic appreciation of his problem and to motivate him to plan treatment goals.

8. *A fourth aspect of classification should be to develop a comprehensive treatment plan with each offender.*

Following the final diagnostic interview, an additional interview should be held by the treatment team with each offender, for the purpose of planning with him a comprehensive treatment plan, including a tentative time schedule for this plan. Key family members also may need to be included in the treatment plan.

The offender should be made to understand that the treatment plan is a joint responsibility, requiring the complete effort and full cooperation of the individual with the team members. The offender by this time should understand enough of his specific diagnostic problem areas to participate intelligently in development of his plan. He also should be made to understand that much of the time required for treatment progress will depend upon his conscious and continuing efforts in carrying out the plan.

9. *The fifth phase of classification should involve implementation of the treatment plan along multidimensional lines.*

The treatment plan should proceed with each offender in each of the four dimensional areas of human behavior. It is likely that each offender will need some correctional and/or developmental treatment in each of the four areas, although more forms of treatment in some dimensions than in others may be needed.

Depending upon the individual diagnosis, the following therapeutics, as indicate in Table 20-2, may be employed:

a. *Mineral-chemical*—Megadoses of selected vitamin therapy, diet therapy, and chemotherapy, or some combination of these three.

b. *Growth and development*—Corrective medicine, especially in the areas of optometry/ophthalmology, orthopedics/chiropractic, physical therapy, speech therapy, hearing therapy, and nutritional-medical therapy to correct endocrine imbalances or allergies.

c. *Intellectual-psychological*—Scholastic training, especially reading, writing, and math skills; development of emotional maturity through use of emotional maturity instruction, reality therapy, and other ego-enhancing methods, development of higher potentialities through use of creative meditation, and art and music therapy.

d. *Social functioning*—Improving interpersonal skills through use of role playing, social education, peer-group interaction training, and psychodrama.

10. *The community program should include all of those elements and staff necessary to implementation of each comprehensive treatment plan.*

Few programs will be able to contain all of the needed elements and staff to carry out the various treatment modalities required for full effectiveness of the program. However, these resources are available in each major-sized community. A major task of the program director, therefore, will be to assemble a basic and continuing full-time staff, while utilizing the laboratories and specialized professional skills in the community on a part-time and/or consultative basis.

11. *The progress of each offender in the treatment program must be closely monitored by staff, and modifications should be made in the treatment plan from time to time as needed.*

Each aspect of the four-dimensional treatment plan should be reduced to some form of quantitative measurement, and measurements should be secured at periodic intervals, i.e., once a day, once a week. This will allow the team members to keep abreast of the degree of progress or failure of each offender in the treatment plan.

At each stage of measurement, the team members should apprise each offender of his progress, and his areas of failure to progress, and an attempt should be made to remotivate or redirect the efforts of the offender along progressive lines. All disciplinary problems of the offender while in the program should also be discussed by the team members with the offender as an aid to behavioral understanding and modification.

12. *Persons should not be released from control in the program until they have shown sufficient progress in treatment.*

Offenders should not be released prematurely, as often is the case today. Premature release does not protect society, nor is it therapeutically wise to release an offender when his chances of success are not very high. Not only should all major abnormalities and deviations be significantly modified, but the offender should demonstrate good probability of socially constructive behavior in the areas of work, family, and/or marriage, and community relations. A probationary period of release could be instituted for borderline cases.

13. *In addition to these early intervention efforts, the program should include strong preventive aspects.*

A number of ideas have been presented by authors of this book on ways in which many of these antisocial types of problems could be prevented. Basically, they involve early detection and remediation at four levels: (1) proper pre- and postnatal care of mothers and their infants; (2) proper nutrition and emotional care of young children; (3) education of teachers, police, and court staff to recognize and refer children with defects/deficiencies and related problems; and (4) education of teen-age youth to help them to understand and correct their own areas of behavior maldevelopment.

The community program for antisocial persons should develop a series of approaches to educate parents, teachers, court personnel, police, and mental health staff in the early detection and prevention of these problems. These should include, for example, use of the mass media, community conferences, professional workshops, parent-teacher programs, youth camps, and development of special publications.

14. *Persons released from the program should be followed up for at least one year to determine the degree to which they have made satisfactory adjustment in the community.*

All offenders released from the program should be followed up for at least one year. This information is needed to evaluate the outcomes of the treatment program. Determination should be made not only of their avoidance of later offenses, but also of constructive social behavior in the areas of work, education, family and/or marriage, and community relations. All follow-up data should be correlated with specific program elements in an attempt to locate those aspects of the program that result in success or failure.

SUMMARY AND CONCLUSIONS

The intent of this writing has been to offer a model solution to the community's need for a specialized program for antisocial persons.

Presented here were 7 important assumptions and 14 basic operational principles related to this model. Some of the operational principles have been tested in practice in isolated programs, but a single program has not yet incorporated all of them. Thus, the unique aspect of this suggested model is in its incorporation of a large number of diverse principles, all of which have shown some degree of pragmatic utility even when used in isolation.

The knowledge of ecologic-biochemical factors in offender behavior presented in this book, it is keenly felt, marks an important bridge in our attempts to find a more effective means of dealing with antisocial forms of behavior. Now it appears that sufficient knowledge exists for us to begin to deal effectively with this most difficult form of human behavior.

A community approach, rather than an institutional approach, is recommended here. Early detection and effective intervention is the primary plan. Education for the long-range goal of prevention is our secondary thrust. It is to be hoped that the new knowledge contained in this book will soon be put to a full test and effective application.

BIBLIOGRAPHY

Book References

Abrahamson, E. M., and Pezet, A. W., *Body, Mind, and Sugar*, New York: Holt, Rinehart and Winston, 1951.

Adams, R., and Murray, F., *Body, Mind and the B Vitamins*, New York: Larchmont Books, 1972.

Adams, Ruth, and Murray, F., *Megavitamin Therapy*, New York: Larchmont Books, 1973.

Alsleben, H. Rudolph, and Shule, Wilfred E., *How To Survive the New Health Catastrophies*, Anaheim, Calif.: Survival Publications, 1973.

Bailey, H., *The Vitamin Pioneers*, Emmaus, Pa.: Rodale Books, Inc., 1968.

Blaine, Tom R., *Goodbye Allergies*, 1st ed., New York: The Citadel Press, 1968.

Blaine, Tom, *Mental Health Through Nutrition*, New York: The Citadel Press, 1969.

Brennon, Richard O., *Nutrigenetics*, New York: M. Evans and Co., 1975.

Brim, M., *Newer Methods of Nutritional Biochemistry*, New York: Academic Press, 1967.

Cheraskin, E., and Ringsdorf, W. M., *Diet and Disease*, Emmaus, Pa.: Rodale Books, Inc., 1968.

Cheraskin, E., and Ringsdorf, W. M., *New Hope for Incurable Diseases*, New York: Exposition Press, 1971.

Cheraskin, E., and Ringsdorf, W. M., *Predictive Medicine*, Mountain View, Calif.: Pacific Press Publ. Assoc., 1973.

Clark, Linda, *Get Well Naturally*, New York: ARC Books, Inc., 1970.

Davis, Adelle, *Let's Eat Right To Keep Fit*, New York: Harcourt Brace Javonovich, Inc., 1954, 1970.

Davis, Adelle, *Let's Have Healthy Children*, Scarborough, Ontario, Canada: The New American Library of Canada, Ltd., 1972.

Eiduson, G., Geller, E., Yuwiler, A., and Eiduson, B. T., *Biochemistry and Behavior*, Princeton, N.J.: D. Van Nostrand Co., Inc., 1964.

Ellis, John M., and Presley, James, *Vitamin B-6—The Doctor's Report*, New York: Harper and Row, 1973.

Fredericks, C., *Eating Right for You*, New York: Grosset and Dunlap, 1972.

Fredericks, C., *Psycho-Nutrition*, New York: Grosset and Dunlap, 1975.

Fredericks, C., and Bailey, H., *Food Facts and Fallacies*, New York: The Julian Press, Inc., 1965.

Fredericks, C., and Goodman, H., *Low Blood Sugar and You*, New York: Constellation International, 1969.

Golos, Natalie, *Management of Complex Allergies*, Norwalk, Conn.: New England Foundation of Allergic and Environmental Diseases, 1974.

Guilford, Carol, *The Diet Book*, New York: Pinnacle Books, 1972.

Hawkins, D. E., and Pauling, L., *Orthomolecular Psychiatry*, San Francisco: W. H. Freeman and Co., 1973.
Hippchen, Leonard J., "Contributions of Biochemical Research to Criminological Theory," in *Theoretical Concerns in Criminology*, Beverly Hills, Calif.: Sage Publications, 1977.
Hoffer, A., and Osmond, H., *The Chemical Basis of Clinical Psychiatry*, Springfield, Ill.: Charles C. Thomas, 1962.
Hoffer, A., and Osmond, H., *The Hallucinogens*, New York: Academic Press, 1967.
Hoffer, A., and Osmond, H., *New Hope for Alcoholics*, New Hyde Park, New York: University Books, 1968.
Lappe, Frances M., *Diet for a Small Planet*, New York: Ballantine Books, 1973.
Nittler, Alan H., *A New Breed of Doctor*, New York: Pyramid House, 1972.
Pauling, Linus, *Vitamin C and The Common Cold*, San Francisco: W. H. Freeman and Co., 1970.
Pawlak, Vic, *Megavitamin Therapy and the Drug Wipeout Syndrome*, Phoenix, Ariz.: Do It Now Foundation, 1972.
Pfeiffer, C., *Neurobiology of the Trace Metals Zinc and Copper*, International Review of Neurobiology, New York: Academic Press, 1972.
Pfeiffer, C., Ward, J., El-Meligi, M., and Cott, A., *The Schizophrenias: Yours and Mine*, New York: Pyramid Books, 1970.
Pugh, K., *Mental Illness: Is It Necessary?* New York: Carlton Press, Inc., 1968.
Randolph, T. G., *Human Ecology and Susceptibility to the Chemical Environment*, Springfield, Ill.: Charles C. Thomas, 1962.
Rimland, B., *High-Dosage Levels of Certain Vitamins in the Treatment of Children with Severe Mental Disorders*, San Diego: Institute for Child Behavior Research, 1968.
Roberts, Sam E., *Exhaustion: Causes and Treatment*, Emmaus, Pa.: Rodale Books, Inc., 1967.
Rodale, J. O., *Natural Health, Sugar, and the Criminal Mind*, New York: Pyramid Books, 1968.
Rosenberg, Harold, and Feldzamen, A. N., *The Book of Vitamin Therapy*, New York: Berkley Windover Edition, 1975.
Rosenberg, Harold, and Feldzamen, A. N., *The Doctors Book of Vitamin Therapy*, New York: G. P. Putnam's Sons, 1974.
Schroeder, H. A., *The Trace Elements and Man*, Old Greenwich, Conn.: Devin-Adair, 1973.
Selye, Hans, *The Stress of Life*, New York: McGraw-Hill Paperbacks, 1956.
Steincrohn, P. J., *Low Blood Sugar*, Chicago: Henry Regnery Co., 1972.
Stone, Irwin, *The Healing Factor: Vitamin C Against Disease*, New York: Grosset and Dunlap, 1972.
Szent-Gyorgyi, A., *The Living State*, New York: Academic Press, 1972.
Turkel, H., *New Hope for the Mentally Retarded*, New York: Vantage, 1972.
Underwood, E. J., *Trace Elements in Human and Animal Nutrition*, New York: Academic Press, 1971.
Walton, G., *Nutrition and Your Mind*, New York: Harper and Row, 1972.
Williams, Roger J., *Biochemical Individuality*, New York: John Wiley & Sons, 1963.
Williams, Roger J., *Nutrition Against Disease*, New York: Pitman Publ. Corp., 1971.

Williams, Roger J., *You Are Extraordinary*, New York: Random House, 1967.
Williams, Roger J., and Kalita, Dwight K., *A Physician's Handbook on Orthomolecular Medicine*, New York: Pergamon Press, 1977.
Winick, Myron, *Nutrition and Development*, New York: John Wiley & Sons, 1971.
Winter, Ruth, *A Consumer's Dictionary of Food Additives*, New York: Crown Publishers, 1970.
Wohl, M. G., and Goodhart, R. S., *Modern Nutrition in Health and Disease*, Philadelphia: Lea and Febiger, 1968.
Wunderlich, Ray C., *Allergy, Brains, and Children Coping*, St. Petersburg, Fla.: Johnny Reads, Inc., 1973.
Wunderlich, Ray C., *Fatigue*, St. Petersburg, Fla.: Johnny Reads, Inc., 1976.
Wunderlich, Ray C., *Improving Your Diet*, St. Petersburg, Fla.: Johnny Reads, Inc., 1976.
Wunderlich, Ray C., *Kids, Brains and Learning*, St. Petersburg, Fla.: Johnny Reads, Inc., 1970.
Yudkin, John, *Sweet and Dangerous*, New York: Peter H. Wyden, Inc., 1972.

Journal References

Buckley, R. E., Nutrition, metabolism, brain functions and learning, *Academic Therapy* 12 (3):321–326, 1977.
Cott, Allan, Orthomolecular approach to the treatment of learning disabilities, *J. Orthomolecular Psychiatry* 1:1–11, 1972.
Davis, V. E., and Walsh, M. J., Alcohol, amimes and alkaloids: a possible biochemical basis for alcohol addiction, *Science* 167:3920, 1970.
Eichenwald, Heinz F., and Fry, P. C., Nutrition and learning, *Science* 163:644–648, 1969.
Goodhart, R. S., The role of nutritional factors in the cause, prevention and cure of alcoholism and associated infirmities, *Am. J. Clin. Nutr.* 5:612, 1957.
Groesbeck, C., D'Asaro, B., and Nigro, C., Polyamine levels in jail inmates, *J. Orthomolecular Psychiatry* 4:149–152, 1975.
Hawley, C., and Buckley, R. E., Food, dyes and hyperkinetic children, *Academic Therapy* 10 (1):27–32, 1974.
Heston, Leonard L., The genetics of schizophrenic and schizoid disease, *Science* 167:249–256, 1970.
Hippchen, Leonard J., Biochemical contributions to offender rehabilitation, *J. Offender Rehabilitation* 1:115–123, 1976.
Hoffer, Abram, The relation of crime to nutrition, *Humanist in Canada* 8:2–9, 1975.
Jani, S. N., and Jani, L. A., Nutritional deprivation and learning disabilities—An appraisal," *Academic Therapy* 10 (2):151–158, 1974.
Krippner, S., Illicit drug usage: Hazards for learning disabled students, *J. Orthomolecular Psychiatry* 1:1, 1972.
Krippner, Stanley, An alternative to drug treatment for hyperactive children, *Academic Therapy* 10 (4):433–439, 1975.
Kromick, Doreen, Learning from living: A case history—sugar, fried oysters and zinc," *Academic Therapy* 11 (1):119–121, 1975.
Mandel, Arnold J., and Spooner, Charles E., Psychochemical research studies in man, *Science* 162:1442–1453, 1968.

Mayron, L. W., Ott, J., Nations, R., and Mayron, E. L., Light, radiation, and academic behavior, *Academic Therapy* 10:33–47, 1974.
Newbolt, H. L., Philpott, W. H., and Mandell, M., Psychiatric syndromes produced by allergies: Ecologic mental illness, presented at annual meeting of Orthomolecular Psychiatry, Dallas, 1972.
Olson, R. E., Gursey, D., and Vester, J. W., Evidence for a defect in tryptophan metabolism in chronic alcoholism, *N. Engl. J. Med.* 263:1169, 1960.
Ott, J. N., Responses of psychological and physiological functions to environmental radiation stress, *J. Learning Disabilities* 1:18–20, 1968.
Ott, John, The eye's dual functions, Parts I, II and III, *The Eye, Ear, Nose and Throat Monthly* 53:42–60, 1974.
Patrick, Jay, Malnutrition and the criminal state of mind, *Let's Live*, Fall 1975.
Pauling, Linus, Orthomolecular psychiatry, *Science* 160:265–271, 1968.
Powers, H. W. S., Jr., Caffeine, behavior and the LD child, *Academic Therapy* 11 (1):5–11, 1975.
Powers, H. W. S., Jr., Dietary measures to improve behavior and achievement, *Academic Therapy* 9 (3):203–214, 1973.
Rolfe, Randall C., Violence and vitamins, *Medical Dimensions*, 39–42, December 1976.
Rosenberg, Harold, and Feldzamen, A. N., Malassimilation and the biochemical individuality of digestion and absorption, *The Osteopathic Annuals* 4 (7), 1976.
Rosenberg, L. D., Vitamin-dependent genetic disease, *Hospital Practice* 15:59, 1970.
Turkel, Henry, Medical amelioration of Down's Syndrome incorporating the orthomolecular approach, *J. Orthomolecular Psychiatry* 4:102–115, 1975.
Von Hilscheimer, G., Koltz, S. D., McFall, G., Lerner, H., Van West, A., and Quirk, D., The use of megavitamin therapy in regulating severe behavior disorders, drug abuse and frank psychoses, *J. Schizophrenia* 3:1, 1967.
Wacker, John A., The dyslogic syndrome, *Texas Key*, September 1975.
Wacker, John A., Eliminating the additives, *Texas Key*, December 1976.
Watson, G., and Currier, W. D., Intensive vitamin therapy in mental illness," *J. Psychology* 49:67, 1960.
Wender, P., Some speculations concerning a possible biochemical basis of minimal brain dysfunction, *Ann. N.Y. Acad. Sci.* 205:21, 1973.
Winick, Myron, Changes in nucleic acid and protein content of the human brain during growth, *Pediat. Res.* 2:352–355, 1968.
Winick, Myron, and Rosso, Pedro, The effects of severe early malnutrition on cellular growth of human brain, *Pediat. Res.* 3:181–184, 1969.
Wunderlich, Ray C., Paranoid schizophrenia as a manifestation of metabolic derangement: Successful management by metabolic therapy," *J. Int. Acad. Prevent. Med.* 3 (1), 1976.
Wunderlich, Ray C., Treatment of the hyperactive child, *Academic Therapy* 8 (4): 375–390, 1973.
Wunderlich, Ray C., Biosocial factors in the child with school problems, *Academic Therapy*, 10 (4):389–399, 1975.
Yaryura-Tobias, J. A., and Neziroglu, F. A., Violent behavior, brain dysrhythmia, and glucose dysfunction: a new syndrome, *J. Orthomolecular Psychiatry* 4:182–188, 1975.

INDEX

Addictions, causes, 128, 320
Adrenochrome-adrenolution, hypothesis, 159
Aggression, theory of causes, 138–139
Alcoholism
   behavioral effects, 23, 27, 28
   causing death, 20
   deficiency, 13, 14
   delinquent use, 146
   diagnosis, 285
   in prison, 274
   offenses, 5, 26
   relation to hypoglycemia, 128
   relation to violence, 144
   social aspects, 284
   social costs, 20, 29
   treatment, 16, 292–295
   Wernicke-Korsakoff disease, 42
Alcoholics Anonymous, treatment, 294, 295
Allergies
   brain, 13, 54, 229
   case histories, 248–252
   causes, 238
   diagnosis, 242–247
   food, 14
   neuroallergy, 229, 238
   reversal effect, 129
   treatment, 130, 247–248
Antisocial behavior
   as hyperactivity, 14
   causes of, 46, 232–238, 372–373
   definition, 42
   malnutrition types, 52
   patterns, 57–58
   relation to crime, 372–373
   treatment philosophy, 374
Ascorbic acid
   side effects, 216
   treatment use, 164
Auditory defects, delinquency research, 88–91

Biochemical individuality
   author of, 32, 34
   nature of, 50

Biochemistry
   contributions, 12, 15
   deficiency types, 13
   definition, v
   research, 13
Biological
   causation concepts, 229
   theories of crime, 9
Biosocial decline, causes, 229–230
Birth defects, identification of, 17
Brain function, areas of, 40

Calcium Pantothenate, side effects, 216
Cerebral allergies, relation to crime, 54
Classification of criminals, procedures, 380–388
Clinical ecology
   definition, 14
   leaders, 33
Correctional institutions
   characteristics, 7
   effects, 8
   populations, 7
   treatment, 276–280
Crime volume
   career, 7
   drug, 6
   prevention of, 297–298
   property, 5
   trends, 3, 4
   violent, 5, 7
   white collar, 11
Criminal behavior
   definition, 11
   psychopathic, 14
   treatment, 276–280
Criminology
   limitations, 8, 9
   theory, 12, 13
Curfew violations, number, 6

Development
   normal, 12
   optimum, 12

Diabetes mellitus
  cause, 122
  definition, 122
  relation to obesity, 134
Diagnostic procedures, initial, 183
Diagnostic testing
  allergies, 199-201
  histamine studies, 191-192
  holistic, 379-386
  hypoglycemia, 196-198
  psychological, 192-196
  screening studies, 187-189
  trace metal studies, 189-191
Diet control
  in treatment, 217-222, 281-283
  of prisoners, 320-323
Diversion of delinquents, early programs, 16
Double blind studies, weaknesses, 31
Down's syndrome (mongolism)
  births annually, 256
  costs, 252
  diagnosis, 257-258
Drug abuse
  by delinquents, 146
  causes, 23, 71
  offenses, 6
  relation to crime, 147
  treatment, 16
Dyslexia, symptoms, 207

Ecologic, definition, v
Electroconvulsive therapy
  case study, 53
  treatment uses, 31
Environment
  behavioral influences, 35
  biochemical aspects, 46
Experiential world inventory
  description, 192-196
  diagnostic use, 192-196, 272
  legal use, 43

Family nutrition, need for, 301-307, 311-312
Food allergies
  case studies, 118-120
  causes, 120
  definition, 14
  symptoms, 116
  treatment, 126, 275

Genetic defects
  identification of, 17
  relation to criminality, 145
  slow learners, 255
Glucose tolerance
  relation to violence, 145
  test, 32

Hallucinations, types, 36, 37
Hoffer-Osmond Diagnostic Test
  description, 162, 163
  diagnostic use, 157, 272
  legal use, 43
Holistic diagnosis, community programs, 379-385
Homocide, relation to alcohol use, 144
Huxley Institute for Biosocial Research, origin, 34
Hyperactivity
  causes, 13, 14, 15
  relation to crime, 271, 272
Hypoglycemia
  causes, 13
  definition, 15, 196, 319
  in children, 218, 318
  relation to alcoholism, 128
  research, 67
  testing for, 197-199

Insanity
  definition, 36
  legal aspects, 43, 44
Intervention approaches, with juvenile delinquents, 352-369

Juvenile court
  case handling, 371-372
  case histories, 365-369
  delinquency intervention, 358-363
  research, 79, 363-365
Juvenile delinquency
  auditory defects, 88
  case histories, 365-368
  causes, 7, 183, 232-238
  definition, 11
  hypoglycemia, 176
  institutions, 7
  intervention, 352-369
  prevention-intervention, 297-299
  problems, 81
  relation to learning disabilities, 75
  research, 92-95, 97
  trends, 4, 5
  vision defects, 82-88

Index   395

Learning disabilities
  biochemical origin, 62
  causation, 61, 206-229
  genetic origin, 62
  nature of, 77
  prenatal influences, 63
  symptoms, 210-214
  treatment, 210-214
Light research
  impact on children, 111
  impact on criminals, 107
  results, 106
Loitering violations, volume annually, 6

Malnutrition
  causes of, 337
  extent of, 32
  symptoms of, 337-340
Malvarian factor
  in schizophrenia, 160
  legal aspects, 161-162
  research on, 161
Megavitamins, use with children, 214-217
Metabolic errors, symptoms, 130, 255-256
Mineral deficiencies, types, 41

Niacinamide
  research, 68
  side effects, 215
  treatment effects, 154
Nicotinic acid (niacin)
  side effects, 215
  treatment effects, 153-156, 164-167
Nutrition
  basics of, 47, 312-315
  deficiency, 125
  fallacies, 315-318
  optimum, 49, 50

Orthomolecular theory
  definition, 13
  leaders, 13
  principles, 33

Panendocrine disorder
  causes, 126
  symptoms, 127
Parole, effectiveness, 8
Pellagra, cause, 217
Perceptual changes
  among delinquents, 348

  among prisoners, 14
  causes, 13, 35
Post-natal influences, deficiencies, 307-311
Prenatal influences
  disorders of, 63
  problems, 305-207
Prevention approaches
  causes of childhood disorders, 328-330
  diagnosis, 330-332
  in children, 327
  treatment, 332-337
Probation, effectiveness, 8
Processing defects, in delinquents, 75
Psychology, theories, 9
Pyridoxine
  research, 70
  side effects, 216
Pyroluria
  description, 201-202
  testing for, 202

Radiation research
  definition, 109
  impact on children, 109, 113
  results, 110
Reading disabilities, research, 78
Recidivism
  rates, 7, 8
  reduction, 16
Rehabilitation
  approaches, 96
  limitations, 76
Rotational diets, four-day type, 126
Runaways, volume, 6

Saccharine disease
  definition, 52
  origin, 52
Schizophrenia
  adrenochrome-adrenolution hypothesis, 159
  case study, 44, 45, 118
  causes, 15, 155
  malvarian factor, 160
  pyroluria factor, 201-204
  relation to diabetes mellitus, 123
  symptoms, 37, 38, 39, 118
  syndromes, 41
  thyroid malfunction, 127
  treatment of, 31, 45
Skills defects, in delinquents, 345-348

Slow learners
  case histories, 263-267
  definition, 254-259
  relation to crime, 267
  treatment, 259-262
Sociological theories, 9, 10
Speech disorders, examination for, 66
Subclinical pellagra
  definition, 269
  in children, 270
  in criminals, 269
  treatment, 275-280
Supernutrition
  definition, 17
  need for, 48
Symptomatic Behavior Rating Scale
  limitations, 173-174
  research use, 158
Syndrome
  definition, 40
  types, 40

Team treatment, community staffing plan, 379
Therapeutic community, for antisocial persons, 375-376, 378
Thyroid disorder, treatment, 127
Toxic metals, diagnosis, 223-227
Trace minerals
  diagnosis, 222-223
  relation to nutrition, 130
  testing for, 189-191

Treatment
  community, 377-388
  diet control, 217-221
  effectiveness, 8-9
  orthomolecular, 16
  violent behavior, 147

Uniform crime report
  source, 18
  statistics, 5, 7

Vandalism, volume, 6
Violent behavior
  animal studies, 139-141
  causes of, 138
  definition, 138-139
  human studies, 141
  treatment, 147
Visual disorders
  case studies, 99-101
  examination for, 66
  of delinquents, 82, 341-350
  treatment of, 96, 97-99
Vitamin deficiency, definition, 13, 14
Vitamin dependency
  B types, 41, 53
  definition, 13, 14
Vitamins
  availability, 216-217
  megadose use, 31